# Introducing Routing and Switching in the Enterprise

## CCNA Discovery Learning Guide

## Part I: Concepts

Allan Reid

Jim Lorenz

Cheryl Schmidt

The CD/CD-ROM has been
removed from this item due
to Copyright restrictions.

**Cisco Press**

800 East 96th Street

Indianapolis, Indiana 46240 USA

# Introducing Routing and Switching in the Enterprise

## CCNA Discovery Learning Guide
## Part I: Concepts

Allan Reid · Jim Lorenz · Cheryl Schmidt

Copyright© 2008 Cisco Systems, Inc.

Published by:
Cisco Press
800 East 96th Street
Indianapolis, IN 46240 USA

Printed in the United States of America

First Printing  April 2008

Library of Congress Cataloging-in-Publication Data:
        Library of Congress Cataloging-in-Publication Data
Reid, Allan.
  Introducing routing and switching in the enterprise / Allan Reid, Jim Lorenz, Cheryl Schmidt.
      p. cm. -- (CCNA discovery learning guide)
  Includes index.
  ISBN-13: 978-1-58713-211-7 (pbk. w/cd)
  ISBN-10: 1-58713-211-7
1.  Routing (Computer network management) 2.  Packet switching (Data transmission)  I. Lorenz, Jim. II. Schmidt, Cheryl A., III. Cisco Systems, Inc. IV. Title. V. Series.
  TK5105.543.R45 2008

  004.6--dc22

2008010656

ISBN-13: 978-1-58713-211-7
ISBN-10: 1-58713-211-7

**This book is part of a two-book set. Not to be sold separately.**

**Publisher**
Paul Boger

**Associate Publisher**
Dave Dusthimer

**Cisco Representative**
Anthony Wolfenden

**Cisco Press Program Manager**
Jeff Brady

**Executive Editor**
Mary Beth Ray

**Managing Editor**
Patrick Kanouse

**Development Editor**
Dayna Isley

**Project Editor**
Jennifer Gallant

**Copy Editors**
Keith Cline
Written Elegance, Inc.

**Technical Editors**
Tony Chen
Tom Knott
Fred Lance
Michael Duane Taylor
Tara Skibar
Marlon Vernon

**Editorial Assistant**
Vanessa Evans

**Book and Cover Designer**
Louisa Adair

**Composition**
Bronkella Publishing

**Indexer**
Heather McNeill

**Proofreaders**
Karen A. Gill
Leslie Joseph

CISCO.

## Warning and Disclaimer

This book is designed to provide information about the Introducing Routing and Switching in the Enterprise CCNA Discovery course. Every effort has been made to make this book as complete and as accurate as possible, but no warranty or fitness is implied.

The information is provided on an "as is" basis. The authors, Cisco Press, and Cisco Systems, Inc. shall have neither liability nor responsibility to any person or entity with respect to any loss or damages arising from the information contained in this book or from the use of the discs or programs that may accompany it.

The opinions expressed in this book belong to the authors and are not necessarily those of Cisco Systems, Inc.

## Trademark Acknowledgments

All terms mentioned in this book that are known to be trademarks or service marks have been appropriately capitalized. Cisco Press or Cisco Systems, Inc. cannot attest to the accuracy of this information. Use of a term in this book should not be regarded as affecting the validity of any trademark or service mark.

## Corporate and Government Sales

The publisher offers excellent discounts on this book when ordered in quantity for bulk purchases or special sales, which may include electronic versions and/or custom covers and content particular to your business, training goals, marketing focus, and branding interests. For more information, please contact: **U.S. Corporate and Government Sales**  1-800-382-3419 corpsales@pearsontechgroup.com

For sales outside the United States please contact: **International Sales**  international@pearsoned.com

## Feedback Information

At Cisco Press, our goal is to create in-depth technical books of the highest quality and value. Each book is crafted with care and precision, undergoing rigorous development that involves the unique expertise of members from the professional technical community.

Readers' feedback is a natural continuation of this process. If you have any comments regarding how we could improve the quality of this book, or otherwise alter it to better suit your needs, you can contact us through e-mail at feedback@ciscopress.com. Please make sure to include the book title and ISBN in your message.

We greatly appreciate your assistance.

| Americas Headquarters | Asia Pacific Headquarters | Europe Headquarters |
|---|---|---|
| Cisco Systems, Inc. | Cisco Systems, Inc. | Cisco Systems International BV |
| 170 West Tasman Drive | 168 Robinson Road | Haarlerbergpark |
| San Jose, CA 95134-1706 | #28-01 Capital Tower | Haarlerbergweg 13-19 |
| USA | Singapore 068912 | 1101 CH Amsterdam |
| www.cisco.com | www.cisco.com | The Netherlands |
| Tel: 408 526-4000 | Tel: +65 6317 7777 | www-europe.cisco.com |
| 800 553-NETS (6387) | Fax: +65 6317 7799 | Tel: +31 0 800 020 0791 |
| Fax: 408 527-0883 | | Fax: +31 0 20 357 1100 |

Cisco has more than 200 offices worldwide. Addresses, phone numbers, and fax numbers are listed on the Cisco Website at **www.cisco.com/go/offices**.

©2007 Cisco Systems, Inc. All rights reserved. CCVP, the Cisco logo, and the Cisco Square Bridge logo are trademarks of Cisco Systems, Inc.; Changing the Way We Work, Live, Play, and Learn is a service mark of Cisco Systems, Inc.; and Access Registrar, Aironet, BPX, Catalyst, CCDA, CCDP, CCIE, CCIP, CCNA, CCNP, CCSP, Cisco, the Cisco Certified Internetwork Expert logo, Cisco IOS, Cisco Press, Cisco Systems, Cisco Systems Capital, the Cisco Systems logo, Cisco Unity, Enterprise/Solver, EtherChannel, EtherFast, EtherSwitch, Fast Step, Follow Me Browsing, FormShare, GigaDrive, GigaStack, HomeLink, Internet Quotient, IOS, IP/TV, iQ Expertise, the iQ logo, iQ Net Readiness Scorecard, iQuick Study, LightStream, Linksys, MeetingPlace, MGX, Networking Academy, Network Registrar, Packet, PIX, ProConnect, RateMUX, ScriptShare, SlideCast, SMARTnet, StackWise, The Fastest Way to Increase Your Internet Quotient, and TransPath are registered trademarks of Cisco Systems, Inc. and/or its affiliates in the United States and certain other countries.

All other trademarks mentioned in this document or Website are the property of their respective owners. The use of the word partner does not imply a partnership relationship between Cisco and any other company. (0609R)

# About the Authors

**Allan Reid** is the curriculum lead and a CCNA/CCNP instructor at the Centennial College CATC in Toronto, Canada. Allan is a professor in the Information and Communications Engineering Technology department and an instructor and program supervisor for the School of Continuing Education at Centennial College. He has developed and taught networking courses for both private and public organizations and has been instrumental in the development and implementation of numerous certificate, diploma, and degree programs in networking. Allan is also a curriculum developer for the Cisco Networking Academy. Outside of his academic responsibilities, he has been active in the computer and networking fields for more than 25 years and is currently a principal in a company specializing in the design, management, and security of network solutions for small and medium-sized companies. Allan authored the first edition of *WAN Technologies CCNA 4 Companion Guide* (Cisco Press, ISBN: 1-58713-172-2) and *Using a Networker's Journal*, which is a supplement to *A Networker's Journal* (Cisco Press, ISBN: 1-58713-158-7). Most recently, Allan coauthored the CCNA Discovery online academy courses Networking for Home and Small Businesses and Introducing Routing and Switching in the Enterprise, with Jim Lorenz.

**Jim Lorenz** is an instructor and curriculum developer for the Cisco Networking Academy. Jim has coauthored several Cisco Press titles, including *Fundamentals of UNIX Companion Guide*, Second Edition (ISBN 1-58713-140-4), *Fundamentals of UNIX Lab Companion*, Second Edition (ISBN 1-58713-139-0), and the third editions of the CCNA Lab Companions. He has more than 20 years of experience in information systems, ranging from programming and database administration to network design and project management. Jim has developed and taught computer and networking courses for numerous public and private institutions. As the Cisco Academy Manager at Chandler-Gilbert Community College in Arizona, he was instrumental in starting the Information Technology Institute (ITI) and developed a number of certificates and degree programs. Most recently, Jim coauthored the CCNA Discovery online academy courses Networking for Home and Small Businesses and Introducing Routing and Switching in the Enterprise, with Allan Reid.

**Cheryl Schmidt** is a professor of network engineering technology at Florida Community College in Jacksonville, Florida, where she has worked for the past 19 years (13 years as a faculty member). Before joining the classroom full time, Cheryl worked in the computer/networking industry, having begun her career in electronics/computers in the U.S. Navy. Cheryl has been active in the Cisco Academy, through which she has taught CCNA, CCNP, wireless, and security classes and has been instrumental in the development and implementation of a converged networking program including VoIP and QoS classes.

# About the Technical Reviewers

**Tony Chen**, CCNP and CCAI, manages Cisco Networking Academy for the College of DuPage in Glen Ellyn, Illinois, and teaches CCNA and CCNP classes at the college. As a manager for a regional academy, he also trains and supports local Cisco networking academies. He also manages the computer network for the Ball Foundation. The Ball Foundation's motto is to discover and develop human potential. Tony Chen has an understanding wife, Joanne, and one wonderful daughter, Kylie.

**Tom Knott** is the technology and communications specialist for the Kenan Institute for Engineering, Technology & Science at North Carolina State University. In that capacity, he works as tech support, manages websites, writes program content, and serves as staff photographer. Mr. Knott was a public school teacher for the previous 17 years, the last 10 teaching Cisco Academy courses at Southeast Raleigh High School, a magnet high school. He is also an author for Cisco Press and has worked on numerous curriculum projects for the Cisco Networking Academy.

**Fred Lance** teaches CCNA, CCNP, and security classes at NHTI in Concord, New Hampshire. After 15 years working in the networking field, he joined the IT faculty of NHTI in 1999 to implement the Cisco Networking Academy for the college. He received both his CCNA and CCNP certifications after moving into the teaching field. He resides in Andover, New Hampshire, with his wife Brenda and their three daughters, Abigail, Becca, and Emily. He has been a volunteer firefighter in Andover for 18 years and enjoys building and painting in his spare time.

**Tara Skibar**, CCNP, was introduced to networking in 1994 when she enlisted in the Air Force. After serving for four years as a network technician, she became an instructor. Tara has worked with major telecom companies in the United States and Europe. She has worked for the Cisco Networking Academy since 2003 as a subject matter expert for the CCNP assessment development team and for the CCNP certification exams. Most recently, Tara was the assessment lead for the newly modified CCNA curriculum and traveled with a group of development folks to Manila, Philippines, for the small market trial. Tara has a bachelor of science degree in information technology and is working toward a master's degree in information systems.

**Marlon Vernon** currently teaches the CCNA and CCNP networking courses. He has been teaching for 23 years in the fields of electronics engineering and computer networking technologies both at the high school and college levels. He has served on the Cisco Advisory Council for the global networking academies for the past four years.

**Michael Duane Taylor** is department head of computer information sciences at the Raleigh Campus of ECPI College of Technology. He has more than seven years of experience teaching introductory networking and CCNA-level curriculum and was awarded the Instructor of the Year Award. Previously, Michael was a lab supervisor with Global Knowledge, working with router hardware configuration and repair. He holds a bachelor's degree in business administration from the University of North Carolina at Chapel Hill and a master of science degree in industrial technology/computer network management from East Carolina University. His certifications include CCNA, CCNP-router, and MCSE.

## Dedications

*This book is dedicated to my children: Andrew, Philip, Amanda, Christopher, and Shaun. You are my inspiration, and you make it all worthwhile. Thank you for your patience and support.*

—Allan Reid

*To the three most important people in my life: my wife, Mary, and my daughters, Jessica and Natasha. Thanks for your patience and support.*

—Jim Lorenz

*In addition to my thankfulness for the production team and my family (my husband, Karl, and my daughters, Raina and Kara), I would like to thank my students and coworkers for their continued support in my projects, classes, and ideas. It truly takes a team to have success.*

—Cheryl Schmidt

## Acknowledgments

From Allan, Jim, and Cheryl:

We want to thank Mary Beth Ray and Dayna Isley with Cisco Press for their help and guidance in putting this book together. We also want to thank the technical editors: Tony Chen, Tom Knott, Fred Lance, Tara Skibar, Mike Taylor, and Marlon Vernon. Their attention to detail and suggestions made a significant contribution to the accuracy and clarity of the content.

We also want to acknowledge the entire CCNA Discovery development team from Cisco Systems for their hard work and dedication to making CCNA Discovery a reality.

Introducing Routing and Switching in the Enterprise, CCNA Discovery Learning Guide

# Contents at a Glance

# Contents

# Icons Used in This Book

# Command Syntax Conventions

The conventions used to present command syntax in this book are the same conventions used in the *IOS Command Reference*. The *Command Reference* describes these conventions as follows:

- **Boldface** indicates commands and keywords that are entered literally as shown. In actual configuration examples and output (not general command syntax), boldface indicates commands that are manually input by the user (such as a **show** command).

- *Italics* indicate arguments for which you supply actual values.

- Vertical bars (|) separate alternative, mutually exclusive elements.

- Square brackets [ ] indicate optional elements.

- Braces { } indicate a required choice.

- Braces within brackets [{ }] indicate a required choice within an optional element.

# Introduction

Cisco Networking Academy is a comprehensive e-learning program that delivers information technology skills to students around the world. The Cisco CCNA Discovery curriculum consists of four courses that provide a comprehensive overview of networking, from fundamentals to advanced applications and services. The curriculum emphasizes real-world practical application, while providing opportunities for you to gain the skills and hands-on experience needed to design, install, operate, and maintain networks in small to medium-sized businesses and in enterprise and Internet service provider environments. The Introducing Routing and Switching in the Enterprise course is the third course in the curriculum.

*Introducing Routing and Switching in the Enterprise, CCNA Discovery Learning Guide* is the official supplemental textbook for the third course in v4.*x* of the CCNA Discovery online curriculum of the Networking Academy. As a textbook, this book provides a ready reference to explain the same networking concepts, technologies, protocols, and devices as the online curriculum. In addition, it contains all the interactive activities, Packet Tracer activities, and hands-on labs from the online curriculum and bonus labs.

This book emphasizes key topics, terms, and activities and provides many alternative explanations and examples as compared with the course. You can use the online curriculum as directed by your instructor and then also use this *Learning Guide*'s study tools to help solidify your understanding of all the topics. In addition, the book includes the following:

- Expanded coverage of CCNA exam material

- Additional key Glossary terms

- Bonus labs

- Additional Check Your Understanding and Challenge questions and activities

- Interactive activities and Packet Tracer activities on the CD-ROM

# Goal of This Book

First and foremost, by providing a fresh, complementary perspective of the online content, this book helps you learn all the required materials of the third course in the Networking Academy CCNA Discovery curriculum. As a secondary goal, individuals who do not always have Internet access can use this text as a mobile replacement for the online curriculum. In those cases, you can read the appropriate sections of this book, as directed by your instructor, and learn the topics that appear in the online curriculum. Another secondary goal of this book is to serve as your offline study material to help prepare you for the CCNA exams.

# Audience for This Book

This book's main audience is anyone taking the third CCNA Discovery course of the Networking Academy curriculum. Many Networking Academies use this textbook as a required tool in the course, whereas other Networking Academies recommend the learning guides as an additional source of study and practice materials.

# Book Features

The educational features of this book focus on supporting topic coverage, readability, and practice of the course material to facilitate your full understanding of the course material.

## Topic Coverage

The following features give you a thorough overview of the topics covered in each chapter so that you can make constructive use of your study time:

- **Objectives**: Listed at the beginning of each chapter, the objectives reference the core concepts covered in the chapter. The objectives match the objectives stated in the corresponding chapters of the online curriculum; however, the question format in the *Learning Guide* encourages you to think about finding the answers as you read the chapter.

- **"How-to" feature**: When this book covers a set of steps that you need to perform for certain tasks, the text lists the steps as a how-to list. When you are studying, the icon helps you easily refer to this feature as you skim through the book.

- **Notes, tips, cautions, and warnings**: These short sidebars point out interesting facts, timesaving methods, and important safety issues.

- **Chapter summaries**: At the end of each chapter is a summary of the chapter's key concepts. It provides a synopsis of the chapter and serves as a study aid.

## Readability

The authors have compiled, edited, and in some cases rewritten the material so that it has a more conversational tone that follows a consistent and accessible reading level. In addition, the following features have been updated to assist your understanding of the networking vocabulary:

- **Key terms**: Each chapter begins with a list of key terms, along with a page-number reference from inside the chapter. The terms are listed in the order in which they are explained in the chapter. This handy reference allows you to find a term, flip to the page where the term appears, and see the term used in context. The Glossary defines all the key terms.

- **Glossary**: This book contains an all-new Glossary with more than 300 computer and networking terms.

## Practice

Practice makes perfect. This new *Learning Guide* offers you ample opportunities to put what you learn to practice. You will find the following features valuable and effective in reinforcing the instruction that you receive:

- **Check Your Understanding questions and answer key**: Updated review questions are presented at the end of each chapter as a self-assessment tool. These questions match the style of questions that you see in the online course. Appendix A, "Check Your Understanding and Challenge Questions Answer Key," provides an answer key to all the questions and includes an explanation of each answer.

- (*New*) **Challenge questions and activities**: Additional, and more challenging, review questions and activities are presented at the end of chapters. These questions are purposefully designed to be similar to the more complex styles of questions you might see on the CCNA exam. This section might also include activities to help prepare you for the exams. Appendix A provides the answers.

- **Packet Tracer activities**: Interspersed throughout the chapters, you'll find many activities to work with the Cisco Packet Tracer tool. Packet Tracer enables you to create networks, visualize how packets flow in the network, and use basic testing tools to determine whether the network would work. When you see this icon, you can use Packet Tracer with the listed file to perform a task suggested in this book. The activity files are available on this book's CD-ROM; Packet Tracer software, however, is available through the Academy Connection website. Ask your instructor for access to Packet Tracer.

- **Interactive activities**: These activities provide an interactive learning experience to reinforce the material presented in the chapter.

- **Labs**: Part II of this book contains all the hands-on labs from the curriculum plus additional labs for further practice. Part I includes references to the hands-on labs, as denoted by the lab icon, and Part II of the book contains each lab in full. You may perform each lab when it is referenced in the chapter or wait until you have completed the entire chapter.

## A Word About Packet Tracer Software and Activities

Packet Tracer is a self-paced, visual, interactive teaching and learning tool developed by Cisco. Lab activities are an important part of networking education. However, lab equipment can be a scarce resource. Packet Tracer provides a visual simulation of equipment and network processes to offset the challenge of limited equipment. Students can spend as much time as they like completing standard lab exercises through Packet Tracer, and have the option to work from home. Although Packet Tracer is not a substitute for real equipment, it allows students to practice using a command-line interface. This "e-doing" capability is a fundamental component of learning how to configure routers and switches from the command line.

Packet Tracer v4.*x* is available only to Cisco Networking Academies through the Academy Connection website. Ask your instructor for access to Packet Tracer.

## A Word About the Discovery Server CD

The CCNA Discovery series of courses is designed to provide a hands-on learning approach to networking. Many of the CCNA Discovery labs are based on Internet services. Because it is not always possible to allow students access to these services on a live network, the Discovery Server has been developed to provide them.

The Discovery Server CD is a bootable CD that transforms a regular PC into a Linux server running several preconfigured services for use with Discovery labs. Your instructor can download the CD files, burn a CD, and show you how to use the server. Hands-on labs that use the Discovery Server are identified within the labs themselves.

Once booted, the server provides many services to clients, including the following:

- Domain Name Services
- Web services
- FTP
- TFTP
- Telnet

- SSH

- DHCP

- Streaming video

# How This Book Is Organized

This book covers the major topics in the same sequence as the online curriculum for the CCNA Discovery Introducing Routing and Switching in the Enterprise course. The online curriculum has ten chapters for this course, so this book has ten chapters, with the same names and numbers as the online course chapters.

To make it easier to use this book as a companion to the course, the major topic headings in each chapter match, with just a few exceptions, the major sections of the online course chapters. However, the *Learning Guide* presents many topics in slightly different order inside each major heading. In addition, the book occasionally uses different examples than the course. As a result, students get more detailed explanations, a second set of examples, and different sequences of individual topics, all to aid the learning process. This new design, based on research into the needs of the Networking Academies, helps typical students lock in their understanding of all the course topics.

## Chapters and Topics

Part I of this book has ten chapters, as follows:

- **Chapter 1, "Networking in the Enterprise,"** describes the goals of the enterprise network and compares enterprise LANs, WANs, intranets, and extranets. Types of enterprise applications are identified, including traffic flow patterns and prioritization. This chapter also focuses on the needs of teleworkers and the use of virtual private networks to support them.

- **Chapter 2, "Exploring the Enterprise Network Infrastructure,"** describes the network operations center (NOC), telecommunications rooms, and network documentation used in the enterprise. Requirements for supporting the enterprise edge are introduced, including external service delivery and security considerations. This chapter also provides a good review of switch and router hardware. It reinforces the basic commands necessary to configure switches and routers and verify their operation.

- **Chapter 3, "Switching in an Enterprise Network,"** focuses on the characteristics of switches and issues associated with supporting them in an enterprise environment. These include redundancy and Spanning Tree Protocol (STP). You learn to configure VLANs, trunking, and multiswitch inter-VLAN routing. The chapter also covers the VLAN Trunking Protocol (VTP), support for IP telephony, and wireless and VLAN implementation best practices.

- **Chapter 4, "Addressing in an Enterprise Network,"** compares flat and hierarchical network design with a focus on the structure and advantages of hierarchical IP addressing. This chapter provides a review of subnet masks and basic subnetting and introduces variable-length subnet masks (VLSM) and their benefits. It provides instruction on how to implement VLSM addressing in hierarchical network design. The use and importance of classless routing, classless inter-domain routing (CIDR), and route summarization are explained, along with subnetting best practices. This chapter also provides a review of private IP addressing, Network Address Translation (NAT), and Port Address Translation (PAT), with examples of implementation.

- **Chapter 5, "Routing with a Distance Vector Protocol,"** describes common network topologies and provides a review of static and dynamic routing and default routes. The chapter also provides a review of distance vector routing protocols. The advantages and disadvantages of using Routing Information Protocol (RIP) and Enhanced Interior Gateway Routing Protocol (EIGRP) are discussed. Instructions are provided for the configuration and implementation of the RIPv2 and EIGRP dynamic routing protocols.

- **Chapter 6, "Routing with a Link-State Protocol,"** focuses on link-state routing protocols, specifically the Open Shortest Path First (OSPF) Protocol. OSPF characteristics are described, as are advantages and issues involved with implementing OSPF. Instructions are provided for configuring single-area OSPF. In addition, issues associated with using multiple routing protocols in a network are addressed.

- **Chapter 7, "Implementing Enterprise WAN Links,"** focuses on devices and technology options for connecting the enterprise WAN. Packet- and circuit-switching technologies are compared, as are last-mile and long-range technologies. WAN encapsulations, such as High-Level Data Link Control (HDLC) and PPP, are described. You learn how to configure PPP on a WAN link, including authentication. The chapter also provides an overview of the popular Frame Relay WAN technology.

- **Chapter 8, "Filtering Traffic Using Access Control Lists,"** emphasizes the importance of using access control lists (ACL) in network security and traffic flow control. This chapter describes the various types of Cisco IOS ACLs and how they are configured, including the use of the wildcard mask. Standard, extended, and named ACLs are compared, with suggestions for when to use them and placement in specific scenarios. Details are provided on how to create, edit, and apply various ACLs. Filtering traffic based on specific fields in the IP packet is covered. The use of ACLs with NAT and PAT and inter-VLAN routing is discussed. In addition, ACL logging (and the use of syslog servers) is introduced.

- **Chapter 9, "Troubleshooting an Enterprise Network,"** emphasizes the impact of network failure on an organization and the concept of a failure domain. This chapter describes network monitoring tools and techniques and reviews the troubleshooting process. This chapter identifies common problems associated with switching and connectivity, routing, WAN configurations and ACLs, and ways to troubleshoot these problems.

- **Chapter 10, "Putting It All Together,"** In this summary activity, you use what you have learned about the enterprise network infrastructure, switching technologies, hierarchical IP addressing, routing protocols, WAN technologies, and ACLs to build and configure a multi-switch, multirouter simulated enterprise network.

Part I: Concepts also includes the following:

- **Appendix A, "Check Your Understanding and Challenge Questions Answer Key,"** provides the answers to the Check Your Understanding questions that you find at the end of each chapter. It also includes answers for the Challenge questions and activities that conclude most chapters.

- The **Glossary** provides a compiled list of all the key terms that appear throughout this book, plus additional computer and networking terms.

Part II of this book includes the labs that correspond to each chapter. Part II also includes the following:

- **Appendix B, "Lab Equipment Interfaces and Initial Configuration Restoration,"** provides a table listing the proper interface designations for various routers. Procedures are included for erasing and restoring routers and switches to clear previous configurations. In addition, the steps necessary to restore an SDM router are provided.

## About the CD-ROM

The CD-ROM included with this book provides many useful tools and information to support your education:

- **Packet Tracer Activity files**: These are files to work through the Packet Tracer activities referenced throughout the book, as indicated by the Packet Tracer activity icon.

- **Interactive activities**: The CD-ROM contains the interactive activities referenced throughout the book.

- **Taking Notes**: This section includes a TXT file of the chapter objectives to serve as a general outline of the key topics of which you need to take note. The practice of taking clear, consistent notes is an important skill for not only learning and studying the material, but for on-the-job success, too. Also included in this section is "A Guide to Using a Networker's Journal" PDF booklet providing important insight into the value of the practice of using a journal, how to organize a professional journal, and some best practices on what, and what not, to take note of in your journal.

- **IT Career Information**: This section includes a student guide to applying the toolkit approach to your career development. Learn more about entering the world of information technology as a career by reading two informational chapters excerpted from *The IT Career Builder's Toolkit*: "Communication Skills" and "Technical Skills."

- **Lifelong Learning in Networking**: As you embark on a technology career, you will notice that it is ever changing and evolving. This career path provides new and exciting opportunities to learn new technologies and their applications. Cisco Press is one of the key resources to plug into on your quest for knowledge. This section of the CD-ROM provides an orientation to the information available to you and tips on how to tap into these resources for lifelong learning.

# PART 1

# Concepts

# CHAPTER 1

# Networking in the Enterprise

## Objectives

Upon completion of this chapter, you should be able to answer the following questions:

- What is an enterprise?
- How does traffic flow in an enterprise network?
- How is traffic handled in an enterprise?
- How does an extranet compare to an intranet?
- What is a telecommuter, and what services does a telecommuter require?
- What is the importance of a VPN?

## Key Terms

This chapter uses the following key terms. You can find the definitions in the Glossary.

business enterprise   page 4

enterprise   page 4

enterprise network   page 5

converged   page 5

mission-critical   page 5

enterprise-class   page 5

failover   page 5

hierarchical design model   page 6

access layer   page 6

distribution layer   page 6

core layer   page 6

Enterprise Composite Network Model (ECNM)
  page 8

edge device   page 9

intrusion detection system (IDS)   page 9

intrusion prevention system (IPS)   page 9

failure domain   page 9

downtime   page 10

back-end network   page 10

intranet   page 12

extranet   page 12

packet sniffer   page 13

latency   page 14

Jitter   page 14

Quality of service (QoS)   page 14

Teleworking   page 15

telecommuting   page 15

teleworker   page 15

telecommuter   page 15

teleconferencing   page 15

virtual private network (VPN)   page 16

Enterprise networks provide application and resource support to local and remote users anywhere and at any time. Intranets and extranets form the structure of these networks and often incorporate both LAN and WAN technologies. Traffic flow patterns, both internal and external, must be controlled to provide an efficient and secure network. The enterprise network uses advanced security and networking technology to enable telecommuters to work securely and productively while away from the office.

Part II of this book includes the corresponding labs for this chapter.

## Describing the Enterprise Network

As businesses grow and evolve, so do their networking requirements. A large business environment with many users and locations, as shown in Figure 1-1, or one with many systems, is referred to as a *business enterprise* or more simply an *enterprise*. Common examples of enterprise environments include the following:

- Manufacturers
- Large retail stores
- Restaurant and service franchises
- Utilities and government agencies
- Hospitals
- School systems

**Figure 1-1    An Enterprise**

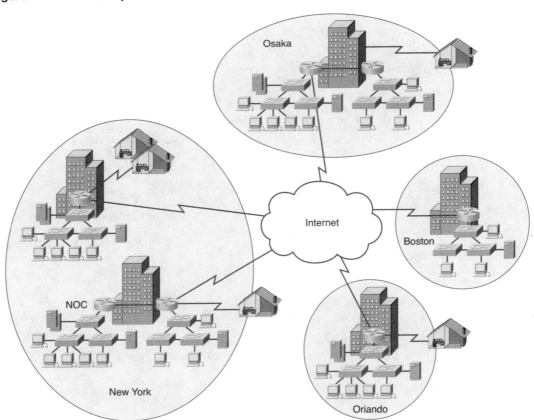

These enterprises rely on their networks to provide access to shared resources and information. Without the network, many of the normal activities of the enterprise cannot be completed, resulting in substantial financial and customer base losses. Enterprise networks must be properly designed and maintained to reduce the chances of any outage.

## Supporting the Business Enterprise

The network used to support the business enterprise is called an *enterprise network*. Enterprise networks are designed to provide support for diverse business requirements and critical applications. They support the exchange of various types of network traffic, including data files, e-mail, voice, and video applications for multiple business units. To efficiently handle this *converged* network traffic, enterprise networks must have centralized control of devices and traffic.

Businesses increasingly rely on their network infrastructure to provide *mission-critical* services. Outages in the enterprise network can prevent the business from performing its normal activities, which can result in lost revenue and lost customers. Users are very intolerant of any outages in network services. In the enterprise environment, users have come to expect that network services will be available as designed 99.999 percent of the time. This means a maximum of just over five minutes of network outage in a year. Many service providers guarantee this level of service and enter into contractual agreements that result in severe financial penalties if this level of service is not maintained.

To obtain this level of reliability, high-end equipment is commonly installed in the enterprise network environment. Equipment installed in an enterprise network normally moves large volumes of network traffic, whereas the volume of traffic that moves in a nonenterprise environment is substantially less. This *enterprise-class* equipment is designed for reliability and stability, with features such as redundant power supplies and *failover* capabilities. Enterprise-class equipment is designed and manufactured to more stringent standards than lower-end devices.

Purchasing and installing enterprise-class equipment does not eliminate the need for proper network design. One objective of good network design is to prevent any single point of failure that could compromise network performance. This is accomplished by building redundancy into the network design as shown in Figure 1-2. When incorporating redundancy into a network design, it is important to consider not only the equipment but also all links. Other key factors in network design include optimizing bandwidth utilization, ensuring security, and network performance.

## Traffic Flow in the Enterprise Network

To optimize available bandwidth on an enterprise network, the network must be organized so that traffic stays localized and is not propagated onto unnecessary portions of the network. Allowing traffic to flow onto network segments where it is not required or desired has many negative affects. The traffic consumes valuable bandwidth, thus decreasing network performance. If this decreased performance is not acceptable, additional bandwidth must be installed to compensate for the unwanted traffic, resulting in increased network costs. In addition, this traffic presents a security hazard in that it may contain confidential information or information about the structure of the network itself. An unscrupulous individual with sufficient technical knowledge could intercept this traffic and use it to compromise the integrity of the network or gain valuable information that could be financially devastating to the organization.

**Figure 1-2    Redundancy in Network Design**

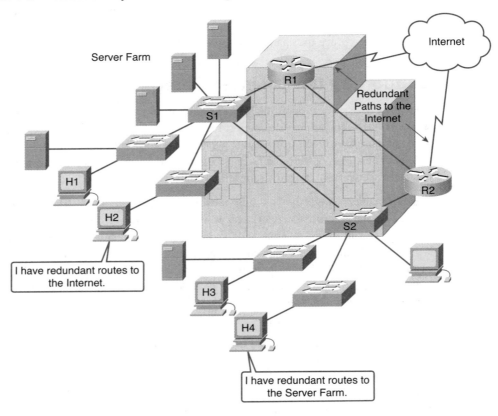

Using the three-layer *hierarchical design model* helps organize the network. This model divides the network functionality into three distinct layers: *access layer*, *distribution layer*, and *core layer*, as shown in Figure 1-3.

Each layer is designed to meet specific functions. The access layer provides connectivity for the users. The distribution layer is used to forward traffic from one local network to another. Finally, the core layer represents a high-speed backbone layer between dispersed end networks. User traffic is initiated at the access layer and passes through the other layers only if the functionality of those layers is required. Even though the hierarchical model has three layers, some enterprise networks use the core layer services offered by an Internet service provider (ISP) to reduce costs.

Each layer is designed to meet specific functions. The access layer performs the following functions:

- Provides a connection point for end-user devices to the network
- Allows multiple hosts to connect to other hosts through a network device such as a switch
- Exists on the same logical network
- Confines traffic destined for a host on the same network to the access layer
- Passes traffic to the distribution layer for delivery if the message is destined for a host on another network

**Figure 1-3    Three-Layer Hierarchical Design Model**

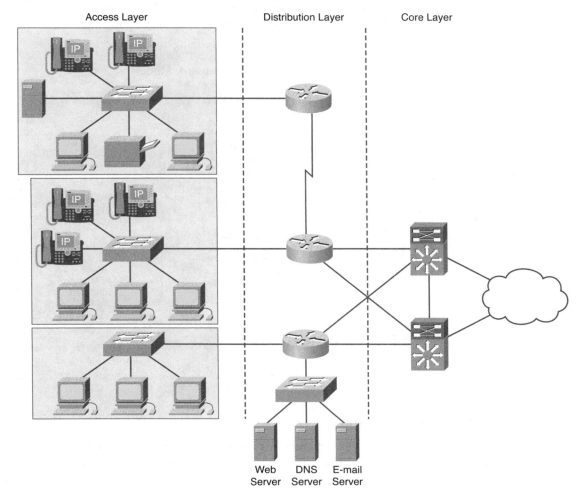

The distribution layer performs the following functions:

- Provides a connection point for separate local networks

- Ensures that traffic between hosts on the same local network stays local

- Passes on traffic destined for other networks

- Filters incoming and outgoing traffic for security and traffic management purposes

- Contains more powerful switches and routers than the access layer

- Passes data to the core layer for delivery to a remote network if the destination network is not directly connected

The core layer performs the following functions:

- Provides a high-speed backbone layer with redundant (backup) connections

- Transports large amounts of data between multiple end networks

- Includes very powerful, high-speed switches and routers

- Transports data quickly and reliably

The Cisco *Enterprise Composite Network Model (ECNM)* divides the network into functional components while still maintaining the concept of core, distribution, and access layers. The functional components of this model are the Enterprise Campus, Enterprise Edge, and Service Provider Edge, as shown in Figure 1-4.

**Figure 1-4    Cisco Enterprise Composite Network Model**

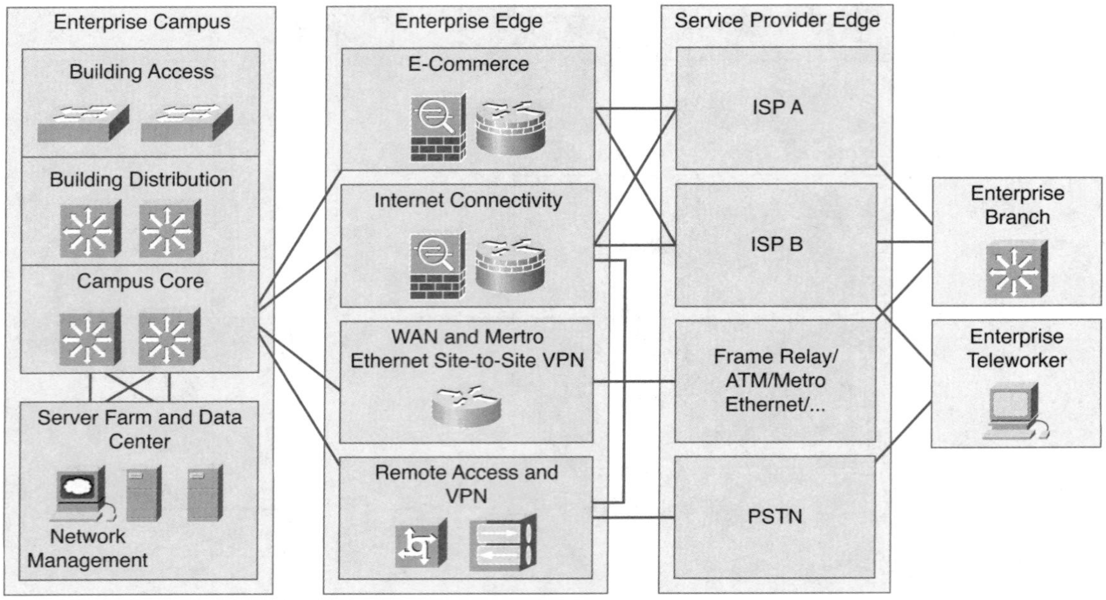

## Enterprise Campus

The Enterprise Campus component consists of the campus infrastructure with server farms and network management. The Building Access module contains both Layer 2 and Layer 3 switches to provide the correct port density for the environment. This module is responsible for the implementation of VLANs and trunk links to the Building Distribution module.

The Building Distribution module uses Layer 3 devices to aggregate traffic from building access layers. Routing, access control, and quality of service (QoS) are all implemented by this module.

Redundancy of devices and links are important design considerations. The Campus Core module provides high-speed connectivity between Building Distribution modules, data center server farms, and the Enterprise Edge. Redundancy, fast convergence, and fault tolerance are the design goals of this module.

Network management continually monitors devices and network performance to ensure optimum operation. The server farm provides high-speed connectivity and protection for servers. It is important to provide redundancy, security, and fault tolerance in this area.

## Enterprise Edge

The Enterprise Edge component consists of the Internet, E-commerce, VPN, and WAN modules connecting the enterprise with the service provider's network. This module extends the enterprise services to remote sites and enables the enterprise to use Internet and partner resources. It provides QoS, policy enforcement, service levels, and security.

All data that enters or exits the ECNM passes through an *edge device*. This is the point at which all packets can be examined and a decision made as to whether the packet should be allowed on the enterprise network. For this reason, this is the location at which an *intrusion detection system (IDS)* or *intrusion prevention system (IPS)* is normally configured. These systems help protect the network against malicious activity.

A well-designed network not only controls traffic but also limits the size of failure domains. A *failure domain* is the area of a network impacted when a key device or service experiences problems. The function of the device that initially fails determines the impact of a failure domain. For example, a malfunctioning switch on a network segment normally impacts only hosts on that segment. However, if the router that connects this segment to others fails, the impact is much greater, as shown in Figure 1-5.

**Figure 1-5    Failure Domains**

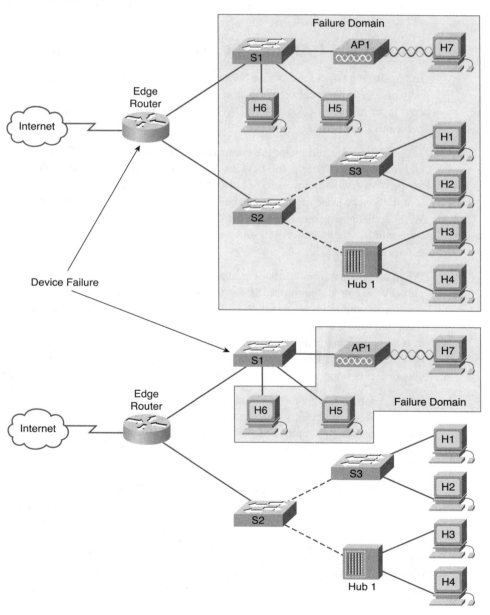

The use of redundant links and reliable enterprise-class equipment minimizes the chance of disruption in a network. Smaller failure domains reduce the impact of a failure on company productivity. They also simplify the troubleshooting process, thereby shortening the *downtime* for all users.

### Service Provider Edge

The Service Provider Edge component provides Internet, public switched telephone network (PSTN), and WAN services to the enterprise. This functional area represents connections to resources external to the campus. It facilitates communications to WAN and ISP technologies.

**Observing the Traffic Flow in an Enterprise Network (1.1.2)**

In this activity, you observe the flow of traffic through a network. Use file d3-112.pka on the CD-ROM that accompanies this book to perform this activity using Packet Tracer.

## Enterprise LANs and WANs

Enterprise networks incorporate both traditional LAN and WAN technologies. In a typical enterprise network, multiple local networks at a single campus interconnect at either the distribution layer or the core layer to form a LAN. These LANs interconnect with other sites that are more geographically dispersed to form a WAN.

LANs are private and under the control of a single organization. The organization installs, manages, and maintains the wiring and devices that are the functional building blocks of the LAN. Some WANs are privately owned; however, because the development and maintenance of a private WAN is expensive, only very large organizations can afford to maintain a private WAN. Most companies purchase WAN connections from a service provider or ISP. The ISP is then responsible for maintaining the *back-end network* connections and network services between the LANs. Figure 1-6 shows a typical enterprise network.

When an organization has many global sites, establishing WAN connections and service can be complex. For example, the major ISP for the organization might not offer service in every location or country in which the organization has an office. As a result, the organization must purchase services from multiple ISPs. Using multiple ISPs often leads to differences in the quality of services provided. In many emerging countries, for example, network designers find differences in equipment availability, WAN services offered, and encryption technology available for security. To support an enterprise network, it is important to have uniform standards for equipment, configuration, and services.

With LAN technology, the organization has the responsibility of installing and managing the infrastructure. This technology functions mainly at the access and distribution layers, with Ethernet being the most commonly deployed LAN technology. The LAN connects users and provides support for localized applications and server farms. Connected devices are usually in the same local area, such as a building or a campus.

With WANs, connected sites are usually geographically dispersed. Connectivity to the WAN requires a device such as a modem or CSU/DSU to put the data in a form acceptable to the network of the service provider. Although some large organizations maintain their own WANs, these services are often provided by an ISP who has the responsibility of installing and managing the infrastructure. WAN services include T1/T3, E1/E3, digital subscriber line (DSL), cable, Frame Relay, and ATM. Figure 1-7 shows how edge devices convert between Ethernet encapsulation and serial WAN encapsulation as the traffic moves from the LAN to the WAN.

**Figure 1-6    An Enterprise Network**

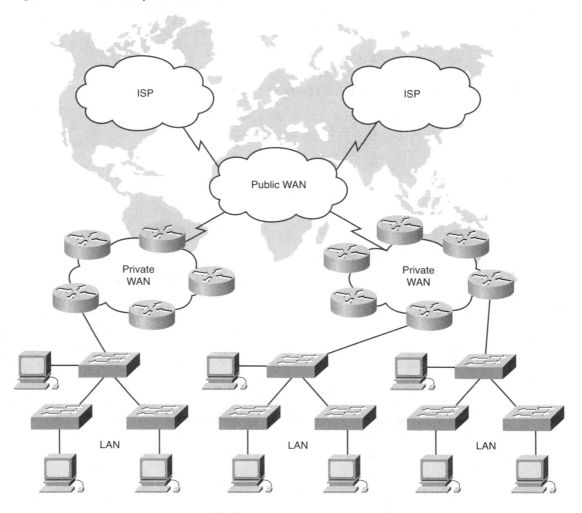

**Figure 1-7    WAN Services**

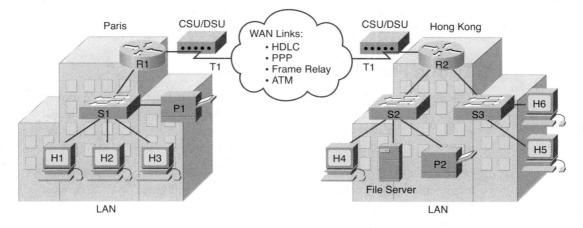

**Interactive Activity 1-1: LAN and WAN Terminology (1.1.3)**

In this activity, you identify the terms relating to LANs and WANs. Use file d3ia-113 on the CD-ROM that accompanies this book to perform this interactive activity.

## Intranets and Extranets

Enterprise networks contain both WAN and LAN technologies. These networks provide many of the services associated with the Internet, including the following:

- E-mail
- Web
- FTP
- Telnet/SSH
- Discussion forums

Many companies use this private network or *intranet* to provide access for local and remote employees via both LAN and WAN technologies. Intranets may have links to the Internet. If connected to the Internet, firewalls control the traffic that enters and exits the intranet. Intranets contain confidential information and are designed for company employees only. The intranet should be protected by a firewall. Remote employees who are not physically connected to the enterprise LAN must authenticate before gaining access to the resources it provides.

In some situations, businesses extend privileged access to their network to key suppliers and customers. This access may be through direct WAN connections, remote login to key application systems, or through virtual private network (VPN) access into a protected network. An *extranet* is a private network (intranet) that allows controlled access to individuals and companies such as suppliers and contractors, outside the organization. An extranet is not a public network.

# Identifying Enterprise Applications

Many different applications are required to support the modern enterprise. Each of these has very specific requirements of the underlying network. Regardless of the type of application, traffic generated by the application should be allowed only on portions of the network where it is required.

## Traffic Flow Patterns

A properly designed enterprise network has well-defined and predictable traffic flow patterns. In some circumstances, traffic stays on the LAN portion of the enterprise network, and at other times it traverses the WAN links. When determining how to design the network, it is important to consider the amount of traffic destined for a specific location and where that traffic most often originates.

Some common traffic types that should remain local to users on the LAN include file sharing, printing, internal backup, mirroring, and intracampus voice. System updates, company e-mail, and transaction processing are also normally seen on a local network but are also sent across the enterprise WAN. In addition to WAN traffic, external traffic is traffic that originates from or is destined for the Internet. VPN and Internet traffic is considered external traffic flow.

Controlling the flow of traffic on a network optimizes available bandwidth and introduces a level of security through monitoring. By understanding traffic patterns and flows, the network administrator can predict the types and amount of traffic to expect on each portion of the network or through each device. When traffic is detected in an area of the network where it is unexpected, that traffic can be filtered and the source of the traffic investigated.

### Interactive Activity 1-2: Traffic Flow Patterns (1.2.1)

In this activity, you identify the flow pattern for each type of traffic. Use file d3ia-121 on the CD-ROM that accompanies this book to perform this interactive activity.

## Applications and Traffic on an Enterprise Network

At one time, voice, video, and data each traveled on separate networks, which could be optimized for the specific type of traffic. Now technology supports a converged network, where voice, video, and data flow across the same medium. This convergence presents many design and bandwidth management challenges. Enterprise networks must support the business enterprise by allowing traffic from a variety of applications, including the following:

- Database transaction processing

- Mainframe or data center access

- File and print sharing

- Authentication services

- Web services

- E-mail and other communications

- VPN services

- Voice calls and voicemail

- Video and videoconferencing

In addition, network management traffic and the control processes required for the underlying operation of the network must also travel across the network.

When trying to determine how to manage network traffic, it is important to understand the type of traffic that is crossing the network and the current traffic flow pattern. If the types of traffic are unknown, a technician can use a *packet sniffer* to capture traffic for analysis. To determine traffic flow patterns, it is important to capture traffic during peak utilization times to get a good representation of the different traffic types and to perform the capture on different network segments, because some traffic will be local to a particular segment.

Using the information obtained from the packet sniffer, network technicians can determine traffic flows. Technicians analyze this information based on the source and destination of the traffic and the type of traffic being sent. Technicians then use this analysis to decide how to manage the traffic more efficiently, such as filtering unnecessary traffic flows or changing flow patterns altogether by relocating a server or service to a different location on the network. Optimizing the network performance might require major redesign and intervention.

**Lab 1-1: Capturing and Analyzing Network Traffic (1.2.2)**

In this lab, you use Wireshark to capture and analyze protocol data packets as they cross the network. Refer to the hands-on lab in Part II of this *Learning Guide*. You may perform this lab now or wait until the end of the chapter.

# Network Traffic Prioritization

Not all types of network traffic have the same requirements or behave in the same manner. For example, voice traffic is much less tolerant to loss and delay than is data traffic. The characteristics of the various types of network traffic must be clearly understood to design and construct a network capable of carrying converged network traffic.

## Data Traffic

Most network applications use data traffic. Some types of online applications transmit data that is sporadic. Other types, such as data storage applications, transmit high volumes of traffic for a sustained period. Some data applications are more concerned about time sensitivity than reliability, and most data applications can tolerate delays. For this reason, data traffic usually uses TCP. TCP uses acknowledgments to determine when lost packets must be retransmitted and thus guarantees delivery. Although the use of acknowledgments makes TCP a more reliable delivery protocol, it also introduces a delay in the delivery of the data.

## Voice and Video Traffic

Voice traffic and video traffic differ from data traffic. Voice and video applications require an uninterrupted stream of data to ensure high-quality conversations and images. The acknowledgment process in TCP introduces delays, which break these streams and degrade the quality of the application. Therefore, voice and video applications use the User Datagram Protocol (UDP) rather than TCP. Because UDP does not incorporate mechanisms for retransmitting lost packets, it minimizes delays.

In addition to understanding the delays of TCP versus UDP, it is necessary to understand the delay, or *latency*, caused by the networking devices that must process the traffic on its path to the destination. Open Systems Interconnection (OSI) Layer 3 devices create more delay than Layer 2 devices because of the number of headers they have to process. Therefore, routers introduce a longer delay than switches. *Jitter*, caused by network congestion, is the variation in the length of time packets take to travel from the source to the destination. It is important to reduce the impact of delay, latency, and jitter on time-sensitive traffic.

*Quality of service (QoS)* is a process used to guarantee adequate bandwidth to a specified data flows. QoS mechanisms sort traffic into different queues, based on priority. For example, voice traffic is given priority over ordinary data. The following list describes this process:

1. Inbound traffic is classified based on type. The traffic type is normally related to the application that generated the traffic and includes things such as voice, video, FTP, and Telnet. Some traffic may be discarded (filtered) at this step.

2. Classified traffic is placed into priority queues based on preconfigured priority levels. For example, voice traffic is very sensitive to delay, so it is placed in a higher-priority queue than FTP data.

3. Traffic in higher-priority queues is sent before traffic in lower-priority queues.

**Interactive Activity 1-3: Traffic Prioritization Terminology (1.2.3)**

In this activity, you match the traffic prioritization term to the correct definition. Use file d3ia-123 on the CD-ROM that accompanies this book to perform this interactive activity.

# Supporting Remote Workers

The development of enterprise networks and remote connection technology has changed the way we work. *Teleworking*, also referred to as *telecommuting* and e-commuting, allows employees to use telecommunications technology to work from their homes or other remote locations. The remote worker using the technology is called a *teleworker* or *telecommuter*.

## Teleworking

An increasing number of companies encourage their employees to consider teleworking. Teleworking provides many advantages and opportunities for both employer and employee. From the employer perspective, when employees work from home, the company does not have to provide them with dedicated physical office space. A single office space can be set up for shared use by employees who need to spend time in the physical office. This arrangement reduces real estate costs and the associated support services. Some companies have even reduced the expense of air travel and hotel accommodations to bring their employees together by using *teleconferencing* and collaboration tools. People from all over the world can work together as if they were in the same physical location.

Employees also benefit from teleworking. Employees save time and money, and reduce stress, by eliminating the daily travel to and from the office. Employees can dress casually at home, and thus save money on business attire. Working from home allows employees to spend more time with their families. Reduced travel for employees also has a favorable effect on the environment. Less airplane and automobile traffic means less pollution.

Not all individuals are suited to a teleworking environment. Teleworkers need to be self-directed and disciplined. Some teleworkers miss the social environment of an office setting and find it difficult to work in physical isolation. Not all jobs can take advantage of teleworking. Some positions require a physical presence in the office during a set period of time. However, more enterprises are taking advantage of technology to increase the frequency of telecommuting. Some of the basic teleworker tools follow:

- **E-mail**: Delivers a written message to a remote user for viewing and response at a later time

- **Chat**: Delivers a written message to a remote user in real time for immediate viewing and response

- **Desktop and Application Sharing**: Allows multiple uses to view and interact with the same applications simultaneously

- **FTP**: Transfers files between computers

- **Telnet**: Connects and starts a terminal session on a remote device

- **VoIP**: Allows real-time voice communication between users over the Internet

- **Videoconferencing**: Allows users in multiple locations to communicate face to face in real time

Application- and screen-sharing tools have improved, and it is now possible to integrate both voice and video into these applications. New technology has enabled more sophisticated levels of online collaboration. Using the enterprise network, this technology creates an environment in which individuals from remote locations meet as though they were in the same room. By combining large video displays and high-quality audio in specially designed rooms, it appears as if all participants, regardless of their physical location, are sitting across the boardroom table from each other.

**Interactive Activity 1-4: Telecommuting Opportunities (1.3.1)**

In this activity, you identify scenarios appropriate for telecommuting. Use file d3ia-131 on the CD-ROM that accompanies this book to perform this interactive activity.

## Virtual Private Networks

One obstacle that teleworkers must overcome is the fact that most of the tools available for working remotely are not secure. Using nonsecure tools allows data to be intercepted or altered during transmission. One solution is to always use the secure forms of applications, if they exist. For example, instead of using Telnet, use Secure Shell (SSH). Unfortunately, secure forms of all applications may not be available. A much easier choice is to encrypt all traffic moving between the remote site and the enterprise network using a *virtual private network (VPN)*.

VPNs are often described as tunnels. Consider the analogy of an underground tunnel versus an open road between two points, as shown in Figure 1-8. Anything that uses the underground tunnel to travel between the two points is surrounded and protected from view. The underground tunnel represents the VPN encapsulation and virtual tunnel.

**Figure 1-8    VPN Analogy**

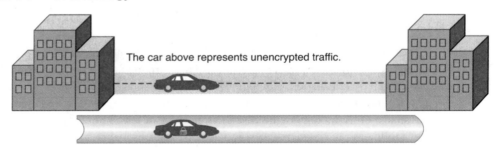

The car above represents unencrypted traffic.

The car below represents encrypted traffic.

When using a VPN, a virtual tunnel is created by linking the source and destination addresses. All data flow between the source and destination is encrypted and encapsulated using a secure protocol such as IPsec, as shown in Figure 1-9. This secure packet is transmitted across the network. When it arrives at the receiving end, it is de-encapsulated and unencrypted.

**Figure 1-9    VPN Tunnel**

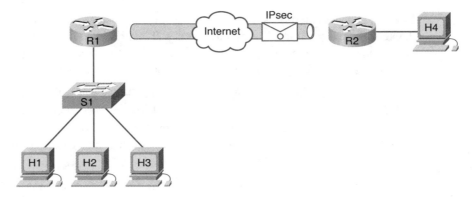

VPNs are a client/server application; therefore, telecommuters must install the VPN client on their computers to form a secure connection with the enterprise network. When telecommuters are connected to the enterprise network through a VPN, they become part of that network and have access to all services and resources that they would have if they were physically attached to the LAN.

**Note**

One of the most common encapsulating protocols for VPNs is IPsec, which is short for IP Security. IPsec is a suite of protocols that provide many services, including the following:

- Data encryption
- Integrity validation
- Peer authentication
- Key management

# Summary

Modern business enterprises rely on their networks for many business-critical applications. Failure of the network can result in both lost customers and lost revenue. For this reason, enterprise-class networks incorporate high-end, enterprise-class equipment and redundancy in their design. Enterprise-class networks are designed to provide an uptime of at least 99.999 percent.

Enterprise networks are composed of both LAN and WAN technology. They must provide services both to those physically connected to the network and to those working remotely. Intranets provide services only to employees of a company or organization. Extranets are intranets that have been extended to provide services to others directly involved in the business of the enterprise but who are not employees.

Enterprise networks can often span continents. Traffic flow patterns in these large enterprise networks must be carefully analyzed and controlled to optimize the available bandwidth and provide a reasonable level of security.

Networks carry many different types of traffic, each of which has different requirements for delivery. Some traffic, such as voice, is very intolerant to delay and must be given priority over more-tolerant traffic such as data packets. QoS is used to provide the prioritization of traffic.

Current network technology and security processes enable network services to be extended outside of the physical boundaries of the corporate office. These services can be made available to anyone at any time, thus enabling many individuals to work from remote locations. This working arrangement is known as teleworking or telecommuting. When working remotely, teleworkers should use the secure form of all applications such as SSH and HTTPS to minimize the possibility that data could be intercepted. Not all applications have a secure form, so VPN technology should be used to encrypt all traffic being sent across a nonsecure network.

# Activities and Labs

**Interactive Activities on the CD-ROM:**

Interactive Activity 1-1: LAN and WAN Terminology (1.1.3)

Interactive Activity 1-2: Traffic Flow Patterns (1.2.1)

Interactive Activity 1-3: Traffic Prioritization Terminology (1.2.3)

Interactive Activity 1-4: Telecommuting Opportunities (1.3.1)

**Packet Tracer Activities on the CD-ROM:**

Observing the Traffic Flow in an Enterprise Network (1.1.2)

**Hands-On Labs in Part II of This Book:**

Lab 1-1: Capturing and Analyzing Network Traffic (1.2.2)

# Check Your Understanding

Complete all the review questions listed here to check your understanding of the topics and concepts in this chapter. Appendix A, "Check Your Understanding and Challenge Questions Answer Key," lists the answers.

1. Which type of network allows a customer to connect to a secure company website to check on a delivery date?

   A. LAN

   B. WAN

   C. Intranet

   D. Extranet

2. Which layer of the three-layer hierarchical design model is used to filter FTP traffic from a specific host?

   A. Access

   B. Distribution

   C. Core

   D. Aggregation

3. In the ECNM, where should an IPS or IDS be configured?

   A. Enterprise Campus

   B. Enterprise Edge

   C. Service Provider Edge

   D. WAN Edge

4. In the ECNM, where should QoS be implemented?

   A. Building Access module

   B. Building Distribution module

   C. Campus Core module

5. Which tool would enable a teleworker to communicate in real time with a colleague?

   A. FTP

   B. E-mail

   C. Chat

   D. Telnet

6. What type of traffic, if found on an enterprise WAN link, indicates a problem with the network design? Choose all that apply.

   A. Departmental file sharing

   B. Printing

   C. Internal backup

   D. Intracampus voice

7. Why should remote workers use VPN technology to connect to the home network?

8. Why does voice traffic use UDP but FTP uses TCP?

9. What should be done if unexpected traffic types are found on a network segment?

10. Why is it important to limit the size of failure domains when designing a network?

## Challenge Questions and Activities

These questions require a deeper application of the concepts covered in this chapter. You can find the answers in Appendix A.

1. You have just been hired by AnyCompany, and your first task is to determine why end users are reporting that the company network is "slow." You quickly analyze the traffic moving on the distribution layer and notice a large number of print requests. What could be causing this, and how would you correct it?

2. You are the network manager for AnyCompany. Company management has decided that they want to allow some people in the accounting department to work from home and have asked you whether this might present any problems. They are especially concerned about the security of their financial data. What recommendations would you make and why?

## Objectives

Upon completion of this chapter, you should be able to answer the following questions:

- What are the main types of network documentation and how are they interpreted?

- What equipment is found in the enterprise Network Operations Center?

- What is the point of presence for service delivery and how is service delivered?

- What are network security considerations and what equipment is used at the enterprise edge?

- What are some characteristics of router and switch hardware?

- What are the most common and useful router and switch CLI configuration and verification commands?

## Key Terms

This chapter uses the following key terms. You can find the definitions in the Glossary.

physical topology    page 22

logical topology    page 22

control plane    page 22

redlined    page 24

as-built    page 24

business continuity plan (BCP)    page 24

business security plan (BSP)    page 25

network maintenance plan (NMP)    page 25

service-level agreement (SLA)    page 25

Network Operations Center (NOC)    page 26

data center    page 26

server farm    page 26

load balancing    page 26

network attached storage (NAS)    page 27

storage-area network (SAN)    page 27

rack units (RU)    page 27

Structured cabling    page 28

electromagnetic interference (EMI)    page 28

telecommunications room    page 29

intermediate distribution facility (IDF)    page 29

access point (AP)    page 29

main distribution facility (MDF)    page 29

extended star    page 29

Power over Ethernet (PoE)    page 31

point of presence (POP)    page 31

service provider (SP)    page 32

(T1/E1)    page 33

punchdown block    page 33

channel service unit/data service unit (CSU/DSU)    page 33

customer premise equipment (CPE)    page 34

form factors    page 36

out-of-band    page 37

in-band    page 37

Port density    page 49

Enterprise networks contain hundreds of sites and support thousands of users worldwide. A well-managed network allows users to work reliably. Network documentation is crucial for maintaining the required 99.999 percent uptime. All Internet traffic flows through the enterprise edge, making security considerations necessary. Routers and switches provide connectivity, security, and redundancy while controlling broadcasts and failure domains.

# Describing the Current Network

The following sections describe network documentation required to support the enterprise and equipment found in the Network Operations Center as well as telecommunications room design considerations.

## Enterprise Network Documentation

One of the first tasks for a new network technician is to become familiar with the current network structure. Enterprise networks can have thousands of hosts and hundreds of networking devices, all of which are interconnected by copper, fiber-optic, and wireless technologies. End-user workstations, servers, and networking devices, such as switches and routers, must all be documented. Various types of documentation show different aspects of the network.

Network infrastructure diagrams, or topology diagrams, keep track of the location, function, and status of devices. Topology diagrams represent either the physical or logical network.

A *physical topology* map uses icons to document the location of hosts, networking devices, and media. It is important to maintain and update physical topology maps to aid future installation and troubleshooting efforts.

A *logical topology* map groups hosts by network usage, regardless of physical location. Host names, addresses, group information, and applications can be recorded on the logical topology map. Connections between multiple sites might be shown but do not represent actual physical locations.

Enterprise network diagrams can also include *control plane* information. Control plane information describes failure domains and defines the interfaces where different network technologies intersect. Figure 2-1 shows a physical topology and Figure 2-2 shows the corresponding logical topology.

**Figure 2-1    Physical Network Topology**

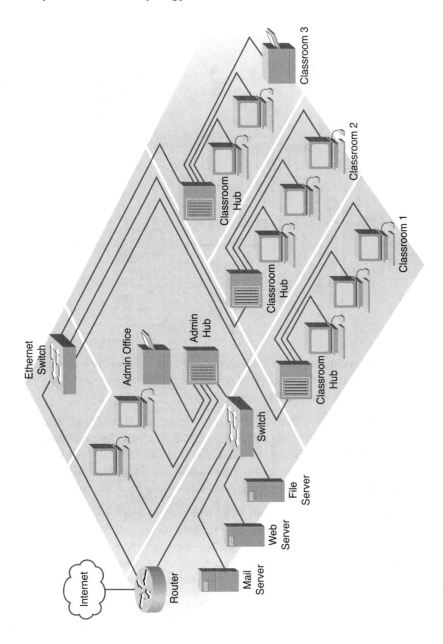

**Figure 2-2    Logical Network Topology**

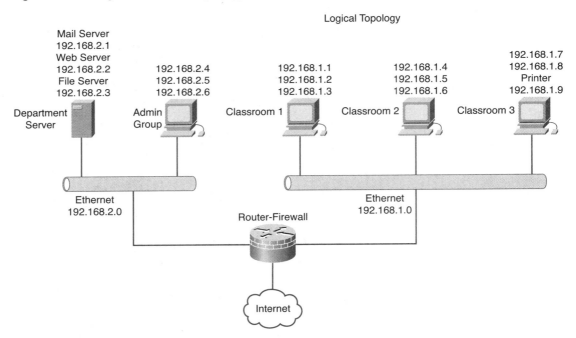

It is crucial that network documentation remain current and accurate. Network documentation is usually accurate at the installation of a network. As the network grows or changes, however, you need to update the documentation.

Network topology maps are frequently based on original floor plans. The current floor plans might have changed since the construction of the building. Blueprints can be marked up, or *redlined*, to show the changes. The modified diagram is known as an *as-built*. An as-built diagram documents how a network was actually constructed, which can differ from the original plans. Always ensure that the current documentation reflects the as-built floor plan and all network topology changes.

Network diagrams are commonly created using graphical drawing software. In addition to being a drawing tool, many network diagramming tools are linked to a database. This feature allows the network support staff to develop detailed documentation by recording information about hosts and networking devices, including manufacturer, model number, purchase date, warranty period, and more. Clicking a device in the diagram opens an entry form with device data listed.

In addition to network diagrams, several other important types of documentation are used in the enterprise network, including a business continuity plan, a business security plan, a network maintenance plan, and a service-level agreement.

## Business Continuity Plan

The *business continuity plan (BCP)* identifies the steps to be taken to continue business operation in the event of a natural or man-made disaster. The BCP helps to ensure business operations by defining procedures that must take place when a disaster strikes. IT support can include

- Off-site storage of backup data

- Alternate IT processing centers

- Redundant communication links

## Business Security Plan

The *business security plan (BSP)* prevents unauthorized access to organizational resources and assets by defining security policies. The BSP includes physical, system, and organizational control measures. The overall security plan must include an IT portion that describes how an organization protects its network and information assets. The IT security plan can contain policies related to

- User authentication
- Permissible software
- Remote access
- Intrusion monitoring
- Incident handling

## Network Maintenance Plan

The *network maintenance plan (NMP)* minimizes downtime by defining hardware and software maintenance procedures. The NMP ensures business continuity by keeping the network up and running efficiently. Network maintenance must be scheduled during specific time periods, usually nights and weekends, to minimize the impact on business operations. The maintenance plan can contain

- Maintenance time periods
- Scheduled downtime
- Staff on-call responsibilities
- Equipment and software to be maintained (OS, IOS, services)
- Network performance monitoring

## Service-Level Agreement

A *service-level agreement (SLA)* ensures service parameters by defining required service provider level of performance. The SLA is a contractual agreement between the customer and a service provider or ISP, specifying items such as network availability and service response time. An SLA can include

- Connection speeds/bandwidth
- Network uptime
- Network performance monitoring
- Problem resolution response time
- On-call responsibilities

Network documentation should be kept in a centrally located area that is available by all who need access to it. Although it is common to store network documentation on network servers in digital form, hard copy versions should also be kept in filing cabinets in the event the network or server is down. Digital and hard copy versions should also be kept in a secure off-site location in the event of a disaster.

**Interactive Activity 2-1: Matching Network Information to Documentation Type (2.1.1)**

In this activity, you identify the network documentation where the information would most likely be found. Use file d3ia-2114 on the CD-ROM that accompanies this book to perform this interactive activity.

## Network Operations Center (NOC)

Most enterprise networks have a *Network Operations Center (NOC)* that allows central management and monitoring of all network resources. The NOC is sometimes referred to as a *data center*.

Employees in a typical enterprise NOC provide support for both local and remote locations, often managing both local- and wide-area networking issues. Larger NOCs can be multiroom areas of a building where network equipment and support staff are concentrated. Figure 2-3 shows a large NOC surrounded by the types of features and equipment found there.

**Figure 2-3    Network Operations Center Components and Features**

The NOC usually has

- Raised floors to allow cabling and power to run under the floor to the equipment
- High-performance UPS systems and air conditioning equipment to provide a safe operating environment for equipment
- Fire suppression systems integrated into the ceiling
- Network monitoring stations, servers, backup systems, and data storage
- Access layer switches and distribution layer routers, if it serves as a main distribution facility (MDF) for the building or campus where it is located

In addition to providing network support and management, many NOCs also provide centralized resources such as servers and data storage. Servers in the NOC are usually clustered together, creating a server farm. The *server farm* is frequently considered as a single resource but, in fact, provides two functions: backup and *load balancing*. If one server fails or becomes overloaded, another server takes over.

The servers in the farm can be rack-mounted and interconnected by very high-speed switches (Gigabit Ethernet or higher). They can also be blade servers mounted in a chassis and connected by a high-speed backplane within the chassis. Figure 2-4 shows a group of rack-mounted servers.

**Figure 2-4    Rack-Mounted Server Farm**

Server Farm

Another important aspect of the enterprise NOC is high-speed, high-capacity data storage. This data storage, or *network attached storage (NAS)*, groups large numbers of disk drives that are directly attached to the network and can be used by any server. An NAS device is typically attached to an Ethernet network and is assigned its own IP address. Figure 2-5 shows an example of multiple rack-mounted NAS drives.

**Figure 2-5    Network Attached Storage (NAS)**

Network Attached Storage (NAS)

A more sophisticated version of NAS is a *storage-area network (SAN)*. A SAN is a high-speed network that interconnects different types of data storage devices over a LAN or WAN.

Equipment in the enterprise NOC is usually mounted in racks. In large NOCs, racks are usually floor-to-ceiling mounted and can be attached to each other. When mounting equipment in a rack, ensure that there is adequate ventilation and access from front and back. Equipment must also be attached to a known good ground.

The most common rack width is 19 inches (48.26 cm). Most equipment is designed to fit this width. The vertical space that the equipment occupies is measured in *rack units (RU)*. A unit equals 1.75 inches (4.4 cm). For example, a 2RU chassis is 3.5 inches (8.9 cm) high. The lower the RU number the less space a device needs; therefore, more devices can fit into the rack. Figure 2-6 shows multiple servers and disk drives in a rack configuration. Each server occupies one RU and the drives typically take two or more RUs.

**Figure 2-6    Network Equipment Height Measured in RUs**

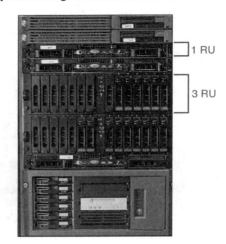

Another consideration is equipment with many connections, like switches. They might need to be positioned near patch panels and close to where the cabling is gathered into cable trays.

In an enterprise NOC, thousands of cables can enter and exit the facility. *Structured cabling* creates an organized cabling system that is easily understood by installers, network administrators, and any other technicians who work with cables.

Cable management serves many purposes. First, it presents a neat and organized system that aids in isolating cabling problems. Second, best cabling practices protect the cables from physical damage and *electromagnetic interference (EMI)*, which greatly reduces the number of problems experienced.

To assist in troubleshooting

- All cables should be labeled at both ends, using a standard convention that indicates source and destination.

- All cable runs should be documented on the physical network topology diagram.

- All cable runs, both copper and fiber, should be tested end to end by sending a signal down the cable and measuring loss.

Cabling standards specify a maximum distance for all cable types and network technologies. For example, the IEEE specifies that, for Fast Ethernet over unshielded twisted-pair (UTP), the cable run from switch to host cannot be greater than 100 meters (approximately 328 ft.). If the cable run is greater than the recommended length, problems could occur with data communications, especially if the terminations at the ends of the cable are poorly completed.

Documentation of the cable plan and testing are critical to network operations. Figure 2-7 shows cabling routed efficiently to the back of a patch panel. Cable bends are minimized, and each cable is clearly labeled for its destination.

**Figure 2-7    Properly Routed and Labeled Cabling**

## Telecommunication Room Design and Considerations

The NOC is the heart of the enterprise. In practice, however, most users connect to a switch in a *telecommunications room*, which is some distance from the NOC. The telecommunications room is also referred to as a wiring closet or *intermediate distribution facility (IDF)*. It contains the access layer networking devices and ideally maintains environmental conditions similar to the NOC, such as air conditioning and UPS. IDFs typically contain

- Fast Ethernet switches
- Gigabit link to MDF
- Wireless access points

Users working with wired technology connect to the network through Ethernet switches or hubs. Users working with wireless technology connect through an *access point (AP)*. Access layer devices such as switches and APs are a potential vulnerability in network security. Physical and remote access to this equipment should be limited to authorized personnel. Network personnel can also implement port security and other measures on switches, as well as various wireless security measures on APs.

Securing the telecommunications room has become even more important because of the increasing occurrence of identity theft. New privacy legislation results in severe penalties if confidential data from a network falls into the wrong hands. Modern networking devices offer capabilities to help prevent these attacks and protect data and user integrity.

Many IDFs connect to a *main distribution facility (MDF)* using an *extended star* design. The MDF is usually located in the NOC or centrally located within the building.

MDFs are typically larger than IDFs. They house high-speed switches, routers, and server farms. The central MDF switches can have enterprise servers and disk drives connected using gigabit copper links. MDFs typically contain

- Point of presence (POP)
- Routers
- Gigabit switches

- Gigabit links to IDFs

- Servers

- Disk storage

IDFs contain lower-speed switches, APs, and hubs. The switches in the IDFs typically have large numbers of Fast Ethernet ports for users to connect at the access layer.

The switches in the IDF usually connect to the switches in the MDF with Gigabit interfaces. This arrangement creates backbone connections, or uplinks. These backbone links, also called vertical cabling, can be copper or fiber-optic. Copper Gigabit or Fast Ethernet links are limited to a maximum of 100 meters and should use CAT5e or CAT6 UTP cable. Fiber-optic links can run much greater distances. Fiber-optic links commonly interconnect buildings, and because they do not conduct electricity, they are immune to lightning strikes, EMI, RFI, and differential grounds. Figure 2-8 illustrates a multi-building Ethernet network design with one MDF in Building A and IDFs in Buildings A, B, and C. The vertical or backbone cabling connecting the MDF and the two IDFs in Building A can be UTP or fiber depending on distance. Vertical (and horizontal) cable runs longer than 100 meters (approx. 328 ft.) should be fiber-optic.

**Figure 2-8    MDFs and IDFs Connect Multiple Buildings and Users**

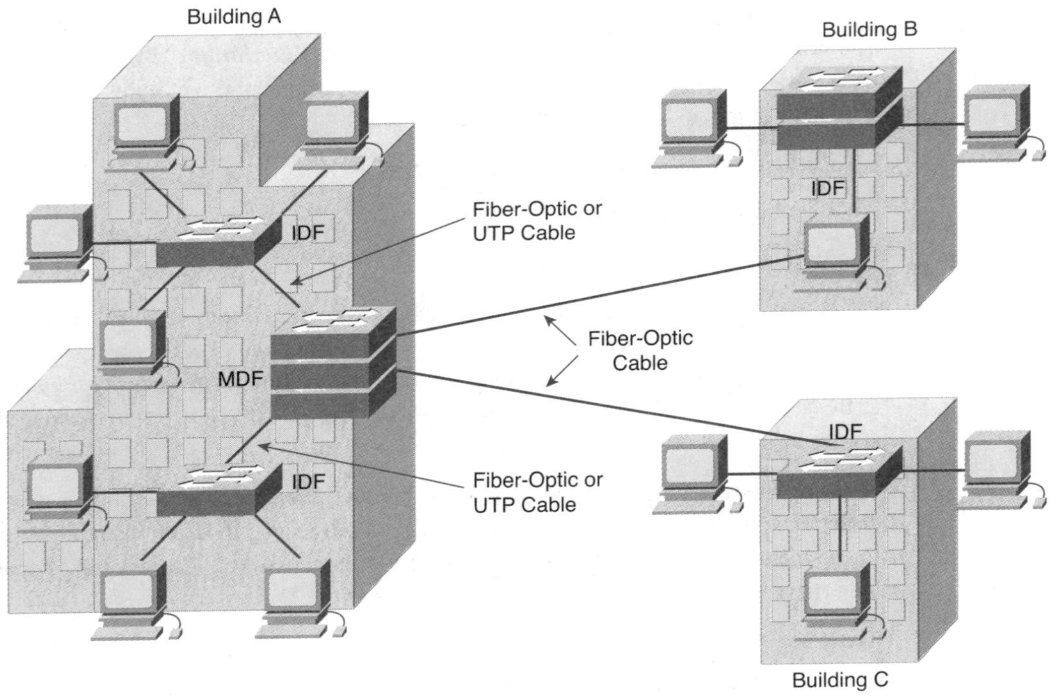

The vertical cabling between the buildings should always be fiber-optic, regardless of distance, to account for the electrical differential between buildings. Inter-building cabling can also be exposed to weather and lightning strikes, which fiber-optic can withstand more easily without damaging equipment connected to it.

In addition to providing basic network access connectivity, it is becoming more common to provide power to end-user devices directly from the Ethernet switches in the telecommunications room. These devices include IP phones, access points, and surveillance cameras.

These devices are powered using the IEEE 802.3af standard, *Power over Ethernet (PoE)*. PoE provides power to a device over the same twisted-pair cable that carries data. This allows an IP phone, for example, to be located on a desk without the need for a separate power cord or a power outlet. To support PoE devices such as the IP phone, the connecting switch must have PoE capability.

PoE can also be provided by power injectors or PoE patch panels for those switches that do not support PoE. Panduit and other suppliers produce PoE patch panels that allow non-PoE-capable switches to participate in PoE environments. Legacy switches connect into the PoE patch panel, which then connects to the PoE-capable device. Figure 2-9 illustrate devices that can be powered by a PoE-capable switch. This allows the devices to be placed without regard to the location of power outlets.

**Figure 2-9    End Devices Receive Power from a PoE Switch**

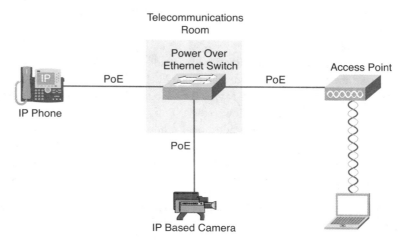

**Interactive Activity 2-2: Placing MDFs, IDFs, and Cabling (2.1.3)**

In this activity, you place the MDFs and IDFs in an appropriate location in the campus diagram and identify appropriate cables to connect them. Use file d3ia-213 on the CD-ROM that accompanies this book to perform this interactive activity.

# Supporting the Enterprise Edge

The enterprise edge is the entry and exit point to the network for external users and services. The following sections describe how external services are delivered as well as security considerations at the edge.

## Service Delivery at the Point of Presence

At the outer edge of the enterprise network is the *point of presence (POP)*, which provides an entry point for services to the enterprise network. Externally provided services coming in through the POP include Internet access, wide-area connections, and telephone services (public switched telephone network [PSTN]).

The POP contains a point of demarcation, or the demarc. The demarc provides a boundary that designates responsibility for equipment maintenance and troubleshooting between the *service provider (SP)* and customer. Equipment from the service provider up to the point of demarcation is the responsibility of the provider; anything past the demarc point is the responsibility of the customer.

In an enterprise, the POP provides links to outside services and sites. The POP can provide a direct link to one or more ISPs, which allows internal users the required access to the Internet. The remote sites of an enterprise are also interconnected through the POPs. The service provider establishes the wide-area links between these remote sites.

The location of the POP and the point of demarcation vary in different countries. While they are often located within the MDF of the customer, they can also be located at the SP.

Figure 2-10 shows an example of a school district with a hub-and-spoke, or star, design. The school district main office is the center of the star or hub and has the primary connections to the Internet and the PSTN. Each of the schools A, B, C, and D connect back to the district office for phone and Internet access to the outside world. The district office and each of the schools have their own POP to make the necessary WAN connections. Each school is connected to the district office with a T1 circuit with a bandwidth of 1.544 Mbps. Because all the schools share the main Internet connection at the district office, the connection to the ISP is a T3 circuit with approximately 45 Mbps bandwidth. This is a scalable design, where additional schools with T1s can connect back to the district office. This design can be applied to businesses and other organizations with multiple remote locations that connect to a central site. If additional remote sites are added to the network, the bandwidth of the Internet and PSTN connections at the central site can be upgraded to higher-speed links, if necessary.

**Figure 2-10   POPs at Each Location Connect Schools to the District Office and External Services**

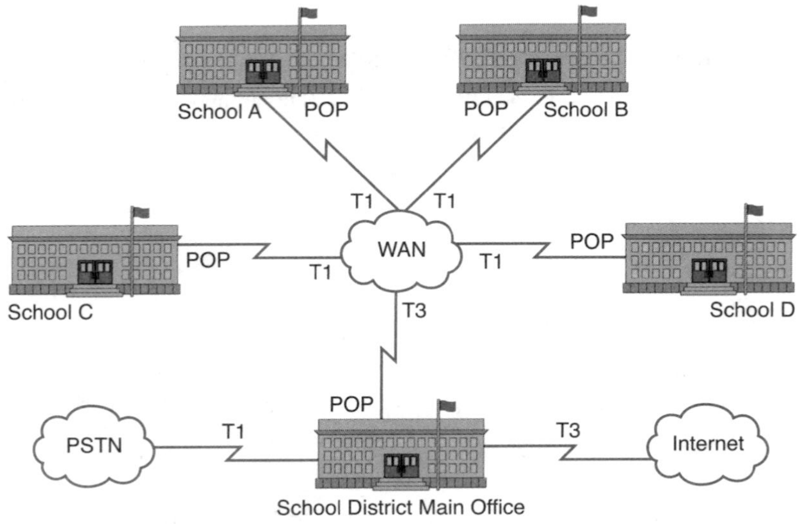

## Security Considerations at the Enterprise Edge

Large enterprises usually consist of multiple sites that interconnect. Multiple locations can have edge connections at each site connecting the enterprise to other individuals and organizations.

The edge is the point of entry for outside attacks and is a point of vulnerability. Attacks at the edge can affect thousands of users. For example, denial of service (DoS) attacks prevent access to resources for legitimate users inside or outside the network, affecting productivity for the entire enterprise.

All traffic into or out of the organization goes through the edge. Edge devices must be configured to defend against attacks and provide filtering based on website, IP address, traffic pattern, application, and protocol.

An organization can deploy a firewall and security appliances with an intrusion detection system (IDS) and intrusion prevention system (IPS) at the edge to protect the network. They can also set up a demilitarized zone (DMZ), an area isolated be firewalls, where web and FTP servers can be placed for external users to access.

External network administrators require access for internal maintenance and software installation. Virtual Private Networks (VPN), access control lists (ACL), user IDs, and passwords provide that access. VPNs also allow remote workers access to internal resources. Figure 2-11 depicts a network with the headquarters (HQ) as the edge, with security protection tools deployed to protect the internal network.

**Figure 2-11    Security Defense Tools at the Enterprise Edge**

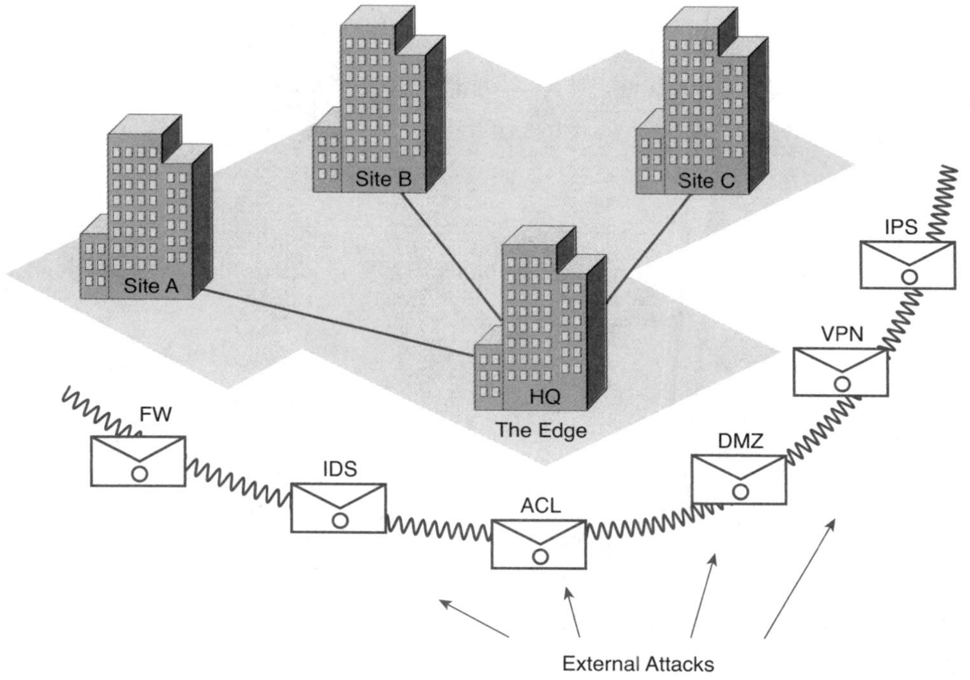

## Connecting the Enterprise Network to External Services

The network connection services commonly purchased by an enterprise include leased lines *(T1/E1)*, Frame Relay, and ATM. Physical cabling brings these services to the enterprise using copper wires, as in the case of T1/E1, or fiber-optic cable for higher-speed services.

The POP must contain certain pieces of equipment to obtain whichever WAN service is required. For example, to obtain T1/E1 service, the customer might require a *punchdown block* to terminate the T1/E1 circuit, as well as a *channel service unit/data service unit (CSU/DSU)* to provide the proper electrical interface and signaling for the service provider. This equipment can be owned and maintained by the service provider or can be owned and maintained by the customer. Regardless of ownership, all equipment located within the POP at the customer site is referred to as *customer premise equipment (CPE)*. The CSU/DSU can be an external standalone device connected to the edge router with a cable or it can be integrated into the router.

Figure 2-12 shows an example of the equipment in the proper sequence required to bring a T1 circuit from a service provider to a customer and finally to the end user. The T1 can be provided by an SP or an ISP and can provide access to the Internet directly or to another site to form a WAN.

**Figure 2-12   Connections and Devices from Service Provider to End User**

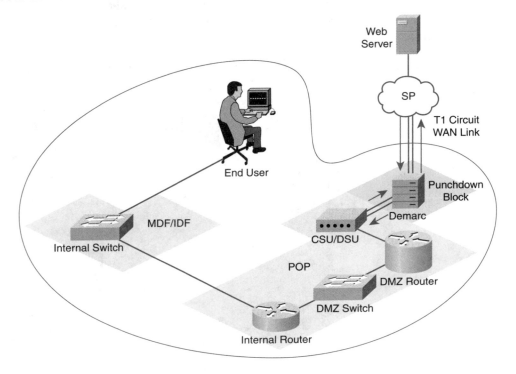

 **Interactive Activity 2-3: Specifying Components to Bring Service to the Internal Network (2.2.3)**

In this activity, you specify the components, in order, needed to connect a service from the edge to the internal network. Use file d3ia-223 on the CD-ROM that accompanies this book to perform this interactive activity.

## Reviewing Routing and Switching

The following sections provide a review of router and switch hardware characteristics. They also serve as a review of router and switch commands most commonly used to display information about and configure these devices.

# Router Hardware

One important device in the distribution layer of an enterprise network is a router. Without the routing process, packets could not leave the local network.

The router provides access to other private networks as well as to the Internet. All hosts on a local network specify the IP address of the local router interface in their IP configuration. This router interface is the default gateway.

Routers play a critical role in networking by interconnecting multiple sites within an enterprise network, providing redundant paths, and connecting ISPs on the Internet. Routers can also act as a translator between different media types and protocols. For example, a router can re-encapsulate packets from an Ethernet to a serial encapsulation.

Routers use the network portion of the destination IP address to route packets to the proper destination. They select an alternate path if a link goes down or traffic is congested. Routers also serve the following other beneficial functions:

- **Provide broadcast containment:** Routers in the distribution layer limit broadcasts to the local network where they need to be heard. Although broadcasts are necessary, too many hosts connected on the same local network generate excessive broadcast traffic and slow the network.

- **Connect remote locations:** Routers in the distribution layer interconnect local networks at various locations of an organization that are geographically separated.

- **Group users logically by application or department:** Routers in the distribution layer logically group users, such as departments within a company, who have common needs or for access to resources.

- **Provide enhanced security (using Network Address Translation [NAT] and ACLs):** Routers in the distribution layer separate and protect certain groups of computers where confidential information resides. Routers also hide the addresses of internal computers from the outside world to help prevent attacks and control who gets into or out of the local network.

With the enterprise and the ISP, the ability to route efficiently and recover from network link failures is critical to delivering packets to their destination. Figure 2-13 depicts each of the main functions the routers can perform.

**Figure 2-13    Functions of Routers**

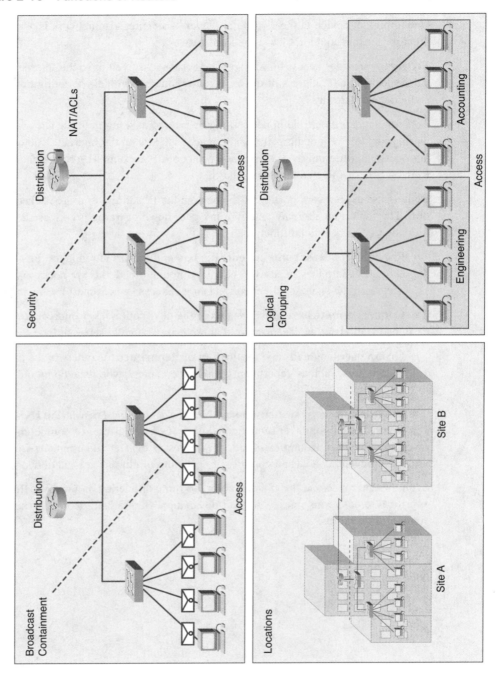

Routers come in many shapes and sizes called *form factors*, as shown in Figure 2-14, and can support a few users or thousands of users, depending on the size and needs of the organization. Network administrators in an enterprise environment should be able to support a variety of routers and switches, from a small desktop to a rack-mounted or blade model.

**Figure 2-14    Router Classes and Form Factors**

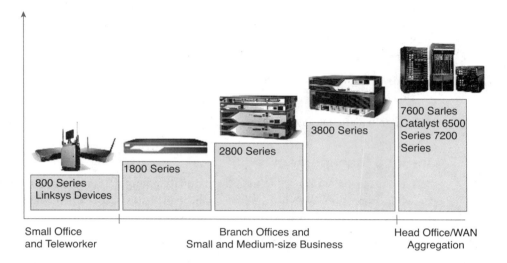

Routers can also be categorized as fixed configuration or modular. With the fixed configuration, the desired router interfaces are built in. Modular routers come with multiple slots that allow a network administrator to change the interfaces on the router. As an example, a Cisco 1841 router comes with two Fast Ethernet RJ-45 interfaces built in and two slots that can accommodate many different network interface modules.

Routers come with a variety of different interfaces, such as Fast and Gigabit Ethernet, serial, and fiber-optic. Router interfaces use the controller/interface or controller/slot/interface conventions. For example, using the controller/interface convention, the first Fast Ethernet interface on a router is numbered as Fa0/0 (controller 0 and interface 0). The second is Fa0/1. The first serial interface on a router using controller/slot/interface is S0/0/0. Figure 2-15 shows the back of an 1841 ISR router with a serial interface card and an integrated 4-port Fast Ethernet switch.

**Figure 2-15    Router Interfaces**

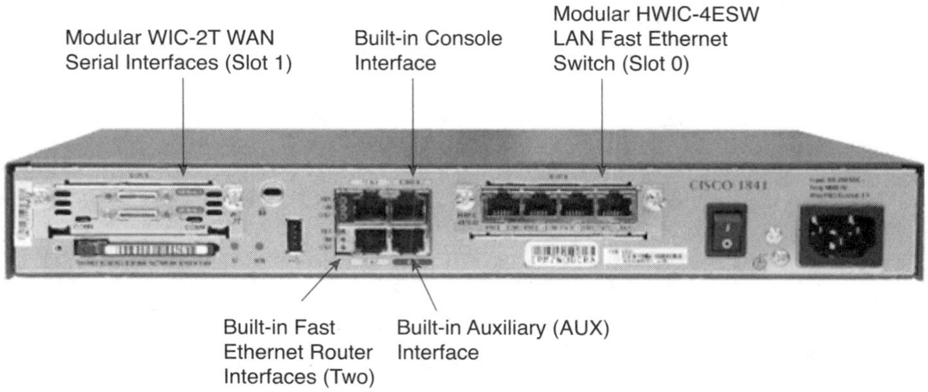

Two methods exist for connecting a PC to a network device for configuration and monitoring tasks: *out-of-band* and *in-band* management.

## Out-of-Band Management

Out-of-band management is used for initial configuration or when a network connection is not unavailable. If there is a problem with access to a network device through the network, it might be necessary to use out-of-band management. For example, a WAN serial interface on a remote router might have been misconfigured so that normal network access is not possible. If the AUX port is properly configured for remote access and a dialup modem is connected, it might be possible to dial in to the modem using out-of-band management and reconfigure the router to correct the problem. Configuration using out-of-band management requires

- Direct connection to the device console port or a direct or remote connection (through dialup) to the AUX port

- Terminal emulation client

### In-Band Management

In-band management is used to monitor and make configuration changes to a network device over a network connection. With in-band, the connection shares network bandwidth with other hosts on the network. Configuration using in-band management requires

- At least one network interface on the device to be connected and operational

- Valid IP configuration on interfaces involved (for an IP-based network)

- Telnet, Secure Shell (SSH), or HTTP to access a Cisco device (these protocols are primarily IP based)

Figure 2-16 shows two forms of out-of-band and two forms of in-band management.

**Figure 2-16  Out-of-Band and In-Band Management Methods**

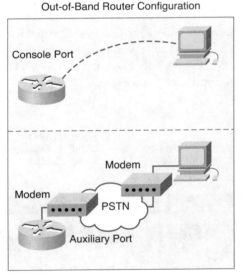
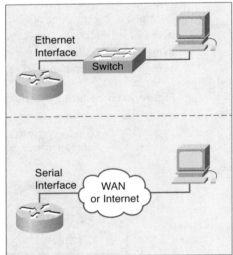

### Basic Router CLI show Commands

This section includes some of the most commonly used Cisco IOS commands to display and verify the operational status of the router and related network functionality. These commands are divided into several categories, as shown in Table 2-1.

Table 2-1 lists these commands with common options used and the minimum abbreviation allowable, along with a description of their function and key information displayed.

**Table 2-1   Common Router show Commands**

| Full Command | Abbreviation | Purpose / Information Displayed |
| --- | --- | --- |
| **General Use** | | |
| **show running-config** | **sh run** | Displays current config running in RAM. Includes host name, passwords, interface IP addresses, routing protocol activated, DHCP, and NAT configuration. Must be issued in EXEC mode. |
| **show startup-config** | **sh star** | Displays backup config in NVRAM. Can be different if running config has not been copied to backup. Must be issued in EXEC mode. |
| **show version** | **sh ve** | Displays IOS version, ROM version, router uptime system image file name, boot method, number and type of interfaces installed, and amount of RAM, NVRAM, and flash. Also shows the Configuration register. |
| **Routing Related** | | |
| **show ip protocols** | **sh ip pro** | Displays information for routing protocols configured including timer settings, version numbers, update intervals, active interfaces, and networks advertised. |
| **show ip route** | **sh ip ro** | Displays routing table information including routing code, networks known, admin distance and metric, how they were learned, last update next hop, interface learned through, and any static routes (including default) configured. |
| **Interface Related** | | |
| **show interfaces (type #)** | **sh int f0/0** | Displays one or all interfaces with line (protocol) status, bandwidth, delay, reliability, encapsulation, duplex, and I/O statistics. |
| **show ip interface brief** | **sh ip int br** | Displays all interfaces with IP address with interface status (up/down/admin down) and line protocol status (up/down). |
| **show protocols** | **sh prot** | Displays all interfaces with IP address and subnet mask (slash notation) with interface status (up/down/admin down) and line protocol status (up/down) . |
| **Connectivity Related** | | |
| **show cdp neighbors (detail)** | **sh cdp ne** | Displays information on directly connected devices including device ID (host name), local interface where device is connected, capability (R=router, S=switch), platform (e.g., 2620XM), and port ID of remote device. The detail option provides the IP address of the other device as well as the IOS version. |
| **show sessions** | **sh ses** | Displays Telnet sessions (VTY) with remote hosts. Displays session number, host name, and address. |
| **show ssh** | **sh ssh** | Displays SSH server connections with remote hosts. |
| **ping (ip / hostname)** | **p** | Sends five ICMP echo requests to an IP address or host name (if DNS is available) and displays the min/max and avg time to respond. |
| **traceroute (ip / hostname)** | **tr** | Sends echo request with varying TTL. Lists routers (hops) in path and time to respond. |

Figure 2-17 shows two networks (192.168.1.0/24 and 192.168.3.0/24) interconnected with a WAN link (network 192.168.2.0/24).

**Figure 2-17    Multi-router and Multi-switch Network**

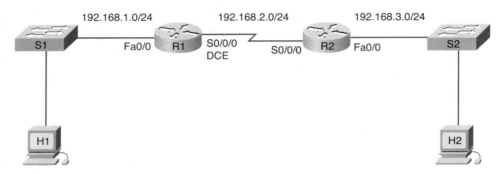

The following examples display the **show** command output for the R1 model 1841 router in the Figure 2-17 network topology. Example 2-1 shows the **show running-config** output for R1.

**Example 2-1  R1 show running-config Command Output**

```
R1# show running-config

<output omitted>
Building configuration...
Current configuration : 1063 bytes
!
version 12.4
service timestamps debug datetime msec
service timestamps log datetime msec
no service password-encryption
hostname R1
enable secret 5 $1$i6w9$dvdpVM6zV10E6tSyLdkR5/
no ip domain lookup
!
interface FastEthernet0/0
 description LAN 192.168.1.0 default gateway
 ip address 192.168.1.1 255.255.255.0
 duplex auto
 speed auto
!
interface FastEthernet0/1
 no ip address
 shutdown
 duplex auto
 speed auto
!
interface Serial0/0/0
 description WAN link to R2
 ip address 192.168.2.1 255.255.255.0
 encapsulation ppp
 clock rate 64000
 no fair-queue
```

```
!
interface Serial0/0/1
 no ip address
 shutdown
!
interface Vlan1
 no ip address
!
router rip
 version 2
 network 192.168.1.0
 network 192.168.2.0
!
banner motd ^CUnauthorized Access Prohibited^C
!
ip http server
!
line con 0
 password cisco
 login
line aux 0
line vty 0 4
 password cisco
 login
```

Example 2-2 presents the **show version** output for R1.

**Example 2-2  R1 show version Command Output**

```
R1# show version

<output omitted>
Cisco IOS Software, 1841 Software (C1841-ADVIPSERVICESK9-M), Version 12.4(10b),
RELEASE SOFTWARE (fc3)
Technical Support: http://www.cisco.com/techsupport
Copyright (c) 1986-2007 by Cisco Systems, Inc.
Compiled Fri 19-Jan-07 15:15 by prod_rel_team

ROM: System Bootstrap, Version 12.4(13r)T, RELEASE SOFTWARE (fc1)
R1 uptime is 43 minutes
System returned to ROM by reload at 22:05:12 UTC Sat Jan 5 2008
System image file is "flash:c1841-advipservicesk9-mz.124-10b.bin"

Cisco 1841 (revision 6.0) with 174080K/22528K bytes of memory.
Processor board ID FTX1111W0QF
6 FastEthernet interfaces
2 Serial(sync/async) interfaces
1 Virtual Private Network (VPN) Module
DRAM configuration is 64 bits wide with parity disabled.
191K bytes of NVRAM.
62720K bytes of ATA CompactFlash (Read/Write)

Configuration register is 0x2102
```

Example 2-3 presents the **show ip protocols** output for R1.

**Example 2-3  R1 show ip protocols Command Output**

```
R1# show ip protocols

Routing Protocol is "rip"
  Outgoing update filter list for all interfaces is not set
  Incoming update filter list for all interfaces is not set
  Sending updates every 30 seconds, next due in 20 seconds
  Invalid after 180 seconds, hold down 180, flushed after 240
  Redistributing: rip
  Default version control: send version 2, receive version 2
    Interface           Send  Recv  Triggered RIP  Key-chain
    FastEthernet0/0      2     2
    Serial0/0/0          2     2
  Automatic network summarization is in effect
  Maximum path: 4
  Routing for Networks:
    192.168.1.0
    192.168.2.0
  Routing Information Sources:
    Gateway          Distance      Last Update
    192.168.2.2         120        00:00:20
  Distance: (default is 120)
```

Example 2-4 presents the **show ip route** output for R1.

**Example 2-4  R1 show ip route Command Output**

```
R1# show ip route

Codes: C - connected, S - static, R - RIP, M - mobile, B - BGP
       D - EIGRP, EX - EIGRP external, O - OSPF, IA - OSPF inter area
       N1 - OSPF NSSA external type 1, N2 - OSPF NSSA external type 2
       E1 - OSPF external type 1, E2 - OSPF external type 2
       i - IS-IS, su - IS-IS summary, L1 - IS-IS level-1, L2 - IS-IS level-2
       ia - IS-IS inter area, * - candidate default, U - per-user static route
       o - ODR, P - periodic downloaded static route

Gateway of last resort is not set
C    192.168.1.0/24 is directly connected, FastEthernet0/0
C    192.168.2.0/24 is directly connected, Serial0/0/0
R    192.168.3.0/24 [120/1] via 192.168.2.2, 00:00:24, Serial0/0/0
```

Example 2-5 presents the **show interfaces** output for R1.

**Example 2-5  R1 show interfaces Command Output**

```
R1# show interfaces

< Some output omitted >
FastEthernet0/0 is up, line protocol is up
  Hardware is Gt96k FE, address is 001b.5325.256e (bia 001b.5325.256e)
  Internet address is 192.168.1.1/24
  MTU 1500 bytes, BW 100000 Kbit, DLY 100 usec,
     reliability 255/255, txload 1/255, rxload 1/255
  Encapsulation ARPA, loopback not set
  Keepalive set (10 sec)
  Full-duplex, 100Mb/s, 100BaseTX/FX
  ARP type: ARPA, ARP Timeout 04:00:00
  Last input 00:00:17, output 00:00:01, output hang never
  Last clearing of "show interface" counters never
  Input queue: 0/75/0/0 (size/max/drops/flushes); Total output drops: 0
  Queueing strategy: fifo
  Output queue: 0/40 (size/max)
  5 minute input rate 0 bits/sec, 0 packets/sec
  5 minute output rate 0 bits/sec, 0 packets/sec
     196 packets input, 31850 bytes
     Received 181 broadcasts, 0 runts, 0 giants, 0 throttles
     0 input errors, 0 CRC, 0 frame, 0 overrun, 0 ignored
     0 watchdog
     0 input packets with dribble condition detected
     392 packets output, 35239 bytes, 0 underruns
     0 output errors, 0 collisions, 3 interface resets
     0 babbles, 0 late collision, 0 deferred
     0 lost carrier, 0 no carrier
     0 output buffer failures, 0 output buffers swapped out

FastEthernet0/1 is administratively down, line protocol is down

Serial0/0/0 is up, line protocol is up
  Hardware is GT96K Serial
  Internet address is 192.168.2.1/24
  MTU 1500 bytes, BW 1544 Kbit, DLY 20000 usec,
     reliability 255/255, txload 1/255, rxload 1/255
  Encapsulation PPP, LCP Listen, loopback not set
  Keepalive set (10 sec)
  Last input 00:00:02, output 00:00:03, output hang never
  Last clearing of "show interface" counters 00:51:52
  Input queue: 0/75/0/0 (size/max/drops/flushes); Total output drops: 0
  Queueing strategy: fifo
  Output queue: 0/40 (size/max)
  5 minute input rate 0 bits/sec, 0 packets/sec
  5 minute output rate 0 bits/sec, 0 packets/sec
     401 packets input, 27437 bytes, 0 no buffer
     Received 293 broadcasts, 0 runts, 0 giants, 0 throttles
     0 input errors, 0 CRC, 0 frame, 0 overrun, 0 ignored, 0 abort
     389 packets output, 26940 bytes, 0 underruns
```

```
        0 output errors, 0 collisions, 2 interface resets
        0 output buffer failures, 0 output buffers swapped out
        6 carrier transitions
        DCD=up  DSR=up  DTR=up  RTS=up  CTS=up

Serial0/0/1 is administratively down, line protocol is down
```

Example 2-6 presents the **show ip interfaces brief** output for R1.

**Example 2-6  R1 show ip interfaces brief Command Output**

```
R1# show ip interface brief

Interface              IP-Address      OK? Method Status                 Protocol
FastEthernet0/0        192.168.1.1     YES manual up                     up
FastEthernet0/1        unassigned      YES unset  administratively down  down
Serial0/0/0            192.168.2.1     YES manual up                     up
Serial0/0/1            unassigned      YES unset  administratively down  down
Vlan1                  unassigned      YES unset  up                     down
```

Example 2-7 presents the **show protocols** output for R1.

**Example 2-7  R1 show protocols Command Output**

```
R1# show protocols

Global values:
  Internet Protocol routing is enabled
FastEthernet0/0 is up, line protocol is up
  Internet address is 192.168.1.1/24
FastEthernet0/1 is administratively down, line protocol is down
FastEthernet0/1/0 is up, line protocol is down
FastEthernet0/1/1 is up, line protocol is down
FastEthernet0/1/2 is up, line protocol is down
FastEthernet0/1/3 is up, line protocol is down
Serial0/0/0 is up, line protocol is up
  Internet address is 192.168.2.1/24
Serial0/0/1 is administratively down, line protocol is down
Vlan1 is up, line protocol is down
```

Example 2-8 presents the **show cdp neighbors** output for R1.

**Example 2-8  R1 show cdp neighbors Command Output**

```
R1# show cdp neighbors

Capability Codes: R - Router, T - Trans Bridge, B - Source Route Bridge
                  S - Switch, H - Host, I - IGMP, r - Repeater

Device ID        Local Intrfce     Holdtme     Capability  Platform  Port ID
R2               Ser 0/0/0         137         R S I       1841      Ser 0/0/0
S1               Fas 0/0           175         S I         WS-C2960- Fas 0/1
```

Example 2-9 presents the **show cdp neighbors detail** output for R1.

**Example 2-9  R1 show cdp neighbors detail Command Output**

```
R1# show cdp neighbors detail

-------------------------
Device ID: R2
Entry address(es):
  IP address: 192.168.2.2
Platform: Cisco 1841,  Capabilities: Router Switch IGMP
Interface: Serial0/0/0,  Port ID (outgoing port): Serial0/0/0
Holdtime : 164 sec
Version :
Cisco IOS Software, 1841 Software (C1841-ADVIPSERVICESK9-M), Version 12.4(10b),
RELEASE SOFTWARE (fc3)
Technical Support: http://www.cisco.com/techsupport
Copyright (c) 1986-2007 by Cisco Systems, Inc.
Compiled Fri 19-Jan-07 15:15 by prod_rel_team
advertisement version: 2
VTP Management Domain: ''

-------------------------
Device ID: S1
Entry address(es):
  IP address: 192.168.1.5
Platform: cisco WS-C2960-24TT-L,  Capabilities: Switch IGMP
Interface: FastEthernet0/0,  Port ID (outgoing port): FastEthernet0/1
Holdtime : 139 sec
Version :
Cisco IOS Software, C2960 Software (C2960-LANBASE-M), Version 12.2(25)SEE3, RELE
ASE SOFTWARE (fc2)
Copyright (c) 1986-2007 by Cisco Systems, Inc.
Compiled Thu 22-Feb-07 13:57 by myl
advertisement version: 2
Protocol Hello:  OUI=0x00000C, Protocol ID=0x0112; payload len=27, value=0000000
0FFFFFFFF010221FF000000000000001D46350C80FF0000
VTP Management Domain: ''
Native VLAN: 1
Duplex: full
```

**Interactive Activity 2-4: Matching the Command to the Information Needed (2.3.2)**

In this activity, you identify the command that can provide the information indicated. Use file d3ia-232 on the CD-ROM that accompanies this book to perform this interactive activity.

## Basic Router Configuration Using CLI

A basic router configuration includes the host name for identification, passwords for security, and assignment of IP addresses to interfaces for connectivity. Verify and save configuration changes using the **copy running-config startup-config** command. To clear the router configuration, use the **erase startup-config** command and then the **reload** command. Table 2-2 shows common IOS commands used to configure routers. Also listed are the abbreviation, the purpose of the command, and the required mode to execute the command.

**Table 2-2    Common Router Configuration Commands**

| Full Command / Example | Abbreviation | Purpose / Mode |
|---|---|---|
| **Configuration Management** | | |
| enable | en | Changes from user EXEC mode (>) to privileged EXEC mode (#) |
| configure terminal | conf t | Changes from privileged EXEC mode to global configuration mode |
| copy running-config startup-config | cop r s | Copies the running configuration from RAM to the startup configuration file in NVRAM |
| erase startup-config | era sta | Deletes the startup configuration file (startup-config) |
| reload | rel | Performs a software reboot |
| **Global Settings** | | |
| hostname R1 | ho | Sets the device host name to R1 |
| banner motd #XYZ# | ban m | Sets the banner message of the day, which is displayed at login, to XYZ |
| enable secret itsasecret | ena s | Sets the privileged mode encrypted password to itsasecret |
| **Line Settings** | | |
| line con 0 | lin c | Enters line config mode for console port 0 |
| line aux 0 | lin a | Enters line config mode for auxiliary port 0 |
| line vty 0 4 | lin v | Enters line config mode for VTY lines 0 through 4 |
| login | login | Allows login to a line in line config mode |
| password | pas | Sets line login password in line config mode |

| Full Command / Example | Abbreviation | Purpose / Mode |
|---|---|---|
| **Interface Settings** | | |
| **interface S0/0/0** | **int** | Enters interface config mode for interface Serial 0/0/0 (specifies the interface as type/number) |
| **description XYZ** | **des** | Specifies a description for the interface as XYZ (in interface config mode) |
| **ip address 192.168.1.1 255.255.255.0** | **ip add** | Specifies an IP address and subnet mask for the interface (in interface config mode) |
| **no shutdown** | **no sh** | Brings up the interface (in interface config mode). Use **shutdown** to disable the interface. |
| **clock rate 64000** | **clo r** | Sets the clock rate for a serial interface, with a DCE cable connected, to 64000 (in interface config mode) |
| **encapsulation ppp** | **enc** | Specifies the encapsulation for the interface as ppp (in interface config mode) |
| **Routing Settings** | | |
| **router rip** | **router** | Enters router config mode for the RIP routing protocol |
| **network 172.16.0.0** | **net** | Specifies network 172.16.0.0 to be advertised by RIP (in RIP router config mode) |
| **ip route 172.16.0.0 255.255.0.0 S0/0/0** | **ip route** | Specifies a static route to network 172.16.0.0 through exit interface Serial 0/0/0 |
| **ip route 0.0.0.0 0.0.0.0 192.168.2.2** | **ip route** | Specifies a static default route through next-hop IP address 192.168.2.2 |

Example 2-10 shows the configuration commands used to configure the R1 router in Figure 2-18. Refer to Example 2-1 to see the results of the commands as displayed with the **show running-config** command. The resulting running configuration frequently has a number of commands inserted automatically by the IOS that were not entered during the configuration process.

**Example 2-10    Router R1 Basic Configuration Commands**

```
Router> enable
Router# configure terminal

Enter configuration commands, one per line.  End with CNTL/Z.
Router(config)# hostname R1
R1(config)# banner motd %Unauthorized Access Prohibited%
R1(config)# enable secret class
R1(config)# line con 0
R1(config-line)# password cisco
R1(config-line)# login
R1(config-line)# line aux 0
R1(config-line)# line vty 0 4
R1(config-line)# password cisco
R1(config-line)# login
```

```
R1(config-line)# exit
R1(config)# no ip domain-lookup

R1(config)#
R1(config)# interface FastEthernet0/0
R1(config-if)# description LAN 192.168.1.0 default gateway
R1(config-if)# ip address 192.168.1.1 255.255.255.0
R1(config-if)# no shutdown
R1(config-if)#
R1(config-if)# interface Serial0/0/0
R1(config-if)# description WAN link to R2
R1(config-if)# ip address 192.168.2.1 255.255.255.0
R1(config-if)# encapsulation ppp
R1(config-if)# clock rate 64000
R1(config-if)# no shutdown
R1(config-if)#
R1(config-if)# router rip
R1(config-router)# version 2
R1(config-router)# network 192.168.1.0
R1(config-router)# network 192.168.2.0
```

It is common to copy the running configuration of a device, such as the R1 router, and paste it into a text editor file for backup or use it as a starting point for modification. The text file can then be edited as necessary so that it can be used to reconfigure the router or configure another router.

### Note

After a device has been configured, it is critical to copy the running configuration to the startup configuration using the **copy run start** command. Otherwise, changes will be lost if the router is restarted using the **reload** command or if it loses power.

### Basic Router Configuration Using CLI (2.3.3)

In this activity, you practice basic router configuration and verification commands. Use file d3-233.pka on the CD-ROM that accompanies this book to perform this activity using Packet Tracer.

## Switch Hardware

Although all three layers of the hierarchical design model contain switches and routers, the access layer generally has more switches. The main function of switches is to connect hosts such as end-user workstations, servers, IP phones, web cameras, access points, and routers. This means that there are many more switches in an organization than routers.

As shown in Figure 2-18, switches come in many form factors:

- Small standalone models sit on a desk or mount on a wall.

- Integrated routers include a switch built into the chassis that is rack mounted.

- High-end switches mount into a rack and are often a chassis-and-blade design to allow more blades to be added as the number of users increases.

**Figure 2-18    Switch Classes and Form Factors**

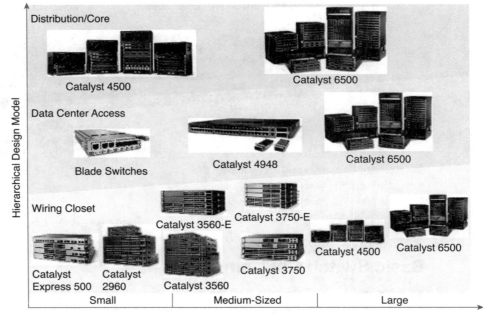

High-end enterprise and service provider switches support ports of varying speeds, from 100 MB to 10 GB.

An enterprise switch in an MDF connects other switches from IDFs using Gigabit fiber or copper cable. An IDF switch typically needs both RJ-45 Fast Ethernet ports for device connectivity and at least one Gigabit Ethernet port (copper or fiber) to uplink to the MDF switch. Some high-end switches have modular ports that can be changed if needed. For example, it might be necessary to switch from multimode fiber to single-mode fiber, which would require a different port.

Like routers, switch ports are also designated using the controller/port or controller/slot/port convention. For example, using the controller/port convention, the first Fast Ethernet port on a switch is numbered as Fa0/1 (controller 0 and port 1). The second is Fa0/2. The first port on a switch that uses controller/slot/port is Fa0/0/1. Gigabit ports are designated as Gi0/1, Gi0/2, and so on.

*Port density* on a switch is an important factor. In an enterprise environment where hundreds or thousands of users need switch connections, a switch with a 1RU height and 48 ports has a higher port density than a 1RU 24-port switch. Figure 2-19 shows a Cisco Catalyst 4948 switch with 48 access ports capable of operating at 10 Mbps (regular Ethernet), 100 Mbps (Fast Ethernet), or 1000 Mbps (Gigabit Ethernet). In addition, it has two built-in 10-Gbps UTP ports and two modular ports that can accept various fiber-optic Ethernet interfaces, including 10-Gbps multimode or single-mode.

**Figure 2-19    Ethernet Switch Ports: Built-in and Modular**

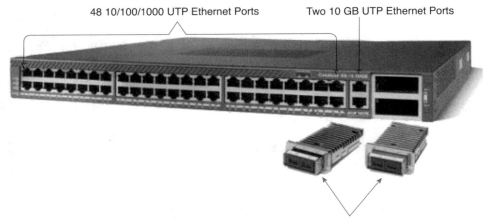

48 10/100/1000 UTP Ethernet Ports    Two 10 GB UTP Ethernet Ports

Two 10 GB Fiber Optic Modular Ethernet Ports

## Basic Switch CLI Commands

Switches make use of common IOS commands for configuration, to check for connectivity and to display current switch status. These commands can be divided into several categories, as shown in Table 2-2.

Table 2-3 lists these commands with common options used and the minimum abbreviation allowable, along with a description of their function and key information displayed.

**Table 2-3    Common Switch show Commands**

| Full Command | Abbreviation | Purpose / Information Displayed |
|---|---|---|
| **General Use** | | |
| **show running-config** | **sh run** | Displays current config running in RAM. Includes host name, passwords, interface IP addresses (if present), port numbers, and characteristics (duplex/speed). |
| **show startup-config** | **sh star** | Displays backup config in NVRAM. Can be different if running config has not been copied to backup. |
| **show version** | **sh ve** | Displays IOS version, ROM version, switch uptime, system image file name, boot method, number and type of interfaces installed, and amount of RAM, NVRAM, and flash. Also shows the Configuration register. |
| **Interface / Port Related** | | |
| **show interfaces (type and number)** | **sh int f0/1** | Displays one or all interfaces with line (protocol) status, bandwidth, delay, reliability, encapsulation, duplex, and I/O statistics. |
| **show ip interface brief** | **sh ip int br** | Displays all interfaces with IP address with interface status (up/down/admin down) and line protocol status (up/down). |

| Full Command | Abbreviation | Purpose / Information Displayed |
|---|---|---|
| **Interface / Port Related** | | |
| **show port-security** | **sh por** | Displays any ports where security has been activated, along with max address allowed, current count, security violation count, and action to take (normally shut-down). |
| **show mac-address-table** | **sh mac-a** | Displays all MAC addresses the switch has learned, how learned (dynamic/static), the port number, and VLAN the port is in. |
| **Connectivity Related** | | |
| **show cdp neighbors (detail)** | **sh cdp ne** | Displays information on directly connected devices, including device ID (host name), local interface where device is connected, capability (R=router, S=switch), platform (e.g., WS-2950-2), and port ID of remote device. The detail option provides the IP address of the other device as well as the IOS version. |
| **show sessions** | **sh ses** | Displays Telnet sessions (VTY) with remote hosts. Displays session number, host name, and address. |
| **show ssh** | **sh ssh** | Displays SSH server connections with remote hosts. |
| **ping (ip / hostname)** | **p** | Sends five ICMP echo requests to an IP address or host name (if DNS is available) and displays the min/max and avg time to respond. |
| **traceroute (ip / hostname)** | **tr** | Sends echo request with varying TTL. Lists routers (hops) in path and time to respond. |

The same in-band and out-of-band management techniques that apply to routers also apply to switch configuration.

The following examples display **show** command output for the S1 model 2960 switch in the Figure 2-18 network topology. This switch has 24 10/100 Ethernet UTP ports and two Gigabit ports. Port Fa0/3 has a host attached and port security has been set. If the **mac-address sticky** option is used with the **switchport port-security** command, the running configuration is automatically updated when the MAC address of the host attached to that port is learned.

Example 2-11 presents the **show running-config** output for S1.

**Example 2-11    S1 show running-config Command Output**

```
S1# show running-config

< output omitted >
Building configuration...
Current configuration : 1373 bytes
!
version 12.2
```

```
no service pad
service timestamps debug uptime
service timestamps log uptime
no service password-encryption
!
hostname S1
enable secret 5 $1$9y6K$CE6oM7XmLRg6ISQPAJOk10
no ip domain-lookup
spanning-tree mode pvst
!
interface FastEthernet0/1
interface FastEthernet0/2
interface FastEthernet0/3
 switchport mode access
 switchport port-security
 switchport port-security mac-address sticky
 switchport port-security mac-address sticky 000b.db04.a5cd
!
< Output for ports Fa0/4 through Fa0/21 omitted >
!
interface FastEthernet0/22
interface FastEthernet0/23
interface FastEthernet0/24
!
interface GigabitEthernet0/1
interface GigabitEthernet0/2
!
interface Vlan1
 ip address 192.168.1.5 255.255.255.0
 no ip route-cache
!
ip default-gateway 192.168.1.1
ip http server
!
banner motd ^CUnauthorized Access Prohibited^C
!
line con 0
 password cisco
 login
line vty 0 4
 password cisco
 login
line vty 5 15
 password cisco
 login
!
end
```

Example 2-12 presents the **show version** command output for S1.

**Example 2-12   S1 show version Command Output**

```
S1#  show version

< output omitted >
Cisco IOS Software, C2960 Software (C2960-LANBASE-M), Version 12.2(25)SEE3, RELEASE SOFTWARE
  (fc2)
Copyright (c) 1986-2007 by Cisco Systems, Inc.
Compiled Thu 22-Feb-07 13:57 by myl
Image text-base: 0x00003000, data-base: 0x00AA3380

ROM: Bootstrap program is C2960 boot loader
BOOTLDR: C2960 Boot Loader (C2960-HBOOT-M) Version 12.2(25r)SEE1, RELEASE SOFTWARE (fc1)

S1 uptime is 55 minutes
System returned to ROM by power-on
System image file is "flash:c2960-lanbase-mz.122-25.SEE3/c2960-lanbase-mz.122-25.SEE3.bin"

cisco WS-C2960-24TT-L (PowerPC405) processor (revision D0) with 61440K/4088K bytes of memory.
Processor board ID FOC1129X56L
Last reset from power-on
1 Virtual Ethernet interface
24 FastEthernet interfaces
2 Gigabit Ethernet interfaces
The password-recovery mechanism is enabled.

64K bytes of flash-simulated non-volatile configuration memory.
Base ethernet MAC Address       : 00:1D:46:35:0C:80
Motherboard assembly number     : 73-10390-04
Power supply part number        : 341-0097-02
Motherboard serial number       : FOC11285HJ7
Power supply serial number      : AZS11280656
Model revision number           : D0
Motherboard revision number     : A0
Model number                    : WS-C2960-24TT-L
System serial number            : FOC1129X56L
Top Assembly Part Number        : 800-27221-03
Top Assembly Revision Number    : A0
Version ID                      : V03
CLEI Code Number                : COM3L00BRB
Hardware Board Revision Number  : 0x01

Switch   Ports  Model         SW Version      SW Image
------   -----  -----         ----------      ----------
*   1    26     WS-C2960-24TT-L  12.2(25)SEE3   C2960-LANBASE-M

Configuration register is 0xF
```

Example 2-13 presents the **show interfaces** command output for S1.

**Example 2-13    S1 show interfaces Command Output**

```
S1# show interfaces

< output omitted >
Vlan1 is up, line protocol is up
  Hardware is EtherSVI, address is 001d.4635.0cc0 (bia 001d.4635.0cc0)
  Internet address is 192.168.1.5/24
  MTU 1500 bytes, BW 1000000 Kbit, DLY 10 usec,
      reliability 255/255, txload 1/255, rxload 1/255
  Encapsulation ARPA, loopback not set
  ARP type: ARPA, ARP Timeout 04:00:00
  Last input 00:00:09, output 00:47:51, output hang never
  Last clearing of "show interface" counters never
  Input queue: 0/75/0/0 (size/max/drops/flushes); Total output drops: 0
  Queueing strategy: fifo
  Output queue: 0/40 (size/max)
  5 minute input rate 0 bits/sec, 0 packets/sec
  5 minute output rate 0 bits/sec, 0 packets/sec
     216 packets input, 23957 bytes, 0 no buffer
     Received 0 broadcasts (0 IP multicast)
     0 runts, 0 giants, 0 throttles
     0 input errors, 0 CRC, 0 frame, 0 overrun, 0 ignored
     25 packets output, 5161 bytes, 0 underruns
     0 output errors, 1 interface resets
     0 output buffer failures, 0 output buffers swapped out
FastEthernet0/1 is up, line protocol is up (connected)
  Hardware is Fast Ethernet, address is 001d.4635.0c81 (bia 001d.4635.0c81)
  MTU 1500 bytes, BW 100000 Kbit, DLY 100 usec,
      reliability 255/255, txload 1/255, rxload 1/255
  Encapsulation ARPA, loopback not set
  Keepalive set (10 sec)
  Full-duplex, 100Mb/s, media type is 10/100BaseTX
  input flow-control is off, output flow-control is unsupported
  ARP type: ARPA, ARP Timeout 04:00:00
  Last input 00:00:28, output 00:00:00, output hang never
  Last clearing of "show interface" counters never
  Input queue: 0/75/0/0 (size/max/drops/flushes); Total output drops: 0
  Queueing strategy: fifo
  Output queue: 0/40 (size/max)
  5 minute input rate 0 bits/sec, 0 packets/sec
  5 minute output rate 0 bits/sec, 0 packets/sec
     564 packets input, 57713 bytes, 0 no buffer
     Received 197 broadcasts (0 multicast)
     0 runts, 0 giants, 0 throttles
     0 input errors, 0 CRC, 0 frame, 0 overrun, 0 ignored
     0 watchdog, 195 multicast, 0 pause input
     0 input packets with dribble condition detected
     2515 packets output, 195411 bytes, 0 underruns
     0 output errors, 0 collisions, 1 interface resets
     0 babbles, 0 late collision, 0 deferred
     0 lost carrier, 0 no carrier, 0 PAUSE output
     0 output buffer failures, 0 output buffers swapped out
< output omitted >
```

Example 2-14 presents the **show ip interface brief** command output for S1.

**Example 2-14    S1 show ip interface brief Command Output**

```
S1# show ip interface brief

< output omitted >
Interface              IP-Address      OK? Method Status            Protocol
Vlan1                  192.168.1.5     YES manual up                up
FastEthernet0/1        unassigned      YES unset  up                up
FastEthernet0/2        unassigned      YES unset  down              down
FastEthernet0/3        unassigned      YES unset  up                up
< Output for ports Fa0/4 through Fa0/21 omitted >
FastEthernet0/22       unassigned      YES unset  down              down
FastEthernet0/23       unassigned      YES unset  down              down
FastEthernet0/24       unassigned      YES unset  down              down
GigabitEthernet0/1     unassigned      YES unset  down              down
GigabitEthernet0/2     unassigned      YES unset  down              down
```

Example 2-15 presents the **show mac-address-table** output for S1.

**Example 2-15    S1 show mac-address-table Command Output**

```
S1# show mac-address-table

          Mac Address Table
-------------------------------------------

Vlan    Mac Address       Type        Ports
----    -----------       --------    -----
 All    0100.0ccc.cccc    STATIC      CPU
< Output for some CPU ports omitted >
 All    0180.c200.0010    STATIC      CPU
 All    ffff.ffff.ffff    STATIC      CPU
   1    000b.db04.a5cd    DYNAMIC     Fa0/3
   1    001b.5325.256e    DYNAMIC     Fa0/1
Total Mac Addresses for this criterion: 22
```

Example 2-16 presents the **show port-security** output for S1.

**Example 2-16    S1 show port-security Command Output**

```
S1# show port-security

Secure Port  MaxSecureAddr  CurrentAddr  SecurityViolation  Security Action
             (Count)        (Count)      (Count)
-----------------------------------------------------------------------
     Fa0/9        1              1              0           Shutdown
-----------------------------------------------------------------------
Total Addresses in System (excluding one mac per port)    : 0
Max Addresses limit in System (excluding one mac per port) : 8320
```

Example 2-17 presents the **show cdp neighbors** output for S1.

**Example 2-17   S1 show cdp neighbors Command Output**

```
S1# show cdp neighbors

Capability Codes: R - Router, T - Trans Bridge, B - Source Route Bridge
                  S - Switch, H - Host, I - IGMP, r - Repeater, P - Phone

Device ID          Local Intrfce       Holdtme    Capability    Platform   Port ID
R1                   Fas 0/1             122        R S I         1841       Fas0/0
```

A basic switch configuration includes the host name for identification, passwords for security, and assignment of IP addresses for connectivity. In-band access requires the switch to have an IP address.

Verify and save the switch configuration using the **copy running-config startup-config** command. To clear the switch configuration, use the **erase startup-config** command and then the **reload** command. You might also need to erase any VLAN information using the **delete flash:vlan.dat** command. Table 2-4 shows common IOS commands used to configure switches. Also listed is a short abbreviation, the purpose of the command, and the required mode to execute the command.

**Table 2-4   Common Switch Configuration Commands**

| Full Command / Example | Abbreviation | Purpose / Mode |
| --- | --- | --- |
| **Configuration Management** | | |
| **enable** | **en** | Changes from user EXEC mode (>) to privileged EXEC mode (#) |
| **configure terminal** | **conf t** | Changes from privileged EXEC mode to global configuration mode |
| **copy running-config startup-config** | **cop r s** | Copies the running configuration from RAM to the startup configuration file in NVRAM |
| **erase startup-config** | **era sta** | Deletes the startup configuration file (startup-config) |
| **delete vlan.dat** | **del** | Removes the VLAN configuration from the switch |
| **reload** | **rel** | Performs a software reboot |
| **Global Settings** | | |
| **hostname S1** | **ho** | Sets the device host name to S1 |
| **banner motd #XYZ#** | **Ban m** | Sets the banner message of the day, which is displayed at login, to XYZ |
| **enable secret itsasecret** | **Ena s** | Sets the privileged mode encrypted password to itsasecret |
| **ip default gateway** | **ip def ga** | Specifies the router gateway the switch will use (in global config mode) |

| Full Command / Example | Abbreviation | Purpose / Mode |
|---|---|---|
| **Line Settings** | | |
| **line con 0** | **Lin c** | Enters line config mode for console port 0 |
| **line vty 0 4** | **Lin v** | Enters line config mode for VTY lines 0 through 4 |
| **login** | **login** | Allows login to a line in line config mode |
| **password** | **Pas** | Sets line login password in line config mode |
| **Interface Settings** | | |
| **interface vlan 1** | **Int** | Enters interface config mode for logical interface management VLAN 1 (default native VLAN) |
| **ip address 192.168.1.1 255.255.255.0** | **ip add** | Specifies an IP address and subnet mask for the interface (in VLAN interface config mode) |
| **interface f0/1** | **Int** | Enters interface config mode for physical port Fast Ethernet 0/1 |
| **speed 100** | **Spe** | Sets the speed of the interface at 100 Mbps (in interface config mode) |
| **duplex full** | **Du** | Sets the duplex mode of the interface to full (in interface config mode) |
| **switchport mode access** | **switch m a** | Sets the switch port to access mode unconditionally (in interface config mode) |
| **switchport port-security** | **switch po** | Sets basic default port security on a port (in interface config mode) |

Example 2-18 shows the configuration commands used to configure the S1 switch in Figure 2-18. Refer to Example 2-11 to see the results of the commands as displayed with the **show running-config** command. As with the router configuration, the resulting running configuration frequently has a number of commands inserted automatically by the IOS that were not entered during the configuration process.

**Example 2-18    Switch S1 Basic Configuration Commands**

```
Switch> enable
Switch# configure terminal

Enter configuration commands, one per line.  End with CNTL/Z.
Switch(config)# hostname S1
S1(config)# banner motd %Unauthorized Access Prohibited%
S1(config)# enable secret class
S1(config)# line con 0
S1(config-line)# password cisco
S1(config-line)# login
S1(config-line)# line vty 0 4
S1(config-line)# password cisco
```

```
S1(config-line)# login
S1(config-line)# line vty 5 15
S1(config-line)# password cisco
S1(config-line)# login
S1(config-line)# exit
1(config)# no ip domain-lookup
S1(config)# interface FastEthernet0/3
S1(config-if)# switchport mode access
S1(config-if)# switchport port-security
S1(config-if)# switchport port-security mac-address sticky
S1(config-if)# interface Vlan1
S1(config-if)# ip address 192.168.1.5 255.255.255.0
S1(config-line)# exit
S1(config)# ip default-gateway 192.168.1.1
```

### Basic Switch Configuration Using CLI (2.3.5)

In this activity, you configure a switch in a switching environment. Use file d3-235.pka on the CD-ROM that accompanies this book to perform this interactive activity using Packet Tracer.

### Lab 2-1: Configuring Basic Routing and Switching (2.3.5)

In this lab, you will connect and configure a multirouter network. Refer to the hands-on lab in Part II of this *Learning Guide*. You can perform this lab now or wait until the end of the chapter.

# Summary

Network infrastructure diagrams document devices in a network. Network documentation includes the business continuity plan, business security plan, network maintenance plan, and service-level agreements.

The enterprise NOC manages and monitors all network resources. End users connect to the network through access layer switches and wireless APs in the IDF, and PoE provides power to devices over the same UTP cable that carries data.

The enterprise edge provides Internet access and service for users inside the organization. Edge devices provide security against attacks.

The POP at the edge provides a direct link to an SP or ISP and connects remote sites. The POP contains a demarc line of responsibility between the service provider and customer. Services are brought to the enterprise POP by copper wires or fiber-optic cable.

Distribution layer routers move packets between locations and the Internet and can control broadcasts. Routers and switches use in-band and out-of-band management.

# Activities and Labs

This summary outlines the activities and labs you can perform to help reinforce important concepts described in this chapter. You can find the activity and Packet Tracer files on the CD-ROM accompanying this book. The complete hands-on labs appear in Part II.

**Interactive Activities on the CD-ROM:**

Interactive Activity 2-1: Matching Network Information to Documentation Type (2.1.1)

Interactive Activity 2-2: Placing MDFs, IDFs, and Cabling (2.1.3)

Interactive Activity 2-3: Specifying Components to Bring Service to the Internal Network (2.2.3)

Interactive Activity 2-4: Matching the Command to the Information Needed (2.3.2)

**Packet Tracer Activities on the CD-ROM:**

Basic Router Configuration Using CLI (2.3.3)

Basic Switch Configuration Using CLI (2.3.5)

**Hands-on Labs in Part II of this book:**

Lab 2-1: Configuring Basic Routing and Switching (2.3.5)

# Check Your Understanding

Complete all the review questions listed here to check your understanding of the topics and concepts in this chapter. Appendix A, "Check Your Understanding and Challenge Questions Answer Key," lists the answers.

1. Draw a line from each term on the left to its correct description on the right. (Not all terms are used.)

   **Term**    **Description**

   POP      Maliciously prevents access to network resources by legitimate users

   VPN      Boundary that designates responsibility for equipment maintenance and troubleshooting

   DoS      Physical link to outside networks at the enterprise edge

   CPE      An area of the network accessible to external users and protected by firewalls

   DM       A telecommunications room to which IDFs connect

   Demarc   A method of providing electrical power to Ethernet end devices

            Allows remote workers to access the internal network securely

            Equipment located at the customer facility

2. What information can you find by using the **show mac-address-table** command on a Cisco Catalyst switch?

   A. The MAC address of the console interface on the Catalyst switch

   B. The MAC addresses of the hosts connected to the switch ports

   C. The IP addresses of directly connected network devices

   D. The mapping between MAC address and IP address for network hosts

3. While troubleshooting a network problem, the network administrator issues the **show version** command on a router. What information can be found using this command?

   A. The amount of NVRAM, DRAM, and flash memory installed on the router

   B. The bandwidth, encapsulation, and I/O statistics on the interfaces

   C. Differences between the backup configuration and the current running configuration

   D. The version of the routing protocols running on the router

4. After gathering a thorough list of network applications, the traffic generated by these applications, and the priority of this traffic, a network engineer wants to integrate this information into a single document for analysis. How can this be accomplished?

   A. Create a physical topology map of the network and annotate it with the network application data.

   B. Create a logical topology map of the network and annotate it with the network application data.

   C. Create a blueprint of the facility, including network cabling and telecommunications rooms, and annotate it with the network applications data.

   D. Take a photograph of the facility, and annotate it with the network application data.

5. One evening a network administrator attempted to access a recently deployed website and received a "Page not found" error. The next day the administrator checked the web server logs and noticed that during the same hour that the site failed to load, there were hundreds of requests for the website home page. All the requests originated from the same IP address. Given this information, what might the network administrator conclude?

   A. It is normal web-surfing activity.

   B. It is likely that someone attempted a DoS attack.

   C. The link to the website does not have enough capacity and needs to be increased.

   D. The web server was turned off and was not able to service requests.

6. What type of media typically connects an MDF switch to an IDF switch in another building with an Ethernet network?

   A. Fiber-optic

   B. Coaxial cable

   C. Unshielded twisted-pair

   D. Shielded twisted-pair

7. Which of the following devices can receive power over the same twisted-pair Ethernet cable that carries data? (Choose three.)

   A. Wireless access points

   B. Monitors

   C. Web cameras

   D. IP phones

   E. Network switches

   F. Laptops

8. Indicate which type of hardware each characteristic describes by marking with an R (router) or S (switch).

   A. Defines broadcast domains

   B. Connects IP phones and access points to the network

   C. Enhances security with ACLs

   D. Interconnects networks

   E. Appears more commonly at the access layer

   F. Connects hosts to the network

   G. First Fast Ethernet interface designation is Fa0/0

   H. First Fast Ethernet interface designation is Fa0/1

9. Which of the following protocols are normally used to access a Cisco router for in-band management? (Choose two.)

   A. ARP

   B. SSH

   C. FTP

   D. SMTP

   E. Telnet

10. A network analyst is documenting the existing network at ABC-XYZ Corporation. The analyst decides to start at the core router to identify and document the Cisco network devices attached to the core. Which command executed on the core router provides the required information?

    A. **show version**

    B. **show ip route**

    C. **show tech-support**

    D. **show running-config**

    E. **show cdp neighbors detail**

11. A network administrator suspects that there is a problem with the configuration of the RIP routing protocol. She investigates the interfaces and finds that all interfaces are up/up. Which of the following commands could help to identify the problem? (Choose two.)

    A. **show cdp neighbors**

    B. **show ip route**

    C. **show sessions**

    D. **show ip protocols**

    E. **show version**

12. As a network technician, you are troubleshooting a router configuration. You want to get a concise display of the status of the router interfaces. You also want to verify the IP address of each interface and the subnet mask in slash format (/XX). Which command would you use?

    A. **show protocols**

    B. **show ip route**

    C. **show running-config**

    D. **show ip protocols**

    E. **show ip interfaces brief**

13. What is the correct sequence of devices and connections for providing a T1 service to an organization's end user? Number each term in the proper sequence.

    A. DMZ router

    B. T1 circuit line

    C. Internal switch

    D. CSU/DSU

    E. DMZ switch

    F. Punchdown block

    G. Internal router

    H. Service provider

    I. End-user PC

14. Which of the following is not a type of network protection device or technique to help security?

   A. DoS

   B. Firewall

   C. ACL

   D. IDS

   E. IPS

   F. DMZ

   G. VPN

# Challenge Questions and Activities

These questions require a deeper application of the concepts covered in this chapter. You can find the answers in Appendix A.

1. Routers R1 and R2 are connected by a serial link. As a network administrator, you entered the following commands to configure the Serial 0/0/0 interface on Router R1. From Router R1 you are unable to ping the R2 S0/0/0 interface. What interface-related issues could be causing the problem, and what commands would you use on which routers to help isolate the problem?

   ```
   R1(config-if)# interface Serial0/0/0
   R1(config-if)# description WAN link to R2
   R1(config-if)# ip address 192.168.2.1 255.255.255.0
   R1(config-if)# encapsulation ppp
   R1(config-if)# clock rate 64000
   R1(config-if)# no shutdown
   ```

2. ISP or WAN Link Investigation Interview Activity (optional)

   In this activity, you will talk with your instructor or a network administrator at the institution where you work or other organization. Use the following form to ask a few questions to learn more about the organization's ISP service or service provider being used for a WAN connection.

   Organization: _____

   Person's name: _____

   Position/title: _____

   ISP or service provider name: _____

   Internet or WAN: _____

   Connection type/speed (DSL, cable, T1/E1, fractional T1, Frame Relay, and so on): _____

   CPE device (CSU/DSU, cable modem, DSL modem, and so on): _____

   If CSU/DSU, location of device (standalone or integrated into router): _____

   Location of POP: _____

   Is there a DMZ? _____

   Is there an SLA? _____

# CHAPTER 3

# Switching in an Enterprise Network

## Objectives

Upon completion of this chapter, you should be able to answer the following questions:

- What types of switches are found in an enterprise network?

- How does Spanning Tree Protocol prevent switching loops?

- What is a VLAN and what purpose does it serve?

- How is a VLAN configured on a Cisco switch?

- What is inter-VLAN routing and how is it configured?

- What is VLAN Trunking Protocol and how does it help maintain VLANs in an enterprise network?

## Key Terms

This chapter uses the following key terms. You can find the definitions in the Glossary.

*wire speed*    page 67

*content addressable memory (CAM)*    page 67

*aging time*    page 67

*microsegmentation*    page 67

*virtual circuit*    page 68

*symmetric switching*    page 68

*asymmetric switching*    page 68

*uplink ports*    page 68

*multilayer switching*    page 69

*application-specific integrated circuit (ASIC)*
  page 69

*store-and-forward switching*    page 70

*cut-through switching*    page 70

*fast-forward switching*    page 70

*fragment-free switching*    page 70

*runts*    page 70

*adaptive cut-through switching*    page 70

*Redundancy*    page 72

*congestion*    page 72

*availability*    page 72

*load balancing*    page 72

*switching loops*    page 72

*broadcast storm*    page 72

*Spanning Tree Protocol (STP)*    page 75

*bridge protocol data units (BPDU)*    page 76

*blocking state*    page 77

*listening state*    page 77

*learning state*    page 77

*forwarding state*    page 77

*disabled*    page 77

*Access ports*    page 77

*Trunking ports*    page 77

*root bridge*    page 78

*bridge-ID (BID)*    page 78

*Root ports*    page 79

*least-cost path*    page 79

*Designated ports*    page 79

*Blocked ports*    page 79

*continues*

*continued*

Enterprise networks rely on switches in the access, distribution, and core layers to provide network segmentation and high-speed connectivity between users and networks. Spanning Tree Protocol (STP) is used in a hierarchical network to prevent switching loops that can seriously degrade network performance. Virtual LANs logically segment networks and contain broadcasts to improve network performance and security. Switches configured with trunking enable VLANs to span multiple geographic locations. VLAN Trunking Protocol (VTP) is used to simplify the configuration and management of VLANs in a complex, enterprise-level switched network.

Part II of this book includes the corresponding labs for this chapter.

# Describing Enterprise-Level Switching

Although you can create an enterprise network with both routers and switches, the network design of most enterprises relies heavily on switches. Switches are cheaper per port than routers and provide fast forwarding of frames at *wire speed*. Transmission at wire speed indicates that little overhead is associated with the transmission and that it occurs at the maximum speed of the hardware.

## Switching and Network Segmentation

A switch is a very adaptable Layer 2 device. In its simplest role, it is used to replace a hub as the central point of connection for multiple hosts. In a more complex role, a switch connects to one or more other switches to create, manage, and maintain redundant links and VLAN connectivity. Regardless of the role a switch plays in a network, it processes all types of traffic in the same way.

A switch moves traffic based on MAC addresses. Each switch maintains a MAC address table in high-speed memory, called *content addressable memory (CAM)*. The switch re-creates this table every time it is activated, using the source MAC addresses of incoming frames and the port number through which the frame entered the switch. The switch deletes entries from the MAC address table if they are not used within a certain period of time. The name given to this period is the *aging time*; removal of an entry is called aging out.

As a unicast frame enters a port, the switch finds the source MAC address in the frame. It then searches the MAC table, looking for an entry that matches the address. If the source MAC address is not in the table, the switch adds a MAC address and port number entry and sets the aging timer. If the source MAC address already exists, the switch resets the aging timer associated with that entry. Next, the switch checks the table for the destination MAC address. If an entry exists, the switch forwards the frame out the appropriate port number. If the entry does not exist, the switch floods the frame out every active port except the port on which the frame was received.

High availability, speed, and throughput of the network are critical in an enterprise environment. These variables are affected by the size of the broadcast domain and the collision domain. In general, larger broadcast and collision domains negatively impact these mission-critical variables.

If a switch receives a broadcast frame, the switch floods it out every active interface, just as it does for an unknown destination MAC address. All devices that receive this broadcast make up the broadcast domain. As more switches are connected together, the size of the broadcast domain increases.

Collision domains create a similar problem. The more devices participating in a collision domain, the more collisions occur and the slower the throughput. Hubs create large collision domains. Switches, however, use a feature called *microsegmentation* to reduce the size of collision domains to a single switch port. When a host connects to a switch port, the switch creates a dedicated connection. When two connected hosts communicate with each other, the switch consults the switching table and establishes a virtual circuit, or microsegment, between the ports. The switch maintains the *virtual circuit* until the session terminates. Multiple virtual circuits can be active at the same time.

This process improves bandwidth utilization by reducing collisions and by allowing multiple simultaneous connections. Figure 3-1 shows the difference between a network that uses a hub versus one that uses a switch to connect hosts.

**Figure 3-1    Connecting Hosts Using a Hub or a Switch**

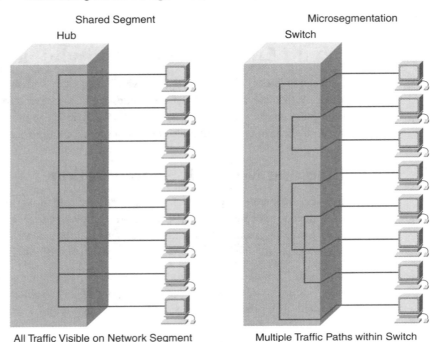

Many switches can support both *symmetric switching* and *asymmetric switching*. Switches that have ports of all the same speeds are termed symmetric. Many switches, however, have two or more high-speed ports. These high-speed, or *uplink ports*, connect to areas that have a higher demand for bandwidth. Typically, these areas include server farms or other networks. Connections between ports of different speeds use asymmetric switching. If necessary, a switch stores information in memory to provide a buffer between ports of different speeds. Asymmetric switches are common in the enterprise environment.

**Interactive Activity 3-1: Switch Frame Forwarding (3.1.1)**

In this activity, you determine to which ports a frame will be forwarded based on the information in the switch MAC table. Use file d3ia-311 on the CD-ROM that accompanies this book to perform this interactive activity.

## Multilayer Switching

Traditionally, networks have been composed of separate Layer 2 and Layer 3 devices. Each device uses a different technique for processing and forwarding traffic and has a very specific role in the network design and functionality. Figure 3-2 compares Layer 2 switching and Layer 3 routing.

**Figure 3-2    Layer 2 Switching and Layer 3 Routing**

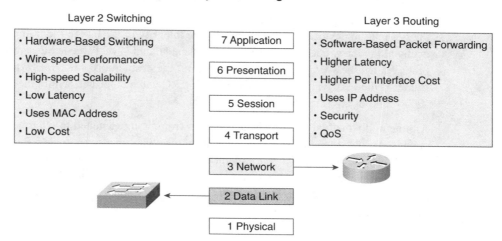

## Layer 2

Layer 2 switches are hardware based. They forward traffic at wire speeds, using the internal circuits that physically connect each incoming port to every other port. The forwarding process uses the MAC address and relies on the existence of the destination MAC address in the MAC address table. A Layer 2 switch limits the forwarding of traffic to within a single network segment or subnet. Traffic that must pass from one network segment to another must pass through a Layer 3 device.

## Layer 3

Routers are software based and use microprocessors to execute routing based on IP addresses. Layer 3 routing allows traffic to be forwarded between different networks and subnets. As a packet enters a router interface, the router uses software to find the destination IP address and select the best path toward the destination network. The router then switches the packet to the correct output interface.

Layer 3 switching, or *multilayer switching*, combines hardware-based switching and hardware-based routing in the same device. A multilayer switch combines the features of a Layer 2 switch and a Layer 3 router. Layer 3 switching occurs in special *application-specific integrated circuit (ASIC)* hardware. The frame- and packet-forwarding functions use the same ASIC circuitry.

Multilayer switches often save, or cache, source and destination routing information from the first packet of a conversation. Subsequent packets do not have to execute a routing lookup, because they find the routing information in memory. This caching feature adds to the high performance of these devices.

## Types of Switching

When switching was first introduced, a switch could support one of two major methods to forward a frame from one port to another. The two methods are store-and-forward and cut-through switching. Each of these methods has distinct advantages as well as some disadvantages. With recent advances in the speed of switching hardware, store-and-forward techniques have become the standard in many networked environments.

## Store-and-Forward

In *store-and-forward switching*, the entire frame is read and stored in memory before being sent to the destination device. The switch checks the integrity of the bits in the frame by recalculating the cyclic redundancy check (CRC) value. If the calculated CRC value is the same as the CRC field value in the frame, the switch forwards the frame out the destination port. The switch does not forward frames if the CRC values do not match. The CRC value is located within the frame check sequence (FCS) field of an Ethernet frame.

Although this method keeps damaged frames from being switched to other network segments, it introduces the highest amount of latency of any of the switching technologies. Because of the latency incurred by the store-and-forward method, it is typically only used in environments where errors are likely to occur. For example, an environment that has a high probability of electromagnetic interference (EMI) would create a large number of defective frames and would be appropriate for store-and-forward switching.

## Cut-Through Switching

The other major method of switching is *cut-through switching*. Cut-through switching subdivides into two other methods: *fast-forward switching* and *fragment-free switching*. In both of these methods the switch forwards the frame before all of it is received. Because the switch does not calculate or check the CRC value before forwarding the frame, damaged frames can be switched.

Fast-forward is the fastest method of switching. The switch forwards the frames out the destination port as soon as it reads the destination MAC address. This method has the lowest latency but also forwards collision fragments and damaged frames. This method of switching works best in a stable network with few errors.

In fragment-free switching, the switch reads the first 64 bytes of the frame before it begins to forward it out the destination port. The shortest valid Ethernet frame is 64 bytes. Smaller frames are usually the result of a collision and are called *runts*. Checking the first 64 bytes ensures that the switch does not forward collision fragments.

Store-and-forward has the highest latency and fast-forward has the lowest. The latency introduced by fragment-free switching is in the middle of these other methods. The fragment-free switching method works best in an environment where many collisions occur. In a properly constructed switched network, collisions are not a problem; therefore, fast-forward switching would be the preferred method.

Some newer Layer 2 and Layer 3 switches can adapt their switching method to changing network conditions. This is known as *adaptive cut-through switching*. The switches begin by forwarding traffic using the fast-forward method to achieve the lowest latency possible. Even though the switch does not check for errors before forwarding the frame, it recognizes errors in the frames as they pass through the switch. The switch stores this value in an error counter in memory. It compares the number of errors found to a predefined threshold value. If the number of errors exceeds the threshold value, the switch has forwarded an unacceptable number of errors. In this situation, the switch modifies itself to perform store-and-forward switching. If the number of errors drops back below the threshold, the switch reverts back to fast-forward mode.

# Switch Security

It is important to keep your network secure, regardless of the switching method used. Network security often focuses on routers and blocking traffic from the outside. Switches are internal to the organization and designed to allow ease of connectivity. For this reason, only limited or no security measures are applied in many switched environments. The following list includes some of the security measures that you should take to ensure that only authorized people have access to the switches in a network:

- **Physically secure the device.** Switches are a critical link in the network. Secure them physically, by mounting them in a rack and installing the rack in a secure room. Limit access to authorized network staff.

- **Use secure passwords.** Configure all passwords (user mode, privilege mode, and vty access) with a minimum of six nonrepeating characters. Change passwords on a regular basis. Never use words found in a dictionary.

  Use the **enable secret command** for privileged-level password protection, because it uses advanced encryption techniques. Encrypt all passwords in the display of the running configuration file using the IOS command **service password-encryption**.

- **Enable SSH access.** Secure Shell (SSH) is a client-server protocol used to log in to another device over a network. It provides strong authentication and secure communication over insecure channels. SSH encrypts the entire login session, including password transmission.

- **Monitor access and traffic.** Monitor all traffic passing through a switch to ensure that it complies with company policies. Additionally, record the MAC address of all devices connecting to a specific switch port and all login attempts on the switch. If the switch detects malicious traffic or unauthorized access, take action according to the security policy of the organization.

- **Disable HTTP access.** Disable HTTP access so that no one modifies the switch configuration through the web. The command to disable HTTP access is **no ip http server.**

- **Disable unused ports.** Disable all unused ports on the switch to prevent unknown PCs or wireless access points from connecting to an available port on the switch. Accomplish this by issuing a **shutdown** command on the interface.

- **Enable port security.** Port security restricts access to a switch port to a specific list of MAC addresses. Enter the MAC addresses manually or have the switch learn them dynamically. The specific switch port associates with the MAC addresses, allowing only traffic from those devices. If a device with a different MAC address plugs into the port, the switch automatically disables the port.

- **Disable Telnet.** A Telnet connection sends data over the public network in clear text. This includes usernames, passwords, and data. Disable Telnet access to all networking devices by not configuring a password for any vty sessions at login.

**Lab 3-1: Applying Basic Switch Security (3.1.4)**

In this lab, you configure and test basic switch security. Refer to the lab in Part II of this *Learning Guide*. You can perform this lab now or wait until the end of the chapter.

# Preventing Switching Loops

Modern enterprises rely more and more on their networks for their very existence. The network is the lifeline of many organizations. Network downtime translates into potentially disastrous loss of business, income, and customer confidence. The failure of a single network link, a single device, or a critical port on a switch causes network downtime.

# Redundancy in a Switched Network

*Redundancy* is required in the network design to maintain a high degree of reliability and eliminate any single point of failure. Redundancy is accomplished by installing duplicate equipment and network links for critical areas. Figure 3-3 shows a network that incorporates redundancy.

**Figure 3-3    Redundancy in a Network**

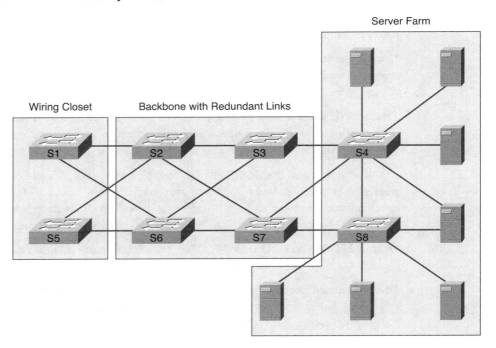

Sometimes, providing complete redundancy of all links and devices in a network becomes very expensive. Network engineers are often required to balance the cost of redundancy with the need for network availability. Network downtime translates into potential loss of business, income, and customer confidence. This loss must be assessed in the context of the business environment. Each company or organization can tolerate different levels of network outage. For most enterprise environments a 99.999 percent uptime is expected, and the network must be designed to provide this level of reliability.

Redundancy refers to having two different pathways to a particular destination. Examples of redundancy in nonnetworking environments include two roads into a town, two bridges to cross a river, or two doors to exit a building. If one way is blocked, another is still available. Redundancy in a switched network is achieved by connecting switches with multiple links. Redundant links in a switched network reduce *congestion* and support high *availability* and *load balancing*.

Connecting switches together, however, can cause problems. For example, the broadcast nature of Ethernet traffic creates *switching loops*. The broadcast frames go around and around in all directions, causing a *broadcast storm*, as shown in Figure 3-4.

In this example, a host sends a broadcast into a switched network. Any switch that receives the broadcast sends it out all ports except the one on which it was originally received. In this case, the first switch forwards the broadcast message across multiple links to a second switch. The second switch repeats the process and forwards the broadcast message back to the first switch. The first switch then forwards the message to the second switch and the process continues to repeat itself, consuming large amounts of bandwidth and creating a broadcast storm.

**Figure 3-4    Broadcast Storm**

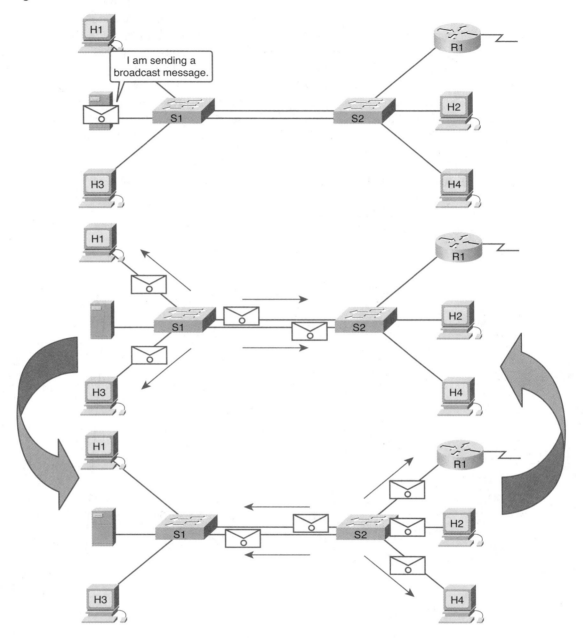

Broadcast storms use up all the available bandwidth, can prevent network connections from being established, and can cause existing network connections to be dropped.

Broadcast storms are not the only problem created by redundant links in a switched network. Unicast frames sometimes produce problems, such as multiple frame transmissions and MAC database instability.

## Multiple Frame Transmissions

If a host sends a unicast frame to a destination host and the destination MAC address is not included in any of the connected switch MAC tables, every switch floods the frame out all ports. The process repeats, creating multiple copies of the frame on the network. Eventually the destination host receives multiple copies of the frame, as shown in Figure 3-5. In this example, a copy of the frame is sent across each link to the destination switch. The destination switch receives two copies of the frame addresses to the destination host and forwards both. This causes three problems: wasted bandwidth, wasted CPU time, and potential duplication of transaction traffic. Imagine the problems that could be caused if two invoices were issued or two buy requests placed in the stock market because of multiple frame transmissions.

**Figure 3-5    Multiple Frame Transmission on a Looped Network**

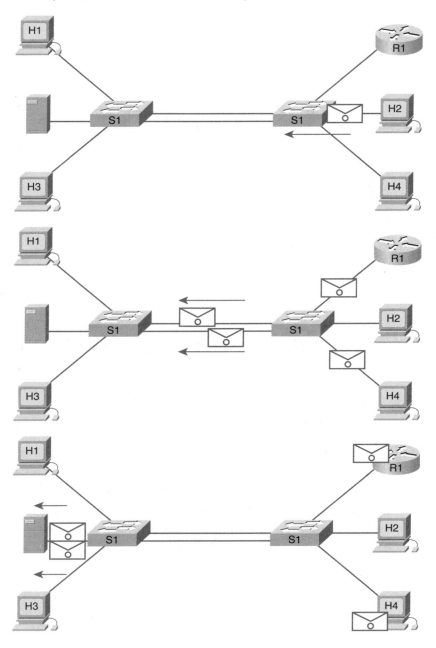

## MAC Database Instability

Switches in a redundant network can learn the wrong information about the location of a host. If a loop exists, one switch might associate the destination MAC address with two separate ports. This is because the switch receives information from the same source on two different ports, causing the switch to continually update its MAC address table. This causes suboptimal forwarding of frames.

### Disabling Redundant Links to Avoid Switching Loops (3.2.1)

In this activity, you disable redundant links in a network to avoid switching loops. Use file d3-321.pka on the CD-ROM that accompanies this book to perform this activity using Packet Tracer.

# Spanning Tree Protocol (STP)

*Spanning Tree Protocol (STP)* provides a mechanism for disabling redundant links in a switched network. STP provides the redundancy required for reliability without creating switching loops. STP is an open standard protocol, used in a switched environment to create a loop-free logical topology.

STP is relatively self-sufficient and requires little configuration. When switches are first powered up with STP enabled, they check the switched network for the existence of loops. Switches detecting a potential loop block some of the connecting ports, while leaving other ports active to forward frames, as shown in Figure 3-6.

**Figure 3-6    Spanning Tree Protocol Preventing a Switching Loop**

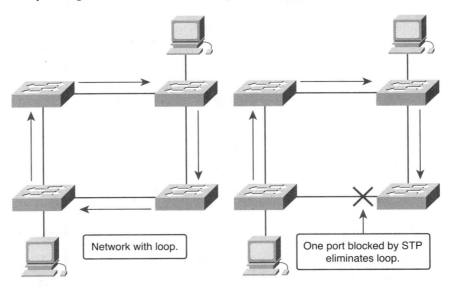

STP defines a tree that spans all the switches in an extended star switched network. Switches are constantly checking the network to ensure that no loops exist and that all ports function as required. To prevent switching loops, STP does the following:

- Forces certain interfaces into a blocked state
- Leaves other interfaces in a forwarding state
- Reconfigures the network by activating the appropriate path, if the forwarding path becomes unavailable

In STP terminology, the term *bridge* is frequently used to refer to a switch. For example, the root bridge is the primary switch or focal point in the STP topology. The root bridge communicates with the other switches using *bridge protocol data units (BPDU)*. BPDUs are frames that multicast every 2 seconds to all other switches. BPDUs contain information such as

- Identity of the source switch
- Identity of the source port
- Cumulative cost to the root bridge
- Value of aging timers
- Value of the hello timer

The structure of a BPDU is shown in Figure 3-7, and the individual fields are described in Table 3-1.

**Figure 3-7    Bridge Protocol Data Unit Structure**

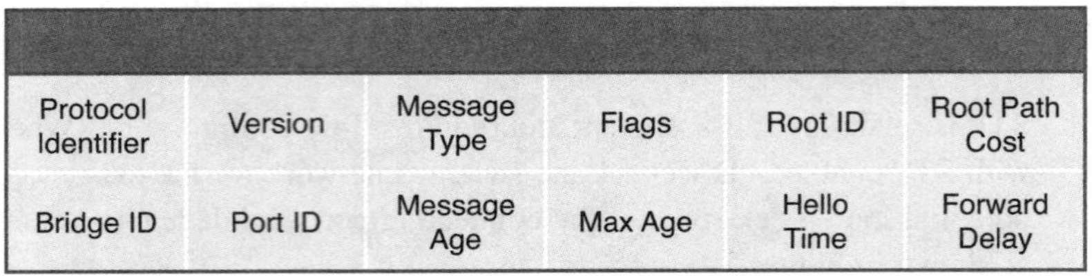

| Protocol Identifier | Version | Message Type | Flags | Root ID | Root Path Cost |
| --- | --- | --- | --- | --- | --- |
| Bridge ID | Port ID | Message Age | Max Age | Hello Time | Forward Delay |

**Table 3-1    BPDU Fields**

| Field | Octets | Description |
| --- | --- | --- |
| Protocol Identifier | 1–2 | Always 0. |
| Version | 3 | Always 0. |
| Message Type | 4 | Specifies the type of BPDU (Configuration or Topology Change Notification) that the frame contains. |
| Flags | 5 | Used to handle changes in active topology. |
| Root ID | 6–13 | Contains the bridge ID of the root bridge. This value is the same for all BPDUs in a bridged network after the network has converged. |
| Root Path Cost | 14–17 | Reflects the cumulative cost of all links leading to the root bridge. |
| Bridge ID | 18–25 | Contains the BID of the bridge that created the current BPDU. |
| Port ID | 26–27 | Contains a unique value for every port. For example, this field contains the value 0x8001 for port 1/1, whereas port 1/2 contains 0x8002. |
| Message Age | 28–29 | Records the time since the root bridge originally generated the information from which the current BPDU is derived. |
| Max Age | 30–31 | Shows the maximum time that a BPDU is saved. This influences the bridge table aging timer during the Topology Change Notification process. |

| Field | Octets | Description |
|---|---|---|
| Hello Time | 32–33 | Shows the time between periodic configuration BPDUs. |
| Forward Delay | 34–35 | Shows the time spent in the listening and learning states. |
| | | This influences timers during the Topology Change Notification process. |

As a switch powers on, each port cycles through a series of four states: blocking, listening, learning, and forwarding. A fifth state, disabled, indicates that the administrator has shut down the switch port. As the port cycles through these states, the LEDs on the switch change from flashing orange to steady green. It can take as long as 50 seconds for a port to cycle through all of these states and be ready to forward frames.

## Blocking

When a switch powers on, it first goes into a *blocking state* to immediately prevent the formation of a loop. In this state, the bridge receives BPDUs but discards all data frames. In this state, the bridge does not learn new addresses and the port status light is steady amber. This phase can last up to 20 seconds before the port transitions to the listening state.

## Listening

In the *listening state*, the switch continues to listen to BPDUs but does not forward data frames or learn addresses. During this state, the switch determines which ports can forward frames without creating a loop. If enabling the port would create a loop, the switch returns the port to the blocking state. If no loop would be created, the switch transitions the port to the learning state. It takes 15 seconds to transition to the learning state, during which time the port indicator flashes amber.

## Learning

In the *learning state*, the switch receives and processes both BPDUs and data frames. It does not forward data frames while in this state but does learn MAC addresses from the data received. The port LED continues to flash amber during this state, which takes 15 seconds to complete before transitioning to the forwarding state.

## Forwarding

In the *forwarding state*, the switch continues to process both BPDUs and learn MAC addresses. It also now forwards data frames on the network. While in this state, the port status LED blinks green.

## Disabled

If the administrator shuts down a port, it is considered to be *disabled*. The port status indicator on a disabled port is off.

*Access ports* are ports that connect to an end host and carry the data for only a single VLAN. Because they do not normally connect to other switches, they do not create loops in a switched network. These ports always transition to forwarding if they have a host attached. *Trunking ports* can connect to other switches and normally carry data for multiple VLANs. These ports can potentially create a looped network and transition to either a forwarding or blocking state.

**Interactive Activity 3-2: Spanning Tree (3.2.2)**

In this activity, you associate the process with the correct spanning-tree state. Use file d3ia-322 on the CD-ROM that accompanies this book to perform this interactive activity.

# Root Bridges

For STP to function, the switches in the network determine a switch that is the focal point in that network. STP uses this focal point, called a *root bridge* or root switch, to determine which ports to block and which ports to put into the forwarding state. The root bridge sends out BPDUs containing network topology information to all other switches. This information allows the network to reconfigure itself in the event of a failure.

Only one root bridge exists on each switched network, and it is elected based on the *bridge-ID (BID).* The bridge priority value plus the MAC address create the BID, as shown in Figure 3-8. Bridge priority has a default value of 32,768. If a switch has a MAC address of AA-11-BB-22-CC-33, the BID for that switch would be 32768: AA-11-BB-22-CC-33. The root bridge is based on the lowest BID value. Because switches typically use the same default priority value, the switch with the lowest MAC address becomes the root bridge.

**Figure 3-8    Bridge ID**

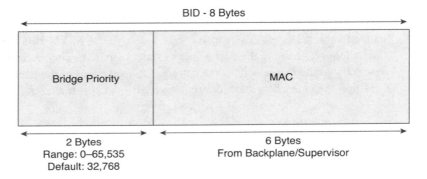

As each switch powers on, it assumes that it is the root bridge and sends out BPDUs containing its own BID. Consider the network shown in Figure 3-9. If S2 advertises a root ID that is a lower number than S1, S1 stops the advertisement of its root ID and accepts the root ID of S2. S2 is now the root bridge.

**Figure 3-9    Port Designations**

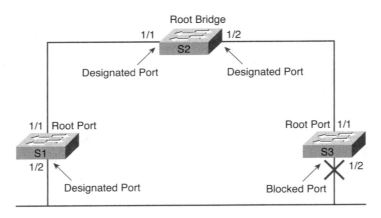

STP designates three types of ports, as shown in Figure 3-9:

■ *Root ports*: A port that provides the least-cost path back to the root bridge becomes the root port. Switches calculate the *least-cost path* using the bandwidth cost of each link required to reach the root bridge.

■ *Designated ports*: A designated port is a port that forwards traffic toward the root bridge but does not connect to the least-cost path. One designated port is elected per link (segment). The designated port is the port closest to the root bridge.

■ *Blocked ports*: A blocked port is a port that does not forward traffic.

Before configuring STP, the network technician plans and evaluates the network to select the best switch to become the root of the spanning tree. If the root switch selection is allowed to default to the one with the lowest MAC address, forwarding might not be optimal. A centrally located switch works best as the root bridge. A blocked port situated at the extreme edge of the network might cause traffic to take a longer route to get to the destination than if the switch is centrally located.

To specify the root bridge, the BID of the chosen switch is configured with the lowest priority value. The bridge priority command is used to configure the bridge priority. The range for the priority is from 0 to 65535, but values are in increments of 4096. The default value is 32768. The global **spanning-tree vlan VLAN-ID priority <0-61440>** command is used to set the priority of a switch.

### Lab 3-2: Building a Switched Network with Redundant Links (3.2.3)

In this lab, you configure the BID on a switch to control which one becomes the root bridge. You also observe the spanning tree and traffic flow patterns as different switches are configured as root. Refer to the lab in Part II of this *Learning Guide*. You can perform this lab now or wait until the end of the chapter.

## Spanning Tree in a Hierarchical Network

After establishing the root bridge, root ports, designated ports, and blocked ports, STP sends BPDUs throughout the switched network at 2-second intervals. STP continues to listen to these BPDUs to ensure that no links fail and no new loops appear. If a link failure occurs, STP recalculates as follows:

■ Changing some blocked ports to forwarding ports

■ Changing some forwarding ports to blocked ports

■ Forming a new STP tree to maintain the loop-free integrity of the network

STP is not instantaneous. When a link goes down, STP detects the failure and recalculates the best paths across the network. This calculation and transition period takes about 30 to 50 seconds on each switch. During this recalculation, no user data passes through the recalculating ports. Figure 3-10 shows how the port designations are altered after a link failure.

Some user applications time out during the recalculation period, which can result in lost productivity and revenue. Frequent STP recalculations negatively impact uptime. A high-volume, enterprise server is normally connected to a switch port. If that port recalculates because of STP, the server is down for 50 seconds. It would be difficult to imagine the number of transactions lost during that time frame.

**Figure 3-10    STP Recalculation**

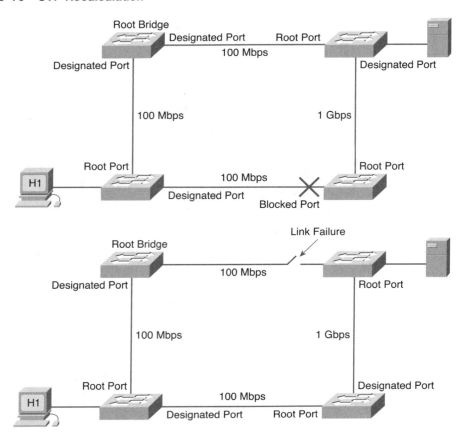

In a stable network, STP recalculations are infrequent. In an unstable network, it is important to check the switches for stability and configuration changes. One of the most common causes of frequent STP recalculations is a faulty power supply or power feed to a switch. A faulty power supply causes the device to reboot unexpectedly.

Several proprietary enhancements to STP exist to minimize the downtime incurred during an STP recalculation. These include PortFast, UplinkFast, and BackboneFast. These enhancements are Cisco proprietary; therefore, they cannot be used if the network includes switches from other vendors. In addition, all of these features require configuration. The following sections describe each enhancement and then conclude with **show** commands that provide information about STP on a network.

## PortFast

STP *PortFast* causes an access port to enter the forwarding state immediately, bypassing the listening and learning states. Using PortFast on access ports that are connected to a single workstation or server allows those devices to connect to the network immediately, instead of waiting for STP to converge.

## UplinkFast

STP *UplinkFast* accelerates the choice of a new root port when a link or switch fails or when STP reconfigures itself. The root port transitions to the forwarding state immediately without going through the listening and learning states, as it would do with normal STP procedures.

## BackboneFast

*BackboneFast* provides fast convergence after a spanning-tree topology change occurs. It quickly restores backbone connectivity. BackboneFast is used at the distribution and core layers, where multiple switches connect.

## STP Diagnostic show Commands

You can use a number of **show** commands to obtain information about the functionality of STP on a network. Sample output from some of the more useful commands is provided in Examples 3-1 to 3-6.

The **show spanning-tree** command displays root ID, bridge ID, and port states. A sample output is shown in Example 3-1.

**Example 3-1  STP show spanning tree Sample Output**

```
milfeet3548# show spanning-tree

VLAN0140
  Spanning tree enabled protocol ieee
  Root ID    Priority    32768
             Address     0004.4d3f.02c0
             Cost        8
             Port        49 (GigabitEthernet0/1)
             Hello Time   2 sec  Max Age 20 sec  Forward Delay 15 sec

  Bridge ID  Priority    32908  (priority 32768 sys-id-ext 140)
             Address     000a.8a53.2200
             Hello Time   2 sec  Max Age 20 sec  Forward Delay 15 sec
             Aging Time 300

Interface        Role Sts Cost      Prio.Nbr Type
---------------- ---- --- --------- -------- --------------------------------
Gi0/1            Root FWD 4         128.49   P2p


VLAN0145
  Spanning tree enabled protocol ieee
  Root ID    Priority    32768
             Address     0004.4d3f.02c1
             Cost        8
             Port        49 (GigabitEthernet0/1)
             Hello Time   2 sec  Max Age 20 sec  Forward Delay 15 sec

  Bridge ID  Priority    32913  (priority 32768 sys-id-ext 145)
             Address     000a.8a53.2200
             Hello Time   2 sec  Max Age 20 sec  Forward Delay 15 sec
             Aging Time 300

Interface        Role Sts Cost      Prio.Nbr Type
---------------- ---- --- --------- -------- --------------------------------
Gi0/1            Root FWD 4         128.49   P2p
<output omitted>
```

The **show spanning-tree summary** command displays a summary of the port states. Example 3-2 shows sample output from this command.

**Example 3-2  STP show spanning-tree summary Sample Output**

```
milfeet3548# show spanning-tree summary

Switch is in pvst mode
Root bridge for: none
EtherChannel misconfig guard is enabled
Extended system ID         is enabled
Portfast Default           is disabled
PortFast BPDU Guard Default  is disabled
Portfast BPDU Filter Default is disabled
Loopguard Default          is disabled
UplinkFast                 is disabled
BackboneFast               is disabled
Configured Pathcost method used is short


Name                  Blocking Listening Learning Forwarding STP Active
--------------------- -------- --------- -------- ---------- ----------
VLAN0140                  0        0        0         1          1
VLAN0145                  0        0        0         1          1
VLAN0151                  0        0        0         1          1
VLAN0152                  0        0        0         1          1
VLAN0153                  0        0        0         1          1
VLAN0155                  0        0        0         1          1
VLAN0157                  0        0        0         1          1
VLAN0231                  0        0        0         1          1
VLAN0262                  0        0        0         3          3
VLAN0420                  0        0        0         1          1
VLAN0430                  0        0        0         1          1
VLAN0900                  0        0        0         1          1
VLAN0901                  0        0        0         1          1
--------------------- -------- --------- -------- ---------- ----------
13 vlans                  0        0        0        15         15
```

Example 3-3 shows sample output from the **show spanning-tree root** command. Use this command to obtain information on the status and configuration of the root bridge.

**Example 3-3  STP show spanning-tree root Sample Output**

```
milfeet3548# show spanning-tree root

                                   Root Hello Max Fwd
Vlan              Root ID          Cost Time Age Dly  Root Port
----------------- ---------------- ----- ----- --- --- ----------------
VLAN0140          32768 0004.4d3f.02c0    8    2  20  15  Gi0/1
VLAN0145          32768 0004.4d3f.02c1    8    2  20  15  Gi0/1
VLAN0151          32768 0004.4d3f.02c2    8    2  20  15  Gi0/1
VLAN0152          32768 0004.4d3f.02c3    8    2  20  15  Gi0/1
VLAN0153          32768 0004.4d3f.02d1    8    2  20  15  Gi0/1
VLAN0155          32768 0004.4d3f.02c4    8    2  20  15  Gi0/1
```

| VLAN0157 | 32768 0004.4d3f.02c5 | 8 | 2 | 20 | 15 | Gi0/1 |
| VLAN0231 | 32768 0004.4d3f.02c6 | 8 | 2 | 20 | 15 | Gi0/1 |
| VLAN0262 | 32768 0004.4d3f.02c7 | 8 | 2 | 20 | 15 | Gi0/1 |
| VLAN0420 | 32768 0004.4d3f.02cc | 8 | 2 | 20 | 15 | Gi0/1 |
| VLAN0430 | 32768 0004.4d3f.02cd | 8 | 2 | 20 | 15 | Gi0/1 |
| VLAN0900 | 32768 0004.4d3f.02cf | 8 | 2 | 20 | 15 | Gi0/1 |
| VLAN0901 | 32768 0004.4d3f.02d0 | 8 | 2 | 20 | 15 | Gi0/1 |

To obtain detailed information on the spanning-tree ports, use the **show spanning-tree detail** command, as shown in Example 3-4.

**Example 3-4  STP show spanning-tree detail Sample Output**

```
milfeet3548# show spanning-tree detail

 VLAN0140 is executing the ieee compatible Spanning Tree protocol
  Bridge Identifier has priority 32768, sysid 140, address 000a.8a53.2200
  Configured hello time 2, max age 20, forward delay 15
  Current root has priority 32768, address 0004.4d3f.02c0
  Root port is 49 (GigabitEthernet0/1), cost of root path is 8
  Topology change flag not set, detected flag not set
  Number of topology changes 15 last change occurred 4w5d ago
  Times:  hold 1, topology change 35, notification 2
          hello 2, max age 20, forward delay 15
  Timers: hello 0, topology change 0, notification 0, aging 300

 Port 49 (GigabitEthernet0/1) of VLAN0140 is forwarding
   Port path cost 4, Port priority 128, Port Identifier 128.49.
   Designated root has priority 32768, address 0004.4d3f.02c0
   Designated bridge has priority 32768, address 0015.c79e.0d8c
   Designated port id is 128.165, designated path cost 4
   Timers: message age 2, forward delay 0, hold 0
   Number of transitions to forwarding state: 1
   Link type is point-to-point by default
   BPDU: sent 16, received 3186595


 VLAN0145 is executing the ieee compatible Spanning Tree protocol
  Bridge Identifier has priority 32768, sysid 145, address 000a.8a53.2200
  Configured hello time 2, max age 20, forward delay 15
  Current root has priority 32768, address 0004.4d3f.02c1
  Root port is 49 (GigabitEthernet0/1), cost of root path is 8
  Topology change flag not set, detected flag not set
  Number of topology changes 12 last change occurred 4w5d ago
  Times:  hold 1, topology change 35, notification 2
          hello 2, max age 20, forward delay 15
  Timers: hello 0, topology change 0, notification 0, aging 300

 Port 49 (GigabitEthernet0/1) of VLAN0145 is forwarding
   Port path cost 4, Port priority 128, Port Identifier 128.49.
   Designated root has priority 32768, address 0004.4d3f.02c1
```

```
    Designated bridge has priority 32768, address 0015.c79e.0d91
    Designated port id is 128.165, designated path cost 4
    Timers: message age 2, forward delay 0, hold 0
    Number of transitions to forwarding state: 1
    Link type is point-to-point by default
    BPDU: sent 12, received 3186349
<output omitted>
```

To view STP status and configuration information on a specific interface, use the **show spanning-tree interface** command, as illustrated in Example 3-5.

**Example 3-5  STP show spanning-tree interface Sample Output**

```
milfeet3548# show spanning-tree interface gigabitEthernet 0/1

Vlan              Role Sts Cost      Prio.Nbr Type
----------------- ---- --- --------- -------- -------------------------------
VLAN0140          Root FWD 4         128.49   P2p
VLAN0145          Root FWD 4         128.49   P2p
VLAN0151          Root FWD 4         128.49   P2p
VLAN0152          Root FWD 4         128.49   P2p
VLAN0153          Root FWD 4         128.49   P2p
VLAN0155          Root FWD 4         128.49   P2p
VLAN0157          Root FWD 4         128.49   P2p
VLAN0231          Root FWD 4         128.49   P2p
VLAN0262          Root FWD 4         128.49   P2p
VLAN0420          Root FWD 4         128.49   P2p
VLAN0430          Root FWD 4         128.49   P2p
VLAN0900          Root FWD 4         128.49   P2p
VLAN0901          Root FWD 4         128.49   P2p
```

The **show spanning-tree blockedports** command is used to view any ports that are currently blocked by STP. This is shown in Example 3-6.

**Example 3-6  STP show spanning-tree blockedports Sample Output**

```
milfeet3548# show spanning-tree blockedports

Name                Blocked Interfaces List
------------------- -----------------------------------


Number of blocked ports (segments) in the system : 0

milfeet3548#
```

**Lab 3-3: Verifying STP with show Commands (3.2.4)**

In this lab, you use various **show** commands to verify STP operation. Refer to the lab in Part II of this *Learning Guide*. You can perform this lab now or wait until the end of the chapter.

## Rapid Spanning Tree Protocol (RSTP)

When the IEEE developed the original 802.1D Spanning Tree Protocol (STP), recovery time of 1 to 2 minutes was acceptable. Today, Layer 3 switching and advanced routing protocols provide a faster alternative path to the destination. The need to carry delay-sensitive traffic, such as voice and video, requires that switched networks converge quickly to keep up with the new technology. *Rapid Spanning Tree Protocol (RSTP)*, defined in IEEE 802.1w, significantly speeds the recalculation of the spanning tree. Unlike PortFast, UplinkFast, and BackboneFast, RSTP is not proprietary.

RSTP requires a full-duplex, point-to-point connection between switches to achieve the highest reconfiguration speed. Reconfiguration of the spanning tree by RSTP occurs in less than 1 second, as compared to 50 seconds in STP. RSTP eliminates the requirements for features such as PortFast and UplinkFast. RSTP can revert to STP to provide services for legacy equipment.

To speed the recalculation process, RSTP reduces the number of port states to three: discarding, learning, and forwarding. The *discarding state* is similar to three of the original STP states: blocking, listening, and disabled. RSTP also introduces the concept of *active topology*. All ports that are not discarding, or are blocked, are considered to be part of the active topology and will immediately transition to the forwarding state.

## Configuring VLANs

Hosts and servers that are connected to Layer 2 switches are part of the same network segment. This arrangement poses two significant problems:

- Switches flood broadcasts out all ports, which consumes unnecessary bandwidth. As the number of devices connected to a switch increases, more broadcast traffic is generated and more bandwidth is wasted.

- Every device that is attached to a switch can forward and receive frames from every other device on that switch.

As a network design best practice, broadcast traffic is contained to the area of the network in which it is required. There are business reasons why certain hosts access each other while others do not. As an example, members of the accounting department might be the only users who need to access the accounting server. In a switched network, virtual local-area networks (VLAN) are created to contain broadcasts and group hosts together in communities of interest.

### Virtual LAN

A *virtual local-area network (VLAN)* is a logical broadcast domain that can span multiple physical LAN segments. It allows an administrator to group stations by logical function, by project teams, or by applications, without regard to physical location of the users. This is shown in Figure 3-11.

**Figure 3-11    VLANs**

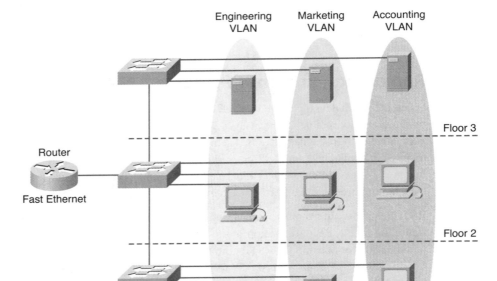

To understand the difference between a physical and a logical network, consider the following example. The students in a school are divided into two groups. In the first group, each student is given a red card, for identification. In the second group, each student is given a blue card. The principal announces that students with red cards can only speak to other students with red cards and that students with blue cards can only speak to other students with blue cards. The students are now logically separated into two virtual groups, which function as VLANs do in a network. Using this logical grouping, a broadcast goes out only to the red card group, even though both the red card group and the blue card group are physically located within the same school.

This example also shows another feature of VLANs. Broadcasts do not forward between VLANs; they are contained within the VLAN. Each VLAN functions as a separate LAN. A VLAN spans one or more switches, which allows host devices to behave as if they were on the same network segment. A VLAN has two major functions: It contains broadcasts and groups devices. Devices located on one VLAN are not visible to devices located on another VLAN. To move traffic between different VLANs requires the use of a Layer 3 device.

In a switched network, a device can be assigned to a VLAN based on its location, MAC address, IP address, or the applications that the device most frequently uses. Administrators assign membership in a VLAN either statically or dynamically.

## Static VLANs

Static VLAN membership requires an administrator to manually assign each switch port to a specific VLAN. As an example, port Fa0/3 might be assigned to VLAN 20. Any device that plugs into port Fa0/3 automatically becomes a member of VLAN 20. This type of VLAN membership is the easiest to configure and is also the most popular; however, it requires the most administrative support for adds, moves, and changes. For example, moving a host from one VLAN to another requires either the switch port to be manually reconfigured to the new VLAN or the workstation cable to be plugged into a different switch port on the new VLAN. Membership in a specific VLAN is transparent to the users. Users working on a device plugged into a switch port have no knowledge that they are members of a VLAN.

### Dynamic VLANs

Dynamic VLAN membership requires a *VLAN management policy server (VMPS)*. The VMPS contains a database that maps MAC addresses to VLAN assignments. When a device plugs into a switch port, the VMPS searches the database for a match of the MAC address and temporarily assigns that port to the appropriate VLAN. Dynamic VLAN membership requires more organization and configuration but creates a structure with much more flexibility than static VLAN membership. In dynamic VLAN, moves, adds, and changes are automated and do not require intervention from the administrator.

**Note**

Not all Catalyst switches support the use of VMPSs.

**Interactive Activity 3-3: Implementing VLANs (3.3.1)**

In this activity, you decide whether VLANs can solve the stated problem. Use file d3ia-331 on the CD-ROM that accompanies this book to perform this interactive activity.

## Configuring a Virtual LAN

Whether VLANs are created statically or dynamically, the maximum number of VLANs depends on the type of switch and the IOS. By default, VLAN1 is the *management VLAN*. An administrator will use the IP address of the management VLAN to configure the switch remotely. When accessing the switch remotely, the network administrator can configure and maintain all VLAN configurations. Additionally, the management VLAN is used to exchange information, such as Cisco Discovery Protocol (CDP) traffic and VLAN Trunking Protocol (VTP) traffic, with other networking devices.

When a VLAN is created, it is assigned a number and a name. The VLAN number is any number from the range available on the switch, except for VLAN1. Some switches support approximately 1000 VLANs; others support more than 4000. Naming a VLAN is considered a network management best practice. To create a VLAN on a switch and give it a name, issue the following commands in global configuration mode:

```
Switch(config)# vlan vlan_number
Switch(config-vlan)# name vlan_name
Switch(config-vlan)# exit
```

After the VLAN is created, ports can be assigned either individually or as a range. By default, all ports are initially members of VLAN1. Use the following commands to assign individual ports to VLANs:

```
Switch(config)# interface fa#/#
Switch(config-if)# switchport access vlan vlan_number
Switch(config-if)# exit
```

Use the following commands to assign a range of ports to a VLAN:

```
Switch(config)# interface range fa#/start_of_range - end_of_range
Switch(config-if)# switchport access vlan vlan_number
Switch(config-if)# exit
```

Example 3-7 shows the creation of an accounting and production VLAN on a switch and the assignment of ports Fa0/3 and Fa0/5 to the accounting VLAN and ports Fa0/6 to Fa0/11 to the production VLAN.

**Example 3-7  Creating VLANs and Assigning Ports**

```
Switch(config)# vlan 101
Switch(config-vlan)# name accounting
Switch(config-vlan)# exit
Switch(config)# vlan 102
Switch(config-vlan)# name production
Switch(config-vlan)# exit
Switch(config)# interface fa0/3
Switch(config-if)# switchport access vlan 101
Switch(config)# interface fa0/5
Switch(config-if)# switchport access vlan10
Switch(config)# interface range fa0/6 - 11
Switch(config-if)# switchport access vlan 102
Switch(config-if)# exit
```

When working with VLANs, it is important to understand the key **show** commands that are available in the Cisco IOS. Sample output from some of the more important **show** commands used to verify, maintain, and troubleshoot VLANs is given in Examples 3-8 to 3-11.

The **show vlan** command displays a detailed list of all the VLAN numbers and names currently active on the switch, along with the ports associated with each one. This command also displays STP statistics if configured on a per-VLAN basis. Example 3-8 provides sample output from this command.

**Example 3-8  show vlan Sample Output**

```
Switch# show vlan

VLAN Name                             Status    Ports
---- -------------------------------- --------- -------------------------------
1    default                          active    Fa0/1, Fa0/2, Fa0/3, Fa0/4
                                                Fa0/5, Fa0/14, Fa0/15, Fa0/16
                                                Fa0/17, Fa0/18, Fa0/19, Fa0/20
                                                Fa0/21, Fa0/22, Fa0/23, Fa0/24
                                                Gi0/1, Gi0/2
27   accounting                       active    Fa0/13
28   engineering                      active    Fa0/6, Fa0/7, Fa0/8, Fa0/9
                                                Fa0/10, Fa0/11, Fa0/12

1002 fddi-default                     act/unsup
1003 token-ring-default               act/unsup
1004 fddinet-default                  act/unsup
1005 trnet-default                    act/unsup
```

```
VLAN Type  SAID       MTU   Parent RingNo BridgeNo Stp  BrdgMode Trans1 Trans2
---- ----- ---------- ----- ------ ------ -------- ---- -------- ------ ------
1    enet  100001     1500  -      -      -        -    -        0      0
27   enet  100027     1500  -      -      -        -    -        0      0
28   enet  100028     1500  -      -      -        -    -        0      0
1002 fddi  101002     1500  -      -      -        -    -        0      0
1003 tr    101003     1500  -      -      -        -    -        0      0

VLAN Type  SAID       MTU   Parent RingNo BridgeNo Stp  BrdgMode Trans1 Trans2
---- ----- ---------- ----- ------ ------ -------- ---- -------- ------ ------
1004 fdnet 101004     1500  -      -      -        ieee -        0      0
1005 trnet 101005     1500  -      -      -        ibm  -        0      0

Remote SPAN VLANs
--------------------------------------------------------------------------


Primary Secondary Type              Ports
------- --------- ----------------- ------------------------------------------

Switch#
```

Sometimes detailed VLAN information is not required. In cases such as this, the **show vlan brief** command might be more appropriate. As shown in Example 3-9, this command displays a summarized list showing only the active VLANs and the ports associated with each one.

**Example 3-9** `show vlan brief` **Sample Output**

```
Switch# show vlan brief

VLAN   Name                             Status    Ports
------ -------------------------------- --------- -----------------
1      default                          active    Fa0/1, Fa0/4, Fa0/5,
                                                  Fa0/14, Fa0/15, Fa0/16, Fa0/17
                                                  Fa0/18, Fa0/19, Fa0/20, Fa0/21
                                                  Fa0/22, Fa0/23, Fa0/24
27     accounting                       active    Fa0/13
28     engineering                      active    Fa0/6, Fa0/7, Fa0/8, Fa0/9
                                                  Fa0/10, Fa0/11, Fa0/12
1002   fddi-default                     active
1003   token-ring-default               active
1004   fddinet-default                  active
1005   trnet-default
```

If information is required on only a single VLAN, the **show vlan id** or **show vlan name** command can be used to display information on the VLAN by VLAN ID number or VLAN name, respectively. Examples 3-10 and 3-11 provide sample output from these two commands.

**Example 3-10   `show vlan id` Sample Output**

```
Switch# show vlan id 28

VLAN  Name                              Status    Ports
----- --------------------------------  --------  ----------------
28    engineering                       active    Fa0/6, Fa0/7, Fa0/8, Fa0/9



VLAN  Type  SAID    MTU   Parent  RingNo  BridgeNo  Stp  BrdgMode  Tran1  Trans2
----- ----- ------- ----- ------- ------- --------- ---- --------- ------ ----------
28    enet  100028  1500  -       -       -         -    -         0      0


Remote  SPAN VLANS
-----------------
Disabled


Primary  Secondary  Type   Ports
-------  ---------  ------ ---------------------------------------
```

**Example 3-11   `show vlan name` Sample Output**

```
Switch# show vlan name engineering

VLAN  Name                              Status    Ports
----- --------------------------------  --------  -------------------------
28    engineering                       active    Fa0/6, Fa0/7, Fa0/8, Fa0/9



VLAN  Type  SAID    MTU   Parent  RingNo  BridgeNo  Stp  BrdgMode  Tran1  Trans2
----- ----- ------- ----- ------- ------- --------- ---- --------- ------ -----
28    enet  100028  1500  -       -       -         -    -         0      0


Remote  SPAN VLANS
-----------------
Disabled


Primary Secondary  Type     Ports
-------  ---------  ------   ---------------------------------------
```

In an organization, employees are frequently added, removed, or moved to a different department or project. This constant movement requires VLAN maintenance, including removal or reassignment to different VLANs. The removal of VLANs and the reassignment of ports to different VLANs are two separate and distinct functions. When a port is disassociated from a specific VLAN, it returns to VLAN1. If a VLAN is deleted, the interfaces assigned to that VLAN will become inactive until assigned to another VLAN.

To delete a VLAN use the following command:

```
Switch(config)# no vlan vlan_number
```

To disassociate a port from a specific VLAN use these commands:

```
Switch(config)# interface fa#/#
Switch(config-if)# no switchport access vlan vlan_number
```

**Lab 3-4: Configuring, Verifying, and Troubleshooting VLANs (3.3.2)**

In this lab, you configure, verify, and troubleshoot VLANs on a switch. Refer to the lab in Part II of this *Learning Guide*. You can perform this lab now or wait until the end of the chapter.

## Identifying VLANs

Devices connected to a VLAN only communicate with other devices in the same VLAN, regardless of whether those devices are on the same switch or different switches. A switch associates each port with a specific VLAN number. If VLANs are to span multiple switches or traffic must be routed between VLANs, trunking is used to carry the traffic from multiple VLANs over a single physical link. The trunking device inserts a tag into the original frame before sending the frame over the trunk link. The tag contains the *VLAN ID (VID)*, which identifies the VLAN to which the traffic belongs. At the receiving end, the tag is removed and the frame is forwarded to the assigned VLAN. The addition of the VLAN ID number into the Ethernet frame is called *frame tagging*.

The most commonly used frame-tagging standard is *IEEE 802.1Q*. The 802.1Q standard, sometimes abbreviated to *dot1q*, inserts a 4-byte tag field into the Ethernet frame. This tag sits between the source address and the type/length field. Untagged Ethernet frames have a minimum size of 64 bytes and a maximum size of 1518 bytes. This tag field increases the minimum Ethernet frame from 64 to 68 bytes. The maximum size increases from 1518 to 1522 bytes. The switch recalculates the FCS because the number of bits in the frame has been modified. The FCS field provides error checking to ensure the integrity of all the bits within the frame.

An 802.1Q tagged Ethernet frame is shown in Figure 3-12. Table 3-2 describes the fields in the 801.1Q tag.

**Figure 3-12    802.1Q Tagged Ethernet Frame**

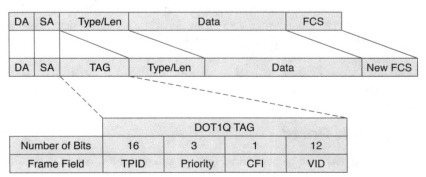

**Table 3-2    802.1Q Tag Fields**

| Field | Description |
|-------|-------------|
| Tag Protocol Identifier (TPID) | Set to a value of 0x8100 to identify the frame as an IEEE 802.1Q tagged frame. |
| Priority | Known as user priority. |
| | This 3-bit field refers to the IEEE 802.1Q priority. |
| | The field indicates the frame priority level used for the prioritization of traffic. |
| | The field can represent 8 levels (0 through 7). |
| Canonical Format Identifier (CFI) | A 1-bit indicator used for compatibility between Ethernet and Token Ring networks. |
| | Always set to 0 for Ethernet switches. |
| VLAN Identifier (VID) | Uniquely identifies the VLAN to which the frame belongs. |
| | The field has a value between 0 and 4095. |

If an 802.1Q-compliant port is connected to another 802.1Q-compliant port, the VLAN tagging information passes between them. If a non-802.1Q-enabled device or an access port receives an 802.1Q frame, the tag data is ignored, and the packet is switched at Layer 2 as a standard Ethernet frame. This allows the placement of Layer 2 intermediate devices, such as other switches or bridges, along the 802.1Q trunk path. To process an 802.1Q tagged frame, a device must allow an MTU of 1522 or higher. Some older devices and network cards that are not 802.1Q compatible view a tagged Ethernet frame as too large. These devices drop the frame and log it as an error, called a baby giant.

**Interactive Activity 3-4: Frame Delivery (3.3.3)**

In this activity, you decide whether a frame can be delivered based on the VLAN and port configurations. Use file d3ia-333 on the CD-ROM that accompanies this book to perform this interactive activity.

# Trunking and Inter-VLAN Routing

A VLAN limits the size of broadcast domains. This has the effect that there is less traffic on an area of the network, which improves network performance. It also provides a level of security by containing traffic within a certain area of the network. A Layer 3 device is required to move traffic between VLANs. This Layer 3 device can filter traffic as it passes between VLANs, thus allowing the network administrator to have complete control over which traffic is allowed to move between VLANs. To take full advantage of the benefits of VLANs, they are extended across multiple switches in the enterprise network.

## Trunk Ports

Switch ports can be configured for two different roles. A port is classified as either an access port or a trunk port, as shown in Figure 3-13.

**Figure 3-13    Access and Trunk Ports**

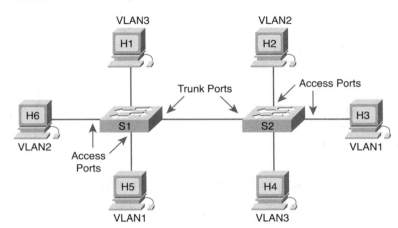

## Access Port

An access port belongs to only one VLAN. Typically, single devices such as PCs or servers connect to this type of port. If a hub connects multiple PCs to the single access port, each device connected to the hub is a member of the same VLAN.

## Trunk Port

A trunk port is a point-to-point link between the switch and another networking device. Trunks carry the traffic of multiple VLANs over a single link and allow VLANs to reach across an entire network. Trunk ports are necessary to carry the traffic from multiple VLANs between devices when connecting either two switches together, a switch to a router, or a host NIC that supports 802.1Q trunking.

Without trunk ports, each VLAN requires a separate connection between switches. For example, an enterprise with 100 VLANs requires 100 connecting links. This type of arrangement does not scale well and is very expensive. Trunk links provide a solution to this problem by transporting traffic from multiple VLANs on the same physical link. When multiple VLANs travel on the same link, they need VLAN identification. A trunk port supports frame tagging. Frame tagging adds VLAN information to the frame.

IEEE 802.1Q is the standardized and approved method of frame tagging. Cisco developed a proprietary frame-tagging protocol called *Inter-Switch Link (ISL).* Higher-end switches, such as the Catalyst 6500 series, still support both tagging protocols; however, most LAN switches, such as the 2960, support only 802.1Q.

Switch ports are access ports by default. To configure a switch port as a trunk port, use the following commands:

```
Switch(config)# interface fa(controller # / port #)
Switch(config-if)# switchport mode trunk
Switch(config-if)# switchport trunk encapsulation {dot1q ¦ isl ¦ negotiate}
```

Switches that support both 802.1Q and ISL require the last configuration statement. The 2960 does not require that statement because it only supports 802.1Q. The negotiate parameter is the default mode on many Cisco switches. This parameter automatically detects the encapsulation type of the neighbor switch.

Newer switches can detect the type of link configured at the other end. Based on the attached device, the link configures itself as either a trunk port or an access port. To turn on this feature use the following command:

```
Switch(config-if)# switchport mode dynamic {desirable ¦ auto}
```

In desirable mode, the port becomes a trunk port if the other end is set to either trunk, desirable, or auto. In auto mode, the port becomes a trunk port if the other end is set to either trunk or desirable. To return a trunk port to an access port, issue either of the following commands:

```
Switch(config-if)# no switchport mode trunk
Switch(config-if)# switchport mode access
```

 **Lab 3-5: Creating VLANs and Assigning Ports (3.4.1)**

In this lab, you create VLANs on a switch and assign ports. Refer to the lab in Part II of this *Learning Guide*. You can perform this lab now or wait until the end of the chapter.

## Extending VLANs Across Switches

Trunking enables VLANs to forward traffic between switches using only a single port. A trunk link configured with 802.1Q on both ends allows traffic that has a 4-byte tag field added to the frame. This frame tag contains the VLAN ID. When a switch receives a tagged frame on a trunk port, it removes the tag before sending it out an access port. This is shown in Figure 3-14. The switch forwards the frame only if the access port is a member of the same VLAN as the tagged frame.

**Figure 3-14    VLAN Tags**

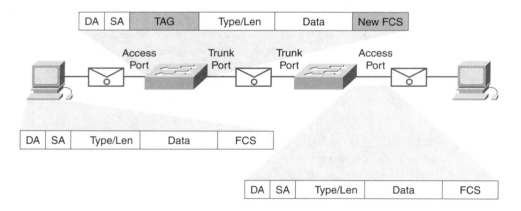

Some traffic however, needs to cross the 802.1Q configured link without a VLAN ID. Traffic with no VLAN ID is called untagged. Examples of untagged traffic are Cisco Discovery Protocol (CDP), VTP, and certain types of voice traffic. Untagged traffic minimizes the delays associated with inspection of the VLAN ID tag. To accommodate untagged traffic, a special VLAN called a *native VLAN* is available. Untagged frames received on the 802.1Q trunk port will become members of the native VLAN. On Cisco Catalyst switches, VLAN 1 is the native VLAN by default.

Any VLAN can be configured as the native VLAN. Ensure that the native VLAN for an 802.1Q trunk is the same on both ends of the trunk line. If they are different, switching loops might result. On an 802.1Q trunk, use the following command to assign the native VLAN ID on a physical interface:

```
Switch(config-if)# switchport trunk native vlan vlan-id
```

**Lab 3-6: Configuring Trunk Ports to Connect Switches (3.4.2)**

In this lab, you configure trunk ports to connect two switches and verify connectivity across the trunk link. Refer to the lab in Part II of this *Learning Guide*. You can perform this lab now or wait until the end of the chapter.

## Inter-VLAN Switching

Although VLANs extend to span multiple switches, only members of the same VLAN can communicate without the assistance of a Layer 3 device. This arrangement enables the network administrator to strictly control the type of traffic that flows from one VLAN to another. One method of accomplishing the inter-VLAN routing requires a separate interface connection to the Layer 3 device for each VLAN, as shown in Figure 3-15.

**Figure 3-15    Inter-VLAN Routing**

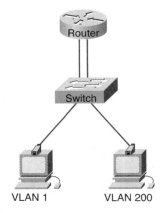

Another method for providing connectivity between different VLANs requires a feature called *subinterfaces*, as shown in Figure 3-16. Subinterfaces logically divide one physical interface into multiple logical pathways. Configure one pathway or subinterface for each VLAN. Supporting inter-VLAN communication using subinterfaces requires configuration on both the switch and the router.

The switch interface connecting to the router must be configured as an 802.1Q trunk link. The router interfaces must be a minimum of 100-Mbps Fast Ethernet and support 802.1Q encapsulation. A separate subinterface must be configured for each VLAN. These subinterfaces allow each VLAN to have its own logical pathway and default gateway into the router.

The host from the sending VLAN forwards traffic to the router using the default gateway. The subinterface for the VLAN specifies the default gateway for all hosts in that VLAN. The router locates the destination IP address and does a routing table lookup. If the destination VLAN is on the same switch as the source VLAN, the router forwards the traffic back down to the source switch using the subinterface parameters of the destination VLAN ID. This type of configuration is often referred to as a *router-on-a-stick*.

**Figure 3-16   Inter-VLAN Routing Using Subinterfaces**

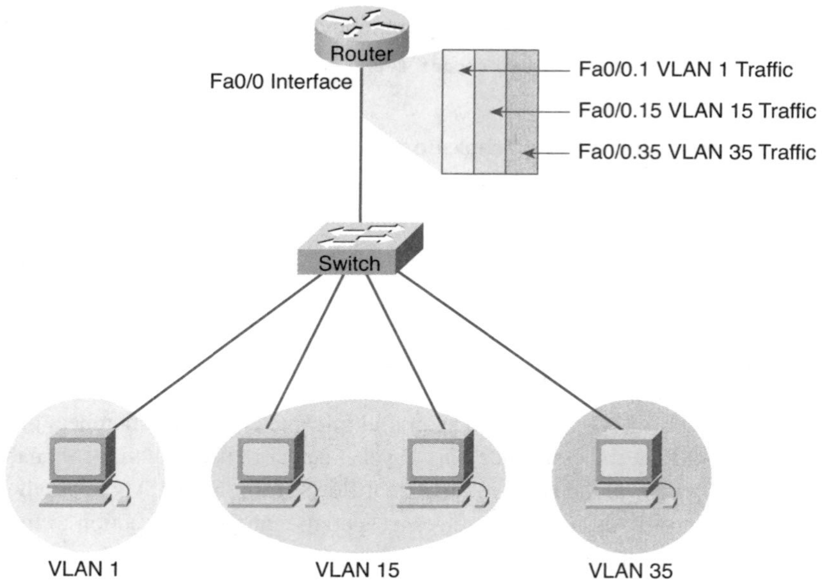

Router
Fa0/0 Interface
Fa0/0.1 VLAN 1 Traffic
Fa0/0.15 VLAN 15 Traffic
Fa0/0.35 VLAN 35 Traffic
Switch
VLAN 1                VLAN 15                VLAN 35

If the exit interface of the router is 802.1Q compatible, the frame retains its 4-byte VLAN tag. If the outbound interface is not 802.1Q compatible, the router strips the tag from the frame and returns the frame to its original Ethernet format.

Consider an example where port Fa0/1 on a router is connected to Fa0/2 on a switch. To configure inter-VLAN routing, use the following steps:

**Step 1.**   Configure a trunk port on the switch.

```
Switch(config)# interface fa0/2
Switch(config-if)# switchport mode trunk
```

**Step 2.**   On the router, configure a Fast Ethernet interface with no IP address or subnet mask.

```
Router(config)# interface fa0/1
Router(config-if)# no ip address
Router(config-if)# no shutdown
```

**Step 3.**   On the router, configure one subinterface with an IP address and subnet mask for each VLAN. Each subinterface has an 802.1Q encapsulation. The number following the dot1q statement is the VLAN ID. Each subinterface must be assigned an IP address because it will act as the default gateway for that subnet.

```
Router(config)# interface fa0/1.10
Router(config-subif)# encapsulation dot1q 10
Router(config-subif)# ip address 192.168.10.1 255.255.255.0
```

**Step 4.**    Use the following commands to verify the inter-VLAN routing configuration and functionality:

```
Switch# show trunk


Router# show ip interfaces
Router# show ip interfaces brief
Router# show ip route
```

**Note**

If inter-VLAN routing fails to function as expected, make certain that no IP address is assigned to the physical Ethernet interface and that the physical interface has been activated.

**Lab 3-7: Part A: Configuring Inter-VLAN Routing (3.4.3)**

In this lab, you configure inter-VLAN routing using separate interfaces for each VLAN. Refer to the lab in Part II of this *Learning Guide*. You can perform this lab now or wait until the end of the chapter.

**Lab 3-7: Part B: Configuring Inter-VLAN Routing (3.4.3)**

In this lab, you configure inter-VLAN routing using a router on-a-stick configuration. Refer to the lab in Part II of this *Learning Guide*. You can perform this lab now or wait until the end of the chapter.

# Maintaining VLANs on an Enterprise LAN

As networks grow in size and complexity, centralized management of the VLAN structure becomes crucial. If there is no automated way to manage an enterprise network with hundreds of VLANs, manual configuration of each VLAN on each switch is necessary. Any change to the VLAN structure requires further manual configuration. One incorrectly keyed number causes inconsistencies in connectivity throughout the entire network. To resolve this issue, Cisco created VTP to automate many of the VLAN configuration functions.

## VLAN Trunking Protocol (VTP)

*VLAN Trunking Protocol (VTP)* is a Layer 2 messaging protocol that provides a method for the distribution and management of the VLAN database from a centralized server in a network segment. Routers do not forward VTP updates. VTP ensures that VLAN configuration is consistently maintained across the network and reduces the task of VLAN management and monitoring.

VTP is a client/server messaging protocol that adds, deletes, and renames VLANs in a single VTP domain. All switches under a common administration are part of a domain. Each domain has a unique name. VTP switches only share VTP messages with other switches in the same domain. Two different versions of VTP exist: Version 1 and Version 2. Version 1 is the default and it is not compatible with Version 2. All switches must be configured with the same version.

With VTP, each switch advertises messages on its trunk ports. Messages include the management domain, configuration revision number, known VLANs, and parameters for each VLAN. These advertisement frames are sent to a multicast address so that all neighbor devices receive the frames.

## VTP Modes

VTP has three modes: server, client, and transparent. The following sections describe each.

### VTP Server Mode

By default, all Cisco switches are in *VTP server* mode. In this mode, the administrator can create, modify, and delete VLANs and VLAN configuration parameters for the entire domain. A VTP server saves VLAN configuration information in the switch NVRAM and sends out VTP messages on all trunk ports. It is good practice to have at least two switches configured as servers on a network to provide backup and redundancy.

### VTP Client Mode

A switch in *VTP client* mode does not create, modify, or delete VLAN information for the VTP domain. It accepts VTP messages from the VTP server and modifies its own database with this information. A VTP client sends VTP messages out all trunk ports.

### VTP Transparent Mode

A switch in *VTP transparent* mode ignores information in the VTP messages. It does not modify its database with information received from the VTP server but does forward VTP advertisements. A switch in VTP transparent mode will not send out an update that indicates a change in its own VLAN database. Therefore, all VLAN created on a switch in this mode remain local to the switch.

 **Challenge Lab 3-8: VTP Modes**

In this lab, you configure VTP and propagate VLAN information through a network. Refer to the lab in Part II of this *Learning Guide*. You can perform this lab now or wait until the end of the chapter.

## VTP Revision Numbers

Each VTP switch saves a VLAN database in NVRAM that contains a revision number. If a VTP receives an update message that has a higher revision number than the one stored in the database, the switch updates its VLAN database with this new information. The VTP configuration revision number begins at 0. As changes occur, the configuration revision number increases by 1. The revision number continues to increment until it reaches 2,147,483,648. When it reaches that point, the counter resets to 0.

There are two ways to reset the VTP revision number to 0. The first is to set the switch you are inserting into the network to VTP transparent mode and then set it back to either a VTP client or server. A second method is to change the VTP domain name to something else and then change it back again.

A problem situation can occur related to the revision number if someone inserts a switch with a higher revision number into the network without first resetting the VTP revision number. Because a switch is a server by default, this results in new, but incorrect, information overwriting the legitimate VLAN information on all the other switches. Another way to protect against this critical situation is to configure a VTP password to validate the switch. When adding a new switch to an existing network, always reset the revision number. In addition, when adding a switch and when a server switch already exists, make sure that the new switch is configured in client or transparent mode.

## VTP Message Types

VTP messages come in three varieties: summary advertisements, subset advertisements, and advertisement requests.

### Summary Advertisements

Catalyst switches issue *summary advertisements* every 5 minutes or whenever a change to the VLAN database occurs. Summary advertisements contain the current VTP domain name and the configuration revision number. If VLANs are added, deleted, or changed, the server increments the configuration revision number and issues a summary advertisement.

When a switch receives a summary advertisement packet, it compares the VTP domain name to its own VTP domain name. If the domain name is the same, the switch compares the configuration revision number to its own number. If it is lower or equal, the switch ignores the packet. If the revision number is higher, an advertisement request is sent.

### Subset Advertisements

A *subset advertisement* follows the summary advertisement. A subset advertisement contains a list of VLAN information. The subset advertisement contains the new VLAN information based on the summary advertisement. If several VLANs exist, they require more than one subset advertisement.

### Advertisement Requests

Catalyst switches use an *advertisement request* to ask for VLAN information. Advertisement requests are required if the switch has been reset or if the VTP domain name has been changed. The switch receives a VTP summary advertisement with a higher configuration revision number than its own.

**Interactive Activity 3-5: VTP Mode Characteristics (3.5.1)**

In this activity, you select the characteristics of VTP client, server, and transparent modes. Use file d3ia-351 on the CD-ROM that accompanies this book to perform this interactive activity.

## Configuring VTP

Switches are servers by default. If a switch in server mode issues an update with a higher revision number than the number currently in place, all switches will modify their databases to match the new switch.

When adding a new switch to an existing VTP domain, use the following steps:

**Step 1.**   Configure VTP off-line as follows:

```
Switch(config)# vtp domain domain_name
Switch(config)# vtp mode {server ¦ client ¦ transparent}
Switch(config)# vtp password password
Switch(config)# end
Switch# copy running-config startup-config
```

**Step 2.**    Verify the VTP configuration using the following commands. Ensure that the revision number is not higher than the network the switch is joining.

```
Switch# show vtp status
```

```
VTP Version                  : 2
Configuration Revision       : 6
Maximum VLANs supported locally : 64
Number of existing VLANs     : 9
VTP Operating Mode           : Server
VTP Domain Name              : headoffice
VTP Pruning Mode             : Disabled
VTP V2 Mode                  : Disabled
VTP Traps Generation         : Disabled
MD5 digest                   : 0x24 0xF1 0xB2 0xF8 0xC9 0x0E 0x9F 0x96
Configuration last modified by 0.0.0.0 at 3-1-93 00:10:17
Local updater ID is 0.0.0.0 (no valid interface found)
```

```
Switch# show vlan
```

```
VLAN Name                         Status    Ports
---- -------------------------- --------- ----------------------------
---
1    default                      active    Fa0/1, Fa0/13, Fa0/14,
Fa0/15

                                            Fa0/16, Fa0/17, Fa0/18,
Fa0/19

                                            Fa0/20, Fa0/21, Fa0/22,
Fa0/23

                                            Fa0/24
10   inventory                    active    Fa0/6
20   marketing                    active    Fa0/4, Fa0/5
30   sales                        active    Fa0/7, Fa0/8, Fa0/9, Fa0/10
                                            Fa0/11, Fa0/12
50   administrators               active
1002 fddi-default                 act/unsup
1003 token-ring-default           act/unsup
1004 fddinet-default              act/unsup
1005 trnet-default                act/unsup
```

```
VLAN Type  SAID       MTU   Parent RingNo BridgeNo Stp  BrdgMode Trans1
Trans2
---- ----- ---------- ----- ------ ------ -------- ---- -------- ------ ----
--
1    enet  100001     1500  -      -      -        -    -        0      0
10   enet  100010     1500  -      -      -        -    -        0      0
20   enet  100020     1500  -      -      -        -    -        0      0
30   enet  100030     1500  -      -      -        -    -        0      0

VLAN Type  SAID       MTU   Parent RingNo BridgeNo Stp  BrdgMode Trans1
Trans2
---- ----- ---------- ----- ------ ------ -------- ---- -------- ------ ----
--
50   enet  100050     1500  -      -      -        -    -        0      0
1002 fddi  101002     1500  -      -      -        -    -        0      0
1003 tr    101003     1500  -      -      -        -    -        0      0
1004 fdnet 101004     1500  -      -      -        ieee -        0      0
1005 trnet 101005     1500  -      -      -        ibm  -        0      0

Switch# show vtp password

VTP Password: itsasecret

Switch# show vtp counters

VTP statistics:
Summary advertisements received    : 4
Subset advertisements received     : 4
Request advertisements received    : 2
Summary advertisements transmitted : 6
Subset advertisements transmitted  : 6
Request advertisements transmitted : 0Number of config revision errors   : 0
Number of config digest errors     : 0
Number of V1 summary errors        : 0

VTP pruning statistics:

Trunk            Join Transmitted Join Received    Summary advts received
from
```

```
                                                        non-pruning-capable
        device
        --------------- --------------- --------------- -----------------------
        --
        Fa0/2            0               1               0
        Fa0/3            0               1               0
```

**Step 3.**   Reboot the switch:

```
Switch# reload
```

### Building and Testing a VTP Domain (3.5.2.2)

In this activity, you build and test a VTP domain. Use file d3-3522.pka on the CD-ROM that accompanies this book to perform this activity using Packet Tracer.

### Adding a Switch to a VTP Domain (3.5.2.3)

In this activity, you add a new switch to an existing VTP domain. Use file d3-3523.pka on the CD-ROM that accompanies this book to perform this activity using Packet Tracer.

## VLAN Support for IP Telephony and Wireless

The main purpose of VLANs is to separate traffic into logical groups. Traffic from one VLAN will not impact traffic from another VLAN. A common network design is to separate voice and wireless traffic from the rest of the traffic. This is shown in Figure 3-17.

A VLAN environment is ideal for traffic that is sensitive to time delays, such as voice. Voice traffic must be given priority over normal data traffic to avoid jerky or jittery conversations. Providing a dedicated VLAN for voice traffic prevents voice traffic from having to compete with data for available bandwidth.

An IP phone usually has two ports, one for voice and one for data. Packets traveling to and from the PC and the IP phone share the same physical link to the switch and the same switch port. To segment the voice traffic, enable a separate voice VLAN on the switch.

Wireless is another type of traffic that benefits from VLANs. Wireless is, by nature, very insecure and prone to attacks by hackers. VLANs created for wireless traffic isolate some of the problems that can occur. A compromise to the integrity of the wireless VLAN has no effect on any other VLAN within the organization. Most wireless deployments place the user in a VLAN on the outside of the firewall for added security. Users have to authenticate to gain entry into the internal network from the wireless network.

In addition, many organizations provide guest access to their wireless network. Guest accounts provide anyone, within a limited range, temporary wireless services such as web access, e-mail, ftp, and SSH. Guest accounts are either included in the wireless VLAN or reside in a VLAN of their own.

**Figure 3-17    Separating Voice and Wireless Traffic**

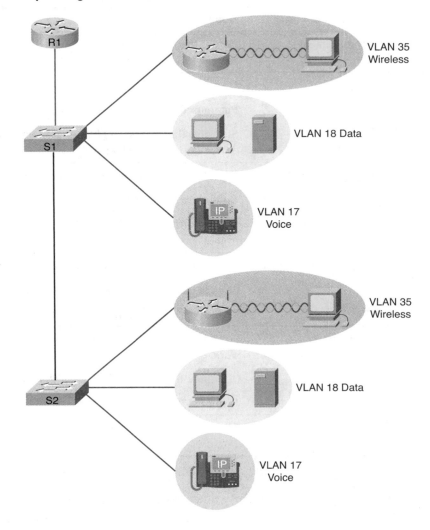

**Packet Tracer**
☐ **Activity**

**Configuring Wireless and Voice VLANs (3.5.3)**

In this activity, you create separate VLANs for voice and wireless traffic. Use file d3-353.pka on the CD-ROM that accompanies this book to perform this activity using Packet Tracer.

## VLAN Best Practices

When carefully planned and designed, VLANs provide security, conserve bandwidth, and localize traffic on an enterprise network. All of these features combine to improve network performance. VLANs, however, are not the answer to every problem. If VLANs are not correctly implemented, they can overly complicate a network, resulting in inconsistent connectivity and slow network performance. VLANs isolate certain types of traffic for reasons of security. Moving traffic between VLANs requires a Layer 3 device, which increases the cost of implementation and introduces an increased level of latency into the network.

Table 3-3 presents some recommended best practices for configuring VLANs in an enterprise network.

**Table 3-3    VLAN Best Practices**

| Best Practice | Description |
| --- | --- |
| Server placement | Ensure that all servers required by a particular group are members of the same VLAN. |
| Unused ports | Disable unused ports. |
| | Put unused ports in an unused VLAN. |
| | Stop unauthorized access by not granting connectivity or by placing a device into an unused VLAN. |
| Management VLAN | By default, the management VLAN and the native VLAN are VLAN1. |
| | Do not use VLAN1 for in-band management traffic. |
| | Select a different, dedicated VLAN to keep management traffic separate from user data and protocol traffic. |
| VLAN Trunking Protocol | Standardize the VLAN configuration across the enterprise. |
| | Provide easy VLAN management and maintenance. |
| | Reduce the time required for VLAN administration and maintenance. |
| VTP domains | Prevent the risk of an administrator error propagating to the entire network. |
| | Configure the VTP domains carefully and consistently. |
| | Turn off VTP when not required. |
| VTP revision number | Ensure that any new switch added to the network has a revision number of 0. |

Packet Tracer
☐ Activity

**Planning and Building an Enterprise Network (3.5.4)**

In this activity, you plan and build a switched network to meet client specifications. Use file d3-354.pka on the CD-ROM that accompanies this book to perform this activity using Packet Tracer.

## Summary

Modern enterprise networks rely on switches for their basic functionality. Switches use microsegmentation to limit the size of the broadcast domain to a single switch port. Traditionally, switches used either store-and-forward or cut-through techniques. Improvements in technology allow some switches to automatically adapt their switching technique to match network conditions.

Redundancy is incorporated into network design to minimize downtime in the network. Spanning Tree Protocol is used to prevent the formation of switching loops in these redundant networks. Spanning Tree elects a root bridge based on the lowest bridge ID. Spanning Tree can take 50 seconds to reach the state where it is forwarding packets through the network. Rapid Spanning Tree Protocol has been developed to greatly shorten this convergence time.

A VLAN is a collection of hosts that are on the same local-area network, even though they might be physically separated from each other. A 4-byte 802.1Q header is inserted into a standard Ethernet frame to identify the VLAN to which the frame belongs. By default, VLAN 1 is the management VLAN.

An access port connects a device to a switch and is a member of a single VLAN. A trunk port carries traffic from multiple VLANs and normally connects a switch to another switch or a router. The native VLAN is the VLAN that uses untagged traffic. A Layer 3 device is required to move traffic between VLANs. Routers are usually configured with subinterfaces to handle multiple VLANs on a single physical link.

VTP provides a mechanism for the centralized control, distribution, and maintenance of the VLAN database. Switches can either be server, client, or transparent. VTP updates contain a revision number. A higher revision number update will overwrite information from a lower revision number.

VLANs are suitable for delay-sensitive traffic such as voice. They are also beneficial when it is important to keep different types of traffic off different areas of the network to provide a level of security and bandwidth management. When implementing VLANs, a number of best practices should be followed, including using a VTP password, consistent domain name, and revision control.

## Activities and Labs

This summary outlines the activities and labs you can perform to help reinforce important concepts described in this chapter. You can find the activity and Packet Tracer files on the CD-ROM accompanying this book. The complete hands-on labs appear in Part II.

**Interactive Activities on the CD-ROM:**

Interactive Activity 3-1: Switch Frame Forwarding (3.1.1)

Interactive Activity 3-2: Spanning Tree (3.2.2)

Interactive Activity 3-3: Implementing VLANs (3.3.1)

Interactive Activity 3-4: Frame Delivery (3.3.3)

Interactive Activity 3-5: VTP Mode Characteristics (3.5.1)

**Packet Tracer Activities on the CD-ROM:**

Disabling Redundant Links to Avoid Switching Loops (3.2.1)

Building and Testing a VTP Domain (3.5.2.2)

Adding a Switch to a VTP Domain (3.5.2.3)

Configuring Wireless and Voice VLANs (3.5.3)

Planning and Building an Enterprise Network (3.5.4)

**Hands-on Labs in Part II of this book:**

Lab 3-1: Applying Basic Switch Security (3.1.4)

Lab 3-2: Building a Switched Network with Redundant Links (3.2.3)

Lab 3-3: Verifying STP with **show** Commands (3.2.4)

Lab 3-4: Configuring, Verifying, and Troubleshooting VLANs (3.3.2)

Lab 3-5: Creating VLANs and Assigning Ports (3.4.1)

Lab 3-6: Configuring a Trunk Port to Connect Switches (3.4.2)

Lab 3-7: Part A: Configuring Inter-VLAN Routing (3.4.3)

Lab 3-7: Part B: Configuring Inter-VLAN Routing (3.4.3)

Challenge Lab 3-8: VTP Modes

# Check Your Understanding

Complete all the review questions listed here to check your understanding of the topics and concepts in this chapter. Appendix A, "Check Your Understanding and Challenge Questions Answer Key," lists the answers.

1. What does a switch do with a frame if the destination address is not in the MAC address database?

   A. It floods the frame out all ports except the one on which it was received.

   B. It forwards the frame out each port until it receives a receipt acknowledgment from the destination.

   C. It discards the frame.

   D. It buffers the frame until the destination address is learned.

2. What type of switching technology is most often used by modern LAN switches?

   A. Store-and-forward

   B. Fast-forward

   C. Fragment-free

   D. Adaptive

3. What type of switching is most appropriate for connecting multiple hosts to a server farm?

   A. Symmetric

   B. Asymmetric

   C. Cut-through

   D. Store-and-forward

4. Which type of switching would not switch runts? (Select all that apply.)

   A. Store-and-forward

   B. Fragment-free

   C. Fast-forward

   D. Adaptive

5. Which are security measures that should be implemented in a switched network? (Select all that apply.)

   A. Disable Telnet and HTTP access

   B. Disable unused ports

   C. Enable port security

   D. Restrict access to the physical switch

6. Which can be the result of redundancy in a switched network? (Select all that apply.)

   A. MAC database instability

   B. Broadcast storms

   C. Multiple frame transmission

   D. Increased availability

7. Which protocol is used to create a loop-free environment in a switched network that has redundant links?

   A  BPDU

   B. STP

   C. VLAN

   D. VTP

8. Which open standard was developed to reduce the time required for a switched network to reach convergence?

   A. BackboneFast

   B. PortFast

   C. UplinkFast

   D. RSTP

9. When a new host is connected to a switch with STP enabled, what mode is the port placed into?

   A. Blocking

   B. Listening

   C. Learning

   D. Forwarding

   E. Disabled

10. In which STP mode does the switch listen for BPDUs? (Select all that apply.)

 A. Blocking

 B. Listening

 C. Learning

 D. Forwarding

11. In a switched network, what is used to contain broadcasts and group physically separated hosts together in communities of interest.

 A. Switch

 B. Router

 C. VLAN

 D. Active topology

12. On a Cisco switch, which VLAN is used for untagged traffic?

 A. VLAN 1

 B. Management VLAN

 C. Native VLAN

 D. Untagged VLAN

13. What are three types of VTP messages and what are they used for?

14. How does STP elect a root bridge?

15. What are the three modes in VTP and how does each function?

# Challenge Questions and Activities

These questions require a deeper application of the concepts covered in this chapter. You can find the answers in Appendix A.

1. You have just been hired by AnyCompany as its network administrator. Your first task is to centralize all the internal company servers into a server farm and to set up a method by which certain hosts can be denied access to this server farm based on a statically assigned IP address. What equipment would you need to purchase and what high-level configuration would you implement to accomplish this?

2. The AnyCompany network has grown to over 200 switches and 43 different VLANs. To simplify the management of this network, you are using VTP. You have just received a call from the company president, who is complaining that she no longer has access to the company network. After a bit of investigating, you determine that the VLAN configuration on the network has been altered. At the same time you are informed by the junior network administrator that he replaced a switch in the engineering department. What could have caused the VLAN configuration change and how would you prevent it in the future?

# CHAPTER 4

# Addressing in an Enterprise Network

## Objectives

After completion of this chapter, you should be able to answer the following questions:

- What are the features and benefits of a hierarchical IP addressing structure?

- How is a VLSM IP address scheme planned and implemented?

- How is classless routing and CIDR used in planning a network?

- How are static and dynamic NAT configured and verified?

## Key Terms

This chapter uses the following key terms. You can find the definitions in the Glossary.

*broadcast domain*    *page 110*

*flat network*    *page 110*

*hierarchical network*    *page 111*

*Variable-length subnet masks (VLSM)*    *page 122*

*route summarization*    *page 122*

*sub-subnets*    *page 123*

*Internet Engineering Task Force (IETF)*    *page 131*

*classless interdomain routing (CIDR)*    *page 131*

*classless routing protocol*    *page 131*

*prefix length*    *page 131*

*interior gateway protocols*    *page 131*

*exterior gateway protocols*    *page 131*

*route aggregation*    *page 132*

*network boundary*    *page 132*

*supernetting*    *page 133*

*discontiguous*    *page 136*

*Private addresses*    *page 140*

*Public addresses*    *page 140*

*Network Address Translation (NAT)*    *page 142*

*Static NAT*    *page 142*

*inside local address*    *page 142*

*Dynamic NAT*    *page 143*

*inside global address*    *page 143*

*access control list (ACL)*    *page 145*

*Port Address Translation (PAT)*    *page 146*

*NAT overload*    *page 146*

Well-designed enterprise networks with many locations and users use a logical addressing hierarchy. The use of classless addresses and variable-length subnet masks (VLSM) facilitate network scalability. Classless routing and classless interdomain routing (CIDR) address the problems of route summarization. Private addressing and Network Address Translation (NAT) preserve IPv4 addresses, providing flexibility and security in network design.

Part II of this book includes the corresponding labs for this chapter.

# Using a Hierarchical IP Network Address Scheme

Enterprise networks make use of hierarchical network design and hierarchical addressing to improve network performance and manageability. The following sections discuss the different flat hierarchical networks and the benefits of using subnetting and hierarchical addressing to structure the network in an organized and logical way.

## Flat and Hierarchical Networks

Implementing switches reduces the number of collisions that occur within a local network. However, having an all-switched network often creates a single *broadcast domain*. In a single broadcast domain, or *flat network*, every device is in the same network and receives each broadcast. In small networks, a single broadcast domain is acceptable.

With large numbers of hosts, a flat network becomes less efficient. As the number of hosts increases in a switched network, so do the number of broadcasts sent and received. Broadcast packets take up a lot of bandwidth, causing traffic delays and timeouts.

Figure 4-1 shows several interconnected switches, each with multiple hosts attached. This creates one large broadcast domain where all hosts must receive and process every broadcast. Broadcasts, such as Address Resolution Protocol (ARP) requests, are essential in an IP/Ethernet network, but too many of them can clog the network and slow it. If switches are used to connect hosts, they eliminate collisions but must still pass along broadcasts or the ARP process would not work. If hubs are attached to switch ports, the problems of a flat network are compounded because of the fact that they allow collisions to occur.

Creating VLANs provides one solution to a large, flat network. Each VLAN is its own broadcast domain.

**Figure 4-1    Flat Switched Network—Single Broadcast Domain**

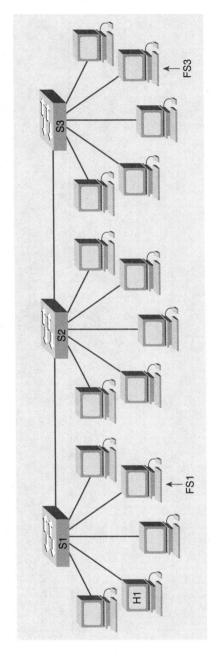

Implementing a *hierarchical network* using routers is another solution. Figure 4-2 shows the same network with the addition of routers at the distribution and core layers to create a hierarchical network design. Distribution layer Router R1 connects to each of the three switches and creates three separate broadcast domains.

To illustrate how routers control broadcasts, consider an example. With the flat network shown in Figure 4-1, if Host H1 on Switch S1 needs to obtain a file from the File Server FS1 on S1, it first broadcasts an ARP request to obtain the MAC address of the server. All hosts on all switches receive and must process the ARP broadcast to determine whether it is for them, even though Host H1 and Server FS1 are on the same switch.

**Figure 4-2    Hierarchical Routed Network—Multiple Broadcast Domains**

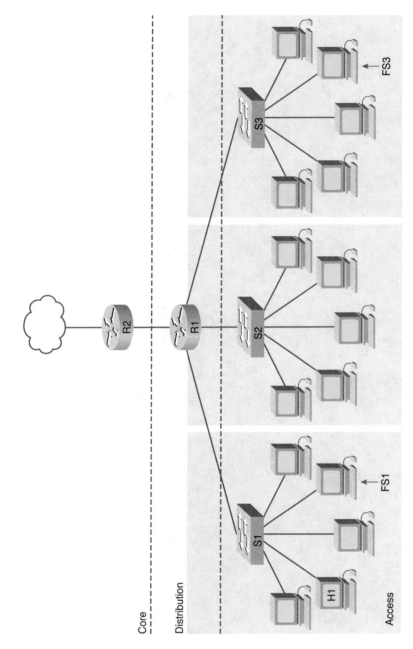

With the hierarchical design shown in Figure 4-2, only hosts on Switch S1 receive the broadcast. The router isolates the S1 broadcast traffic from hosts on Switches S2 and S3. If Host H1 needs access to File Server FS3 on Switch S3, the router forwards the packets to S3. If Host H1 needs access to a web server on the Internet, R1 forwards the packets to R2. Router R1 routes traffic between the hosts on the three switches and to core layer Router R2 when necessary.

## Hierarchical Network Addressing

Enterprise networks are large and benefit from a hierarchical network design and address structure. A hierarchical addressing structure logically groups networks into smaller subnetworks.

An effective hierarchical address scheme consists of a classful network address in the core layer that is subdivided into successively smaller subnets in the distribution and access layers.

It is possible to have a hierarchical network without hierarchical addressing. Although the network still functions, the effectiveness of the network design decreases and certain routing protocol features, such as route summarization, do not work properly.

In enterprise networks with many geographically separate locations, a hierarchical network design and address structure simplify network management and troubleshooting and also improve scalability and routing performance. Figure 4-3 shows a physical hierarchical design with nonhierarchical logical addressing. The S1 network is 192.168.1.0/24, the S2 network is 10.22.5.0/24, and the S3 network is 172.16.8.0/24. The network numbers are mixed and do not summarize because they have no common bits in the network portion of the address.

**Figure 4-3    Nonhierarchical Addressing**

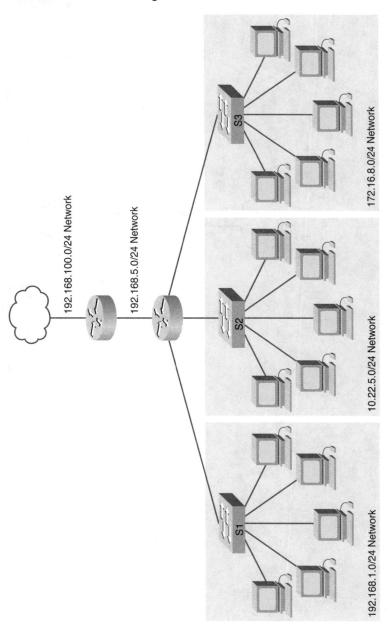

Figure 4-4 shows a physical hierarchical design with hierarchical logical addressing. The S1 network is 10.1.1.32/27, the S2 network is 10.1.1.64/27, and the S3 network is 10.1.1.96/27. Because the first 24 bits of the network address are the same, these three networks are contiguous and can be summarized to 10.1.1.0/24 and advertised as a single network. Multiple 10.1.x.0/24 networks could be summarized and advertised as a single 10.1.0.0/16 network. This is the nature of hierarchical logical addressing.

**Figure 4-4    Hierarchical Addressing**

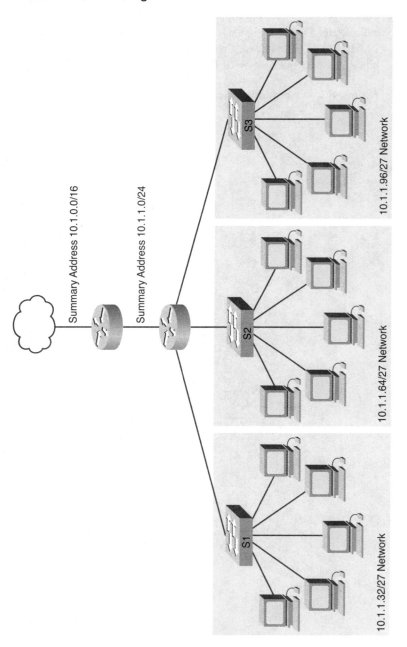

## Using Subnetting to Structure the Network

There are many reasons to divide the network into subnets, including

- Physical location
- Logical grouping
- Security
- Application requirements
- Broadcast containment
- Hierarchical network design

For example, if an organization uses a 10.0.0.0 network for the enterprise, it might use an addressing scheme such as 10.$X$.$Y$.0, where $X$ represents a geographical location and $Y$ represents a building or floor within a building for that location. This addressing scheme allows

- 255 different geographical locations
- 255 buildings or floors in each location
- 254 hosts within each building or floor

Figure 4-5 shows the use of routers in the distribution layer to control broadcasts, provide security, group users logically by department, and link geographically separate locations.

**Interactive Activity 4-1: Deciding When to Use a Hierarchical Addressing Scheme (4.1.3)**

In this interactive activity, you indicate whether a hierarchical addressing scheme using subnets should be used to structure the network. Use file d3ia-4132 on the CD-ROM that accompanies this book to perform this interactive activity.

**Figure 4-5    Functions of Routers**

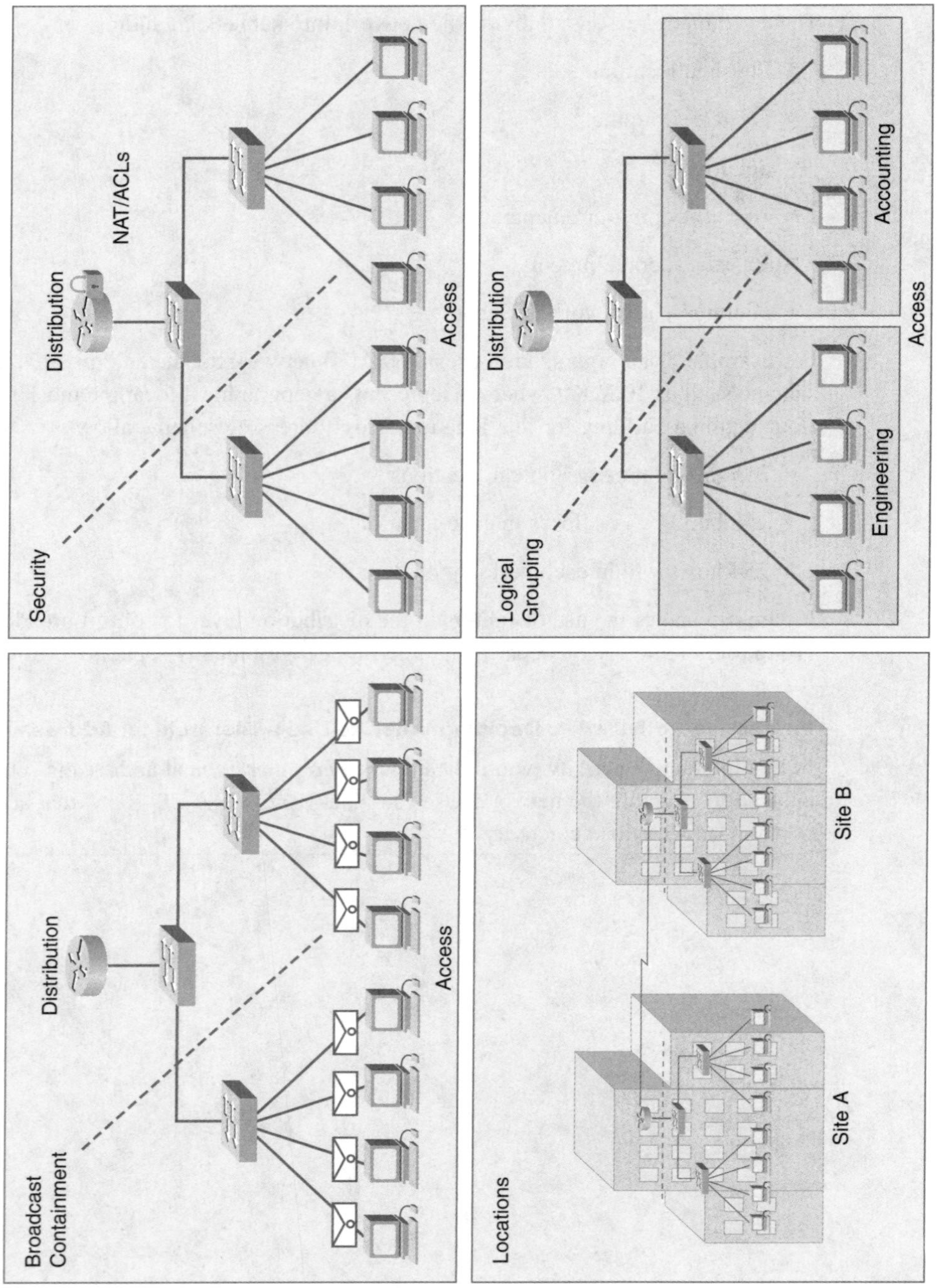

## Using VLSM

Variable-length subnet masking is a key technology to making the most efficient use of IP address space. The following sections review the basic subnetting process and compare it to VLSM. The process of planning and applying a VLSM design to a network is described.

# Subnet Mask

To use subnetting to create a hierarchical design, it is crucial to have a clear understanding of the structure of the subnet mask.

The subnet mask indicates whether hosts are in the same network. The subnet mask is a 32-bit value that distinguishes between the network bits and the host bits. It consists of a string of 1s followed by a string of 0s. The 1 bits represent the network portion and the 0 bits represent the host portion. The following are the main classful addresses and the default or standard mask associated with each:

- Class A addresses use a default subnet mask of 255.0.0.0 or a slash notation of /8.

- Class B addresses use a default mask of 255.255.0.0 or /16.

- Class C addresses use a default mask of 255.255.255.0 or /24.

The /x refers to the number of bits in the subnet mask that comprise the network portion of the address and is often called *slash notation*. CIDR, which is covered later in this chapter in the section "Using Classless Routing and CIDR," refers to the number of network bits specified by the /x format as a network prefix.

In an enterprise network, subnet masks vary in length. LAN segments often contain varying numbers of hosts; therefore, it is not efficient to have the same subnet mask length for all subnets created. Table 4-1 shows the subnet masks from 255.0.0.0 through 255.255.255.255 using dotted decimal notation. Although it is possible to have a mask of less than 8 bits, it is not common. In the table, the binary equivalent mask and the CIDR prefix (slash notation) are shown along with the number of host bits left after applying the mask and the number of hosts possible.

**Table 4-1    Subnet Masks and Number of Hosts**

| Dotted Decimal Subnet Mask | Binary Subnet Mask | Slash Notation (CIDR Prefix) | Number of Host Bits | Hosts Possible (Subtract 2) |
|---|---|---|---|---|
| 255.0.0.0 | 11111111.00000000.00000000.00000000 | /8 | 24 | 16777216 |
| 255.128.0.0 | 11111111.10000000.00000000.00000000 | /9 | 23 | 8388608 |
| 255.192.0.0 | 11111111.11000000.00000000.00000000 | /10 | 22 | 4194304 |
| 255.224.0.0 | 11111111.11100000.00000000.00000000 | /11 | 21 | 2097152 |
| 255.240.0.0 | 11111111.11110000.00000000.00000000 | /12 | 20 | 1048576 |
| 255.248.0.0 | 11111111.11111000.00000000.00000000 | /13 | 19 | 524288 |
| 255.252.0.0 | 11111111.11111100.00000000.00000000 | /14 | 18 | 262144 |
| 255.254.0.0 | 11111111.11111110.00000000.00000000 | /15 | 17 | 131072 |
| 255.255.0.0 | 11111111.11111111.00000000.00000000 | /16 | 16 | 65536 |
| 255.255.128.0 | 11111111.11111111.10000000.00000000 | /17 | 15 | 32768 |
| 255.255.192.0 | 11111111.11111111.11000000.00000000 | /18 | 14 | 16384 |
| 255.255.224.0 | 11111111.11111111.11100000.00000000 | /19 | 13 | 8192 |

*continues*

**Table 4-1    Subnet Masks and Number of Hosts**    *continued*

| Dotted Decimal Subnet Mask | Binary Subnet Mask | Slash Notation (CIDR Prefix) | Number of Host Bits | Hosts Possible (Subtract 2) |
|---|---|---|---|---|
| 255.255.240.0 | 11111111.11111111.11110000.00000000 | /20 | 12 | 4096 |
| 255.255.248.0 | 11111111.11111111.11111000.00000000 | /21 | 11 | 2048 |
| 255.255.252.0 | 11111111.11111111.11111100.00000000 | /22 | 10 | 1024 |
| 255.255.254.0 | 11111111.11111111.11111110.00000000 | /23 | 9 | 512 |
| 255.255.255.0 | 11111111.11111111.11111111.00000000 | /24 | 8 | 256 |
| 255.255.255.128 | 11111111.11111111.11111111.10000000 | /25 | 7 | 128 |
| 255.255.255.192 | 11111111.11111111.11111111.11000000 | /26 | 6 | 64 |
| 255.255.255.224 | 11111111.11111111.11111111.11100000 | /27 | 5 | 32 |
| 255.255.255.240 | 11111111.11111111.11111111.11110000 | /28 | 4 | 16 |
| 255.255.255.248 | 11111111.11111111.11111111.11111000 | /29 | 3 | 8 |
| 255.255.255.252 | 11111111.11111111.11111111.11111100 | /30 | 2 | 4 |
| 255.255.255.254 | 11111111.11111111.11111111.11111110 | /31 | 1 | 2 |
| 255.255.255.255 | 11111111.11111111.11111111.11111111 | /32 | 0 | 0 |

To determine the number of IP addresses that can be assigned to hosts, take the number 2 to the power of the number of host bits available and then subtract 2.

As an example, if you use a subnet mask of 255.255.254.0 (/23 CIDR prefix) or binary 11111111.11111111.11111110.00000000 with any network number, 9 bits are left for host addresses. The calculation for the number of usable IP addresses is $2^2 = 512 - 2 = 510$. The default masks of /8, /16, and /24 are highlighted.

**Interactive Activity 4-2: Analyzing a Decimal Subnet Mask to Determine the Number of Hosts (4.2.1)**

In this interactive activity, you enter the slash notation, number of host bits, and number of hosts possible based on the subnet mask displayed. Use file d3ia-421 on the CD-ROM that accompanies this book to perform this interactive activity.

## Calculating Subnets Using Binary Representation

When one host needs to communicate with another, the IP address and subnet mask of the source host are compared to the IP address and subnet mask of the destination. This is done to determine whether the two addresses are on the same local network.

The subnet mask is a 32-bit value used to distinguish between the network bits and the host bits of the IP address.

The network bits are compared between the source and destination. If the resulting networks are the same, the packet can be delivered locally. If they do not match, the packet is sent to the default gateway.

Figure 4-6 shows the ANDing process for two hosts. With ANDing, the 32 subnet mask bits are compared one by one to the 32 bits of an IP host address to determine the network address of the host. The router does this comparison in microseconds. If a 1 bit and a 1 bit are compared, the result is a 1 bit. If a 0 bit and a 1 bit are compared, the result is a 0. If a 0 bit and a 0 bit are compared, the result is a 0 bit. The 1 bits in the resulting 32-bit address determine the network that the host is on.

**Figure 4-6     Two Hosts on the Same Subnet**

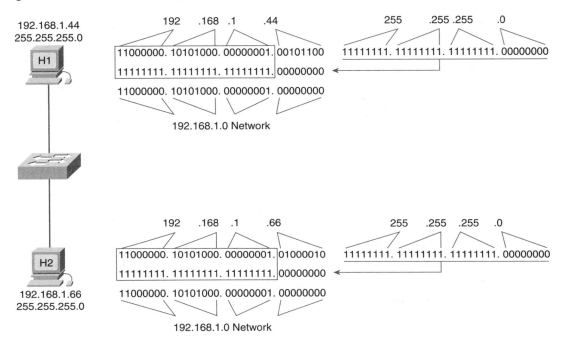

In Figure 4-6, H1 has IP address 192.168.1.44 and subnet mask 255.255.255.0, or /24. If H1 needs to send a message to H2, with IP address 192.168.1.66 and subnet mask 255.255.255.0, are they on the same network or will a router be necessary for them to communicate? In this instance, both hosts have a default subnet mask of 255.255.255.0, which means that the network bits end on the octet boundary, the third octet. Both hosts have the same network bits of 192.168.1 and therefore are on the same network.

While it is fairly easy to see the network and host portion of an IP address when the subnet mask ends on the network boundary, the process of determining the network bits is the same, even when the network portion does not take up the entire octet. In Figure 4-7, H1 has IP address 192.168.13.21 with subnet mask 255.255.255.248, or /29. This means that of the 32 bits, 29 of them make up the network portion. The network bits take up all the first three octets and extend into the fourth octet. In this instance, the value of the network ID for Host H1 is 192.168.13.16.

If H1, with IP address of 192.168.13.21/29 needed to communicate with another host, H2, with IP address 192.168.13.25/29, the network portion of the two hosts must be compared to determine whether the two are on the same local network. In this case, H1 has a network value of 192.168.13.16, whereas H2 has a network value of 192.168.13.24. H1 and H2 are not on the same network and require the use of a router to communicate.

**Figure 4-7    Two Hosts on Different Subnets**

```
H1 = 192.168.13.21/29
Subnet Mask: 255.255.255. 1 1 1 1 1|0 0 0 (Decimal 248)
IP Address:   192.168.13   0 0 0 1 0|1 0 1 (Decimal 21)
------------------------------------|----------
Subnetwork:  192.168.13   0 0 0 1 0|0 0 0 (Decimal 16)

H1 is on Subnetwork: 192.168.13.16
```

```
H2 = 192.168.13.25/29
Subnet Mask: 255.255.255. 1 1 1 1 1|0 0 0 (decimal 248)
IP Address:   192.168.13   0 0 0 1 1|0 0 1 (decimal 25)
------------------------------------|----------
Subnetwork:  192.168.13   0 0 0 1 1|0 0 0 (decimal 24)

H2 is on Subnetwork: 192.168.13.24
```

## Alternative Subnet Calculation

Another way to determine the network portion of the IP address is to look at the number of host bits to determine the valid subnets. For example, if 3 host bits are left, you take $2^2$, which = 8. Because eight addresses exist on each subnet, the subnet numbers will increase by multiples of 8. Starting at subnet 0, the first five valid subnets are

- 192.168.13.0 /29

- 192.168.13.8 /29

- 192.168.13.16 /29

- 192.168.13.24 /29

- 192.168.13.32 /29

Because the host address of 192.168.13.21 falls between the subnets of 192.168.13.16 and 192.168.13.24, it belongs to the 192.168.13.16 network. Host address 192.168.13.25 falls between the subnets of 192.168.13.24 and 192.168.13.32; therefore, it belongs to the 192.168.13.24 network.

**Interactive Activity 4-3: Determining Whether Two Hosts Are on the Same Network (4.2.2)**

In this interactive activity, you choose whether the hosts are on the same network or a different network. Use file d3ia-422 on the CD-ROM that accompanies this book to perform this interactive activity.

# Basic Subnetting Process

Using a hierarchical addressing scheme, much information can be determined by looking at only an IP address and slash notation (/x) subnet mask. For example, an IP address of 192.168.1.75 /26 shows the following information:

- **Decimal subnet mask:** The /26 translates to a subnet mask of 255.255.255.192.

- **Number of subnets created:** Assuming that you started with the default /24 subnet mask, borrow 2 additional host bits for the network. This creates four subnets ($2^2 = 4$).

- **Number of usable hosts per subnet:** Six bits are left on the host side, creating 62 hosts per subnet ($2^6 = 64 - 2 = 62$).

- **Network address:** Using the subnet mask to determine the placement of network bits, the value of the subnetwork address can be determined. In this example, the subnet value is 192.168.1.64.

- **First usable host address:** A host cannot have all 0s within the host bits, because that represents the network address of the subnet. Therefore, the first usable host address within the .64 subnet is .65.

- **Broadcast address:** A host cannot have all 1s within the host bits because that represents the broadcast address of the subnet. In this case, the broadcast address is .127. 128 starts the network address of the next subnet.

Table 4-2 shows an example of the 192.168.1.0/24 network being subnetted into four subnets by borrowing 2 bits from the 8 host bits ($2^2 = 4$). The four resulting subnetwork addresses are shown in the table. Each of these subnets has 6 bits for hosts, which results in 62 possible hosts per subnet ($2^6 = 64 - 2 = 62$). For each of the four subnets created, the table shows the subnet sequence number (0 through 4), the base or starting subnetwork address, the range of valid host addresses, and the broadcast address (last address of the range) for the subnet.

**Table 4-2    Subnetting a /24 Network into Four /26 Subnets**

| Subnet | Network Address | Host Range | Broadcast Address |
|--------|-----------------|------------|-------------------|
| 0 | 192.168.1.0/26 | 192.168.1.1–192.168.1.62 | 192.168.1.63 |
| 1 | 192.168.1.64/26 | 192.168.1.65–192.168.1.126 | 192.168.1.127 |
| 2 | 192.168.1.128/26 | 192.168.1.129–192.168.1.190 | 192.168.1.191 |
| 3 | 192.168.1.192/26 | 192.168.1.193–192.168.1.254 | 192.168.1.255 |

**Note**

The first subnet is often referred to as the zero (0) subnet but can also be referred to as subnet 1.

**Lab 4-1: Designing and Applying an IP Addressing Scheme (4.2.3)**

In this lab, you will design and apply an IP addressing subnet scheme for a given topology. Refer to the lab in Part II of this *Learning Guide*. You can perform this lab now or wait until the end of the chapter.

**Challenge Lab 4-2: Calculating a Network IP Addressing Scheme**

In this lab, you will gain additional practice in calculating network IP addressing. Refer to the lab in Part II of this *Learning Guide*. You can perform this lab now or wait until the end of the chapter.

# Variable-Length Subnet Masks (VLSM)

Basic subnetting is sufficient for smaller networks but does not provide the flexibility needed in larger enterprise networks. *Variable-length subnet masks (VLSM)* provide efficient use of address space. They also allow hierarchal IP addressing, which allows routers to take advantage of *route summarization*. Route summarization reduces the size of routing tables in distribution and core routers. Smaller routing tables require less CPU time for routing lookups.

VLSM is the use of subnet masks of varying lengths within the same internetwork, or basically the use of different masks instead of the same mask for all network segments. VLSM also supports the subnetting of a subnet. It was initially developed to maximize addressing efficiency. With the advent of private addressing, the primary advantage of VLSM now is organization and summarization.

Not all routing protocols support VLSM. Classful routing protocols, such as RIPv1, do not include a subnet mask field with a routing update. A router with a subnet mask assigned to its interface assumes that all packets within that same class have the same subnet mask assigned.

Classless routing protocols support the use of VLSM because the subnet mask is sent with all routing update packets. Classless routing protocols include RIPv2, EIGRP, and OSPF.

Benefits of VLSM include the following:

- Allows efficient use of address space
- Allows the use of multiple subnet mask lengths
- Breaks up an address block into smaller blocks
- Allows route summarization
- Provides more flexibility in network design
- Supports hierarchical enterprise networks

Figure 4-8 shows a topology diagram with seven subnetworks based on the 192.168.20.0/24 network. There are four LANs and three WANs. Each of the LANs has a requirement for approximately 20 host IP addresses. The WAN links only require two IP addresses each.

**Figure 4-8   Using VLSM to Address the Network**

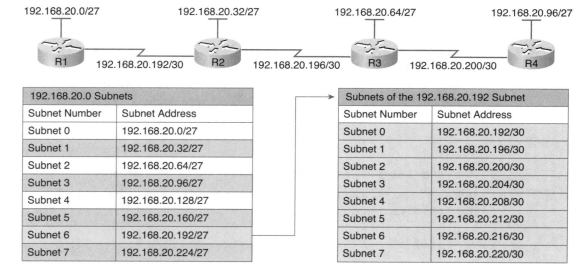

| 192.168.20.0 Subnets | |
|---|---|
| Subnet Number | Subnet Address |
| Subnet 0 | 192.168.20.0/27 |
| Subnet 1 | 192.168.20.32/27 |
| Subnet 2 | 192.168.20.64/27 |
| Subnet 3 | 192.168.20.96/27 |
| Subnet 4 | 192.168.20.128/27 |
| Subnet 5 | 192.168.20.160/27 |
| Subnet 6 | 192.168.20.192/27 |
| Subnet 7 | 192.168.20.224/27 |

| Subnets of the 192.168.20.192 Subnet | |
|---|---|
| Subnet Number | Subnet Address |
| Subnet 0 | 192.168.20.192/30 |
| Subnet 1 | 192.168.20.196/30 |
| Subnet 2 | 192.168.20.200/30 |
| Subnet 3 | 192.168.20.204/30 |
| Subnet 4 | 192.168.20.208/30 |
| Subnet 5 | 192.168.20.212/30 |
| Subnet 6 | 192.168.20.216/30 |
| Subnet 7 | 192.168.20.220/30 |

The 192.168.20.0/24 network is subdivided into eight subnets by borrowing 3 bits from the host portion of the address ($2^2 = 8$). This leaves 5 bits for hosts on each of the eight subnets, which allows 30 valid host addresses ($2^5 = 32 - 2 = 30$) on each subnet. Because the network design only requires four LANs, we assign the first four subnets (0–3), with 30 hosts each, to the LANs. There are still three WAN serial links to account for. We could use the next three subnets (4–6) for WAN links, but point-to-point WAN links require only two IP addresses. Using a /27 subnet with 30 IP addresses for a WAN link that requires only two wastes most of the IP addresses for that subnet.

Instead, we can use VLSM to further subnet one of the /27 30-host subnets by borrowing another 3 bits. In this case, we use subnet 6, the 192.168.20.192/27 subnet, and borrow 3 more bits, which results in another eight subnets ($2^2 = 8$). Each of the eight /30 subnets has four addresses, but only two are usable. This is exactly what we need for each WAN link network. The first three of these (0–2) can be used for the WAN links, which leaves three 30-host /27 subnets (4, 5, and 7) for future use.

We now have two subnet masks in use with this network, the /27 (255.255.255.224) for the LANs and the /30 (255.255.255.252) for the WAN links. All LAN devices will be configured with the 255.255.255.224 subnet mask. All router WAN link interfaces will be configured with the 255.255.255.252 subnet mask. This is the basis of VLSM, the use of multiple masks to create variably sized subnets based on the number of host IP addresses required in each subnet.

VLSM allows the use of different masks for each subnet. After a network address is subnetted, further division of those subnets creates *sub-subnets*. Refer to Figure 4-9 for the following example of subnetting.

**Figure 4-9    Subnetting a Large Network with VLSM**

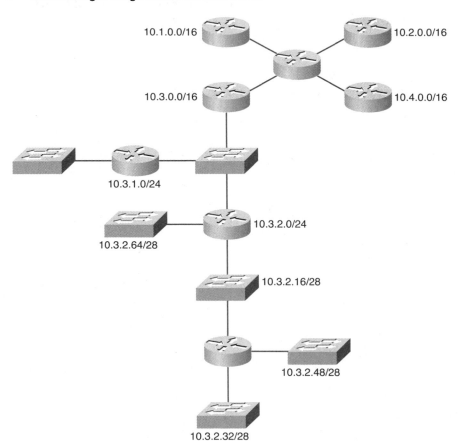

10.1.0.0/16

10.2.0.0/16

10.3.0.0/16

10.4.0.0/16

10.3.1.0/24

10.3.2.0/24

10.3.2.64/28

10.3.2.16/28

10.3.2.48/28

10.3.2.32/28

We begin with network 10.0.0.0/8 and apply a subnet mask of /16, which subdivides the 10.0.0.0/8 address space into 256 subnets, each capable of addressing 16,382 hosts:

- 10.0.0.0/16

- 10.1.0.0/16

- 10.2.0.0/16 up to 10.255.0.0/16

Applying a subnet mask of /24 to any one of these /16 subnets, such as 10.1.0.0/16, results in a subdivision of 256 subnets. Each one of these new subnets is capable of addressing 254 hosts:

- 10.1.1.0/24

- 10.1.2.0/24

- 10.1.3.0/24 up to 10.1.255.0/24

Applying a subnet mask of /28 to any one of these /24 subnets, such as 10.1.3.0/28, results in a subdivision of 16 subnets. Each one of these new subnets is capable of addressing 14 hosts:

- 10.1.3.0/28

- 10.1.3.16/28

- 10.1.3.32/28 up to 10.1.3.240/28

**Interactive Activity 4-4: Determining the Slash Format Mask to Support Hosts (4.2.4)**

In this interactive activity, you determine the slash notation of the subnet mask necessary to accommodate the required number of hosts. Use file d3ia-424 on the CD-ROM that accompanies this book to perform this interactive activity.

## Implementing VLSM Addressing

Designing an IP addressing scheme with VLSM takes practice and planning. As a practice example, a network has the following requirements. This network is shown in Figure 4-10.

- Atlanta HQ = 42 host addresses

- Perth HQ = 26 host addresses

- Sydney HQ = 10 host addresses

- Corpus HQ = 10 host addresses

- WAN links = 2 host addresses (each)

A subnet of /26 is required to accommodate the largest network segment of 420 hosts. A /26 mask borrows 2 bits from the base /24 address. This results in four subnetworks and 6 bits for hosts on each subnetwork, or 62 possible host IP addresses ($2^6 = 64 - 2 = 62$) per subnet. Using a basic subnetting scheme is not only wasteful but also creates only four subnets. This is not enough to address each of the required seven LAN/WAN segments. A VLSM addressing scheme resolves this problem. Table 4-3 shows how many addresses would be wasted for each network segment if we applied a /26 mask with 62 hosts for each segment.

**Figure 4-10    VLSM Practice Example Network Topology**

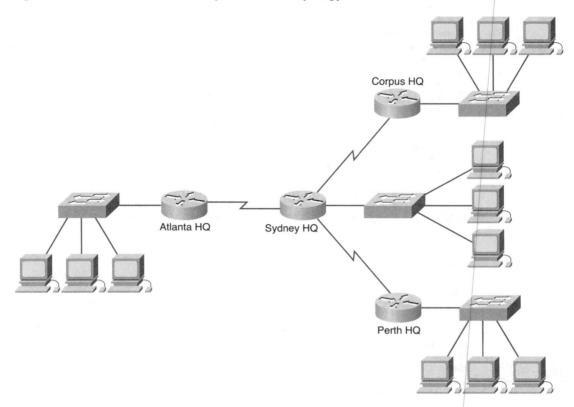

**Table 4-3    Network Subnetting Requirements**

| Headquarters | Requirements (No. of Host Addresses) | Total Wasted Addresses |
|---|---|---|
| Atlanta HQ | 42 | 20 |
| Perth HQ | 26 | 36 |
| Sydney HQ | 10 | 52 |
| Corpus HQ | 10 | 52 |
| *WAN links (3) | 2 (each) | 60 |

*With a /26 mask, there are not enough subnets to cover the three WAN links.

The first step in planning the use of VLSM in addressing the requirements of a particular network is to list the network requirements from largest to smallest, as shown in Table 4-4. Doing so allows you to select the proper number of bits to use for the mask to create the number of host addresses needed. The table shows the number of host addresses required, the size of the CIDR block required, the subnet address and mask, and the range of addresses on each subnet. Host IP addresses can be selected from the address range for each subnet.

**Table 4-4    Network Subnetting Requirements**

| Name (Required Addresses) | VLSM Address Block Size | Subnet Address/Prefix (Dotted Decimal Mask) | Address Range | Broadcast Address |
|---|---|---|---|---|
| Atlanta HQ LAN (58) | $2^6$=64 | 192.168.15.0/26 (255.255.255.192) | .1–.62 | .63 |
| Perth HQ LAN (26) | $2^5$=32 | 192.168.15.64/27 (255.255.255.224) | .65–.94 | .95 |
| Sydney HQ LAN (10) | $2^4$=16 | 192.168.15.96/28 (255.255.255.240) | .97–.110 | .111 |
| Corpus HQ LAN (10) | $2^4$=16 | 192.168.15.112/28 (255.255.255.240) | .113–.126 | .127 |
| WAN link 1 Atl-Syd (2) | $2^2$=4 | 192.168.15.128/30 (255.255.255.252) | .129–.130 | .131 |
| WAN link 2 Syd-Corp (2) | $2^2$=4 | 192.168.15.132/30 (255.255.255.252) | .133–.134 | .135 |
| WAN link 3 Syd-Perth (2) | $2^2$=4 | 192.168.15.136/30 (255.255.255.252) | .137–.138 | .139 |

**Note**

Always remember to subtract 2 from the CIDR address block size to get the actual number of hosts that can be supported. With a block size of 64, 62 hosts can actually be assigned addresses.

The basic process of planning and assigning VLSM subnets and addresses to a physical network is listed here:

**Step 1.** Determine the total size of the address block available.

The network described in Figure 4-10 and Table 4-4 starts with the 192.168.15.0/24 base address. A /24 mask yields 256 possible addresses, two of which are not usable, for a total of 254 usable addresses. This address space will be subdivided into smaller chunks as appropriate based on the number of hosts in each segment of the network (LAN or WAN).

**Step 2.** Determine the size of each VLSM block to accommodate users in each segment.

This information is in column 2 of Table 4-4. Look at the number of users for each area or subnet and determine the smallest power of 2 that will cover the requirement. Atlanta HQ has a requirement for 42 host addresses. A VLSM block of 64 ($2^6$) would be needed. The next smallest power of 2 is 32 ($2^5$), which does not cover the requirement for Atlanta but does cover the requirement for Perth, which has 26 hosts.

**Step 3.** Sort the block sizes from largest to smallest.

Atlanta HQ has the largest number of hosts and requires a block of 64 addresses (42 hosts). Perth is next with a block of 32 addresses (26 hosts), followed by Sydney and Corpus, each with blocks of 16 addresses (10 hosts each). The WAN links are last, each requiring a block of four addresses (two hosts each).

**Step 4.** Determine subnet addresses for the VLSM block.

Determine which blocks of VLSM address space to assign to each segment of the network. Start with the largest segment and work toward the smaller segments. Use a tabular or pie VLSM chart, as described later in this section, to allocate specific blocks of addresses. Column 3 of Table 4-4 shows each segment and the base address assigned. Atlanta HQ is assigned 192.168.15.0/26, which uses up the first 64 addresses (.0–.63) of the original 256 address space. The next group of addresses is assigned to Perth, starts at 192.168.15.64/27, uses up the next 32 addresses, and so on.

How To

**Step 5.**    Select IP addresses for use when configuring devices.

Column 4 of Table 4-4 lists the host IP address range for each segment of the network (LAN or WAN). Hosts in a particular segment are assigned an IP address from this range and are configured with the dotted decimal mask listed in column 3. It is common to use the first IP address for the router interface on the LAN. This IP address becomes the default gateway with which each host on the LAN is configured. Remaining hosts are assigned addresses starting with the next one available. These addresses and devices can be recorded in a device interface/IP address chart similar to the one shown in Table 4-5. An example is shown for the Perth router (Perth-HQ) interfaces and hosts on that subnetwork.

**Table 4-5    Perth HQ Device Interface/IP Address Chart**

| Device Name | Interface | IP Address/Subnet Mask | Default Gateway |
|---|---|---|---|
| Perth-HQ | Fa0/1 | 192.168.15.65 255.255.255.224 | — |
| | S0/0/0 | 192.168.15.137 255.255.255.252 | — |
| H1 | NIC | 192.168.15.66 255.255.255.224 | 192.168.15.65 |
| H2 | NIC | 192.168.15.67 255.255.255.224 | 192.168.15.65 |
| H3 | NIC | 192.168.15.68 255.255.255.224 | 192.168.15.65 |

Multiple tools exist to assist with address planning, including subnet calculators, VLSM tabular charts, and VLSM pie charts. These methods prevent assigning addresses that are already allocated. They also help to avoid assigning address ranges that overlap:

- **Subnet calculator:** Many subnet calculators exist, including one on the Cisco Networking Academy website, for determining subnets. These are normally interactive tools where you typically enter the base network address and mask you are starting with and then the number of subnets or hosts per subnet you need. If you give it the largest requirement first, the subnet calculator gives you the subnet numbers and the mask required. You can then take any of these subnets and repeat the process to calculate the subnets and masks for the remaining sub-subnets.

- **VLSM tabular chart:** One method you can use for address planning is a VLSM tabular chart to identify which blocks of addresses are available and which ones are already assigned. Figure 4-11 shows the subnets as divided in the example network using a tabular chart, which can be easily created using a spreadsheet program.

- **VLSM pie chart:** Another method uses a pie chart or circle approach. The circle is cut into increasingly smaller segments, representing the smaller subnets.

Figure 4-12 shows an example network where the subnets are planned using the pie or circle chart. In this example, the base network address of 192.168.1.0/24 is first subdivided into a /25, which leaves 7 bits for hosts or 126 addresses ($2^7 = 128 - 2 = 126$). This uses addresses 192.168.1.1 through 192.168.1.127 (the broadcast address) and consumes half the circle or pie for the first subnet. The next subnet is a /26 subnet 192.168.1.128/26, which leaves 6 bits for hosts or 62 addresses ($2^6 = 64 - 2 = 62$). This uses addresses 192.168.1.129 through 192.168.1.191 (the broadcast address) and consumes the next quarter of the circle or pie for the second subnet. The third and fourth subnet each consume an eighth of the pie (14 usable addresses), and the last subnet, a WAN link, consumes 1/64 of the pie (two usable addresses).

**Figure 4-11   VLSM Tabular Chart**

| | A | B | C | D | E | F | G | H |
|---|---|---|---|---|---|---|---|---|
| 1 | Base Address: 192.168.15.0 Subnet Mask: 255.255.255.0 | | | | | | | |
| 2 | CIDR Mask | /24 | /25 | /26 | /27 | /28 | /29 | /30 |
| 3 | Dot Mask (Octets 3 & 4) | 255.0 | 255.128 | 255.192 | 255.224 | 255.240 | 255.248 | 255.252 |
| 4 | No. Hosts Possible | 256 | 128 | 64 | 32 | 16 | 8 | 4 |
| 5 | | | | | | | | |
| 6 | Subnet # (Octets 3 & 4) | 15.0 | 15.0 | 15.0 | 15.0 | 15.0 | 15.0 | 15.0 |
| 7 | | | | | | | | 15.4 |
| 8 | | | | | | | 15.8 | 15.8 |
| 9 | | | | | | | | 15.12 |
| 10 | | | | | | 15.16 | 15.16 | 15.16 |
| 11 | | | | | | | | 15.20 |
| 12 | | | | | | | 15.24 | 15.24 |
| 13 | | | Atlanta HQ | | | | | 15.28 |
| 14 | | | | | 15.32 | 15.32 | 15.32 | 15.32 |
| 15 | | | | | | | | 15.36 |
| 16 | | | | | | | 15.40 | 15.40 |
| 17 | | | | | | | | 15.44 |
| 18 | | | | | | 15.48 | 15.48 | 15.48 |
| 19 | | | | | | | | 15.52 |
| 20 | | | | | | | 15.56 | 15.56 |
| 21 | | | | | | | | 15.60 |
| 22 | | | | 15.64 | 15.64 | 15.64 | 15.64 | 15.64 |
| 23 | | | | | | | | 15.68 |
| 24 | | | | | | | 15.72 | 15.72 |
| 25 | | | | | | | | 15.76 |
| 26 | | | Perth HQ | | | 15.80 | 15.80 | 15.80 |
| 27 | | | | | | | | 15.84 |
| 28 | | | | | | | 15.88 | 15.88 |
| 29 | | | | | | | | 15.92 |
| 30 | | | | | 15.96 | 15.96 | 15.96 | 15.96 |
| 31 | | | | | | | | 15.100 |
| 32 | | | | Sydney HQ | | | 15.104 | 15.104 |
| 33 | | | | | | | | 15.108 |
| 34 | | | | Corpus HQ | | 15.112 | 15.112 | 15.112 |
| 35 | | | | | | | | 15.116 |
| 36 | | | | | | | 15.120 | 15.120 |
| 37 | | | | | | | | 15.124 |
| 38 | | | 15.128 | 15.128 | 15.128 | 15.128 | 15.128 | 15.128 |
| 39 | | | | | | WAN Links | | 15.132 |
| 40 | | | | | | | 15.136 | 15.136 |
| 41 | | | | | | | | 15.140 |

**Interactive Activity 4-5: Creating a VLSM Addressing Scheme (4.2.5)**

In this interactive activity, you create an IP addressing scheme for the specified requirements. Use file d3ia-425 on the CD-ROM that accompanies this book to perform this interactive activity.

**Lab 4-3: Calculating a VLSM Addressing Scheme (4.2.5)**

In this lab, you will use VLSM to provide the IP addressing for a given topology. Refer to the lab in Part II of this *Learning Guide*. You can perform this lab now or wait until the end of the chapter.

**Figure 4-12    VLSM Pie Chart**

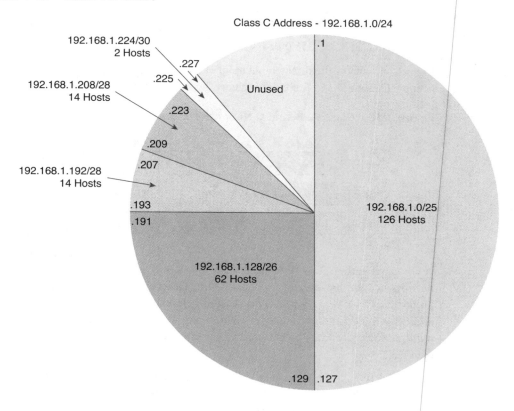

**Challenge Lab 4-4: Calculating a VLSM Network IP Addressing Scheme**

In this lab, you will gain additional practice in working with VLSM to develop an IP addressing scheme. Refer to the lab in Part II of this *Learning Guide*. You can perform this lab now or wait until the end of the chapter.

# Using Classless Routing and CIDR

Early routing protocols depended on the class of a network address to be able to process and route packets. Classless interdomain routing (CIDR) allows better use of the IP address space and improves Internet routing efficiency. The following sections compare classful and classless routing and describe CIDR and its benefits in route summarization and reducing the size of Internet routing table. The process of calculating summary routes is described and issues involved with discontiguous subnet are addressed. Finally, a list of subnetting best practices is provided.

## Classful and Classless Routing

Technology such as VLSM enables the classful IPv4 addressing system to evolve into a classless system. Classless addressing has made the exponential growth of the Internet possible.

Classful addresses consist of the three major classes of assignable IP addresses and an associated default subnet mask:

- Class A (255.0.0.0 or /8)

- Class B (255.255.0.0 or /16)

- Class C (255.255.255.0 or /24)

Figure 4-13 shows the three commercial classes of addresses and the octets of the 32-bit address they occupy. Classes D and E are not included because they do not consist of assignable addresses.

**Figure 4-13   Class A, B, and C Network Octets**

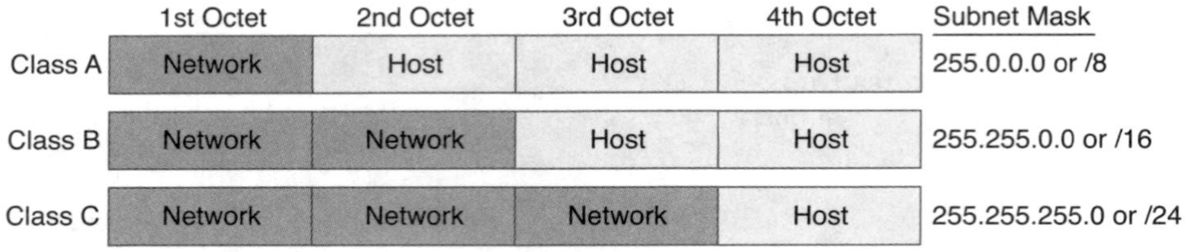

| | 1st Octet | 2nd Octet | 3rd Octet | 4th Octet | Subnet Mask |
|---|---|---|---|---|---|
| Class A | Network | Host | Host | Host | 255.0.0.0 or /8 |
| Class B | Network | Network | Host | Host | 255.255.0.0 or /16 |
| Class C | Network | Network | Network | Host | 255.255.255.0 or /24 |

A company with a Class A network address has over 16 million host addresses available, a Class B network address has over 65,000 hosts, and a Class C has only 254 hosts. Because there is a limited number of Class A and Class B addresses in circulation, many companies purchase multiple Class C addresses to obtain enough addresses to satisfy their network requirements. As a result, purchasing multiple Class C addresses has used up the Class C address space more quickly than originally planned.

In classful IP addresses, the value of the first octet, or the first 3 bits, determines whether the major network is a Class A, B, or C. Table 4-6 shows the binary and decimal range of the first octet, the number of networks possible, and the number of hosts per network, for each address class. For a Class A address, the first bit of the first octet is always a 0. For a Class B address, the first 2 bits of the first octet are always a 1 and a 0. For a Class C address, the first 3 bits of the first octet are always 1, 1, and 0.

**Table 4-6    Class A, B, and C Address Characteristics**

| Address Class | First Octet Binary Range | First Octet Decimal Range | Number of Possible Networks | Number of Hosts per Network |
|---|---|---|---|---|
| Class A | 00000000–01111111 | 0–127 | 128 (2 are reserved) | 16,777,214 |
| Class B | 10000000–10111111 | 128–191 | 16,384 | 65,534 |
| Class C | 11000000–11011111 | 192–223 | 2,097,152 | 254 |

Classful routing protocols, such as RIPv1, do not include the subnet mask in routing updates. Because the subnet mask is not included, the receiving router makes certain assumptions. These include the application of the mask associated with an interface in routing updates and the automatic summarization to classful addresses.

Using a classful protocol, if a router sends an update about a subnetted network, such as 172.16.1.0/24, to a router whose connecting interface is on the same major network as that in the update, such as 172.16.2.0/24, the following occurs, as shown in Figure 4-14:

1. The sending router advertises the full network address but without a subnet mask. In this case, the network address is 172.16.1.0.

2. The receiving router, with a configured interface of 172.16.2.0/24, adopts the subnet mask of the configured interface and applies it to the advertised network. Therefore, in the example, the receiving router assumes the subnet mask of 255.255.255.0 applies to the 172.16.1.0 network.

**Figure 4-14    Classful Routing Updates**

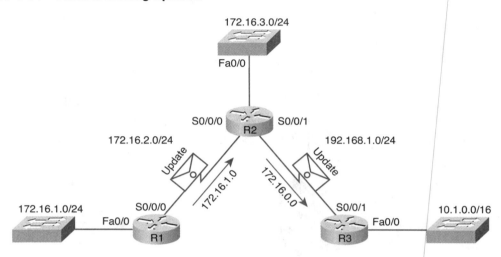

If the router sends an update about a subnetted network, such as 172.16.1.0/24, to a router whose connecting interface is in a different major network, such as 192.168.1.0/24, the following occurs:

1. The sending router advertises the major classful network address only, not the subnetted address. In this case, the address advertised is 172.16.0.0.

2. The receiving router assumes the default subnet mask for this network. The default subnet mask for a Class B address is 255.255.0.0.

With the rapid depletion of IPv4 addresses, the *Internet Engineering Task Force (IETF)* developed *classless interdomain routing (CIDR)*. CIDR (pronounced *cider*) uses IPv4 address space more efficiently and for network address aggregation or summarizing, which reduces the size of routing tables.

The use of CIDR requires the use of a *classless routing protocol*, such as Routing Information Protocol version 2 (RIPv2), Enhanced IGRP (EIGRP), or static routing. To CIDR-compliant routers, address class is meaningless. The network subnet mask determines the network portion of the address. This is also known as the network prefix, or *prefix length*. The class of the address no longer determines the network address.

ISPs assign blocks of IP addresses to a network based on the requirements of the customer, ranging from a few hosts to hundreds or thousands of hosts. With CIDR and VLSM, ISPs are no longer limited to using prefix lengths of /8, /16, or /24. In Figure 4-15, the ISP assigns a /22 CIDR block from its /16 CIDR block of addresses to Company 1, which leaves 10 bits for hosts ($32 - 22 = 10$). With 10 host bits, the address block can provide IP addresses for 1022 hosts ($2^{10} = 1024 - 2 = 1022$). For Company 2, the ISP allocates a /23 block, which leaves 9 bits and can provide 510 hosts ($2^2 = 512 - 2 = 510$).

Classless routing protocols that can support VLSM and CIDR include *interior gateway protocols (IGP)* RIPv2, EIGRP, Open Shortest Path First (OSPF), and Intermediate System–to–Intermediate System (IS-IS). ISPs also use *exterior gateway protocols (EGP)* such as Border Gateway Protocol (BGP) .

**Figure 4-15    ISPs Assign Blocks of Addresses Based on Customer Needs**

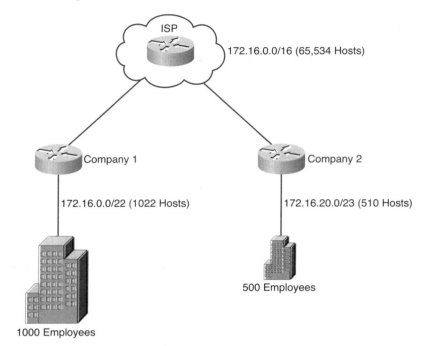

The difference between the classful routing protocols and classless routing protocols is that the classless routing protocols include subnet mask information with the network address information in the routing updates. Classless routing protocols are necessary when the mask cannot be assumed or determined by the value of the first octet.

In a classless protocol, if a router sends an update about a network, such as 172.16.1.0, to a router whose connecting interface is on the same major network as that in the update, such as 172.16.2.0/24, the following occurs, as shown in Figure 4-16:

1. The sending router advertises all subnetworks with subnet mask information.

2. If the router sends an update about a subnetted network, such as 172.16.1.0/24, to a router whose connecting interface is in a different major network, such as 192.168.1.0/24, the sending router, by default, summarizes all the subnets and advertises the major classful network. This process is often referred to as *summarizing on a network boundary*.

3. While most classless routing protocols enable summarization on the network boundary by default, the process of summarizing can be disabled. When summarization is disabled, the sending router advertises all subnetworks with subnet mask information.

## CIDR and Route Summarization

The rapid growth of the Internet has caused the number of routes to networks around the world to increase dramatically. This growth results in heavy loads on Internet routers. A VLSM addressing scheme allows route summarization, which reduces the number of routes advertised.

Route summarization groups contiguous subnets or networks using a single address. Route summarization is also known as *route aggregation* and occurs at a *network boundary* on a boundary router.

**Figure 4-16    Classless Routing Updates**

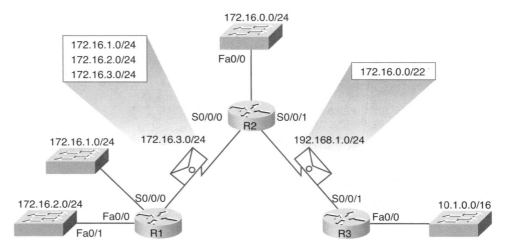

Summarization decreases the number of entries in routing updates and reduces the number of entries in local routing tables. It also reduces bandwidth utilization for routing updates and results in faster routing table lookups.

Route summarization and the term *supernetting* are used interchangeably. However, supernetting generally refers to joining multiple smaller contiguous classful networks, whereas summarization groups contiguous networks or subnets, whether they are classful or classless. Supernetting is the opposite of subnetting.

If the network bits are greater than the default value for that class, this represents a subnet. An example is 172.16.3.0/26. For a Class B address, any network prefix value greater than /16 is a subnet.

If the network bits are less than the default value for the class value, this represents a supernet. An example is 172.16.0.0/14. For a Class B address, any network prefix less than /16 represents a supernet.

In Figure 4-17, Router R1 supports four Class C LANs, 192.168.48.0/24 through 192.168.51.0/24. These can be summarized as 192.168.48.0/22 because the first 22 bits of these Class C networks are the same. This allows Router R1 to advertise just one route to Router R4. Router R2 also summarizes four Class C networks and advertises one route to R4. Router R3 summarizes eight Class C networks, 192.168.56.0/24 through 192.168.63.0/24, and advertises one route to R4, 192.168.56.0/21. Router R4 then combines all the network routes received by Routers R1, R2, and R3; further summarizes them into a single 192.168.48.0/20 network; and advertises a single route to the ISP. The ISP only needs to keep one route in its routing table to reach any host on Routers R1, R2, R3, or R4 (the 192.168.48.0/20 network). Combining multiple classful networks is known as supernetting.

Figure 4-18 shows how the bits in four /24 network addresses can be summarized into a single address with a /22 prefix.

An edge or border router advertises all the known networks within an enterprise to the ISP. If there are eight different networks, the router would have to advertise all eight. If every enterprise followed this pattern, the routing table of the ISP would be huge.

Using route summarization, a router groups the networks if they are contiguous and advertises them as one large group. For example, a company has a single listing in the phone book for its main office, even though you can dial individual employee extensions directly.

**Figure 4-17 Route Summarization (Supernetting) Example**

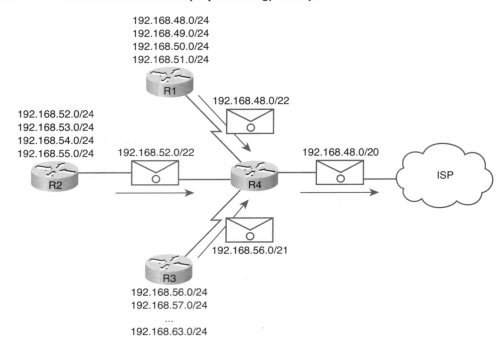

**Figure 4-18 Summarizing Is Based on Common Bits**

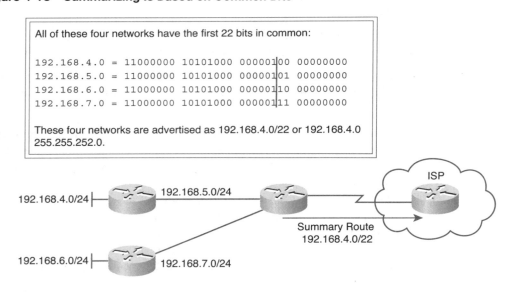

It is easier to perform summarization if the addressing scheme is hierarchical. Assign similar networks to the same enterprise so that grouping them using CIDR is possible.

**Interactive Activity 4-6: Determining Subnets and Summary Routes (4.3.2)**

In this interactive activity, you determine whether the IP address with CIDR information is a subnet or a route summary. Use file d3ia-432 on the CD-ROM that accompanies this book to perform this interactive activity.

## Calculating Route Summarization

Calculating a route summary requires summarizing networks into a single address. This process is performed in three steps and is shown in Figure 4-19.

**Step 1.**   List the networks in binary format.

**Step 2.**   Count the number of leftmost matching bits to determine the mask for the summary route. This number represents the network prefix or subnet mask for the summarized route. An example is /14 or 255.252.0.0.

**Step 3.**   Determine the summarized network address. Copy the matching bits and then add 0 bits to the end. A quicker method is to use the lowest network value.

**Figure 4-19    Network Summarization Process**

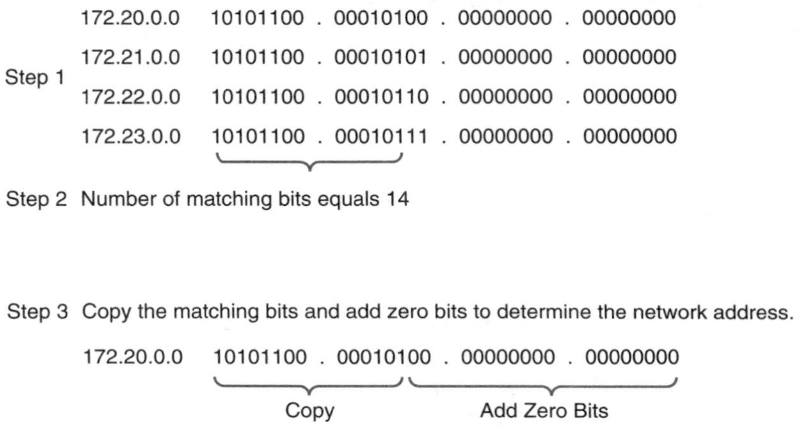

```
             172.20.0.0   10101100 . 00010100 . 00000000 . 00000000
             172.21.0.0   10101100 . 00010101 . 00000000 . 00000000
    Step 1
             172.22.0.0   10101100 . 00010110 . 00000000 . 00000000

             172.23.0.0   10101100 . 00010111 . 00000000 . 00000000
                                    _____/

    Step 2  Number of matching bits equals 14



    Step 3  Copy the matching bits and add zero bits to determine the network address.

             172.20.0.0   10101100 . 00010100 . 00000000 . 00000000
                          _____/  _____/
                             Copy            Add Zero Bits
```

If a contiguous hierarchical addressing scheme is not used, it might not be possible to summarize routes. If the network addresses do not have common bits from left to right, a summary mask cannot be applied.

**Interactive Activity 4-7: Selecting a Summary Route for a Contiguous Address Group (4.3.3)**

In this interactive activity, you select the best summary route for the contiguous address groups shown. Use file d3ia-433 on the CD-ROM that accompanies this book to perform this interactive activity.

**Lab 4-5: Calculating Summarized Routes (4.3.3)**

In this lab, you will determine summarized routes to reduce the number of entries in routing tables. Refer to the lab in Part II of this *Learning Guide*. You can perform this lab now or wait until the end of the chapter.

**Challenge Lab 4-6: Route Summarization Practice**

In this lab, you will gain additional practice in performing route summarization. Refer to the lab in Part II of this *Learning Guide*. You can perform this lab now or wait until the end of the chapter.

## Discontiguous Subnets

Either an administrator configures route summarization manually or certain routing protocols perform the same function automatically. RIPv1 and EIGRP are examples of routing protocols that perform automatic summarization. It is important to control the summarization so that routers do not advertise misleading networks.

Suppose that three routers each connect to Ethernet interfaces with addresses using subnets from a Class C network, such as 192.168.3.0. The three routers also connect to each other through serial interfaces configured using another major network, such as 172.16.100.0/24. Classful routing results in each router advertising the major Class C network without a subnet mask. As a result, the middle router receives advertisements about the same network from two different directions. This scenario is called a *discontiguous* network and is illustrated in Figure 4-20.

**Figure 4-20    Discontiguous Networks**

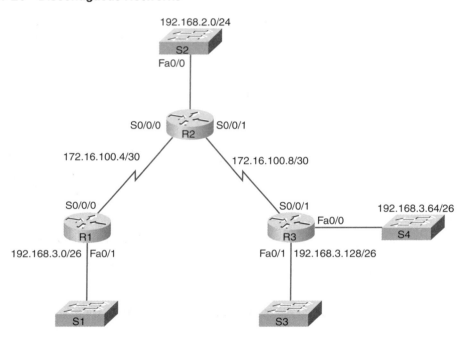

Discontiguous networks cause unreliable or suboptimal routing. To avoid this condition, an administrator can do one of the following:

- Modify the addressing scheme, if possible
- Use a classless routing protocol, such as RIPv2 or OSPF
- Turn automatic summarization off
- Manually summarize at the classful boundary

Even after careful planning, it is still possible to have a situation in which a discontiguous network exists. The following traffic and routing patterns help to identify this situation and are illustrated in Figure 4-21:

- Host H1 needs to send a message to host H2 (192.168.3.130/26).

- Router R1 has one subnet 192.168.3.0/26 attached. Router R3 has two subnets, 192.168.3.64/26 and 192.168.3.128/26. R2 does not have any routes to the LAN subnets attached to Router R1 or R3 because both of these routers advertise classful network 192.168.3.0/24. Example 4-1 shows the routing table contents for R2.

**Example 4-1  R2 show ip route Command Output**

```
Gateway of last resort is not set
     172.16.0.0/30 is subnetted, 2 subnets
C        172.16.100.8 is directly connected, Serial0/1
C        172.16.100.4 is directly connected, Serial0/0
C        192.168.2.0/24 is directly connected, FastEthernet0/0
R        192.168.3.0/24 [120/1] via 172.16.100.10, 00:00:05, Serial0/1
                        [120/1] via 172.16.100.5, 00:00:15, Serial0/0
```

- As can be seen in Example 4-1, Router R2 has two equal-cost paths to major network 192.168.3.0/24, as shown by the RIP entry in its routing table, although the subnets are separated on several network segments.

- Router R2 is load-balancing traffic destined for any subnet of a major network.

- Router R3 appears to be receiving only half of the traffic destined for host H2.

**Figure 4-21    Effects of Discontiguous Networks**

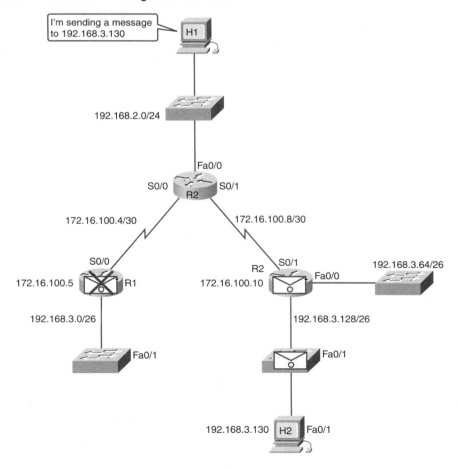

**Lab 4-7: Configuring a LAN with Discontiguous Subnets (4.3.4)**

In this lab, you will configure a LAN with discontiguous networks to view results. Refer to the lab in Part II of this *Learning Guide*. You can perform this lab now or wait until the end of the chapter.

## Subnetting and Addressing Best Practices

Properly implementing a VLSM addressing scheme is essential for creating a hierarchical network. When creating a VLSM addressing scheme, follow these basic guidelines:

- Use newer routing protocols that support VLSM and discontiguous subnets.

- Disable auto-summarization if necessary.

- Use the same routing protocol throughout the network.

- Keep the router IOS up to date to support the use of subnet 0.

- Avoid intermixing private network address ranges in the same internetwork.

- Avoid discontiguous subnets where possible.

- Use VLSM to maximize address efficiency.

- Assign VLSM ranges based on requirements from the largest to the smallest.

- Plan for summarization using hierarchical network design and contiguous addressing design.

- Summarize at network boundaries.

- Use /30 ranges for WAN links.

- Allow future growth when planning for the number of subnets and hosts supported.

Figure 4-22 shows an example of a hierarchical network with hierarchal addressing that uses VLSM. All routes from all remote networks can be summarized up to the edge router and advertised to the ISP as 10.0.0.0/13. Only four /16 networks—172.1.0.0/16, 172.2.0.0/16, 172.3.0.0/16, and 172.4.0.0/16—are currently attached to the edge router. Summarizing to 172.0.0.0/13 actually advertises an eight-network range from 10.0.0.0/16 to 10.7.0.0/16. This allows other networks to be added in the future.

**Figure 4-22    Hierarchical Addressing Scheme**

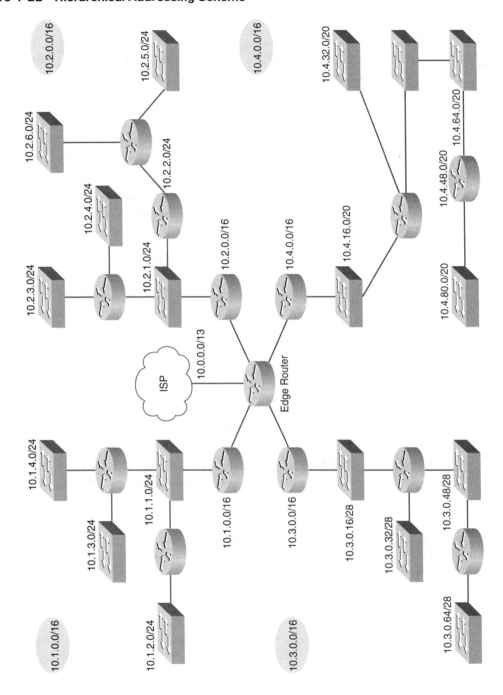

# Using NAT and PAT

In addition to VLSM and CIDR, another key technology that has improved the scalability and extended the life of the IPv4 protocol and addressing is Network Address Translation (NAT). In combination with private IP addressing, NAT has been the main factor in allowing organizations to grow their networks without the need for more public IP addresses. The following sections describe private addressing and the various forms of NAT. Instructions are provided for configuring static NAT, dynamic NAT, and Port Address Translation (PAT) on a router.

## Private IP Address Space

*Private addresses* are available for anyone to use in enterprise networks because private addresses route internally; they never appear on the Internet. *Public addresses* are legitimate IP addresses that are registered for use on the Internet. Private addresses are unregistered and cannot be used on the Internet, but they are reserved for use internally.

RFC 1918 governs the use of the private address space as follows:

- Class A: 10.0.0.0–10.255.255.255

- Class B: 172.16.0.0–172.31.255.255

- Class C: 192.168.0.0–192.168.255.255

Using private addressing has the following benefits:

- It alleviates the high cost associated with the purchase of public addresses for each host.

- It allows thousands of internal employees to use a few public addresses.

- It provides a level of security, because users from other networks or organizations cannot see the internal addresses.

Figure 4-23 shows three private networks, each using a different class of private addresses to connect to the Internet. Without routers and NAT at the edge of these networks, the private addresses would be rejected by Internet routers.

### Note

Most of the examples of IP addressing given in this course use private addressing, even though they are often intended to represent real public IP addresses. This is because it is not appropriate to use real IP addresses in training material because they are assigned to real organizations in many cases.

When implementing a private addressing scheme for the internal network, apply the same hierarchical design principles that are associated with VLSM. Although private addresses are not routed on the Internet, they are frequently routed in the internal network. Problems associated with discontiguous networks still occur when using private addresses; therefore, carefully design the addressing scheme.

**Figure 4-23    Private Address Space**

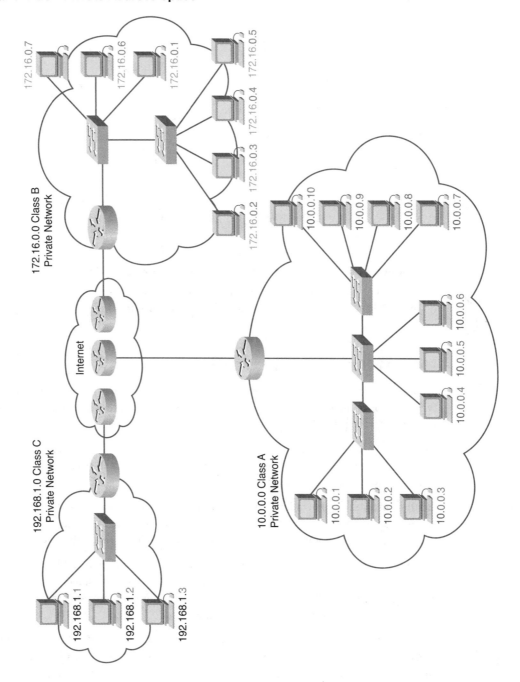

Be sure that the addresses are properly distributed according to the concepts of VLSM. Also, use valid boundaries and hierarchical IP addressing best practices for effective use of address summarization. Figure 4-24 shows an example of hierarchical addressing using private addressing, where multiple /16 networks are summarized to a single /8.

**Figure 4-24    Hierarchical Addressing Scheme with Private Addressing**

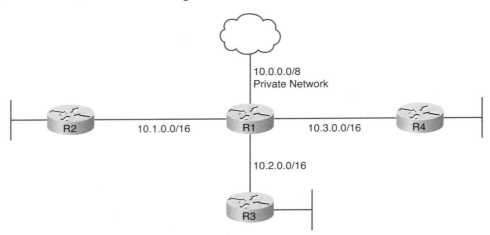

**Interactive Activity 4-8: Determining Public and Private Addresses (4.4.1)**

In this interactive activity, you determine whether the IP address is public or private. Use file d3ia-441 on the CD-ROM that accompanies this book to perform this interactive activity.

## NAT at the Enterprise Edge

Many organizations want the benefits of private addressing while connecting to the Internet. Organizations create huge LANs and WANs with private addressing and connect to the Internet using *Network Address Translation (NAT)*.

NAT translates internal private addresses into one or more public addresses for routing onto the Internet. NAT changes the private IP source address inside each packet to a publicly registered IP address before sending it out onto the Internet.

Small to medium organizations connect to their ISPs through a single connection. The local boundary or edge router configured with NAT connects to the ISP. Larger organizations can have multiple ISP connections, and the boundary router at each of these locations performs NAT.

Using NAT on boundary routers improves security. Internal private addresses translate to different public addresses each time. This hides the actual address of hosts and servers in the enterprise. Most routers that implement NAT also block packets coming from outside the private network unless they are a response to a request from an inside host.

Figure 4-25 shows an example of host H1 with a private source IP address (inside local address) of 192.168.1.106 being translated by the router into one of the external public inside global addresses, in this case 209.165.202.129, before sending the packet onto the Internet.

## Static and Dynamic NAT

NAT can be configured statically or dynamically.

*Static NAT* maps a single *inside local address* to a single global, or public, address. The static NAT entry is configured manually and remains permanently in the table. This mapping ensures that a particular inside local address always associates with the same public address. Static NAT ensures that outside devices consistently reach an internal device. Examples include web and FTP servers accessible to the public.

**Figure 4-25    Network Address Translation**

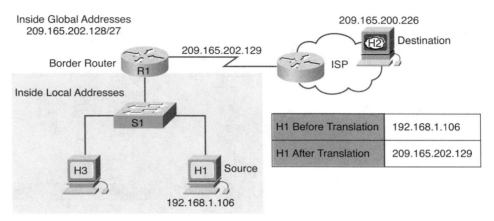

Figure 4-26 shows the use of static NAT to permanently map the web server internal private address 192.168.1.200 to a public (inside global) address 209.165.200.225. When packets are received from host H3 at R1's external interface destined for 209.165.200.225, they are forwarded to the web server.

**Figure 4-26    Static NAT**

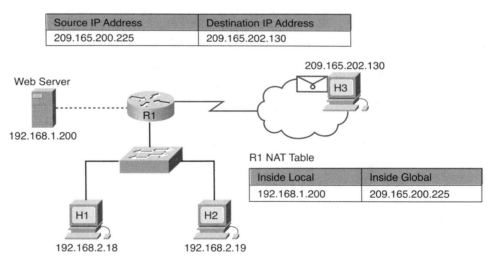

*Dynamic NAT* uses an available pool of Internet public addresses and assigns them to inside local addresses. Dynamic NAT assigns the first available IP address in the pool of public addresses to an inside device. That host uses the assigned global IP address throughout the length of the session. When the session ends, the outside global address returns to the pool for use by another host.

The address that one internal host uses to connect to another internal host is the inside local address. The public address assigned to the organization is called the inside global address. The *inside global address* is sometimes used as the address of the external interface of the border router.

The NAT router manages the translations between the inside local addresses and the inside global addresses by maintaining a table that lists each address pair. Figure 4-27 illustrates dynamic NAT. In the figure, the web server with IP address 192.168.1.200 is statically mapped to 209.165.200.225. When host H2, with source IP address of 192.168.2.19, sends a packet, its source address is translated to the next address in the pool, which is 209.165.200.226. If host H1 sends a packet, source address 192.168.2.18 will be translated to the next address in the pool, which is 209.165.200.227.

**Figure 4-27 Dynamic NAT**

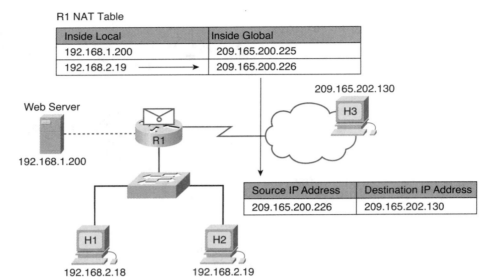

When configuring either static or dynamic NAT, you need to do the following:

- List any servers that require a permanent outside address.

- Determine which internal hosts require translation.

- Determine which interfaces source the internal traffic. These will become the inside interfaces.

- Determine which interface sends traffic to the Internet. This will become the outside interface.

- Determine the range of public addresses available.

The next sections describe configuring static NAT and dynamic NAT.

## Configuring Static NAT

To configure static NAT, follow these steps:

**Step 1.** Determine the public IP address that outside users should use to access the inside device/server. Administrators tend to use addresses from either the beginning or end of the range for static NAT.

**Step 2.** Map the inside, or private, address to the public address.

**Step 3.** Configure the inside and outside interfaces.

Example 4-2 shows the running configuration for a static NAT router entry.

**Example 4-2 R1 show running-config Command Output**

```
R1# show running-config

< output omitted >
!
ip nat inside source static 172.31.232.14 209.165.202.130
!
```

```
interface FastEthernet0/0
ip address 172.31.232.182 255.255.255.0
ip nat inside
!
interface Serial0/0/0
 ip address 209.165.202.1 255.255.255.0
 ip nat outside
```

## Configuring Dynamic NAT

An important part of configuring dynamic NAT is the use of the standard *access control list (ACL)*. The standard ACL is used to specify the range of hosts that require translation. This is done in the form of a permit or deny statement. The ACL can include an entire network, a subnet, or just a specific host. The ACL can range from a single line to several permit and deny statements.

To configure dynamic NAT, follow these steps:

**Step 1.** Identify the pool of public IP addresses available for use.

**Step 2.** Create an access control list (ACL) to identify hosts that require translation.

**Step 3.** Link the access list with the address pool.

**Step 4.** Assign interfaces as either inside or outside.

Example 4-3 shows the running configuration for a dynamic NAT router. The NAT pool being defined is ten addresses, from 209.165.202.131 to 209.165.202.140.

**Example 4-3  R1 show running-config Command Output**

```
R1# show running-config

< output omitted >
!
access-list 1 permit 172.31.232.0 0.0.0.255
ip nat pool pub-addr 209.165.202.131  209.165.202.140 netmask 255.255.255.0
ip nat inside source list 1 pool pub-addr

interface FastEthernet0/0
ip address 172.31.232.182 255.255.255.0
ip nat inside
!
interface Serial0/0/0
 ip address 209.165.202.1 255.255.255.0
 ip nat outside
```

**Lab 4-8: Configuring and Verifying Static NAT (4.4.3)**

In this lab, you will configure and verify static NAT. Refer to the lab in Part II of this *Learning Guide*. You can perform this lab now or wait until the end of the chapter.

**Lab 4-9: Configuring and Verifying Dynamic NAT (4.4.3)**

In this lab, you will configure and verify dynamic NAT. Refer to the lab in Part II of this *Learning Guide*. You can perform this lab now or wait until the end of the chapter.

## Using PAT

One of the more popular variations of dynamic NAT is known as *Port Address Translation (PAT)*, also referred to as *NAT overload*. PAT dynamically translates multiple inside local addresses to a single public address.

When a source host sends a message to a destination host, it uses an IP address and port number combination to keep track of each individual conversation. In PAT, the gateway router translates the local source address and port number combination to a single global IP address and a unique port number above 1024.

A table in the router contains a list of the internal IP address and port number combinations that are translated to the external address. Although each host translates into the same global IP address, the port number associated with the conversation is unique. Because over 64,000 ports are available, a router is unlikely to run out of addresses.

Both enterprise and home networks take advantage of PAT functionality. PAT is built into integrated routers and is enabled by default. Figure 4-28 shows PAT in action. The same external public IP address (209.165.201.2) is used by both H1 and H2, but with differing internal port numbers to distinguish between the two conversations. The upper table shows the router's NAT table entries. The lower table shows the IP packet header in the HTTP request sent from host H1 to the web server, with source/destination IP addresses and source/destination port numbers.

**Figure 4-28   PAT Process**

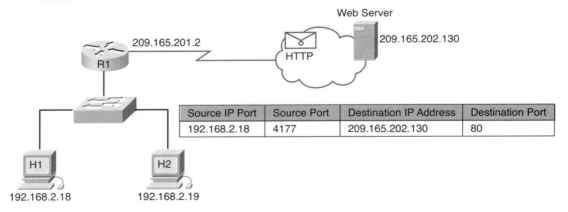

Configuring PAT requires the same basic steps and commands as configuring NAT. However, instead of translating to a pool of addresses, PAT translates to a single address. The following command translates the inside addresses to the IP address of the serial interface:

```
ip nat inside source list 1 interface serial 0/0/0 overload
```

Example 4-4 shows the running configuration for a PAT router.

**Example 4-4  R1 show running-config Command Output**

```
R1# show running-config

< output omitted >
!
access-list 1 permit 172.31.232.0 0.0.0.255
ip nat inside source list 1 interface serial 0/0/0 overload

interface FastEthernet0/0
ip address 172.31.232.182 255.255.255.0
ip nat inside
!
interface Serial0/0/0
 ip address 209.165.202.1 255.255.255.0
 ip nat outside
```

Verify NAT and PAT functionality with the following commands:

- **show ip nat translations**

- **show ip nat statistics**

The **show ip nat translations** command displays active translations. If the translation is not used, it ages out after a period of time. Static NAT entries remain in the table permanently. A dynamic NAT entry requires some action from the host to a destination on the outside of the network. If configured correctly, a simple ping or trace creates an entry in the NAT table.

Example 4-5 shows the output from the **show ip nat translations** command.

**Example 4-5  R1 show ip nat translations Command Output**

```
R1# show ip nat translations

Pro    Inside global       Inside local        Outside local        Outside global
---    209.165.202.130     172.31.232.14       ------
icmp   209.165.202.131:512  172.31.232.1:512   209.165.200.1:512    209.165.200.1:512
udp    209.165.202.131:1067 172.31.232.2:1067  209.165.200.2:53     209.165.200.2:53
tcp    209.165.202.131:1028 172.31.232.2:1028  209.165.200.3:80     209.165.200.3:80
```

The **show ip nat statistics** command displays translation statistics, including the number of addresses used and the number of hits and misses. The output also includes the access list that specifies internal addresses, the global address pool, and the range of addresses defined.

Example 4-6 shows the output from the **show ip nat statistics** command.

**Example 4-6  R1 show ip nat statistics Command Output**

```
R1# show ip nat statistics

Total active translations: 0 (0 static, 0 dynamic; 0 extended)
Outside interfaces:
```

```
    Serial 0/0/0
Inside interfaces:
  FastEthernet 0/0
Hits: 47  Misses: 0
Expired translations: 5
Dynamic mappings:
-- Inside Source
[Id: 1] access-list 1 pool pub-addr refcount 4
 Pool pub-addr: netmask 255.255.255.0
      Start 209.165.202.131 end 209.165.202.140
      Type generic, total addresses 10, allocated 2 (20%), misses 0
Queued Packets: 0
```

### Lab 4-10: Configuring and Verifying PAT (4.4.4)

In this lab, you will configure and verify PAT. Refer to the lab in Part II of this *Learning Guide*. You can perform this lab now or wait until the end of the chapter.

# Summary

A single broadcast domain is a nonhierarchical or flat network. A hierarchical addressing structure logically groups networks into smaller subnetworks. A hierarchical network design simplifies network management and improves scalability and performance.

With basic or standard subnetting, each subnet is the same size and has the same number of hosts. Variable-length subnet masking (VLSM) enables routers to use route summarization to reduce the size of routing tables but requires classless routing protocols.

VLSM enables different masks for each subnet, which can be further subnetted, creating sub-subnets. When implementing VLSM, ensure room for growth in the number of subnets and hosts available.

Classful IP addressing determines the subnet mask of a network address by the value of the first octet. The use of classful routing protocols can create the issue of discontiguous networks. The CIDR network address is not determined by the class of the address; instead it is determined by the prefix length.

Route summarization groups contiguous subnets using a single address and shorter mask to reduce the number of routes advertised. Route summarization, route aggregation, or supernetting are done at network boundaries on a boundary router.

Private addresses are used and routed internally but are not routed onto the Internet. NAT translates private addresses into public addresses that route onto the Internet. Static NAT maps a single inside local address to a single inside global (public) address. Dynamic NAT uses an available pool of public addresses and assigns them to inside local addresses. PAT translates multiple local addresses to a single global IP address.

# Activities and Labs

This summary outlines the activities and labs you can perform to help reinforce important concepts described in this chapter. You can find the activity files on the CD-ROM accompanying this book. The complete hands-on labs appear in Part II.

**Interactive Activities on the CD-ROM:**

Interactive Activity 4-1: Deciding When to Use a Hierarchical Addressing Scheme (4.1.3)

Interactive Activity 4-2: Analyzing a Decimal Subnet Mask to Determine the Number of Hosts (4.2.1)

Interactive Activity 4-3: Determining Whether Two Hosts Are on the Same Network (4.2.2)

Interactive Activity 4-4: Determining the Slash Format Mask to Support Hosts (4.2.4)

Interactive Activity 4-5: Creating a VLSM Addressing Scheme (4.2.5)

Interactive Activity 4-6: Determining Subnets and Summary Routes (4.3.2)

Interactive Activity 4-7: Selecting a Summary Route for a Contiguous Address Group (4.3.3)

Interactive Activity 4-8: Determining Public and Private Addresses (4.4.1)

**Labs in Part II of this book:**

Lab 4-1: Designing and Applying an IP Addressing Scheme (4.2.3)

Challenge Lab 4-2: Calculating a Network IP Addressing Scheme

Lab 4-3: Calculating a VLSM Addressing Scheme (4.2.5)

Challenge Lab 4-4: Calculating a VLSM Network IP Addressing Scheme

Lab 4-5: Calculating Summarized Routes (4.3.3)

Challenge Lab 4-6: Route Summarization Practice

Lab 4-7: Configuring a LAN with Discontiguous Subnets (4.3.4)

Lab 4-8: Configuring and Verifying Static NAT (4.4.3)

Lab 4-9: Configuring and Verifying Dynamic NAT (4.4.3)

Lab 4-10: Configuring and Verifying PAT (4.4.4)

# Check Your Understanding

Complete all the review questions listed here to check your understanding of the topics and concepts in this chapter. Appendix A, "Check Your Understanding and Challenge Questions Answer Key," lists the answers.

1. What is the best route summarization for the following list of networks?

    209.48.200.0

    209.48.201.0

    209.48.202.0

    209.48.203.0

    A.  209.48.200.0/20

    B.  209.48.200.0/22

    C.  209.48.201.0/20

    D.  209.48.201.0/21

2. Given a host with IP address 172.32.65.13 and a default subnet mask, to which network does the host belong?

    A.  172.32.65.0

    B.  172.32.65.32

    C.  172.32.0.0

    D.  172.32.32.0

3. A Class C network address has been subnetted into eight subnetworks. Using VLSM, the last subnet will be divided into eight smaller subnetworks. What bit mask must be used to create eight small subnetworks, each having two usable host addresses?

   A. /26

   B. /27

   C. /28

   D. /29

   E. /30

   F. /31

4. Which address is a valid subnet if a 26-bit mask is used for subnetting?

   A. 172.16.43.16

   B. 172.16.128.32

   C. 172.16.243.64

   D. 172.16.157.96

   E. 172.16.47.224

   F. 172.16.192.252

5. Refer to Figure 4-29. A network technician is trying to determine the correct IP address configuration for Host A. What is a valid configuration for Host A?

**Figure 4-29    Question 5 Network Topology Diagram**

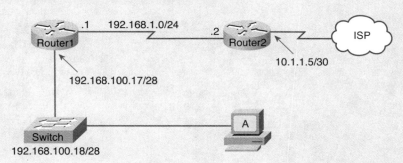

   A. IP address: 192.168.100.19; subnet mask: 255.255.255.248; default gateway: 192.16.1.2

   B. IP address: 192.168.100.20; subnet mask: 255.255.255.240; default gateway: 192.168.100.17

   C. IP address: 192.168.100.21; subnet mask: 255.255.255.248; default gateway: 192.168.100.18

   D. IP address: 192.168.100.22; subnet mask: 255.255.255.240; default gateway: 10.1.1.5

   E. IP address: 192.168.100.30; subnet mask: 255.255.255.240; default gateway: 192.168.1.1

   F. IP address: 192.168.100.31; subnet mask: 255.255.255.240; default gateway: 192.168.100.18

6. Which of the following is true regarding the differences between NAT and PAT?

   A. PAT uses the word *overload* at the end of the **access-list** statement to share a single registered address.

   B. Static NAT allows an unregistered address to map to multiple registered addresses.

   C. Dynamic NAT allows hosts to receive the same global address each time external access is required.

   D. PAT uses unique source port numbers to distinguish between translations.

7. For each characteristic on the left, indicate to which NAT technique it applies: static NAT, dynamic NAT, or NAT overload (PAT).

| Characteristic | NAT Technique |
| --- | --- |
| Provides one-to-one fixed mappings of local and global addresses | Static NAT |
| Assigns the translated addresses of IP hosts from a pool of public addresses | Dynamic NAT |
| Assigns unique source port numbers of an inside global address on a session-by-session basis | NAT overload (PAT) |
| Allows external hosts to establish sessions with an internal host | Static NAT |
| Defines translations on a host-to-host basis | Dynamic NAT |
| Can map multiple addresses to a single address of the external interface | NAT Overload (PAT) |

8. Refer to Figure 4-30. Which address is an inside global address?

**Figure 4-30   Question 8 Network Topology Diagram**

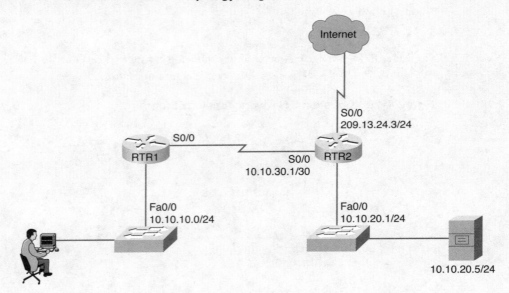

A. 10.10.20.1

B. 10.10.20.5

C. 10.10.30.1

D. 209.13.24.3

9. Refer to Example 4-7. The **show ip nat translations** command has been issued. Which type of NAT translation is being performed?

**Example 4-7  R1 show ip nat translations Command Output**

```
R1# show ip nat translations

Pro     Inside global        Inside local        Outside local        Outside global
icmp    209.165.202.131:512  172.31.232.1:512    209.165.200.1:512    209.165.200.1:512
udp     209.165.202.131:1067 172.31.232.2:1067   209.165.200.2:53     209.165.200.2:53
tcp     209.165.202.131:1028 172.31.232.2:1028   209.165.200.3:80     209.165.200.3:80
```

   A.  NAT static configuration

   B.  NAT simple configuration

   C.  NAT overloading configuration

   D.  NAT overlapping configuration

10. What is the purpose of a subnet mask in a network?

   A.  A subnet mask is necessary when a default gateway is not specified.

   B.  A subnet mask is required only when bits are borrowed on a network.

   C.  A subnet mask is used to identify the network portion of an IP address.

   D.  A subnet mask is used to separate the 48-bit address into the OUI and the vendor serial number.

11. How many addresses will be available for dynamic NAT translation when a router is configured with the following commands?

```
Router(config)# ip nat pool TAME 10.186.2.24 10.186.2.30 netmask 255.255.255.224
Router(config)# ip nat inside source list 9 pool TAME
```

   A.  6

   B.  7

   C.  8

   D.  9

   E.  10

12. Given a host with IP address 192.168.200.75 and a subnet mask of 255.255.255.224, to which subnetwork does the host belong?

   A.  192.168.200.0

   B.  192.168.200.32

   C.  192.168.200.64

   D.  192.168.200.96

**13.** You have been assigned a Class C address 192.168.2.0/24. You need to subnet it to provide multiple network segments. The first (and largest) subnet has 100 hosts. What is the VLSM block required for the first subnet, and what subnet mask will be configured for hosts on that subnet?

    A. VLSM block: 512, mask: 255.255.255.0

    B. VLSM block: 128, mask: 255.255.255.128

    C. VLSM block: 256, mask: 255.255.255.192

    D. VLSM block: 64, mask: 255.255.255.224

    E. VLSM block: 128, mask: 255.255.255.224

**14.** Using the slash format (CIDR prefix notation) subnet mask given, write the decimal subnet mask (dot format), the number of host bits available, and the number of hosts that can be assigned IP addresses (valid hosts).

| Subnet Mask (Slash Format) | Subnet Mask (Dot Format) | Number of Host Bits | Number of Valid Host IP Addresses |
|---|---|---|---|
| /22 | | | |
| /23 | | | |
| /24 | | | |
| /25 | | | |
| /26 | | | |
| /27 | | | |
| /28 | | | |
| /29 | | | |
| /30 | | | |

**15.** What is the name of the standard developed by the IETF that eliminates the dependence on network address classes, helps to make more efficient use of Internet addresses, and reduces the size of Internet routing tables?

# Challenge Questions and Activities

These questions require a deeper application of the concepts covered in this chapter. You can find the answers in Appendix A.

  **1.** Given the following host IP addresses and the subnet mask, indicate whether they are on the same subnet and should be able communicate. Use the ANDing process and compare each IP address to the subnet mask to determine the network or subnet number each host is on.

| Host 1 IP Address | Host 2 IP Address | Subnet Mask | Same Subnet? |
|---|---|---|---|
| 10.10.10.10<br>Net: 10.10.10.0 | 10.10.10.20<br>Net: 10.10.10.0 | 255.255.255.0 | Yes |
| 172.19.50.20<br>Net: 172.19.0.0 | 172.19.139.50<br>Net: 172.19.128.0 | 255.255.192.0 | No |

| Host 1 IP Address | Host 2 IP Address | Subnet Mask | Same Subnet? |
|---|---|---|---|
| 192.168.15.1<br>Net: 192.168.15.0 | 192.168.15.252<br>Net: 192.168.15.0 | 255.255.255.0 | Yes |
| 172.30.28.120<br>Net: 172.30.28.64 | 172.30.28.133<br>Net: 172.30.28.128 | 255.255.255.192 | No |
| 192.168.20.61<br>Net: 192.168.20.32 | 192.168.20.76<br>Net: 192.168.20.64 | 255.255.255.224 | No |

2. Examine the commands shown in the **show running-config** output in Example 4-8 and answer the questions that follow.

**Example 4-8  R1 show running-config Command Output**

```
R1# show running-config

< output omitted >
!
access-list 1 permit 172.31.232.0 0.0.0.255
ip nat pool pub-addr 209.165.202.131  209.165.202.145 netmask 255.255.255.0
ip nat inside source list 1 pool pub-addr

interface FastEthernet0/0
ip address 172.31.232.182 255.255.255.0
ip nat inside
!
interface Serial0/0/0
 ip address 209.165.202.1 255.255.255.0
 ip nat outside
```

A. What type of NAT is being configured with these commands?

B. How many addresses are being reserved in the NAT pool?

C. What type of NAT address is the one assigned to Serial 0/0/0?

D. What is the range of private addresses being permitted by access-list 1?

E. What would happen if the IP address of Fa0/0 were changed from 172.31.232.182/24 to 172.31.235.182/24?

F. One of the addresses that an internal host could have assigned as an inside global address for use on the Internet is 172.31.232.182. True or false? Briefly explain your answer.

3. Organization IP Addressing, VLSM, and NAT Interview Activity (optional)

In this activity, you will talk with your instructor or a network administrator at your institution, where you work, or at another organization. Use the following form to ask a few questions to learn more about the organization's IP addressing scheme.

Organization: _____

Person's name: _____

Position/title: _____

Size of network (No. of hosts): _____

Is public IP addressing used for internal hosts? (Y/N) _____

Public address used: _____

Is private addressing used for internal hosts? (Y/N) _____

Private address used: _____

Is VLSM used? (Y/N) _____

How many different subnet masks are used, and how are they applied to areas or segments in the organization's network? _____

_____

Is dynamic NAT used? (Y/N) _____

How many addresses are in the inside global address pool? _____

Is static NAT used? (Y/N) _____

For what types of devices? _____

Is PAT used? (Y/N) _____

What is the inside global address to which inside local addresses are translated?

_____

# CHAPTER 5

# Routing with a Distance Vector Protocol

## Objectives

Upon completion of this chapter, you should be able to answer the following questions:

- What is a hierarchical network and why is it required?

- What is the difference between a static, dynamic, and default route?

- How does RIP function?

- What are the limitations of RIP?

- What are the advantages of RIPv2 over RIPv1?

- What advantages does EIGRP have over RIP?

- What is the purpose of the various packet types used by EIGRP?

- What tables does EIGRP use, and what is their purpose?

## Key Terms

This chapter uses the following key terms. You can find the definitions in the Glossary.

*continued*

Workers today collaborate, communicate, and interact within large companies with complex networks. Network engineers design enterprise networks to provide reliable, high-speed communications channels between remote sites. Data moves through the enterprise hierarchy based on the IP address of the remote network. Routing protocols continually exchange information on the best path through the network. This chapter examines routing in an enterprise network and concentrates on the distance vector routing protocols, specifically Routing Information Protocol (RIP) and Enhanced Interior Gateway Routing Protocol (EIGRP).

Part II of this book includes the corresponding labs for this chapter.

# Managing Enterprise Networks

Hierarchical enterprise networks facilitate the flow of information. Information flows between mobile workers and branch offices. These branch offices connect to corporate offices in cities and countries around the world. The organization must create a hierarchy to meet the different network requirements of each part of the company.

## Enterprise Networks

In an enterprise network, crucial information and services typically reside near the top of the hierarchy, in secured server farms or on storage-area networks. The structure expands into many different departments that are spread across the lower part of the hierarchy. Communication between different levels of the hierarchy requires a combination of LAN and WAN technologies. As the company grows or adds e-commerce operations, a demilitarized zone (DMZ) might be required to house the various servers. Figure 5-1 shows an enterprise network environment. The cloud represents a WAN, which could be either public or private.

Traffic control is essential in an enterprise network. Without it, these networks could not function. Routers forward traffic and prevent broadcasts from clogging the main channels to crucial services. They control the flow of traffic between LANs, allowing only the required traffic to pass through the network.

Enterprise networks provide a high level of reliability and services. To ensure this, network professionals do the following:

- Design networks to provide redundant links to use in case a primary data path fails.

- Deploy quality of service (QoS) to ensure critical data receives priority treatment.

- Use packet filtering to deny certain types of packets, maximize available bandwidth, and protect the network from attacks.

## Enterprise Topologies

Choosing the right physical topology allows a company to expand its networked services without losing reliability and efficiency. Network designers base their topology decisions on the enterprise requirements for performance and reliability. The star and mesh topologies are normally deployed in enterprise environments.

**Figure 5-1    Enterprise Network**

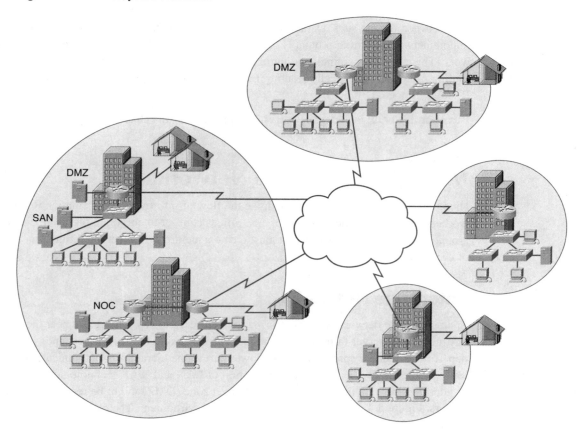

## Star Topology

One popular physical topology is the star, as shown in Figure 5-2. The center of the star corresponds to the top of the hierarchy, which could be the corporate headquarters or head office. Branch offices at multiple locations connect to the center, or hub, of the star.

A *star topology* provides centralized control of the network. All crucial services and technical staff can be located in one place. Star topologies are scalable. Adding a new branch office simply requires one more connection to the central point of the star. If an office adds several branches to its territory, each branch office can connect to a center hub in its own area, which then connects back to the main central point at the central office. In this way, a simple star can grow into an *extended star topology*, with smaller stars radiating out from the main branch offices, as shown in Figure 5-3.

**Figure 5-2    Star Topology**

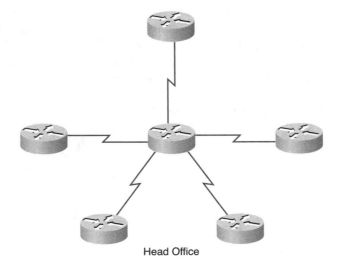

Head Office

**Figure 5-3    Extended Star Topology**

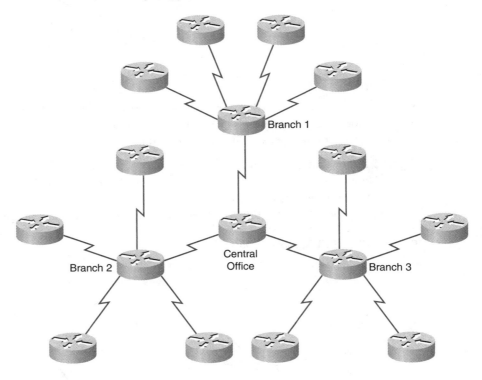

In the star and extended star topologies, failure of a spoke link disrupts only the portions of the network connected to that spoke. If the central node fails, the entire network is affected. Because of this, alternative mesh topologies are often deployed in networks that cannot tolerate downtime.

Each additional link added between endpoints in a network provides an alternate pathway for data and adds reliability to the network. With the addition of links, the topology becomes a mesh of interconnected nodes. Even though each redundant link adds stability and reliability into the network, each additional link adds cost and additional overhead. It also adds to the complexity of managing the network.

## Partial Mesh

Adding redundant links only to a specific area of an enterprise creates a ***partial-mesh topology***. This topology meets uptime and reliability requirements for critical areas such as server farms and storage-area networks (SAN), while minimizing additional expenses. With this topology, the other areas of the network are still vulnerable to failures. Therefore, it is essential to place the mesh where it provides the most benefit. Figure 5-4 shows an example of a partial-mesh topology.

**Figure 5-4    Partial-Mesh Topology**

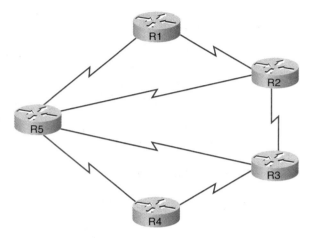

## Full Mesh

When no downtime is acceptable, the network requires a ***full-mesh topology***. Each node in a full-mesh topology connects to every other node in the enterprise. This is the most failure-proof topology, but it is also the most expensive to implement and maintain.

Figure 5-5 shows a full-mesh network. The number of links required in a full mesh network is given by the formula $n * (n - 1) / 2$, where $n$ is the number of network nodes. For example, a full-mesh network with four nodes would require six links ($4 * 3 / 2 = 6$), whereas one with five nodes would require ten links ($5 * 4 / 2 = 10$). All of these links must be installed, managed, and maintained.

**Figure 5-5    Full-Mesh Topology**

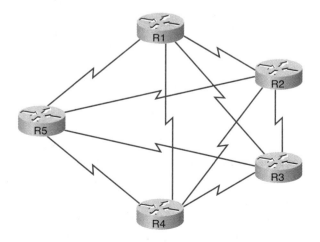

The Internet is an excellent example of a meshed network. Because devices on the Internet are not under the control of any one individual or organization, the topology is constantly changing. Links between nodes come up and go down without warning. Redundant connections balance the traffic and ensure that there is a reliable path to the destination. Enterprise networks face many of the same issues as the Internet. Therefore, processes are put in place that allow devices to adapt to these constantly changing conditions and reroute traffic as appropriate.

**Lab 5.1: Designing and Creating a Redundant Network (5.1.2)**

In this lab, you interconnect network nodes with redundant links to provide reliability at minimal cost. Refer to the lab in Part II of this *Learning Guide*. You may perform this lab now or wait until the end of the chapter.

## Static and Dynamic Routing

The physical topology of an enterprise network provides the structure for forwarding data, and routing provides the mechanism that makes it work. Finding the best path to the destination becomes very difficult in an enterprise network, because a router can have many sources of information from which to build its routing table.

A routing table, as shown in Example 5-1, is a data file that exists in RAM and stores information about directly connected and remote networks. The routing table associates each network with either an *exit interface* or a *next hop*. The exit interface is the physical interface on the local router that the router uses to move the data closer to the destination. The next hop is an interface on a directly connected router that moves the data closer to the final destination.

The routing table also attaches a number to each route that represents the trustworthiness or accuracy of the source of the routing information. This value is the *administrative distance*. Routers maintain information about directly connected, static, and dynamic routes.

**Example 5-1  Routing Table**

```
R1# show ip route
Codes:  C - connected, S - static, I - IGRP, R - RIP, M - mobile, B - BGP
        D - EIGRP, EX - EIGRP external, O - OSPF, IA - OSPF inter area
        N1 - OSPF NSSA external type 1, N2 - OSPF NSSA external type 2
        E1 - OSPF external type 1, E2 - OSPF external type 2
        i - IS-IS, su - IS-IS summary, L1 - IS-IS level-1, L2 - IS-IS level-2,
        ia - IS-IS inter area, * - candidate default, U - per-user static route
        o - ODR, P - periodic downloaded static route

Gateway of last resort is not set

R       192.168.4.0/24 [120/1] via 192.168.2.2, 00:00:26, Serial0/0/0
C       192.168.1.0/24 is directly connected, FastEthernet0/0
C       192.168.2.0/24 is directly connected, Serial0/0/0
S       192.168.3.0/24 [1/0] via 192.168.2.2
```

The first column in the routing table indicates the source of the routing information. Routes may be directly connected (C), manually entered or static (S), or learned from a dynamic routing protocol. Each dynamic routing protocol is identified by a different character in the routing table. The next entry is the destination network. If the route is statically assigned or learned from a dynamic routing protocol, the administrative distance and metric are provided. The administrative distance represents the accuracy or trustworthiness of the metric used for cost calculations. The metric is the value used to calculate the cost to reach the destination. Finally, the exit interface or next hop is specified.

## Directly Connected Routes

A directly connected network attaches to a router interface. Configuring the interface with an IP address and subnet mask allows the interface to become a host on the attached network. The network address and subnet mask of the interface, along with the interface type and number, appear in the routing table as a directly connected network. The routing table designates directly connected networks with a *C*. The output in Example 5-1 shows the following two directly connected networks:

```
C       192.168.1.0/24 is directly connected, FastEthernet0/0
C       192.168.2.0/24 is directly connected, Serial0/0/0
```

## Static Routes

Static routes are routes that a network administrator manually configures. A static route includes the network address and subnet mask of the destination network, along with the exit interface or the IP address of the next-hop router. The routing table designates static routes with an *S*. Static routes have the lowest administrative distance, because static routes are more stable and reliable than routes learned dynamically. The output in Example 5-1 shows one statically assigned route, as follows:

```
S       192.168.3.0/24 [1/0] via 192.168.2.2
```

## Dynamic Routes

Dynamic routing protocols also add remote networks to the routing table. Dynamic routing protocols enable routers to share information about the reachability and status of remote networks through *network discovery*. Each protocol sends and receives data packets while locating other routers and updating and maintaining routing tables. Routes learned through a dynamic routing protocol are identified by the protocol used (for example, R for RIP and D for EIGRP). They are assigned the administrative distance of the protocol. The output in Example 5-1 shows one dynamically learned route, as follows:

```
R       192.168.4.0/24 [120/1] via 192.168.2.2, 00:00:26, Serial0/0/0
```

**Investigating Connected, Static, and Dynamic Routing (5.1.3)**

In this activity, you investigate the various types of routing in a converged network. Use file d3-513.pka on the CD-ROM that accompanies this book to perform this activity using Packet Tracer.

## Comparing Static and Dynamic Routing

Typically, both static and dynamic routes are used in an enterprise network. Static routing addresses specific network needs. Depending on the physical topology, a static route can be used to control the traffic flow. Limiting traffic to a single point of entrance/exit creates a *stub network*. In some enterprise networks, small branch offices have only one possible path to reach the rest of the network. In this situation, it is not necessary to burden the stub router with routing updates and increased overhead by running a dynamic routing protocol; therefore, static routing is beneficial.

Based on their placement and function, specific enterprise routers may also require static routes (see Figure 5-6). Border routers use static routes to provide secure, stable paths to the Internet service provider (ISP). Other routers within the enterprise use either static routing or dynamic routing protocols as necessary to meet their needs.

**Figure 5-6    Static Routes in an Enterprise Network**

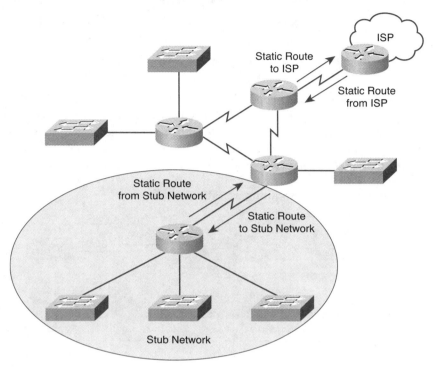

Routers in an enterprise network use bandwidth, memory, and processing resources to provide Network Address Translation / Port Address Translation (NAT/PAT), packet filtering, and other services. Static routing provides forwarding services without the overhead associated with most dynamic routing protocols. Static routing provides more security than dynamic routing, because no routing updates are required. A hacker could intercept a dynamic routing update to gain information about a network.

However, static routing is not without problems. It requires time and accuracy from the network administrator, who must manually enter routing information. A simple typographical error in a static route can result in network downtime and packet loss. When a static route changes, the network may experience routing errors and problems during manual reconfiguration. For these reasons, static routing is impractical for general use in a large enterprise environment.

Table 5-1 compares static and dynamic routing.

**Table 5-1    Static and Dynamic Routing**

|  | Static | Dynamic |
|---|---|---|
| **Configuration Complexity** | Increases with network size. | Generally independent of network size. |
| **Topology Changes** | Administrator intervention required. | Automatically adapts to network changes. |
| **Scaling** | Scalable for simple topologies. | Suitable for simple and complex topologies. |
| **Security** | More secure. | Less secure. |
| **Resource Usage** | No extra resources required. | Uses CPU, memory, link bandwidth. |
| **Predictability** | Route to destination is always the same. | Route depends on current topology. |

## Configuring Static Routes

The global command for configuring most static routes is **ip route**, followed by the destination network, the subnet mask, and the path used to reach it, as follows:

```
Router(config)# ip route [network-address] [subnet mask] [address of next hop OR exit
    interface]
```

Using either the next-hop address or the exit interface, as shown in Figure 5-7, will forward traffic to the proper destination. However, these two parameters behave very differently. Before a router forwards any packet, the routing table process determines which exit interface to use. Static routes configured with exit interfaces require a single routing table lookup. Static routes configured with the next-hop parameter must reference the routing table twice to determine the exit interface.

**Figure 5-7    Configuring a Static Route**

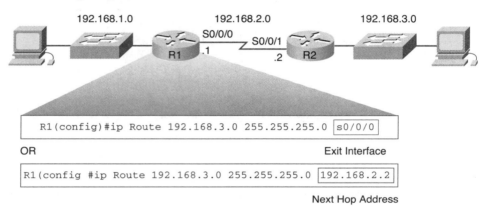

In an enterprise network, static routes configured with exit interfaces are ideal for point-to-point connections like those between a border router and the ISP. Static routes configured with a next-hop interface require two steps to determine the exit interface. This two-step process is called a *recursive lookup*. In a recursive lookup, the following process occurs:

1. The router matches the destination IP address of a packet to the static route.

2. The router then matches the next-hop IP address of the static route to entries in its routing table to determine which interface to use.

Figure 5-8 illustrates a packet moving on a simple network. Example 5-2 shows the routing table on R1 when an exit interface is configured, and Example 5-3 shows the routing table on R1 when a next hop is configured.

**Figure 5-8    Routing to Remote Network: Next Hop or Exit Interface**

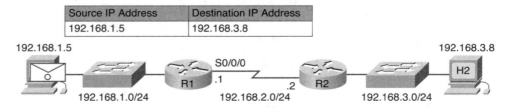

**Example 5-2  Routing Table: Static Route Using Exit Interface**

```
R1# show ip route
Codes:  C - connected, S - static, R - RIP, M - mobile, B - BGP
        D - EIGRP, EX - EIGRP external, O - OSPF, IA - OSPF inter area
        N1 - OSPF NSSA external type 1, N2 - OSPF NSSA external type 2
        E1 - OSPF external type 1, E2 - OSPF external type 2
        i - IS-IS, su - IS-IS summary, L1 - IS-IS level-1, L2 - IS-IS level-2
        ia - IS-IS inter area, * - candidate default, U - per-user static route
        o - ODR, P - periodic downloaded static route


Gateway of last resort is not set

R       192.168.4.0/24 [120/1] via 192.168.2.2, 00:00:05, Serial0/0/0
C       192.168.1.0/24 is directly connected, FastEthernet0/0
C       192.168.2.0/24 is directly connected, Serial0/0/0
S       192.168.3.0/24 is directly connected, Serial0/0/0
```

**Example 5-3  Routing Table: Static Route Using Next Hop**

```
R1# show ip route
Codes:  C - connected, S - static, R - RIP, M - mobile, B - BGP
        D - EIGRP, EX - EIGRP external, O - OSPF, IA - OSPF inter area
        N1 - OSPF NSSA external type 1, N2 - OSPF NSSA external type 2
        E1 - OSPF external type 1, E2 - OSPF external type 2
        i - IS-IS, su - IS-IS summary, L1 - IS-IS level-1, L2 - IS-IS level-2
        ia - IS-IS inter area, * - candidate default, U - per-user static route
        o - ODR, P - periodic downloaded static route

Gateway of last resort is not set

R       192.168.4.0/24 [120/1] via 192.168.2.2, 00:00:26, Serial0/0/0
C       192.168.1.0/24 is directly connected, FastEthernet0/0
C       192.168.2.0/24 is directly connected, Serial0/0/0
S       192.168.3.0/24 [1/0] via 192.168.2.2
```

If an exit interface is disabled, static routes disappear from the routing table. The routing table reinstalls the routes when the interface is re-enabled.

Summarizing several static routes as a single entry reduces the size of the routing table and makes the lookup process more efficient. This process is shown in Figure 5-9 and is called route summarization. A single static route summarizes multiple static routes in the following scenarios:

- The destination networks summarize into a single network address.

- All the static routes use the same exit interface or next-hop IP address.

Without summary routes, routing tables within Internet *core routers* become unmanageable. Enterprise networks encounter the same problem. Summary static routes are an indispensable solution for managing routing table size.

**Figure 5-9    Route Summarization**

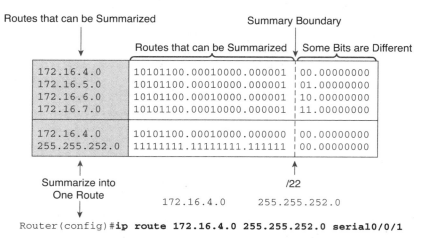

```
Router(config)#ip route 172.16.4.0 255.255.252.0 serial0/0/1
```

**Configuring Static Routes (5.1.4)**

In this activity, you configure static routes in a network. Use file d3-514.pka on the CD-ROM that accompanies this book to perform this activity using Packet Tracer.

Depending on the WAN services used in the enterprise, static routes provide a backup service when the primary WAN link fails. A feature called *floating static routes* can be used to provide this backup service.

By default, a static route has a lower administrative distance than the route learned from a dynamic routing protocol. A floating static route has a higher administrative distance than the route learned from a dynamic routing protocol. For that reason, a floating static route does not display in the routing table. The floating static route entry appears in the routing table only if the dynamic information is lost.

To create a floating static route, add an administrative distance value to the end of the **ip route** command:

```
Router(config)# ip route 192.168.4.0 255.255.255.0 192.168.9.1 200
```

The administrative distance specified must be greater than the administrative distance assigned to the dynamic routing protocol. The router uses the primary route as long as it is active. If the primary route is down, the table installs the floating static route.

## Default Route

Routing tables cannot contain routes to every possible Internet site. As routing tables grow in size, they require more RAM and processing power. A special type of static route, called a *default route*, specifies a gateway to use when the routing table does not contain a path to a destination. It is common for default routes to point to the next router in the path toward the ISP. In a complex enterprise, default routes funnel Internet traffic out of the network. The default route is marked with an asterisk in the routing table.

The command to create a default route is similar to the command used to create either an ordinary or a floating static route. The network address and subnet mask are both specified as 0.0.0.0, making it a *quad zero route*. The command uses either the next-hop address or the exit interface parameters as shown in Figure 5-10 and Example 5-4. The zeros indicate to the router that no bits need to match to use this route. As long as a better match does not exist, the router uses the default static route.

The final default route, located on the border router, sends the traffic to the ISP. This route identifies the last stop within the enterprise as the *gateway of last resort* for packets that cannot be matched. This information appears in the routing tables of all routers. If the enterprise uses a dynamic routing protocol, the border router can send a default route to the other routers as part of a dynamic routing update.

**Figure 5-10    Default Route**

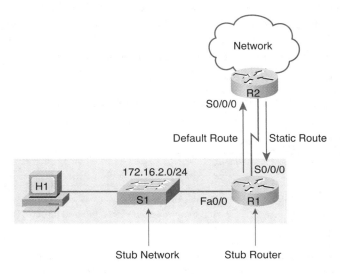

**Example 5-4  Default Route Configuration**

```
R1(config)# ip route 0.0.0.0 0.0.0.0 s0/0/0
R1(config)# end

R1# show ip route
Codes:  C - connected, S - static, I - IGRP, R - RIP, M - mobile, B - BGP
        D - EIGRP, EX - EIGRP external, O - OSPF, IA - OSPF inter area
        N1 - OSPF NSSA external type 1, N2 - OSPF NSSA external type 2
        E1 - OSPF external type 1, E2 - OSPF external type 2
        i - IS-IS, su - IS-IS summary, L1 - IS-IS level-1, L2 - IS-IS level-2
        ia - IS-IS inter area, * - candidate default, U - per-user static route
        o - ODR, P - periodic downloaded static route

Gateway of last resort is 0.0.0.0 to network 0.0.0.0

     172.16.0.0/24 is subnetted, 2 subnets
C       172.16.2.0 is directly connected, Serial0/0/0
C       172.16.3.0 is directly connected, FastEthernet0/0
S*   0.0.0.0/0 is directly connected, Serial0/0/0
```

**Configuring Default Routes (5.1.5)**

In this activity, you configure default routes in a network. Use file d3-515.pka on the CD-ROM that accompanies this book to perform this activity using Packet Tracer.

# Routing Using the RIP Protocol

Dynamic routing protocols are classified into two major categories: *distance vector protocols* and *link-state protocols*. Both types of routing protocols have distant advantages and some serious limitations. Two of the most common distance vector routing protocols are RIP and EIGRP.

## Distance Vector Routing Protocols

Routers running distance vector routing protocols share network information with directly connected neighbors. The neighbor routers then advertise the information to their neighbors, until all routers in the enterprise learn the information. A router running a distance vector protocol does not know the entire path to a destination; it knows only the distance to the remote network and the direction, or *vector*. Its knowledge comes through information from directly connected neighbors, as shown in Figure 5-11.

**Figure 5-11    Distance Vector Routing Protocols**

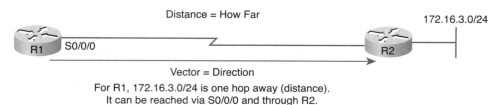

For R1, 172.16.3.0/24 is one hop away (distance).
It can be reached via S0/0/0 and through R2.

Like all routing protocols, distance vector protocols use a *metric* to determine the best route to the destination. Distance vector protocols calculate the best route based on the distance from the local router to the remote network. An example of a metric used is hop count, which is the number of routers, or hops, between the router and the destination.

Distance vector protocols usually require less-complicated configurations and management than link-state protocols. They can run on older, less-powerful routers and require lower amounts of memory and processing.

Routers using distance vector protocols broadcast or multicast their entire routing table to their neighbors at regular intervals. If a router learns more than one route to a destination, it calculates and advertises the route with the lowest metric. This method of moving routing information through large networks is slow. At any given moment, some routers may not have the most current information about the network. This limits the scalability of the protocols and causes issues such as *routing loops*.

RIP Versions 1 and 2 are true distance vector protocols, whereas EIGRP is actually a distance vector protocol with advanced capabilities. *RIPng*, the newest version of RIP, was specifically designed to support IPv6.

## Routing Information Protocol (RIP)

RIPv1 was the first and only IP routing protocol available in the early days of networking. RIPv1 does not send subnet mask information in its routing updates and, therefore, does not support variable-length subnet masking (VLSM) and classless interdomain routing (CIDR). RIPv1 automatically summarizes networks at the *classful boundary*, treating all networks as though they were default Classes A, B, and C. As long as networks are *contiguous*, such as 192.168.1.0, 192.168.2.0, and so on, this feature may not pose a serious problem. However, if networks are discontiguous, for example if the network 10.0.1.0 separates the networks 172.16.10.0 and 172.16.11.0, RIPv1 may not correctly report the routes. In this case, both the 172.16.10.0 and the 172.16.11.0 are seen as the 172.16.0.0/16 network. When the router receives an update with information for the 172.16.0.0/16 network, it checks its routing table. Because it already has a route to that network, it disregards the update.

By default, RIPv1 broadcasts its routing updates to all connected routers every 30 seconds. Figure 5-12 shows a network running RIP, and Example 5-5 shows the specifics for RIP running on R1.

**Figure 5-12    Routing with RIP**

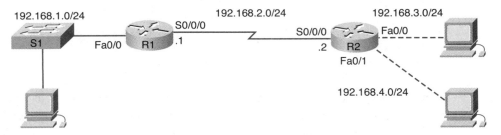

**Example 5-5  RIP Protocol**

```
R1# show ip protocols
Routing Protocol is "rip"
  Outgoing update filter list for all interfaces is not set
  Incoming update filter list for all interfaces is not set
  Sending updates every 30 seconds, next due in 23 seconds
  Invalid after 180 seconds, hold down 180, flushed after 240
  Redistributing: rip
  Default version control: send version 1, receive any version
    Interface          Send  Recv  Triggered RIP  Key-chain
    FastEthernet0/0      1    1 2
    Serial0/0/0          1    1 2
  Automatic network summarization is in effect
  Maximum path: 4
  Routing for Networks:
    192.168.1.0
    192.168.2.0
  Routing Information Sources:
    Gateway         Distance      Last Update
    192.168.2.2        120         00:00:02
  Distance: (default is 120)
```

RIPv2 has many of the features of RIPv1 and includes important enhancements. RIPv2 is a classless routing protocol that supports VLSM and CIDR. A subnet mask field is included in v2 updates, which allows the use of discontiguous networks. RIPv2 also has the ability to turn off automatic summarization of routes.

Both versions of RIP send their entire routing table out all participating interfaces in updates. RIPv1 broadcasts these updates to 255.255.255.255. This requires all devices on a broadcast network such as Ethernet to process the data. RIPv2 multicasts its updates to 224.0.0.9. Multicasts take up less network bandwidth than broadcasts. Devices not configured for RIPv2 discard multicasts at the data link layer. Example 5-6 shows a partial debug output of the RIP updates moving across the network shown in Figure 5-12.

**Example 5-6  Debugging the RIP Process**

```
<output omitted>
*Aug 30 04:37:11.115: RIP: sending v2 update to 224.0.0.9 via FastEthernet0/0 (192.168.1.1)
*Aug 30 04:37:11.115: RIP: build update entries
*Aug 30 04:37:11.115: 192.168.2.0/24 via 0.0.0.0, metric 1, tag 0
*Aug 30 04:37:11.115: 192.168.4.0/24 via 0.0.0.0, metric 1, tag 0
R1#
*Aug 30 04:37:36.697: RIP: sending v1 update to 255.255.255.255 via Serial0/0/0 (192.168.2.1)
*Aug 30 04:37:36.697: RIP: build update entries
*Aug 30 04:37:36.697: network 192.168.1.0 metric 1
*Aug 30 04:37:36.697: RIP: sending v2 update to 224.0.0.9 via Serial0/0/0 (192.168.2.1)
<output omitted>
```

Attackers often introduce invalid updates to trick a router into sending data to the wrong destination or to seriously degrade network performance. Invalid information can also end up in the routing table because of poor configuration or a malfunctioning router. Encrypting routing information hides the content of the routing table from any routers that do not possess the password or authentication data. RIPv2 has an authentication mechanism, whereas RIPv1 does not.

Although RIPv2 provides many enhancements, it is not an entirely different protocol. RIPv2 shares many of the features found in RIPv1, such as the following:

- Hop-count metric

- 15-hop maximum

- TTL equals 16 hops

- Default 30-second update interval

- Route poisoning, poison reverse, split horizon, and holddowns to avoid loops

- Updates using UDP port 520

- Administrative distance of 120

- Message header containing up to 25 routes without authentication

When a router starts up, each RIP-configured interface sends out a *request message*. This message requests that all RIP neighbors send their complete routing tables. RIP-enabled neighbors send a *response message* that includes known network entries. These entries are used to build the routing table.

A router that has just been powered on will not have any dynamic routes in the routing table other than directly connected or static route assignments. If the router has been running for a while, it may also have routes learned through a dynamic process. The receiving router evaluates each route entry based on the following criteria:

- If a route entry is new, the receiving router installs the route in the routing table.

- If the route is already in the table and the entry comes from a different source, the routing table replaces the existing entry if the new entry has a better hop count.

- If the route is already in the table and the entry comes from the same source, it replaces the existing entry even if the metric is not better.

The startup router then sends a *triggered update* out all RIP-enabled interfaces containing its own routing table. RIP neighbors are informed of any new routes.

As long as routers send and process the correct versions of routing updates, RIPv1 and RIPv2 are completely compatible. By default, RIPv2 sends and receives only Version 2 updates. If a network must use both versions of RIP, the network administrator configures RIPv2 to send and receive both Versions 1 and 2. By default, RIPv1 sends Version 1 updates, but receives both Versions 1 and 2.

Within an enterprise, it might be necessary to use both versions of RIP. For example, part of the network may be migrating to RIPv2, whereas another part may be staying with RIPv1. Overriding the global RIP configuration with interface-specific behavior allows routers to support both versions of RIP. Example 5-7 shows the send and receive versions configured on R1 in Figure 5-12.

**Example 5-7  RIP Send and Receive Versions**

```
R1# show ip protocols
Routing Protocol is "rip"
  Outgoing update filter list for all interfaces is not set
  Incoming update filter list for all interfaces is not set
  Sending updates every 30 seconds, next due in 16 seconds
  Invalid after 180 seconds, hold down 180, flushed after 240
  Redistributing: rip
  Default version control: send version 2, receive version 2
    Interface           Send  Recv  Triggered RIP  Key-chain
    FastEthernet0/0     2     2
    Serial0/0/0         1 2   2
  Automatic network summarization is in effect
  Maximum path: 4
  Routing for Networks:
    192.168.1.0
    192.168.2.0
  Routing Information Sources:
    Gateway         Distance       Last Update
    192.168.2.2          120       00:00:03
  Distance: (default is 120)
```

To customize the global configuration of an interface, use the following interface configuration commands:

```
ip rip send version <1 ¦ 2 ¦ 1 2>
ip rip receive version <1 ¦ 2 ¦ 1 2>
```

**Interactive Activity 5-1: RIP Characteristics (5.2.2)**

In this activity, you determine whether a characteristic is that of RIPv1 or RIPv2. Use file d3ia-522 on the CD-ROM that accompanies this book to perform this interactive activity.

# Configuring RIPv2

Before configuring RIP, assign IP addresses and masks to all interfaces that participate in routing and set the clock rate where necessary on the serial links. After the basic configurations are complete, configure RIP.

Basic RIP configuration consists of three steps:

**Step 1.** Enable RIP routing:

Router(config)# **router rip**

**Step 2.** Specify the version to use:

Router(config)# **version 2**

**Step 3.** Identify each directly connected network that should be advertised by RIP:

Router(config-router)# **network** [*network address*]

These steps are illustrated in Figure 5-13, and Example 5-8 shows the configuration.

**Figure 5-13   RIP Configuration**

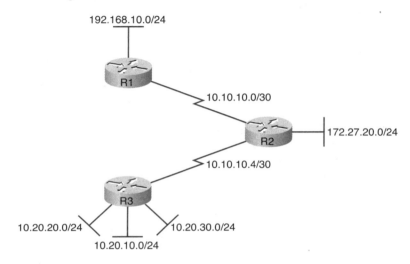

**Example 5-8  RIP Configurations**

```
R1 RIP Configuration


R1(config)# router rip
R1(config-router)# version 2
R1(config-router)# network 192.168.10.0
R1(config-router)# network 10.0.0.0
R2 RIP Configuration


R2(config)# router rip
R2(config-router)# version 2
R2(config-router)# network 172.27.0.0
R2(config-router)# network 10.0.0.0
R3 RIP Configuration


R3(config)# router rip
R3(config-router)# version 2
R3(config-router)# network 10.0.0.0
```

To configure *MD5 authentication*, go to any interface participating in RIPv2 and enter the **ip rip authentication mode md5** command. MD5 authentication uses the one-way, MD5 hash algorithm, acknowledged to be a strong hashing algorithm. In this mode of authentication, the routing update does not carry the password for the purpose of authentication. Rather, a 128-bit message, generated by running the MD5 algorithm on the password, and the message are sent along for authentication. The receiving device uses the same hashing algorithm on the password stored locally. If the two hashed password match, the receiving device accepts the update.

RIPv2 propagates a default route to its neighbor routers as part of its routing updates. To accomplish this, create the default route, and then add **redistribute static** to the RIP configuration.

**Lab 5.2: Configuring RIPv2 with VLSM and Default Route Propagation (5.2.3)**

In this lab, you configure a network using RIPv2. You also create a default route and propagate it through the network. Refer to the lab in Part II of this *Learning Guide*. You may perform this lab now or wait until the end of the chapter.

# Problems with RIP

Various performance and security issues arise when using RIP. The first issue concerns routing table accuracy. Both versions of RIP automatically summarize subnets on the classful boundary. This means that RIP recognizes subnets as a single Class A, B, or C network. Enterprise networks typically use classless IP addressing and a variety of subnets, some of which are not directly connected to each other, which creates discontiguous subnets.

Unlike RIPv1, with RIPv2 you can disable the automatic-summarization feature. With that feature disabled, RIPv2 will report all subnets with subnet mask information as shown in Figure 5-14. This is done to ensure a more accurate routing table. To accomplish this, add the **no auto-summary** command to the RIPv2 configuration:

```
Router(config-router)# no auto-summary
```

**Figure 5-14   Disabling Auto Summarization in RIPv2**

10.1.1.0/16

S0/0/0     S0/0/1
R2

209.165.200.228/30                    209.165.200.232/30

S0/0/0     RIP Update                    RIP Update     S0/0/1
Fa0/0   R1   172.30.1.0/24   172.30.100.0/24   R3   Fa0/0
          1 Hop              1 Hop

172.30.1.0/24                                         172.30.100.0/24

No Auto Summarization

Another issue to consider is the broadcast nature of RIP updates. As soon as the RIP configuration lists a network command for a given network, RIP immediately begins to send advertisements out all interfaces that belong to that network. These updates might not be needed on all portions of a network. For example, an Ethernet LAN interface passes these updates to every device on its network segment, which produces unnecessary traffic. The routing update could also be intercepted by any device. This makes the network less secure. The **passive-interface** command disables routing updates on specified interfaces:

```
Router(config-router)# passive-interface interface-type interface-number
```

In complex enterprise networks running more than one routing protocol, the **passive-interface** command defines which routers learn RIP routes, as shown in Figure 5-15. When the number of interfaces advertising RIP routes is limited, security and traffic control increase.

**Figure 5-15    RIP Passive Interfaces**

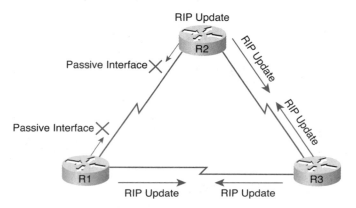

A network running RIP needs time to converge. Some routers may contain incorrect routes in their routing tables until all routers have updated and have the same view of the network. Erroneous network information may cause routing updates and traffic to loop endlessly as they *count to infinity*. In the RIP routing protocol, infinity occurs when the hop count is 16. Routing loops negatively affect network performance. RIP contains several features designed to combat this impact. The anti-loop features of RIP add stability to the protocol, but also add to convergence time. These features are often used in combination:

- Poisoned reverse

- Split horizon

- Holddown timer

- Triggered updates

*Poisoned reverse* sets the metric for a route to 16, making it unreachable. Because RIP defines infinity as 16 hops, any network further away than 15 hops is unreachable. If a network is down, a router changes the metric for that route to 16 so that all other routers see it as unreachable. This feature prevents the routing protocol from sending information via poisoned routes. *Split horizon* prevents the formation of loops. When multiple routers advertise the same network routes to each other, routing loops may form.

Split horizon dictates that a router receiving routing information on an interface cannot send an update about that same network back out the same interface. This prevents two routers from seeing each other as a route to a destination network. If router A receives update from router B saying it has a route to network X, and then router B sends an update to router A saying it now has a route to network X, traffic destined for network X loops between the two routers.

The holddown timer stabilizes routes. The *holddown timer* refuses to accept route updates with a higher metric to the same destination network for a period after a route goes down. If, during the holddown period, the original route comes back up or the router receives route information with a lower metric, the router installs the route in the routing table and immediately begins to use it. The default holddown time is 180 seconds, six times the regular update period. The default can be changed. However, any holddown period increases the convergence time and has a negative impact on network performance.

When a route fails, RIP does not wait for the next periodic update. Instead, RIP sends an immediate update, called a triggered update. It advertises the failed route by increasing the metric to 16, effectively poisoning the route. This update places the route in holddown status while RIP attempts to locate an alternative route with a better metric.

### Routing Between Discontiguous Networks (5.2.4)

In this activity, you configure routing between discontiguous networks using RIP. Use file d3-524.pka on the CD-ROM that accompanies this book to perform this activity using Packet Tracer.

## Verifying RIP

RIPv2 is a simple protocol to configure. However, errors and inconsistencies can occur on any network. There are many **show** commands to assist the technician in verifying a RIP configuration and troubleshooting RIP functionality. The **show ip protocols** and **show ip route** commands are important for verification and troubleshooting on any routing protocol.

To view all the routes known by the RIP protocol, use the command **show ip rip database**. To display RIP routing updates as sent and received in real time, use the **debug ip rip** or **debug ip rip** {**events**} commands. The output of this debug command displays the source address and interface of each update, and the version and the metric, as shown in Figure 5-16 and Example 5-9.

**Figure 5-16    Debugging RIP**

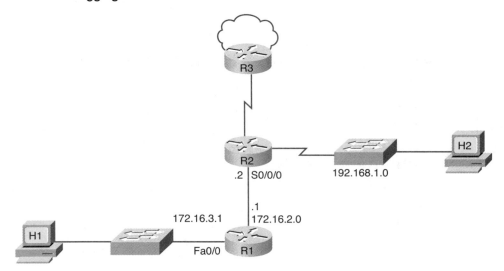

**Example 5-9  Sample debug ip rip Output**

```
R1# debug ip rip
RIP protocol debugging is on
R1#
*Aug 29 12:04:41.653: RIP: sending v1 update to 255.255.255.255 via FastEthernet0/0
   (172.16.3.1)
*Aug 29 12:04:41.653: RIP: build update entries
*Aug 29 12:04:41.653: subnet 172.16.1.0 metric 2
*Aug 29 12:04:41.653: subnet 172.16.2.0 metric 1
*Aug 29 12:04:41.653: network 192.168.1.0 metric 1
*Aug 29 12:04:43.188: RIP: sending v1 update to 255.255.255.255 via Serial0/0/0 (172.16.2.1)
*Aug 29 12:04:43.188: RIP: build update entries
*Aug 29 12:04:43.188: subnet 172.16.3.0 metric 1
*Aug 29 12:04:43.188: RIP: sending v2 update to 224.0.0.9 via Serial0/0/0 (172.16.2.1)
*Aug 29 12:04:43.188: RIP: build update entries
*Aug 29 12:04:43.188: 172.16.3.0/24 via 0.0.0.0, metric 1, tag 0
*Aug 29 12:04:58.665: RIP: received v1 update from 172.16.2.2 on Serial0/0/0
*Aug 29 12:04:58.665: 172.16.1.0 in 1 hops
*Aug 29 12:04:58.665: 192.168.1.0 in 1 hops
*Aug 29 12:04:58.677: RIP: received v2 update from 172.16.2.2 on Serial0/0/0
*Aug 29 12:04:58.677: 172.16.1.0/24 via 0.0.0.0 in 1 hops
*Aug 29 12:04:58.677: 192.168.1.0/24 via 0.0.0.0 in 1 hops
```

As with all debug commands, do not use the **debug ip rip** command more than necessary. Debugging consumes bandwidth and processing power, which slows network performance.

You can use the **ping** command to test for end-to-end connectivity. The **show running-config** command provides a convenient way to verify that you correctly entered all commands.

### Troubleshooting RIPv2 (5.2.5)

In this activity, you troubleshoot and correct issues with RIPv2. Use file d3-525.pka on the CD-ROM that accompanies this book to perform this activity using Packet Tracer.

# Routing Using the EIGRP Protocol

RIP has a number of limitations that make it less than ideal for large networks. Cisco developed an enhanced distance vector protocol to try and overcome some of these limitations. This Cisco proprietary routing protocol is EIGRP.

## Limitations of RIP

Although RIP is easy to configure and requires minimal amounts of router resources to function, its simple hop-count metric is not an accurate way to determine the best path in complex networks. In addition, the RIP limitation of 15 hops can mark distant networks as unreachable, as shown in Figure 5-17.

**Figure 5-17    Network Unreachable Problem with RIP**

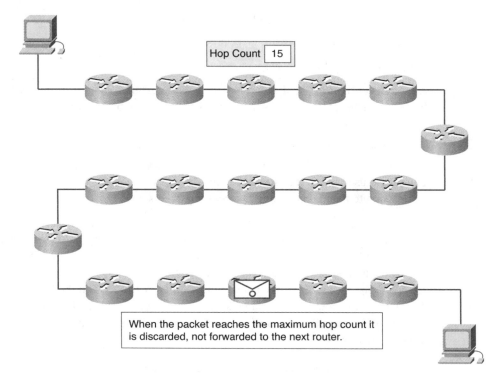

RIP issues periodic updates of its routing table, which consumes bandwidth, even when no network changes have occurred. Routers must accept these updates and process them to see whether they contain updated route information. This uses valuable router resources.

Updates passed from router to router take time to reach all areas of the network. As a result, routers might not have an accurate picture of the network. This slow convergence can lead to the formation of routing loops. These loops waste valuable bandwidth.

## Enhanced Interior Gateway Routing Protocol (EIGRP)

The limitations of RIP led to the development of more advanced protocols. Networking professionals required a protocol that would support VLSM and CIDR, scale easily, and provide faster convergence in complex enterprise networks. Cisco developed EIGRP as a proprietary distance vector routing protocol. It has enhanced capabilities that address many of the limitations of other distance vector protocols. EIGRP shares some of features of RIP, while using many advanced features.

Some of the more advanced features of EIGRP discussed in this section are as follows:

- Supports VLSM and classless routing
- Uses a composite metric
- Uses the DUAL algorithm to prevent routing loops
- Uses bounded updates for fast convergence
- Maintains multiple tables
- Forms neighbor adjacencies
- Maintains successor and feasible successor routes

- Accommodates equal- and unequal-cost load balancing
- Uses multiple packet types for stability and fast convergence
- Supports multiple network layer protocols
- Uses RTP for Layer 4 support

Although configuring EIGRP is relatively simple, the underlying features and options are complex. EIGRP contains many features that are not found in any other routing protocols. All of these factors make EIGRP an excellent choice for large, multiprotocol networks that use primarily Cisco devices.

The two main goals of EIGRP are to provide a loop-free routing environment and to enable rapid convergence. To achieve these goals, EIGRP uses a method other than RIP for calculating the best route. The metric used is a *composite metric* that primarily considers bandwidth and delay. This metric is more accurate than hop count in determining the distance to a destination network.

The *Diffusing Update Algorithm (DUAL)* used by EIGRP guarantees loop-free operation while it calculates routes. When a change occurs in the network topology, DUAL synchronizes all affected routers simultaneously, thus shortening convergence time and preventing routing loops. For these reasons, the administrative distance of EIGRP is 90, whereas the administrative distance of RIP is 120. The lower number reflects the increased reliability of EIGRP and the increased accuracy of the metric. If a router learns routes to the same destination from both RIP and EIGRP, it chooses the EIGRP route over the route learned through RIP. Table 5-2 lists the administrative distances of some of the more common routing protocols.

**Table 5-2    Routing Protocol Administrative Distances**

| Route Source | Administrative Distance |
| --- | --- |
| Connected | 0 |
| Static | 1 |
| EIGRP summary route | 5 |
| External BGP | 20 |
| Internal EIGRP | 90 |
| IGRP | 100 |
| OSPF | 110 |
| IS-IS | 115 |
| RIP | 120 |
| External EIGRP | 170 |
| Internal BGP | 200 |

EIGRP tags routes learned from another routing protocol as external. Because the information used to calculate these routes is not as reliable as the metric of EIGRP, it attaches a higher administrative distance to the routes.

EIGRP is a good choice for complex enterprise networks composed primarily of Cisco routers. Its maximum hop count of 224 supports large networks. EIGRP can display more than one routing table because it can collect and maintain routing information for a variety of routed protocols, such as IP and IPX. The EIGRP routing table reports routes learned both inside and outside the local system.

Unlike other distance vector protocols, EIGRP does not send complete tables in its updates. EIGRP multicasts partial updates about specific changes to only those routers that need the information, not to all routers in the area. These are called *bounded updates* because they reflect specific parameters.

Consider the network shown in Figure 5-18. When the 10.1.0.0 network goes down, R1 notifies R2. R2 updates its routing information, and then sends an update to its neighbor router R3. Also, instead of sending periodic routing updates, EIGRP sends small *hello packets* to maintain knowledge of its neighbors. Because they are limited in size, both bounded updates and hello packets save bandwidth while keeping network information fresh.

**Figure 5-18    EIGRP Bounded Updates**

**Interactive Activity 5-2: Characteristics of RIP and EIGRP (5.3.2)**

In this activity, you sort characteristics into those matching RIP and those matching EIGRP. Use file d3ia-532 on the CD-ROM that accompanies this book to perform this interactive activity.

## EIGRP Terminology and Tables

To store network information from the updates and support rapid convergence, EIGRP maintains multiple tables. EIGRP routers keep route and topology information readily available in RAM so that they can react quickly to changes. EIGRP maintains three interconnected tables:

- Neighbor table
- Topology table
- Routing table

### Neighbor Table

The *neighbor table* lists information about directly connected neighbor routers. EIGRP records the address of a newly discovered neighbor and the interface that connects to it. When a neighbor sends a hello packet, it advertises a hold time. The *hold time* is the length of time that a router treats a neighbor as reachable. If another hello packet is not received within the hold time, the timer expires, and DUAL recalculates the topology. Because fast convergence depends on accurate neighbor information, this table is crucial to EIGRP operation.

### Topology Table

The *topology table* lists all routes learned from each EIGRP neighbor. DUAL takes the information from the neighbor and topology tables and calculates the lowest cost routes to each network. The topology table identifies up to four primary loop-free routes for any one destination. These *successor routes* appear in the routing table. EIGRP load balances, or sends packets to a destination using more than one path. It load balances using successor routes that are both equal cost and unequal cost. This feature avoids overloading any one route with packets.

Backup routes, called *feasible successors*, appear in the topology table but not in the routing table. If a primary route fails, a feasible successor becomes a successor route. This backup occurs as long as the feasible successor has a lower reported distance than the feasible distance of the current successor distance to the destination. Example 5-10 shows a sample topology table.

**Example 5-10    EIGRP Topology Table**

```
R2# show ip eigrp topology
 IP-EIGRP Topology Table for AS(1)/ID(192.168.10.9)

 Codes: P - Passive, A - Active, U - Update, Q - Query, R - Reply,
        r - reply Status, s - sia Status

 P 172.16.1.0/24, 1 successors, FD is 20514560
         via 172.16.3.1 (20514560/28160), Serial0/0/0
         via 192.168.10.10 (21026560/10514432), Serial0/0/1
 P 192.168.10.4/30, 2 successors, FD is 21024000
         via 192.168.10.10 (21024000/10511872), Serial0/0/1
         via 172.16.3.1 (21024000/20512000), Serial0/0/1
 P 192.168.1.0/24, 1 successors, FD is 20514560
         via 192.168.10.10 (20514560/28160), Serial0/0/1
 P 192.168.10.8/30, 1 successors, FD is 20512000
         via Connected, Serial0/0/1
 P 192.168.2.0/24, 1 successors, FD is 28160
         via Connected, FastEthernet0/0
 P 172.16.3.0/30, 1 successors, FD is 20512000
         via Connected, Serial0/0/0
         via 192.168.10.10 (21536000/11023872), Serial0/0/1
```

Each entry provides a significant amount of information. Consider the first entry in Example 5-10. The *P* indicates that DUAL has placed this route in the passive state. When DUAL is recalculating the route, it is placed in an active state. The destination network is 172.16.1.0/24, and DUAL has found one successor with a feasible distance of 20514560. The successor is via the next-hop address of 172.16.3.1, which can be reached out the serial 0/0/0 interface. This neighbor is reporting a distance to the destination network of 28160. There is also a feasible successor to the destination network via the next hop of 192.168.10.10. This route is a feasible successor because the distance to the destination network being reported (10514432) is less than the feasible distance. Only the successor route moves to the routing table.

## Routing Table

Whereas the topology table contains information about many possible paths to a network destination, the routing table displays only the best paths, called the successor routes. EIGRP displays information about routes in two ways. The routing table designates routes learned through EIGRP with a *D*. EIGRP tags dynamic or static routes learned from other routing protocols or from outside the EIGRP network as D EX, or external, because they did not originate from EIGRP routers within the same autonomous system. This is shown in Figure 5-19 and Example 5-11.

**Figure 5-19    EIGRP Routing**

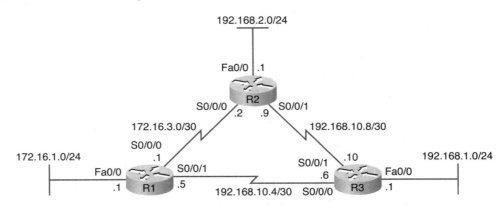

**Example 5-11    EIGRP Network Routing Tables**

```
R1 Routing Table


R1# show ip route
Codes:  C - connected, S - static, R - RIP, M - mobile, B - BGP
        D - EIGRP, EX - EIGRP external, O - OSPF, IA - OSPF inter area
        N1 - OSPF NSSA external type 1, N2 - OSPF NSSA external type 2
        E1 - OSPF external type 1, E2 - OSPF external type 2
        i - IS-IS, su - IS-IS summary, L1 - IS-IS level-1, L2 - IS-IS level-2
        ia - IS-IS inter area, * - candidate default, U - per-user static route
        o - ODR, P - periodic downloaded static route



Gateway of last resort is not set

     192.168.10.0/24 is variably subnetted, 3 subnets, 2 masks
D       192.168.10.0/24 is a summary, 00:04:22, Null0
C       192.168.10.4/30 is directly connected, Serial0/0/1
D       192.168.10.8/30 [90/21024000] via 172.16.3.2, 00:04:22, Serial0/0/0
     172.16.0.0/16 is variably subnetted, 3 subnets, 3 masks
D       172.16.0.0/16 is a summary, 00:04:22, Null0
C       172.16.1.0/24 is directly connected, FastEthernet0/0
C       172.16.3.0/30 is directly connected, Serial0/0/0
D    192.168.1.0/24 [90/20514560] via 192.168.10.6, 00:04:23, Serial0/0/1
D EX 192.168.2.0/24 [170/20514560] via 172.16.3.2, 00:04:23, Serial0/0/0
R2 Routing Table


R2# show ip route
Codes:  C - connected, S - static, R - RIP, M - mobile, B - BGP
        D - EIGRP, EX - EIGRP external, O - OSPF, IA - OSPF inter area
        N1 - OSPF NSSA external type 1, N2 - OSPF NSSA external type 2
        E1 - OSPF external type 1, E2 - OSPF external type 2
        i - IS-IS, su - IS-IS summary, L1 - IS-IS level-1, L2 - IS-IS level-2
        ia - IS-IS inter area, * - candidate default, U - per-user static route
        o - ODR, P - periodic downloaded static route



Gateway of last resort is not set
```

```
           192.168.10.0/24 is variably subnetted, 2 subnets, 2 masks
D             192.168.10.0/24 [90/21024000] via 172.16.3.1, 00:14:48, Serial0/0/0
C             192.168.10.8/30 is directly connected, Serial0/0/1
           172.16.0.0/16 is variably subnetted, 2 subnets, 3 masks
D             172.16.1.0/24 [90/20514560] via 172.16.3.1, 00:24:10, Serial0/0/0
C             172.16.3.0/30 is directly connected, Serial0/0/0
D          192.168.1.0/24 [90/21026560] via 172.16.3.1, 00:19:00, Serial0/0/0
C          192.168.2.0/24 is directly connected, FastEthernet0/0
R3 Routing Table


R3# show ip route
Codes:  C - connected, S - static, R - RIP, M - mobile, B - BGP
        D - EIGRP, EX - EIGRP external, O - OSPF, IA - OSPF inter area
        N1 - OSPF NSSA external type 1, N2 - OSPF NSSA external type 2
        E1 - OSPF external type 1, E2 - OSPF external type 2
        i - IS-IS, su - IS-IS summary, L1 - IS-IS level-1, L2 - IS-IS level-2
        ia - IS-IS inter area, * - candidate default, U - per-user static route
        o - ODR, P - periodic downloaded static route


Gateway of last resort is not set

           192.168.10.0/24 is variably subnetted, 3 subnets, 2 masks
D             192.168.10.0/24 is a summary, 00:13:46, Null0
C             192.168.10.4/30 is directly connected, Serial0/0/0
C             192.168.10.8/30 is directly connected, Serial0/0/1
D          172.16.0.0/16 [90/20514560]via 192.168.10.5, 00:13:44, Serial0/0/0
C          192.168.1.0/24 is directly connected, FastEthernet0/0
D EX 192.168.2.0/24 [170/21026560] via 192.168.10.5, 00:02:11, Serial0/0/0
```

**Interactive Activity 5-3: EIGRP Tables (5.3.3)**

In this activity, you determine in which of the EIGRP tables specific information may be found. Use file d3ia-533 on the CD-ROM that accompanies this book to perform this interactive activity.


## EIGRP Neighbors and Adjacencies

Before EIGRP can exchange packets between routers, it must first discover its neighbors. EIGRP neighbors are other routers running EIGRP on shared, directly connected networks. EIGRP routers use hello packets to discover neighbors and establish *adjacencies* with neighbor routers, as shown in Figure 5-20. By default, hello packets are multicast every 5 seconds on links greater than a T1 and every 60 seconds on T1 or slower links.

On IP networks, the multicast address for EIGRP routing updates is 224.0.0.10. The hello packet contains information about the router interfaces and the interface addresses. An EIGRP router assumes that as long as it is receiving hello packets from a neighbor, the neighbor and its routes are reachable. The hold time is the period that EIGRP waits to receive a hello packet. Generally, the hold time is three times the duration of the *hello interval*. When the hold time expires and EIGRP declares the route as down, DUAL reevaluates the topology and refreshes the routing table.

**Figure 5-20   EIGRP Hello Packets**

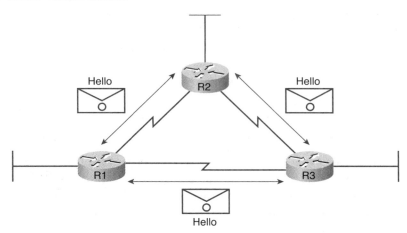

Information discovered through the hello packet provides the information for the neighbor table. A sequence number records the number of the last received hello from each neighbor and time-stamps the time that the packet arrived.

When a neighbor adjacency is established, EIGRP uses various types of packets to exchange and update routing table information. Neighbors learn about new routes, unreachable routes, and rediscovered routes through exchange of these packets:

- Acknowledgment

- Update

- Query

- Reply

When a route is lost, it moves to an active state, and DUAL searches for a new route to the destination. When a route is found, it is moved to the routing table and placed in a passive state. These various packets help DUAL gather the information it requires to calculate the best route to the destination network.

An *acknowledgment packet* indicates the receipt of an update, query, or reply packet. Acknowledgment packets are small hello packets without any data. These types of packets are always unicast packets and carry no data.

An *update packet* sends information about the network topology to its neighbor. That neighbor uses the information in the update packet to update its topology table. Several updates are often required to send all the topology information to a new neighbor. If a new neighbor relationship is formed, these packets are unicast. To indicate a change in the routing, these packets are multicast.

Whenever DUAL places a route in the active state, the router must send a *query packet* to each neighbor. Neighbors must send replies, even if the reply states that no information on the destination is available. The information contained in each *reply packet* helps DUAL to locate a successor route to the destination network. Query packets are unicast when requesting specific information about a neighbor or multicast when looking for a new successor. Reply packets are always unicast in response to a query.

When a hello packet is not received from an EIGRP neighbor for three hello intervals, EIGRP considers routes through that neighbor as being down. If a router loses a route to a network, EIGRP sends an update packet to alert other routers that the route has been lost, and DUAL places the route into an active state. Routers that received the update acknowledge receipt of the information. EIGRP then sends out a query packet to these routers asking whether they have a route to the destination. The routers acknowledge the request, and then send a reply indicating that they either have or do not have a route to the network. Even if the router does not have a route, it responds to the query. DUAL then recalculates the information and determines whether it can find a new successor. If it does, the successor is moved to the routing table.

EIGRP packet types use either a connection-oriented service similar to TCP or a connectionless service similar to User Datagram Protocol (UDP). Update, query, and reply packets use the TCP-like service. Acknowledgments and hello packets use the UDP-like service.

As a routing protocol, EIGRP operates independently of the network layer. Cisco designed *Reliable Transport Protocol (RTP)* as a proprietary Layer 4 protocol. RTP guarantees delivery and receipt of EIGRP packets for all network layer protocols. Because large, complex networks may use a variety of network layer protocols, this protocol makes EIGRP flexible and scalable.

RTP can be used as both a reliable and best effort transport protocol, similar to TCP and UDP. Reliable RTP requires an acknowledgment packet from the receiver to the sender. Update, query, and reply packets are sent reliably; hello and acknowledgment packets are sent best effort and do not require an acknowledgment. RTP uses both unicast and multicast packets. Multicast EIGRP packets use the reserved multicast address of 224.0.0.10.

Each network layer protocol works through a *protocol-dependent module (PDM)*, which is responsible for the specific routing task. Each PDM maintains three tables. For example, a router running IP, IPX, and AppleTalk has three neighbor tables, three topology tables, and three routing tables.

**Interactive Activity 5-4: EIGRP Packet Types (5.3.4)**

In this activity, you match the definition to an EIGRP packet type. Use file d3ia-534 on the CD-ROM that accompanies this book to perform this interactive activity.

## EIGRP Metrics and Convergence

EIGRP uses a composite metric value to determine the best path to a destination. This metric is determined from the bandwidth, delay, reliability, and load. *Maximum transmission unit (MTU)* is another value included in routing updates, but it is not a routing metric. The complete formula to calculate the composite metric is as follows:

Metric = [K1 * Bandwidth + (K2 * Bandwidth) / (256 – Load) + K3 * Delay] * [K5 / (Reliability + K4)]

The composite metric formula consists of *K values*: K1 through K5. By default, K1 and K3 are set to 1. K2, K4, and K5 are set to 0. This simplifies the formula to this:

Metric = [K1 * Bandwidth + K3 * delay]

You can change K values with the **metric weights** command. If the K values are changed on one router in the autonomous system, they must be changed to the same values on all routers:

```
Router(config-router)# metric weights tos k1 k2 k3 k4 k5
```

The bandwidth metric is a static value and is displayed in kilobits per second (kbps). Most serial interfaces use the default bandwidth value of 1544 kbps. This metric reflects the bandwidth of a T1 connection. Sometimes the bandwidth value may not reflect the actual physical bandwidth of the interface. Bandwidth influences the metric calculation and, as a result, the EIGRP path selection. If a

56-kbps link is advertised with a 1544-kbps value, it could interfere with convergence as it struggles to cope with the traffic load.

The other metrics used by EIGRP to calculate the cost of a link are delay, reliability, and load. The *delay* metric is a static value based on the type of exit interface. The default value is 20,000 microseconds for Serial interfaces and 100 microseconds for Fast Ethernet interfaces. Table 5-3 lists the delay values.

**Table 5-3    Interface Delay Values**

| Interface | Delay (microseconds) |
| --- | --- |
| 100-Mbps ATM | 100 |
| Fast Ethernet | 100 |
| FDDI | 100 |
| HSSI | 20,000 |
| 16-Mbps Token Ring | 630 |
| Ethernet | 1000 |
| T1 (Serial default) | 20,000 |
| 512 kbps | 20,000 |
| DS0 | 20,000 |
| 56 kbps | 20,000 |

The delay metric does not represent the actual amount of time packets take to reach the destination. Changing the delay value associated with a specific interface alters the metric but does not physically affect the network.

*Reliability* measures how often the link has experienced errors. Unlike delay, reliability updates automatically, depending on the link conditions. It has a value of between 0 and 255. A reliability of 255/255 represents a 100 percent reliable link.

*Load* reflects the amount of traffic using the link. A lower load value is more desirable than a higher value. As an example, 1/255 is a minimally loaded link, and 255/255 is a link that is 100 percent utilized. Figure 5-21 illustrates an EIGRP network, and Example 5-12 shows these values for the network.

**Figure 5-21    EIGRP Network**

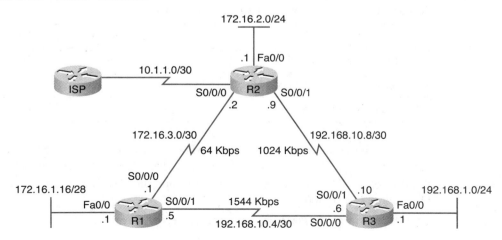

**Example 5-12    EIGRP Metric Values**

```
R1# show interface s0/0/0
Serial0/0/0 is up, line protocol is up
        Hardware is PowerQUICC Serial
        Internet address is 172.16.3.1/30
        MTU 1500 bytes, BW 64 Kbit, DLY 20000 usec,
            reliability 255/255, txload 1/255, rxload 1/255

R1# show interface s0/0/1
Serial0/0/1 is up, line protocol is up
        Hardware is PowerQUICC Serial
        Internet address is 192.168.10.5/30
        MTU 1500 bytes, BW 1544 Kbit, DLY 20000 usec,
            reliability 255/255, txload 1/255, rxload 1/255

R1# show ip protocol
Routing Protocol is "eigrp 1"
        Outgoing update filter list for all interfaces is not set
        Incoming update filter list for all interfaces is not set
        Default networks flagged in outgoing updates
        Default networks accepted from incoming updates
        EIGRP metric weight K1=1, K2=0, K3=1, K4=0, K5=0
        EIGRP maximum hopcount 100
```

The EIGRP topology table uses metrics to maintain values for the following. DUAL uses these values to determine successors and feasible successors:

- *Feasible distance (FD):* Feasible distance is the best EIGRP metric along the path to the destination from the router.

- *Advertised distance (AD):* Advertised distance, also called *reported distance*, is the best metric reported by a neighbor.

The loop-free route with the lowest feasible distance becomes a successor. There can be multiple successors for a destination, depending on the actual topology. A feasible successor is a route with an advertised distance that is less than the feasible distance of a successor. Table 5-4 lists the successor and feasible successor for network Z shown in Figure 5-22.

**Table 5-4    Successor and Feasible Successor**

|  | Feasible Distance | Advertised Distance |
|---|---|---|
| R2 is successor to Network Z. | 15 | 5 |
| R3 is feasible successor to Network Z. | 20 | 6 |
| R4 is a successor to Network Z. | 15 | 5 |

In an EIGRP routing table entry, the word **via** precedes the address of the successor. The feasible distance is the metric listed after the administrative distance of 90. In the following entry, the best path to the 192.168.1.0/24 network is through the next-hop successor's interface 192.168.10.10, and the feasible distance is 3014400:

```
D 192.168.1.0/24 [90/3014400] via 192.168.10.10, 00:00:31, Serial0/0/1
```

**Figure 5-22    Successor and Feasible Successor**

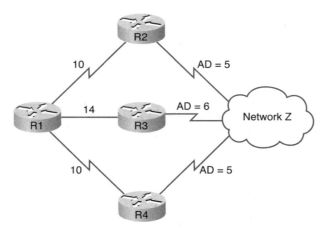

DUAL converges quickly after a change in the topology. DUAL keeps feasible successors in the topology table and promotes the best one to the routing table as a successor route if the original route fails. If no feasible successor exists, the original route moves into active mode, and queries are sent to find a new successor.

### Interactive Activity 5-5: EIGRP Successor (5.3.5)

In this activity, you answer questions about the feasible distance, reported distance, and successor routes. Use file d3ia-535 on the CD-ROM that accompanies this book to perform this interactive activity.

# Implementing EIGRP

Even with all the advanced features of EIGRP, it is relatively simple to configure. It has many similarities to RIPv2. EIGRP is Cisco proprietary and is a routing protocol option between Cisco routers. If non-Cisco routers must be incorporated into the network, you should explore alternative routing protocols.

## Configuring EIGRP

Enabling the EIGRP process requires an autonomous system parameter. This autonomous system parameter can be assigned any 16-bit value and identifies all the routers belonging to a single company or organization. Although EIGRP refers to the parameter as an autonomous system number, it actually functions as a process ID. This autonomous system number is locally significant only and is not the same as the autonomous system number issued and controlled by the Internet Assigned Numbers Authority (IANA). The autonomous system number can have any value between 1 and 65535, but must match on all routers that work within the EIGRP routing process, as shown in Figure 5-23. To enable EIGRP, use the following command:

```
R1(config)# router eigrp AS#
```

**Figure 5-23    EIGRP Autonomous System**

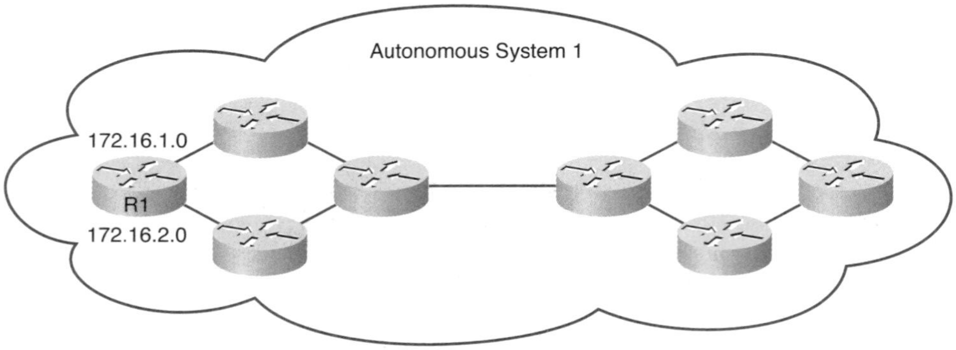

After the EIGRP process has been enabled, network statements for each network to be advertised must be entered. The **network** command tells EIGRP which networks and interfaces participate in the EIGRP process.

Configuring EIGRP on R1 in Figure 5-23 requires the following commands:

```
R1(config)# router eigrp 1
R1(config-router)# network 172.16.0.0
```

The process ID references an instance of EIGRP running in a router. If there were two instances of EIGRP running on the same router at the same time, the process ID, or instance number, would separate and identify each individual process.

To configure EIGRP to advertise only certain subnets, include a *wildcard mask* after the network number. To determine the wildcard mask, subtract the subnet mask from 255.255.255.255. Some versions of the Cisco IOS allow the subnet mask to be specified instead of using the wildcard mask. Even if the subnet mask is used, the **show running-config** command displays the wildcard mask in its output.

Two additional commands complete the typical basic EIGRP configuration. Add the **eigrp log-neighbor-changes** command to view changes in neighbor adjacencies. This feature helps the administrator monitor the stability of the EIGRP network. On serial links that do not match the default EIGRP bandwidth of 1.544 Mbps, add the **bandwidth** command followed by the actual speed of the link expressed in kilobits per second. Inaccurate bandwidth interferes with choosing the best route.

Figure 5-24 illustrates a sample EIGRP network, and Example 5-13 shows the EIGRP configuration for the three routers shown.

**Example 5-13    EIGRP Configuration**

```
R1 Configuration

R1(config)# router eigrp 1
R1(config-router)# network 172.16.0.0
R1(config-router)# network 192.168.10.0
R1(config-router)# exit
R2 Configuration

R2(config)# router eigrp 1
R2(config-router)# network 172.16.0.0
R2(config-router)#
```

```
*Mar  1 07:54:42.475: %DUAL-5-NBRCHANGE: IP-EIGRP(0) 1: Neighbor 172.16.3.1
  (Serial0/0/0) is up: new adjacency
R2(config-router)# network 192.168.10.8 0.0.0.3
R3 Configuration

R3(config)# router eigrp 1
R3(config-router)# network 192.168.10.0
R3(config-router)#
*Mar  1 00:18:11.004: %DUAL-5-NBRCHANGE: IP-EIGRP(0) 1: Neighbor 192.168.10.5
  (Serial0/0/0) is up: new adjacency
*Mar  1 00:18:11.008: %DUAL-5-NBRCHANGE: IP-EIGRP(0) 1: Neighbor 192.168.10.9
  (Serial0/0/1) is up: new adjacency
R3(config-router)# network 192.168.1.0
```

**Figure 5-24    Sample EIGRP Network**

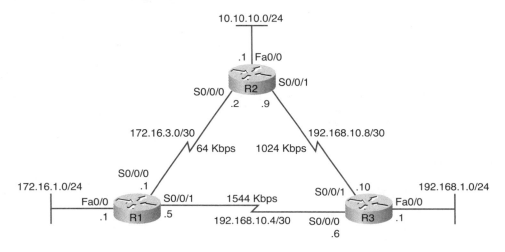

After EIGRP has been enabled, any router configured with EIGRP and the correct autonomous system number can enter the EIGRP network. This means routers with different or conflicting route information can affect and possibly corrupt the routing tables. To prevent this, it is possible to enable authentication within the EIGRP configuration. After neighbor authentication has been configured, the router authenticates the source of all routing updates before accepting them.

EIGRP authentication requires the use of a pre-shared key. EIGRP allows an administrator to manage the keys though a keychain. The configuration of EIGRP authentication consists of two steps: creating the key and enabling authentication to use the key.

## Key Creation

Entering the global configuration command **key chain** *name-of-chain* specifies the name of the keychain and enters the configuration mode for the keychain. The **key** *key-id* syntax identifies the key number and enters the configuration mode for that key ID. The command **key-string** *text* identifies the key string or password. This must be configured to match on all EIGRP routers.

## Enabling Authentication

Once created, the key can be used to enable MD5 authentication for EIGRP. To accomplish this requires that you turn on EIGRP authentication with the following command:

```
ip authentication mode eigrp AS md5
```

After doing so, you must specify the password for an individual autonomous system using the following command:

```
ip authentication key-chain eigrp AS name-of-chain
```

In this command, *AS* specifies the autonomous system of the EIGPR configuration, and *name-of-chain* parameter specifies the keychain that was previously configured. Figure 5-25 illustrates a network using MD5 authentication, and Example 5-14 shows the relevant parts of the running configuration files.

**Figure 5-25   EIGRP MD5 Authentication**

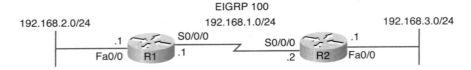

**Example 5-14   EIGRP MD5 Configuration**

```
R1 Configuration

R1# show run
<output omitted>
key chain R1chain
        key 1
                key-string firstkey
        key 2
                key-string secondkey
!
<output omitted>
!
Interface Serial0/0/0
        bandwidth 64
        ip address 192.168.1.1 255.255.255.0
        ip authentication mode eigrp 100 md5
        ip authentication mode key-chain eigrp 100 R1chain

R2 Configuration

R2# show run
<output omitted>
key chain R2chain
        key 1
                key-string secondkey
!
<output omitted>
!
```

```
Interface Serial0/0/0
        bandwidth 64
        ip address 192.168.1.2 255.255.255.0
        ip authentication mode eigrp 100 md5
        ip authentication mode key-chain eigrp 100 R2chain
```

**Lab 5.3: Implementing EIGRP (5.4.1)**

In this lab, you configure EIGRP with MD5 authentication. Refer to the lab in Part II of this *Learning Guide*. You may perform this lab now or wait until the end of the chapter.

## EIGRP Route Summarization

Like RIP, EIGRP automatically summarizes subnetted networks on the classful boundary. EIGRP creates only one entry in the routing table for the summary route. A best path or successor route is associated with the summary route. As a result, all traffic destined for the subnets travels across that one path.

In an enterprise network, the path chosen to reach the summary route might not be the best choice for the traffic that is trying to reach each individual subnet. The only way that all routers can find the best routes for each individual subnet is for neighbors to send subnet information. When default summarization is disabled, updates include subnet information. The routing table installs entries for each of the subnets and also an entry for the summary route. The summary route is called the *parent route*, and the subnet routes are called the *child routes*.

EIGRP installs a Null0 summary route in the routing table for each parent route. The *Null0 interface* indicates that this is not an actual path, but a summary for advertising purposes. If a packet matches one of the child routes, it forwards out the correct interface. If the packet matches the summary route but does not match one of the child routes, it is discarded. Figure 5-26 illustrates EIGRP summary routes, and Example 5-15 shows the summary routes created on R1.

**Figure 5-26    EIGRP Summary Routes**

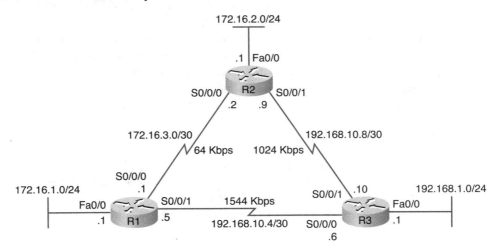

**Example 5-15    EIGRP Summary Routes**

```
R1# show ip route
Codes:  C - connected, S - static, I - IGRP, R - RIP, M - mobile, B - BGP
        D - EIGRP, EX - EIGRP external, O - OSPF, IA - OSPF inter area
        N1 - OSPF NSSA external type 1, N2 - OSPF NSSA external type 2
        E1 - OSPF external type 1, E2 - OSPF external type 2
        i - IS-IS, su - IS-IS summary, L1 - IS-IS level-1, L2 - IS-IS level-2
        ia - IS-IS inter area, * - candidate default, U - per-user static route
        o - ODR, P - periodic downloaded static route

Gateway of last resort is not set

      192.168.10.0/24 is variably subnetted, 3 subnets, 2 masks
D         192.168.10.0/24 is a summary, 00:45:09, Null0
C         192.168.10.4/30 is directly connected, Serial0/0/1
S         192.168.10.8/30 [90/3523840] via 192.168.10.6, 00:44:56, Serial0/0/1
      172.16.0.0/16 is variably subnetted, 4 subnets, 3 masks
D         172.16.0.0/16 is a summary, 00:46:10, Null0
C         172.16.1.0/24 is directly connected, FastEthernet0/0
D         172.16.2.0/24 [90/40514560] via 172.16.3.2, 00:45:09, Serial0/0/0
C         172.16.3.0/24 is directly connected, Serial0/0/0
D      192.168.1.0/24 [90/2172416] via 192.168.10.6, 00:44:55, Serial0/0/1
```

Using default summarization results in smaller routing tables. Turning off the summarization produces larger updates and larger tables. Consideration of the overall network performance and traffic patterns determines whether auto summarization is appropriate.

Use the **no auto-summary** command to disable the default summarization. With auto summarization disabled, all subnets are advertised. An administrator might have a situation in which some of the subnets need to be summarized and some do not. The decision to summarize depends on the placement of the subnets. As an example, four contiguous subnets terminating on the same router are good candidates for summarization.

*Manual summarization* provides a more precise control of EIGRP routes. Using this feature, the administrator determines which subnets on which interfaces are advertised as summary routes. Manual summarization is done on a per-interface basis and gives the network administrator complete control. Figure 5-27 shows a network with manual summarization required, and Example 5-16 shows the configuration. A manually summarized route appears in the routing table as an EIGRP route sourced from a logical, not physical, interface, as follows:

```
D 192.168.0.0/22 is a summary, Null0
```

**Example 5-16    EIGRP Manual Summarization**

```
R3(config)# interface serial 0/0/0
R3(config-if)# ip summary-address eigrp 1 192.168.0.0 255.255.252.0
R3(config-if)# interface serial 0/0/1
R3(config-if)# ip summary-address eigrp 1 192.168.0.0 255.255.252.0
```

**Configuring and Verifying EIGRP and EIGRP Summary Routes (5.4.2)**

In this activity, you configure and verify EIGRP and EIGRP summary routes. Use file d3-542.pka on the CD-ROM that accompanies this book to perform this activity using Packet Tracer.

**Figure 5-27   EIGRP Manual Summarization**

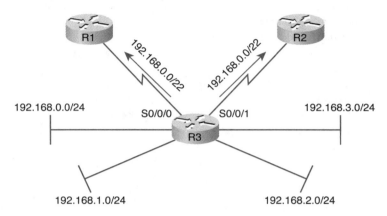

 **Lab 5.4: Configuring Automatic and Manual Route Summarization (5.4.2)**

In this lab, you configure EIGRP with automatic and manual route summarization. Refer to the lab in Part II of this *Learning Guide*. You may perform this lab now or wait until the end of the chapter.

## Verifying EIGRP Operation

Although EIGRP is a relatively simple protocol to configure, it uses sophisticated technologies to overcome the limitations of distance vector routing protocols. It is important to understand these technologies so that you can properly verify and troubleshoot a network configuration that uses EIGRP. Some of the verification commands available are shown in this section, including example output as the commands relate to the network shown in Figure 5-28.

**Figure 5-28   EIGRP Sample Network**

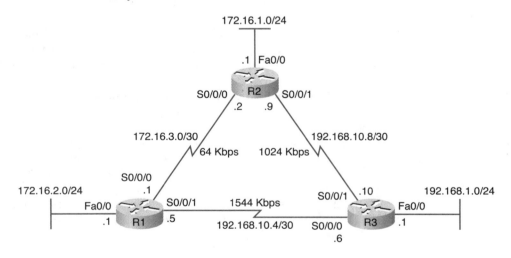

The **show ip protocols** command verifies that EIGRP is advertising the correct networks. It displays the autonomous system number and administrative distance, as shown in Example 5-17.

**Example 5-17    EIGRP Diagnostic Commands: show ip protocols**

```
R1# show ip protocols
Routing Protocol is "eigrp 1"
  Outgoing update filter list for all interfaces is not set
  Incoming update filter list for all interfaces is not set
  Default networks flagged in outgoing updates
  Default networks accepted from incoming updates
  EIGRP metric weight K1=1, K2=0, K3=1, K4=0, K5=0
  EIGRP maximum hopcount 100
  EIGRP maximum metric variance 1
  Redistributing: eigrp 1
  EIGRP NSF-aware route hold timer is 240s
  Automatic network summarization is in effect
  Automatic address summarization:
    192.168.10.0/24 for FastEthernet0/0, Serial0/0/0
      Summarizing with metric 20512000
    172.16.0.0/16 for Serial0/0/1
      Summarizing with metric 28160
  Maximum path: 4
  Routing for Networks:
    172.16.0.0
    192.168.10.0
  Routing Information Sources:
    Gateway          Distance      Last Update
    (this router)          90      00:35:13
    192.168.10.6           90      00:33:48
    Gateway          Distance      Last Update
    172.16.3.2             90      00:33:50
  Distance: internal 90 external 170
```

The **show ip route** command, shown in Example 5-18, verifies that the EIGRP routes are in the routing table. It designates EIGRP routes as D or a D EX, depending on whether they originate within the same autonomous system. Internal EIGRP routes have a default administrative distance of 90.

**Example 5-18    EIGRP Diagnostic Commands: show ip route**

```
R1# show ip route
Codes: C - connected, S - static, R - RIP, M - mobile, B - BGP
       D - EIGRP, EX - EIGRP external, O - OSPF, IA - OSPF inter area
       N1 - OSPF NSSA external type 1, N2 - OSPF NSSA external type 2
       E1 - OSPF external type 1, E2 - OSPF external type 2
       i - IS-IS, su - IS-IS summary, L1 - IS-IS level-1, L2 - IS-IS level-2
       ia - IS-IS inter area, * - candidate default, U - per-user static route
       o - ODR, P - periodic downloaded static route

Gateway of last resort is not set

     192.168.10.0/24 is variably subnetted, 3 subnets, 2 masks
D       192.168.10.0/24 is a summary, 00:37:59, Null0
C       192.168.10.4/30 is directly connected, Serial0/0/1
```

```
D        192.168.10.8/30 [90/21024000] via 192.168.10.6, 00:35:59, Serial0/0/1
         172.16.0.0/16 is variably subnetted, 3 subnets, 3 masks
D        172.16.0.0/16 is a summary, 00:42:00, Null0
C        172.16.1.0/24 is directly connected, FastEthernet0/0
C        172.16.3.0/30 is directly connected, Serial0/0/0
D     192.168.1.0/24 [90/20514560] via 192.168.10.6, 00:35:36, Serial0/0/1
```

The command **show ip eigrp neighbors detail** verifies the adjacencies formed between routers and displays the IP addresses and interfaces of neighbor routers. Example 5-19 shows a sample output from this command.

**Example 5-19    EIGRP Diagnostic Commands: show eigrp neighbors detail**

```
R1# show ip eigrp neighbors detail
IP-EIGRP neighbors for process 1
H   Address              Interface      Hold Uptime    SRTT   RTO  Q  Seq
                                        (sec)          (ms)        Cnt Num
1   192.168.10.6         Se0/0/1          13 00:37:13   20   1140  0  10
    Version 12.4/1.2, Retrans: 0, Retries: 0, Prefixes: 2
0   172.16.3.2           Se0/0/0          13 00:40:07   21   1140  0  13
    Version 12.4/1.2, Retrans: 2, Retries: 0, Prefixes: 2
```

Example 5-20 displays a sample output of the **show ip eigrp topology** command. This command displays successors and all feasible successors and the feasible distance and reported distance.

**Example 5-20    EIGRP Diagnostic Commands: show ip eigrp topology**

```
R1# show ip eigrp topology
IP-EIGRP Topology Table for AS(1)/ID(192.168.10.5)

Codes: P - Passive, A - Active, U - Update, Q - Query, R - Reply,
       r - reply Status, s - sia Status

P 192.168.10.0/24, 1 successors, FD is 20512000
        via Summary (20512000/0), Null0
P 192.168.10.4/30, 1 successors, FD is 20512000
        via Connected, Serial0/0/1
P 192.168.1.0/24, 1 successors, FD is 20514560
        via 192.168.10.6 (20514560/28160), Serial0/0/1
P 192.168.10.8/30, 1 successors, FD is 21024000
        via 192.168.10.6 (21024000/20512000), Serial0/0/1
P 172.16.0.0/16, 1 successors, FD is 28160
        via Summary (28160/0), Null0
P 172.16.1.0/24, 1 successors, FD is 28160
        via Connected, FastEthernet0/0
P 172.16.3.0/30, 1 successors, FD is 20512000
        via Connected, Serial0/0/0
```

The **show ip eigrp interfaces detail** command shown in Example 5-21 verifies which interfaces are using EIGRP. It also provides interface-specific details on the operation of EIGRP.

**Example 5-21    EIGRP Diagnostic Commands: show ip eigrp interfaces detail**

```
R1# show ip eigrp interfaces detail
IP-EIGRP interfaces for process 1

                    Xmit Queue   Mean   Pacing Time   Multicast    Pending
Interface     Peers Un/Reliable  SRTT   Un/Reliable   Flow Timer   Routes
Fa0/0           0      0/0         0        0/1           0           0
  Hello interval is 5 sec
  Next xmit serial <none>
  Un/reliable mcasts: 0/0  Un/reliable ucasts: 0/0
  Mcast exceptions: 0  CR packets: 0  ACKs suppressed: 0
  Retransmissions sent: 0  Out-of-sequence rcvd: 0
  Authentication mode is not set
  Use multicast
Se0/0/0         1      0/0        21        5/190        282          0
  Hello interval is 5 sec
  Next xmit serial <none>
  Un/reliable mcasts: 0/0  Un/reliable ucasts: 4/7
  Mcast exceptions: 0  CR packets: 0  ACKs suppressed: 2
  Retransmissions sent: 2  Out-of-sequence rcvd: 0
  Authentication mode is not set
  Use unicast
Se0/0/1         1      0/0        20        5/190        270          0
  Hello interval is 5 sec
  Next xmit serial <none>

                    Xmit Queue   Mean   Pacing Time   Multicast    Pending
Interface     Peers Un/Reliable  SRTT   Un/Reliable   Flow Timer   Routes
  Un/reliable mcasts: 0/0  Un/reliable ucasts: 2/5
  Mcast exceptions: 0  CR packets: 0  ACKs suppressed: 3
  Retransmissions sent: 0  Out-of-sequence rcvd: 0
  Authentication mode is not set
  Use unicast
```

To obtain information on the number and types of EIGRP packets sent and received, use the **show ip eigrp traffic** command. Example 5-22 shows a sample output from this command.

**Example 5-22    EIGRP Diagnostic Commands: show ip eigrp traffic**

```
R1# show ip eigrp traffic
IP-EIGRP Traffic Statistics for AS 1
  Hellos sent/received: 1941/1179
  Updates sent/received: 11/11
  Queries sent/received: 0/1
  Replies sent/received: 1/0
  Acks sent/received: 6/4
  Input queue high water mark 1, 0 drops
```

```
SIA-Queries sent/received: 0/0
SIA-Replies sent/received: 0/0
Hello Process ID: 108
PDM Process ID: 105
```

One of the primary uses of these **show** commands is to verify the successful formation of EIGRP adjacencies and the successful exchange of EIGRP packets between routers. EIGRP cannot work without forming adjacencies; therefore, you should verify this before any other troubleshooting efforts. If adjacencies appear normal but problems still exist, an administrator should begin troubleshooting using **debug** commands to view real-time information on the EIGRP activities occurring on a router.

Debugging operations use large amounts of bandwidth and router processing power, particularly when debugging a very complex protocol such as EIGRP. These commands provide details that can pinpoint the source of a lost EIGRP route or missing adjacency; however, the use of these commands can also degrade network performance.

Example 5-23 shows a sample debug output from the command **debug eigrp packet**. This command displays transmission and receipt of all EIGRP packets. Careful observation of this output can help pinpoint why EIGRP might not be functioning properly. To understand this output, the troubleshooter must be very familiar with the functionality of EIGRP.

**Example 5-23    EIGRP Diagnostic Commands: debug eigrp packets**

```
R1# debug eigrp packets
EIGRP Packets debugging is on
    (UPDATE, REQUEST, QUERY, REPLY, HELLO, IPXSAP, PROBE, ACK, STUB, SIAQUERY, SIAREPLY)
R1#
*Mar  1 12:22:58.464: EIGRP: Sending HELLO on FastEthernet0/0
*Mar  1 12:22:58.464:    AS 1, Flags 0x0, Seq 0/0 idbQ 0/0 iidbQ un/rely 0/0
*Mar  1 12:23:00.520: EIGRP: Received HELLO on Serial0/0/1 nbr 192.168.10.6
*Mar  1 12:23:00.520:    AS 1, Flags 0x0, Seq 0/0 idbQ 0/0 iidbQ un/rely 0/0 peerQ un/rely 0/0
*Mar  1 12:23:25.300: %LINK-3-UPDOWN: Interface Serial0/0/0, changed state to up
*Mar  1 12:23:25.317: EIGRP: Enqueueing UPDATE on Serial0/0/1 iidbQ un/rely 0/1 serno 10-10
*Mar  1 12:23:25.321: EIGRP: Enqueueing UPDATE on Serial0/0/1 nbr 192.168.10.6 iidbQ un/rely
  0/0 peerQ un/rely 0/0 serno 10-10
*Mar  1 12:23:25.321: EIGRP: Serial0/0/1 multicast flow blocking cleared
*Mar  1 12:23:25.413: EIGRP: Sending HELLO on FastEthernet0/0
*Mar  1 12:23:25.413:    AS 1, Flags 0x0, Seq 0/0 idbQ 0/0 iidbQ un/rely 0/0
*Mar  1 12:23:26.302: %LINEPROTO-5-UPDOWN: Line protocol on Interface Serial0/0/0, changed
  state to up
*Mar  1 12:23:27.720: EIGRP: Received HELLO on Serial0/0/1 nbr 192.168.10.6
*Mar  1 12:23:27.724:    AS 1, Flags 0x0, Seq 0/0 idbQ 0/0 iidbQ un/rely 0/0 peerQ un/rely 0/0

*Mar  1 12:23:29.335: EIGRP: Received HELLO on Serial0/0/0 nbr 172.16.3.2
*Mar  1 12:23:29.335:    AS 1, Flags 0x0, Seq 0/0 idbQ 0/0
*Mar  1 12:23:29.335: %DUAL-5-NBRCHANGE: IP-EIGRP(0) 1: Neighbor 172.16.3.2 (Serial0/0/0) is
  up: new adjacency
*Mar  1 12:23:29.335: EIGRP: Enqueueing UPDATE on Serial0/0/0 nbr 172.16.3.2 iidbQ un/rely
  0/1 peerQ un/rely 0/0
*Mar  1 12:23:29.339: EIGRP: Sending HELLO on Serial0/0/0
*Mar  1 12:23:29.339:    AS 1, Flags 0x0, Seq 0/0 idbQ 0/0 iidbQ un/rely 0/1
```

```
*Mar  1 12:23:29.339: EIGRP: Requeued unicast on Serial0/0/0
*Mar  1 12:23:29.343: EIGRP: Sending UPDATE on Serial0/0/0 nbr 172.16.3.2
*Mar  1 12:23:29.343:    AS 1, Flags 0x1, Seq 14/0 idbQ 0/0 iidbQ un/rely 0/0 peerQ un/rely
   0/1
*Mar  1 12:23:29.347: EIGRP: Enqueueing UPDATE on Serial0/0/0 iidbQ un/rely 0/1 serno 1-10
*Mar  1 12:23:29.351: EIGRP: Enqueueing UPDATE on Serial0/0/0 nbr 172.16.3.2 iidbQ un/rely
   0/0 peerQ un/rely 0/1 serno 1-10
```

To observe information on how DUAL processes information and migrates successor routes to the routing table, use the command **debug eigrp fsm**. The finite state machine displays feasible successor activity to determine whether routes are discovered, installed, or deleted by EIGRP. Example 5-24 shows a sample output from this command.

**Example 5-24   EIGRP Diagnostic Commands: debug eigrp fsm**

```
R1# debug eigrp fsm
EIGRP FSM Events/Actions debugging is on
*Mar  1 12:31:54.443: %LINK-3-UPDOWN: Interface Serial0/0/0, changed state to up
*Mar  1 12:31:54.447: DUAL: lostroute: do nothing
*Mar  1 12:31:54.447: DUAL: dest(172.16.3.0/30) not active
*Mar  1 12:31:54.447: DUAL: rcvupdate: 172.16.3.0/30 via Connected metric 20512000/0
*Mar  1 12:31:54.447: DUAL: Find FS for dest 172.16.3.0/30. FD is 4294967295, RD is
  4294967295 found
*Mar  1 12:31:54.447: DUAL: RT installed 172.16.3.0/30 via 0.0.0.0
*Mar  1 12:31:54.447: DUAL: Send update about 172.16.3.0/30.  Reason: metric chg
*Mar  1 12:31:54.451: DUAL: Send update about 172.16.3.0/30.  Reason: new if
*Mar  1 12:31:54.527: %DUAL-5-NBRCHANGE: IP-EIGRP(0) 1: Neighbor 172.16.3.2 (Serial0/0/0) is
  up: new adjacency
*Mar  1 12:31:54.587: %SYS-5-CONFIG_I: Configured from console by console
*Mar  1 12:31:54.595: DUAL: dest(192.168.1.0/24) not active
*Mar  1 12:31:54.595: DUAL: rcvupdate: 192.168.1.0/24 via 172.16.3.2 metric 21026560/20514560
*Mar  1 12:31:54.595: DUAL: Find FS for dest 192.168.1.0/24. FD is 20514560, RD is 20514560
*Mar  1 12:31:54.595: DUAL: 192.168.10.6 metric 20514560/28160
*Mar  1 12:31:54.595: DUAL: 172.16.3.2 metric 21026560/20514560 found Dmin is 20514560
*Mar  1 12:31:54.599: DUAL: RT installed 192.168.1.0/24 via 192.168.10.6
*Mar  1 12:31:54.599: DUAL: dest(192.168.10.0/24) not active
*Mar  1 12:31:54.599: DUAL: rcvupdate: 192.168.10.0/24 via 172.16.3.2 metric
  21024000/20512000
*Mar  1 12:31:54.599: DUAL: Find FS for dest 192.168.10.0/24. FD is 20512000, RD is 20512000
*Mar  1 12:31:54.599: DUAL: 0.0.0.0 metric 20512000/0
*Mar  1 12:31:54.599: DUAL: 172.16.3.2 metric 21024000/20512000 found Dmin is 20512000
*Mar  1 12:31:54.599: DUAL: RT installed 192.168.10.0/24 via 0.0.0.0
*Mar  1 12:31:55.445: %LINEPROTO-5-UPDOWN: Line protocol on Interface Serial0/0/0, changed
  state to up
```

**Interactive Activity 5-6: EIGRP Troubleshooting Commands (5.4.3)**

In this activity, you match the EIGRP troubleshooting commands to the information they provide. Use file d3ia-543 on the CD-ROM that accompanies this book to perform this interactive activity.

**Packet Tracer**
☐ **Activity**

### Verifying and Troubleshooting EIGRP Operation (5.4.3)

In this activity, you explore the various EIGRP configuration and troubleshooting commands. Use file d3-543.pka on the CD-ROM that accompanies this book to perform this activity using Packet Tracer.

## Issues and Limitations of EIGRP

Although EIGRP is a powerful and sophisticated routing protocol, several considerations limit its use:

- Does not work in a multivendor environment because it is a Cisco proprietary protocol

- Works best with a flat network design

- Must share the same autonomous system among routers and cannot be subdivided into groups

- Can create very large routing tables, which requires large update packets and large amounts of bandwidth

- Uses more memory and processor power than RIP

- Works inefficiently when left on the default settings

- Requires administrators with advanced technical knowledge of the protocol and the network

EIGRP offers the best of distance vector routing, while using additional features typically associated with link-state routing protocols, including bounded updates and neighbor adjacencies. Successful implementation of the many features of EIGRP requires careful configuration, monitoring, and troubleshooting.

### Interactive Activity 5-7: Critical Thinking: EIGRP (5.5.2)

In this activity, you answer a series of question about a supplied EIGRP network. Use file d3ia-552 on the CD-ROM that accompanies this book to perform this interactive activity.

# Summary

Enterprise networks are hierarchical to facilitate the flow of information. Many different topologies exist, including star, extended star, partial mesh, and full mesh. The full-mesh design provides the most reliability but is also the most expensive to install and support.

Regardless of the topology used, routing the information between networks requires that routers have information on routes to these networks. These routes can be learned dynamically using routing protocols, or they may be statically configured. Default routes are usually configured to provide a path for information to follow if no specific route is known.

Routing protocols can be either distance vector or link state in nature. RIP and EIGRP are two common distance vector routing protocols. RIPv1 broadcasts its entire routing table every 30 seconds, and RIPv2 multicasts its table. RIPv1 does not support classless routing, but RIPv2 does. Both RIPv1 and RIPv2 use hop count as their metric and are slow to converge. This causes the formation of routing loops.

EIGRP is a Cisco proprietary distance vector routing protocol that uses a composite metric involving many factors, including bandwidth and delay. EIGRP maintains multiple tables and uses different packet types to establish and maintain neighbor relationships. EIGRP uses DUAL to calculate the successor and feasible successor routes. EIGRP uses bounded updates to notify neighbor routers of any changes in network topology instead of regularly broadcasting its entire routing table. EIGRP is fast to converge, and DUAL prevents the formation of routing loops.

EIGRP makes use of a process ID known as an autonomous system to identify routers that are participating in the same instance. Even though EIGRP is easy to configure, it is difficult to maintain and optimize.

# Activities and Labs

This summary outlines the activities and labs you can perform to help reinforce important concepts described in this chapter. You can find the activity and Packet Tracer files on the CD-ROM accompanying this book. The complete hands-on labs appear in Part II.

**Interactive activities on the CD-ROM:**

Interactive Activity 5-1: RIP Characteristics (5.2.2)

Interactive Activity 5-2: Characteristics of RIP and EIGRP (5.3.2)

Interactive Activity 5-3: EIGRP Tables (5.3.3)

Interactive Activity 5-4: EIGRP Packet Types (5.3.4)

Interactive Activity 5-5: EIGRP Successor (5.3.5)

Interactive Activity 5-6: EIGRP Troubleshooting Commands (5.4.3)

Interactive Activity 5-7: Critical Thinking: EIGRP (5.5.2)

**Packet Tracer activities on the CD-ROM:**

Packet Tracer Activity: Investigating Connected, Static, and Dynamic Routing (5.1.3)

Packet Tracer Activity: Configuring Static Routes (5.1.4)

Packet Tracer Activity: Configuring Default Routes (5.1.5)

Packet Tracer Activity: Routing Between Discontiguous Networks (5.2.4)

Packet Tracer Activity: Troubleshooting RIPv2 (5.2.5)

Packet Tracer Activity: Configuring and Verifying EIGRP and EIGRP Summary Routes (5.4.2)

Packet Tracer Activity: Verifying and Troubleshooting EIGRP Operation (5.4.3)

**Hands-on labs in Part II of this book:**

Lab 5-1: Designing and Creating a Redundant Network (5.1.2)

Lab 5-2: Configuring RIPv2 with VLSM and Default Route Propagation (5.2.3)

Lab 5-3: Implementing EIGRP (5.4.1)

Lab 5-4: EIGRP Configuring Automatic and Manual Route Summarization (5.4.2)

# Check Your Understanding

Complete all the review questions listed here to check your understanding of the topics and concepts in this chapter. Appendix A, "Check Your Understanding and Challenge Questions Answer Key," lists the answers.

1. What measures can a network designer implement to improve the performance of an enterprise network? (Choose all that apply.)

    A. Redundancy

    B. QoS

    C. Packet filtering

    D. Hierarchical network design

2. What type of network topology provides the most reliability?

    A. Star

    B. Extended star

    C. Partial mesh

    D. Full mesh

3. What is the administrative distance?

4. When EIGRP learns a route from the autonomous system in which that route originates, how is that route identified in the routing table?

   A. E

   B. E EX

   C. D

   D. D EX

5. Why is static routing normally used on a stub network?

6. What type of route can provide a backup for the primary WAN route?

   A. default route

   B. dynamic route

   C. static route

   D. floating static route

7. How often does RIPv2 send out its routing table?

   A. RIPv2 uses only triggered updates.

   B. Every 30 seconds.

   C. When asked by a neighbor router.

   D. Every 60 seconds.

8. What happens when a RIP-enabled router interface first comes online?

9. What affect would issuing the following commands have on the routing process?

   ```
   R1(config)# router rip

   R1(config-router)# passive-interface ethernet0
   ```

   A. Ethernet0 will no longer send RIP routing updates, but will accept them.

   B. Ethernet0 will no longer send or receive RIP routing updates.

   C. Ethernet0 will no longer receive RIP routing updates, but will send them.

   D. Ethernet0 will no longer send RIP or receive RIPv1 updates, but will send and receive RIPv2 updates.

10. What command can be used to see all of the routes known to RIP?

    A. **show ip route rip**

    B. **show ip rip route**

    C. **show ip rip database**

    D. **show ip rip protocol**

11. EIGRP maintains which of the following tables? (Choose all that apply.)

    A. Adjacency

    B. Neighbor

    C. Topology

    D. Routing

**12.** Which EIGRP packet type is responsible for establishing adjacencies with neighboring routers?

   A.  Acknowledgment

   B.  Hello

   C.  Query

   D.  Reply

   E.  Update

**13.** EIGRP uses which type of packet transmission? (Choose all that apply.)

   A.  Unicast

   B.  Multicast

   C.  Broadcast

**14.** By default, what factors contribute to the EIGRP composite metric? (Choose all that apply.)

   A.  Bandwidth

   B.  Delay

   C.  Reliability

   D.  Load

**15.** Which Layer 4 protocol is used by EIGRP?

## Challenge Questions and Activities

These questions require a deeper application of the concepts covered in this chapter. You can find the answers in Appendix A.

   **1.** You have been hired by AnyCompany as a network consultant. The company has recently taken over three new firms and has increased the size of their network from 20 to more than 200 Cisco routers. During the integration of the company networks, all routers were configured to use RIPv1. The company is now finding that their network is extremely slow and not always accessible. What might be the cause of these problems, and what solution would you suggest?

   **2.** AnyCompany has decided to join three of their remote office networks together so that employees can share information. Each of the three offices is using a 10.20.x.0/24 network, where x is 1, 2, or 3 depending on the office. All company routers are running RIPv1 and are a mixture of equipment from different vendors. All three of these networks are linked through a service provider network that is using 172.27.20.0/24 for their network. Each router has a network statement for both the 10.20.x.0 and the 172.27.20.0 networks. Unfortunately, the different branch offices cannot route data to each other. What might be the cause of this problem, and what would you do to correct it?

# CHAPTER 6

# Routing with a Link-State Protocol

## Objectives

Upon completion of this chapter, you should be able to answer the following questions:

- How does OSPF routing function?

- What is necessary to plan a network using OSPF?

- How is a single-area OSPF network designed and configured?

- What are multiprotocol environments, and what issues are associated with them?

## Key Terms

This chapter uses the following key terms. You can find the definitions in the Glossary.

Open Shortest Path First (OSPF) Protocol    page 208

open standard    page 208

SPF algorithm    page 211

Dijkstra's algorithm    page 211

SPF tree    page 211

topology database    page 211

Adjacency    page 212

Hello protocol    page 213

dead interval    page 213

designated router (DR)    page 213

backup designated router (BDR)    page 213

DROther    page 213

router ID    page 213

loopback interface    page 214

Broadcast multiaccess networks    page 215

Point-to-point networks    page 215

Nonbroadcast multiaccess (NBMA) networks    page 215

Area 0    page 216

autonomous system    page 217

flapping    page 217

Area Border Router (ABR)    page 217

Autonomous System Boundary Router (ASBR)    page 217

wildcard mask    page 218

area ID    page 218

simple password authentication    page 221

key    page 221

key ID    page 221

fractional T1    page 223

reference bandwidth    page 224

external type route (E2)    page 229

legacy    page 233

administrative distance (AD)    page 233

Enterprise networks need a reliable and scalable routing protocol to maintain communications and select the best path. Link-state routing protocols such as the Open Shortest Path First (OSPF) Protocol are ideally suited to the needs of enterprise networks. Network technicians configure and verify OSPF to support basic routing functionality and authentication. Network engineers configure a hierarchical design for OSPF to access the Internet and for improved routing efficiency.

Part II of this book includes the corresponding labs for this chapter.

# Routing Using the OSPF Protocol

*Open Shortest Path First (OSPF) Protocol* is the most widely used link-state interior gateway routing protocol in enterprise networks. This section describes the operation of link-state protocols in general and OSPF specifically. The structure of OSPF networks, the metrics used, and the process of establishing neighbor adjacencies are covered.

## Link-State Protocol Operation

Enterprise networks and ISPs use link-state protocols because of their hierarchical design and ability to scale for large networks. Link-state routing protocols such as OSPF work well for larger hierarchical networks where fast convergence is important. Distance vector routing protocols, such as Routing Information Protocol (RIP), are usually not the best choice for a complex enterprise network.

OSPF is an example of a link-state routing protocol. OSPF is an *open standard* routing protocol, developed by the Internet Engineering Task Force (IETF) to support IP traffic. OSPF is a classless interior gateway protocol (IGP). It divides the network into different sections, which are referred to as areas. This division allows for greater scalability. Working with multiple areas allows the network administrator to selectively enable route summarization and to isolate routing issues within a single area.

Link-state routing protocols, such as OSPF, do not send frequent periodic updates of the entire routing table. Instead, after the network converges, a link-state protocol sends an update only when a change in the topology occurs, such as a link going down. This can be caused by physical problems with the local router interface, a problem with an interface on the other end of the link, the data link protocol, and other issues.

In Figure 6-1, when a link on R1 goes down, R1 sends an update to R2 informing it of the inactive link. R2 then sends updates to the other OSPF routers to which it is attached. The link-state information is exchanged until all routers participating in the OSPF area become aware of the change. The routers adjust their routing information accordingly. In addition to event-driven or triggered updates, OSPF performs a full update every 30 minutes.

With a distance vector protocol such as RIP, each router exchanges its entire routing table with every adjacent router every 30 seconds, whether there was a change in the network topology or not.

Compared to distance vector protocols, link-state routing protocols require the following:

- More complex network planning and configuration
- Increased router resources
- More memory for storing multiple tables
- More CPU and processing power for the complex routing calculations

**Figure 6-1    Link-State Protocol Operation**

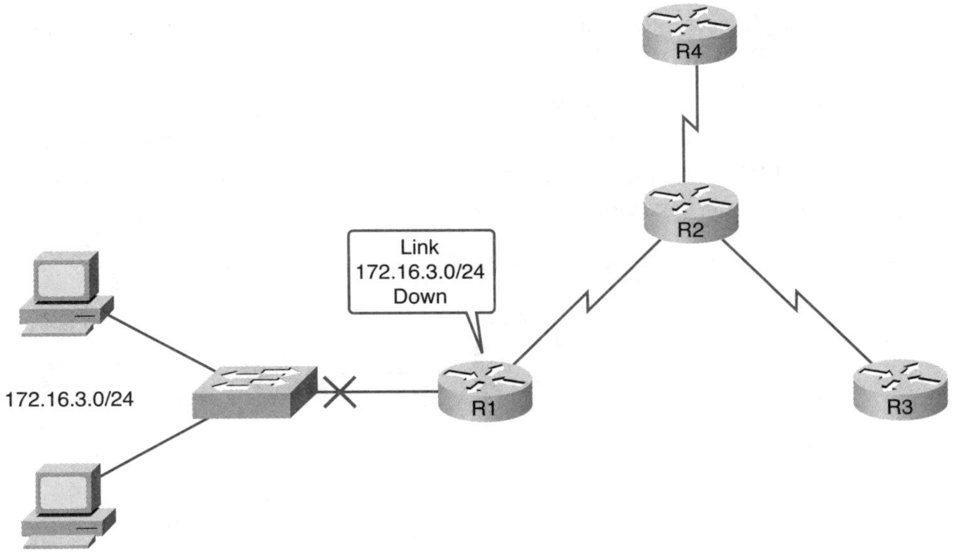

With the high performance of routers available today, however, these requirements are usually not a problem.

**Note**

Some older routers such as the Cisco 2500 series might not have enough DRAM memory to support OSPF operations, and some IOS images might not support OSPF.

Routers running RIP receive updates from their immediate neighbors, but with no details about the network as a whole. Routers running OSPF generate a complete map of the network from their own viewpoint. This map allows them to quickly determine loop-free alternative paths in the case of a network link failure. The overall OSPF topology is similar to having a single map of a country. People in different locations in the country, like each router, have a different view of the map from their own perspective.

Unlike RIP and Enhanced Interior Gateway Routing Protocol (EIGRP), OSPF does not automatically summarize at major network boundaries. In addition, the Cisco implementation of OSPF uses bandwidth to determine the cost of a link. RIP uses hop count, and EIGRP uses bandwidth and delay by default.

## OSPF Metrics and Convergence

OSPF uses a cost metric to determine the best path. A link with higher bandwidth results in a lower cost. The lowest-cost route to a destination is the most desirable path.

The router enabled with OSPF trusts a metric based on bandwidth more than one based on hop count to establish the shortest path. Within the Cisco IOS, the administrative distance of OSPF is 110, compared to RIP's administrative distance of 120. OSPF is given a lower administrative distance because the calculated cost metric is considered more accurate than RIP's hop count metric.

**Note**

Although the *SP* in OSPF stands for shortest path, the path chosen might not actually be the shortest in terms of distance. With OSPF, the shortest path is considered the fastest path.

In Figure 6-2, host H1 needs to send a packet to host H2. If the network is using RIP, the desirability of a route is based solely on hop count (how many routers or hops are between source and destination). Because hop count is the only metric, the packet takes the path with the fewest hops and travels from R1 to R2 over the very slow 56-kbps link.

If the network is using OSPF, the desirability of a route is based on link bandwidth or cost. With OSPF, the packet takes the path from R1 to R3 and then to R2. This path has more hops, but the links are T1 (1.544 Mbps) bandwidth, which is significantly faster than the 56-kbps link, even though the packets must go through two links.

**Figure 6-2    RIP and OSPF Metrics and Route Selection**

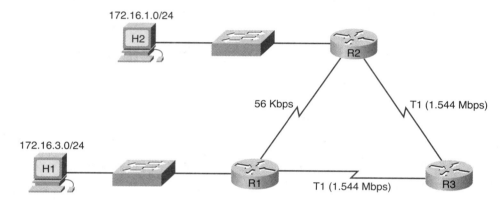

**Interactive Activity 6-1: Identifying the Characteristics of RIP and OSPF (6.1.1)**

In this activity, you indicate whether the characteristic describes RIP or OSPF. Use file d3ia-611 on the CD-ROM that accompanies this book to perform this interactive activity.

With OSPF, the cost metric for an individual link is based on its bandwidth or speed. The metric for a particular destination network is the sum of all link costs in the path. If there are multiple paths to the network, the path with the lowest overall cost is the preferred path and is placed in the routing table.

The equation used to calculate the cost of an OSPF link is as follows:

Cost = 100,000,000 / Bandwidth of link in bps

In other words, the OSPF link cost of an interface is one hundred million divided by the bandwidth of the interface in bits per second (bps). The configured bandwidth on an interface provides the bandwidth value for the equation. Determine the bandwidth of an interface using the **show interfaces** command.

Using this equation presents a problem with link speeds of greater than 100 Mbps, such as Gigabit Ethernet. Comparing a FastEthernet and a Gigabit link, they both calculate to a value of 1. The routing protocol treats them equally even though the Gigabit link is ten times as fast as the FastEthernet link. One way to compensate for this is to configure the interface cost value manually with the **ip ospf cost** command.

Table 6-1 shows common digital link speeds and the associated OSPF cost calculation. If you calculate the cost for the links in Figure 6-2, you can see that the R1-R2 path with a 56-kbps link has a cost of 1785. The R1-R3-R2 path with two T1 links has a much lower cost of 128 (2 × 64), so it is the preferred route from H1 to H2.

**Table 6-1    Interface Types and OSPF Cost Calculation**

| Interface Type | Cost ($10^8$ / bps) |
|---|---|
| FastEthernet (100 Mbps) and faster | $10^8$ / 100,000,000 bps = 1 |
| Ethernet (10 Mbps) | $10^8$ / 10,000,000 bps = 10 |
| E1 | $10^8$ / 2,048,000 bps = 48 |
| T1 | $10^8$ / 1,544,000 bps = 64 |
| 512 kbps | $10^8$ / 512,000 bps = 195 |
| 256 kbps | $10^8$ / 256,000 bps = 390 |
| 128 kbps | $10^8$ / 128,000 bps = 781 |
| 64 kbps | $10^8$ / 64,000 bps = 1562 |
| 56 kbps | $10^8$ / 56,000 bps = 1785 |

OSPF routers within a single area advertise information about the status of their links to their neighbors. Messages called link-state advertisements (LSA) are used to advertise this status information.

When an OSPF router receives LSAs describing all the links within an area, it uses the *SPF algorithm*, also called *Dijkstra's algorithm*, to generate a topological tree, or map of the network. Each router running the algorithm identifies itself as the root of its own SPF tree. Starting from the root, the *SPF tree* identifies the shortest path to each destination network and the total cost of each path.

The OSPF link-state or *topology database* stores the SPF tree information. The router installs the shortest path to each network in the routing table.

Convergence occurs when all routers

- Receive information about every destination on the network
- Process this information with the SPF algorithm
- Update their routing tables

Figure 6-3 shows an OSPF router network with the R1 router SPF tree path information on how to get from R1's local network to Networks A, B, and C on the other three routers. Notice that R1 has two possible paths (routes) to network C on Router R4. The R1-R3-R4 path with a cost of 15 is the preferred route over the R1-R4 path with a cost of 20.

Each router builds an SPF table of information similar to the one for R1 but with itself as the root of the tree and information on how to get to each of the other networks.

### Interactive Activity 6-2: Identifying the Path Through an OSPF Network (6.1.2)

In this activity, you identify the path that packets will take from H1 to H2 in an OSPF network using link cost. Use file d3ia-612 on the CD-ROM that accompanies this book to perform this interactive activity.

**Figure 6-3    SPF Tree and Paths**

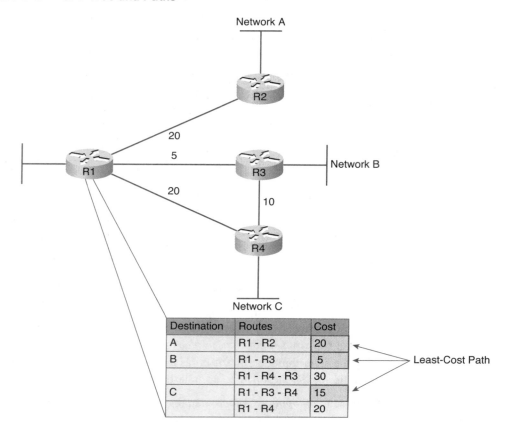

| Destination | Routes | Cost |
|---|---|---|
| A | R1 - R2 | 20 |
| B | R1 - R3 | 5 |
|  | R1 - R4 - R3 | 30 |
| C | R1 - R3 - R4 | 15 |
|  | R1 - R4 | 20 |

Least-Cost Path

## OSPF Neighbors and Adjacencies

With OSPF, link-state updates are sent when network changes occur. But how does a router know when a neighboring router fails? OSPF routers establish and maintain neighbor relationships, or adjacencies, with other connected OSPF routers. *Adjacency* is an advanced form of neighboring between routers that are willing to exchange routing information. When routers initiate an adjacency with neighbors, an exchange of link-state updates begins. Routers reach a full state of adjacency when they have synchronized views on their link-state database.

The router goes through the following state changes before becoming fully adjacent with its neighbor:

- **Init**: The router received an initial hello packet from its neighbor. When a router receives a hello packet from a neighbor, it lists the sending router ID in its own hello packet as an acknowledgment.

- **2-way**: Bidirectional communication is established in that each router has seen the hello packet from each other. This state is attained when the router receiving the hello packet sees its own router ID within the neighbor field of the hello packet. At this state, a router decides whether to become fully adjacent with this neighbor.

- **Exstart**: The routers establish a master-slave relationship and choose the initial sequence number for adjacency formation. Between two routers, the router with the higher router ID becomes the master and starts the exchange.

- **Exchange**: OSPF routers exchange database descriptor (DBD) packets that contain LSA headers only. The DBD describes the contents of the entire link-state database. Each DBD packet has a sequence number that can be incremented only by the master.

- **Loading**: Based on the information provided by the DBDs, routers send link-state request packets for more specific information. The neighbor provides the requested link-state information in link-state update packets. This enables the router to have the exact data needed to complete the recalculation of the least cost/shortest paths without burdening the network link for the whole database.

- **Full**: All the router and network LSAs are exchanged, and the router databases are fully synchronized.

The OSPF *Hello protocol* is used to initially establish and maintain adjacencies. The Hello protocol sends very small data packets, known as hello packets, to directly connected OSPF routers on the multicast address of 224.0.0.5. The packets are sent every 10 seconds on Ethernet and broadcast links and every 30 seconds for nonbroadcast links. Router settings are also included in the hello packets.

The settings in the hello packet include the hello interval, *dead interval*, and network type, and the authentication type and authentication data if configured. For any two routers to form an adjacency, all settings must match. The router records neighbor adjacencies discovered in an OSPF adjacencies database.

Full is the normal adjacency state for an OSPF router. If a router is stuck in another state, this indicates a problem such as mismatched settings. The only exception to this is the 2-way state. In a broadcast environment, such as the Ethernet network shown in Figure 6-4, a router achieves a full state only with a *designated router (DR)* and a *backup designated router (BDR)*. All other neighbors are viewed in the 2-way state.

The purpose of the DR and BDR is to reduce the number of updates sent, unnecessary traffic flow, and processing overhead on all routers. This reduction is accomplished by requiring all routers to accept updates from the DR only. On broadcast network segments, there is only one DR and BDR. All other routers must have a connection to the DR and BDR. When a link fails, the router with information about the link sends the information to the DR, using the multicast address 224.0.0.6. The DR is responsible for distributing the change to all other OSPF routers, using multicast 224.0.0.5. In addition to reducing the number of updates sent across the network, this process ensures that all routers receive the same information at the same time from a single source.

The BDR ensures that there is no single point of failure. Like the DR, the BDR listens to 224.0.0.6 and receives all updates sent to the DR. If the DR fails, the BDR immediately takes over as DR, and a new BDR is elected. Any router not elected as the DR or BDR is known as a *DROther*.

In Figure 6-4, Router R1 forms an adjacency with the DR and BDR only. R1 forwards all route information to the DR and BDR using an LSA. The DR forwards the LSAs containing the route information provided by R1 to all other routers.

Within a local network, the router with the highest *router ID* is elected the DR. The second highest is elected as the BDR. The router ID is used to identify a specific router in an OSPF network. The router ID is sent in all LSA packets so that the receiving router knows who the sending router is.

The router ID is an IP address determined as follows:

1. The value configured with the **router-id** command. This is the preferred method of setting a router ID because it avoids configuring loopback interfaces and gives the administrator manual control over the router ID. To configure **router-id**, the router must be in OSPF routing protocol configuration mode.

**Figure 6-4    DR/BDR Interaction with Other OSPF Routers**

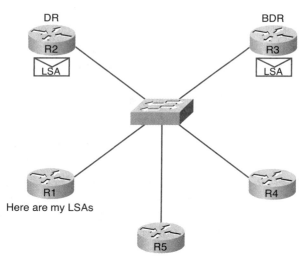

2. If no value is set with the **router-id** command, the highest configured IP address on any *loopback interface*. Because loopback addresses do not experience physical link problems, their status is always up/up, and they do not cause issues with routing table recalculations.

3. If no loopback interface is configured, the highest IP address on any active physical interface.

You can view the router ID by using the following **show** commands:

- **show ip protocols**

- **show ip ospf**

- **show ip ospf interface**

In some cases, an administrator might want specific routers to be the DR and BDR. These might be routers with more processing power or lighter traffic load. An administrator can force the DR and BDR election by configuring a priority using the **ip ospf priority number** interface configuration command.

By default, OSPF routers have a priority value of 1. If the priority value is changed on a router, the highest priority setting wins the election for DR, regardless of highest router ID. The highest value that can be set for router priority is 255. A value of 0 signifies that the router is ineligible to be DR or BDR. Referring to Figure 6-5, Router R3 has the highest priority of 10 and becomes the DR. Router R4, with a priority of 5, becomes the BDR. R1 has its priority set to 0 and will not participate in the DR/BDR election. Router R2, with the default priority of 1, becomes a DROther.

**Note**

Setting the priority number or setting the router ID is preferred over the use of loopback interfaces for controlling the DR/BDR election. The priority number is independent of any IP addresses, and thus offers more flexibility in the manual selection of the DR/BDR by the network administrator. In addition, using a priority number avoids configuring loopback interfaces and accounting for them in the routing table.

**Figure 6-5    Router Priority Can Control Which Routers Become DR and BDR**

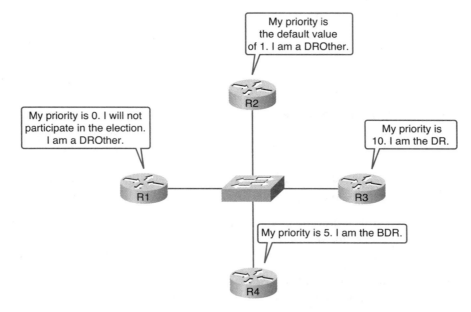

A DR/BDR election is required only on broadcast-type OSPF networks. OSPF detects the link type in use and, if there are multiple routers, determines whether a DR/BDR election is necessary. Link types identified by OSPF include the following:

- *Broadcast multiaccess networks*, such as Ethernet

- *Point-to-point networks*, such as serial and T1/E1

- *Nonbroadcast multiaccess (NBMA) networks*, such as Frame Relay and ATM

On broadcast multiaccess networks, such as Ethernet, the number of neighbor relationships can become large; therefore, a DR election is required. Figure 6-6 shows a typical multirouter Ethernet network.

**Figure 6-6    Broadcast Multiaccess Network: Ethernet Example**

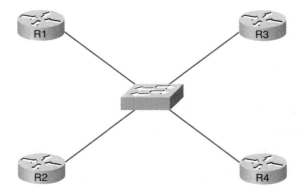

On point-to-point networks, the establishment of full adjacencies is not an issue because, by definition, there can be only two routers on the link. The DR election is not necessary and does not apply. Figure 6-7 shows a typical point-to-point WAN link, such as a T1, where no DR is required.

**Figure 6-7   Point-to-Point Network: T1 Example**

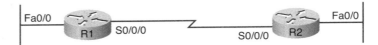

On NBMA networks, OSPF can run in two modes:

- **Simulated broadcast environment**: An administrator can define the network type as broadcast, and the network simulates a broadcast model by electing a DR and a BDR. In this environment, it is generally recommended that the administrator choose the DR and BDR by configuring the priority of the router. This ensures that the DR and BDR have full connectivity to all other neighboring routers. Neighboring routers are also statically defined using the **neighbor** command in the OSPF configuration mode.

- **Point-to-multipoint environment**: In this environment, each nonbroadcast network is treated as a collection of point-to-point links, and a DR is not elected. This environment also requires that neighboring routers are statically defined.

Figure 6-8 shows a typical NBMA network, such as Frame Relay, where a DR might be needed, depending on the type of environment (broadcast or point to point).

**Figure 6-8   Nonbroadcast Multiaccess Network: Frame Relay Example**

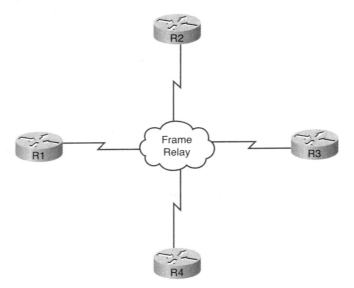

**Interactive Activity 6-3: Determining OSPF Router ID and Designated Router (6.1.3)**

In this activity, you determine the router ID for each router and the designated router for each network. Use file d3ia-613 on the CD-ROM that accompanies this book to perform this interactive activity.

# OSPF Areas

All OSPF networks begin with *Area 0*, also called the backbone area. As the network is expanded, other areas can be created that are adjacent to Area 0. These other areas can be assigned any number, up to 4,294,967,295 ($2^{32}$). The maximum number of routers allowed in one area is 50.

**Note**

The area number is a 4-byte (32-bit) number. This allows areas other than Area 0 to be labeled with an IP address, such as a summary network number, rather than a raw number. This is sometimes easier on the administrator who has multiple areas to manage.

OSPF has a two-layer hierarchical design. Area 0 exists at the top, and all other areas are located at the next level. All nonbackbone areas must directly connect to Area 0. This group of areas creates an OSPF *autonomous system*.

The operation of OSPF within an area is different from operation between that area and the backbone area. For example, when there is a change in the topology, only those routers in the affected area receive the LSA and run the SPF algorithm. Summarization of network information usually occurs between areas. This helps to decrease the size of routing tables in the backbone. Summarization also isolates changes and unstable, or *flapping*, links to a specific area in the routing domain. Flapping refers to a route that consistently goes up and down.

A router that connects an area to the backbone area is called an *Area Border Router (ABR)*. A router that connects an area to a different routing protocol, such as EIGRP or Border Gateway Protocol (BGP), redistributes static routes into the OSPF area, or connects the OSPF autonomous system to another autonomous system, is called an *Autonomous System Boundary Router (ASBR)*. Figure 6-9 shows an OSPF autonomous system with three areas. Areas 1 and 51 connect to backbone Area 0 through the use of ABRs. An ASBR connects this entire multiarea autonomous system to another autonomous system running EIGRP.

**Figure 6-9    OSPF ABR and ASBR Router Placement**

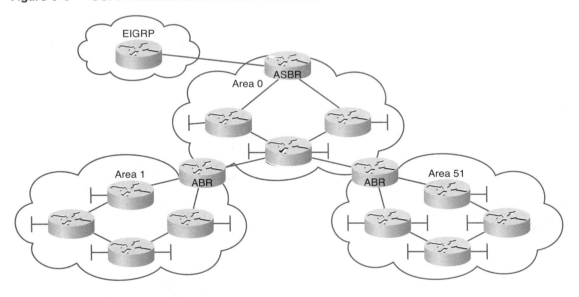

**Interactive Activity 6-4: Matching OSPF Terms and Descriptions (6.1.4)**

In this activity, you match the term to the best description. Use file d3ia-614 on the CD-ROM that accompanies this book to perform this interactive activity.

# Implementing Single-Area OSPF

This section provides instructions for configuring and verifying basic single-area OSPF on Cisco routers. Also covered are OSPF authentication and tuning parameters.

## Configuring Basic OSPF in a Single Area

Configuration of basic OSPF is not a complex task. It requires only two steps. The first step enables the OSPF routing process. The second step identifies the networks to advertise.

**How To ○**

**Step 1:**   Enable OSPF with the following command:

```
router(config)# router ospf <process-id>
```

The process ID is chosen by the administrator and can be any number from 1 to 65535. The process ID is only locally significant and does not have to match the ID of other OSPF routers. This process number is it not an autonomous system number as is the case with EIGRP.

**Step 2:**   Advertise networks with the following command:

```
router(config-router)# network <network-address> <wildcard-mask> area <area-id>
```

The **network** command has the same function as it does in other IGP routing protocols. It identifies the interfaces that are enabled to send and receive OSPF packets. This statement identifies the networks to include in OSPF routing updates.

The OSPF **network** command uses a combination of network address and *wildcard mask*. The network address, along with the wildcard mask, specifies the interface address, or range of addresses, that will be enabled for OSPF.

The *area ID* identifies the OSPF area to which the network belongs. Even if there are no areas specified, there must be an Area 0. In a single-area OSPF environment, the area is always 0.

Figure 6-10 shows a three-router OSPF network with three LANs and three WANs. Because every router has a WAN link to every other router, this is known as a full-mesh design. Example 6-1, Example 6-2, and Example 6-3 show the network statement used to configure Routers R1, R2, and R3, respectively.

**Figure 6-10   OSPF Topology Attached Networks**

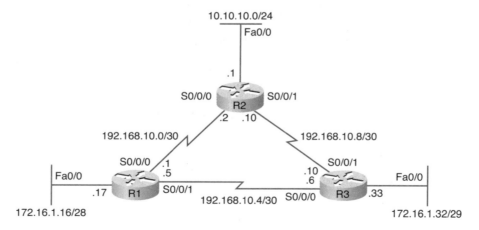

**Example 6-1  R1 OSPF network Configuration Commands**

```
R1(config)# router ospf 1
R1(config-router)# network 172.16.1.16  0.0.0.15 area 0
R1(config-router)# network 192.168.10.0  0.0.0.3 area 0
R1(config-router)# network 192.168.10.4  0.0.0.3 area 0
```

**Example 6-2  R2 OSPF network Configuration Commands**

```
R2(config)# router ospf 1
R2(config-router)# network 10.10.10.0  0.0.0.255 area 0
R2(config-router)# network 192.168.10.0  0.0.0.3 area 0
R2(config-router)# network 192.168.10.8  0.0.0.3 area 0
```

**Example 6-3  R2 OSPF network Configuration Commands**

```
R3(config)# router ospf 1
R3(config-router)# network 172.16.1.32  0.0.0.7 area 0
R3(config-router)# network 192.168.10.4  0.0.0.3 area 0
R3(config-router)# network 192.168.10.8  0.0.0.3 area 0
```

The OSPF **network** statement requires the use of the wildcard mask. When used for network summarization, or supernetting, the wildcard mask is the inverse of the subnet mask.

To determine the wildcard mask for a network or subnet, just subtract the decimal subnet mask for the interface from the all -255s mask (255.255.255.255). As an example, an administrator wants to advertise the 10.10.10.0/24 subnet in OSPF. The subnet mask for this Ethernet interface is /24 or 255.255.255.0. Subtract the subnet mask from the all -255s mask to get the wildcard mask:

> All -255s mask: 255.255.255.255
>
> Subnet mask:      − 255.255.255.0
>
> _____
>
> Wildcard mask:   0 . 0 .  0 .255

The resulting OSPF **network** statement is this:

```
Router(config-router)# network 10.10.10.0 0.0.0.255 area 0
```

The following three examples of OSPF **network** commands show an example interface IP address and the process of creating the OSPF wildcard mask given the interface IP address and slash format (/xx) mask.

**Scenario 1**

```
R1(config-router)# network 172.16.4.0  0.0.0.255 area  0
```

Interface IP:     172.16.4.1 /24

Network:          172.16.4.0 /24

All -255s mask: 255.255.255.255

Subnet mask:   −255.255.255.0

Wildcard mask:   _____

            0 . 0 .0  .255

### Scenario 2

```
R1(config-router)# network 172.16.1.16 0.0.0.15 area  0
```

Interface IP:    172.16.1.17 /28

Network:        172.16.1.16 /28

All -255s mask: 255.255.255.255

Subnet mask:   −255.255.255.240

Wildcard mask:  ─────────────
                0 .  0 .  0 .15

### Scenario 3

```
R1(config-router)# network 192.168.10.4  0.0.0.3 area  0
```

Interface IP:    192.168.10.6 /30

Network:        192.168.10.4 /30

All -255s mask: 255.255.255.255

Subnet mask:   −255.255.255.252

Wildcard mask:  ─────────────
                0 .  0 .  0 . 3

**Note**

Instead of specifying a range of addresses that coincide with the subnet, specify the interface (host) IP address and use a 0.0.0.0 wildcard mask in the **network** statement. Doing this limits OSFP advertisements to that specific interface and address, because all 32 bits of the address must match.

**Interactive Activity 6-5: Determining the Subnet Mask and Wildcard Mask for OSPF (6.2.1)**

In this activity, you determine the subnet mask and wildcard mask required to advertise the specified network addresses in OSPF. Use file d3ia-621 on the CD-ROM that accompanies this book to perform this interactive activity.

**Lab 6-1: Configuring and Verifying Single-Area OSPF (6.2.1)**

In this lab, you configure and verify single-area point-to-point OSPF. Refer to the hands-on lab in Part II of this *Learning Guide*. You may perform this lab now or wait until the end of the chapter.

## Configuring OSPF Authentication

Like other routing protocols, the default configuration of OSPF exchanges information between neighbors in plain text. This poses potential security threats to a network. A hacker on a network could use packet-sniffing software to capture and read OSPF updates and determine network information.

To eliminate this potential security problem, configure OSPF authentication between routers. When authentication is enabled in an area, routers share information only if the authentication information matches.

With *simple password authentication*, configure each router with a password, called a *key*. This method provides only a basic level of security because the key passes between routers in plaintext form. It is just as easy to view the key as it is the plaintext.

A more secure method of authentication is Message Digest 5 or MD5. It requires a key and a *key ID* on each router. The key must match for the neighboring router interfaces. The router uses an algorithm that processes the key, the OSPF packet, and the key ID to generate an encrypted number. Each OSPF packet includes that encrypted number. A packet sniffer cannot be used to obtain the key because it is never transmitted.

Example 6-4 shows how to configure MD5 on a router.

**Example 6-4  OSPF MD5 Authentication Configuration Commands for R1 and R3**

```
Router R1
R1(config)# interface serial0/0/0
R1(config-if)# ip address 10.1.1.1 255.255.255.0
R1(config-if)# ip ospf message-digest-key 10 md5 areapassword

R1(config)# router ospf 18
R1(config-router)# network 10.1.1.0  0.0.0.255 area 0
R1(config-router)# area 0 authentication message-digest

Router R3
R3(config)# interface serial0/0/0
R3(config-if)# ip address 10.1.1.2 255.255.255.0
R3(config-if)# ip ospf message-digest-key 10 md5 areapassword

R3(config)# router ospf 25
R3(config-router)# network 10.1.1.0  0.0.0.255 area 0
R3(config-router)# area 0 authentication message-digest
```

Figure 6-11 shows how authentication encrypts updates sent between OSPF routers. The **ip ospf message-digest-key** command must be used on all router interfaces that participate in OSPF routing.

**Figure 6-11   OSPF Router Authentication**

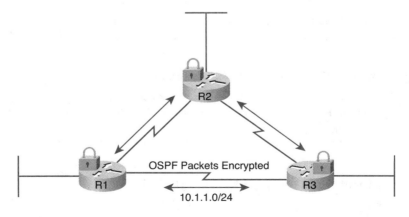

**Lab 6-2: Configuring OSPF Authentication (6.2.2)**

In this lab, you configure and verify single-area point-to-point OSPF authentication using MD5. Refer to the hands-on lab in Part II of this *Learning Guide*. You may perform this lab now or wait until the end of the chapter.

# Tuning OSPF Parameters

In addition to performing the basic configuration of OSPF, administrators often need to modify, or tune, certain OSPF parameters. Parameters include specifying the DR and BDR and modifying the bandwidth value.

## Specifying the DR and BDR

An example is when a network administrator needs to specify which routers become the DR and the BDR. Setting the interface priority or the router ID on specific routers accomplishes this requirement.

The router selects the DR based on the highest value of any one of the following parameters, in the sequence listed:

1. **Interface priority**: The interface priority is set with the **priority** command, as follows:

   ```
   R1(config)# interface fastethernet 0/0
   R1(config-if)# ip ospf priority 50
   ```

2. **Router ID**: The router ID is set with the OSPF **router-id configuration** command, as follows:

   ```
   R1(config)# router ospf 1
   R1(config-router)# router-id 10.1.1.1
   ```

3. **Highest loopback address**: The loopback interface with the highest IP address is used as the router ID by default. OSPF favors loopback interfaces because they are logical interfaces and not physical interfaces. Logical interfaces are always up. Configuration of a loopback follows:

   ```
   R1(config)# interface loopback 1
   R1(config-router)# ip address 10.1.1.1 255.255.255.255
   ```

4. **Highest physical interface address**: The router uses the highest active IP address from one of its interfaces as the router ID. This option poses a problem if interfaces go down or are reconfigured.

After changing the ID of a router or interface priority, reset neighbor adjacencies. Use the **clear ip ospf process** command. This command ensures that the new values take effect.

**Lab 6-3: Controlling a DR/BDR Election (6.2.3)**

In this lab, you configure OSPF loopback addresses in a multiaccess topology to control DR/BDR election. Refer to the hands-on lab in Part II of this *Learning Guide*. You may perform this lab now or wait until the end of the chapter.

## Modifying Bandwidth Values

Bandwidth is another parameter that often requires modification. On Cisco routers, the bandwidth value on most serial interfaces defaults to 1.544 Mbps, the speed of a T1. This bandwidth value determines the cost of the link but does not actually affect its speed.

In some circumstances, an organization receives a *fractional T1* from the service provider. One-fourth of a full T1 connection is 384 kbps and is an example of a fractional T1. The IOS assumes a T1 bandwidth value on serial links even though the interface is actually only sending and receiving at 384 kbps. This assumption results in improper path selection because the routing protocol determines that the link is faster than it is.

When a serial interface is not actually operating at the default T1 speed, the interface requires manual modification. Configure both sides of the link to have the same value.

In OSPF, modification using the **bandwidth interface** command or the **ip ospf cost interface** command achieves the same result. Both commands specify an accurate value for use by OSPF to determine the best route.

The **bandwidth** command modifies the bandwidth value used to calculate the OSPF cost metric. To directly modify the cost of an interface, use the **ip ospf cost** command.

Example 6-5 shows the use of the **bandwidth** command on Router R1 to set the actual bandwidth of the R1 router interfaces in Figure 6-12. The S0/0/0 interface is set to 64 kbps, and the S0/0/1 interface is set to 256 kbps. Without the use of the **bandwidth** command, these interfaces default to T1 or faster speeds. The routing protocol would think the links are faster than they actually are, which could result in improper routing decisions. Setting the bandwidth on R1 S0/0/1 to 256 results in a cost of 390 for that interface/link.

**Example 6-5  R1 OSPF bandwidth Configuration Commands**

```
R1(config)# interface serial 0/0/0
R1(config-if)# bandwidth 64
R1(config)# interface serial 0/0/1
R1(config-if)# bandwidth 256
```

**Figure 6-12   Configuring OSPF Bandwidth and Cost**

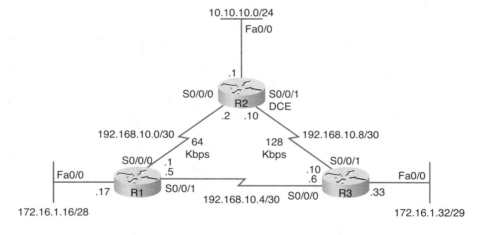

Example 6-6 shows the use of the **ip ospf cost** command on Router R3 to directly set the cost of S0/0/0 to 390, instead of using the **bandwidth** command.

**Example 6-6  R3 OSPF cost Configuration Commands**

```
R3(config)# interface serial 0/0/0
R3(config-if)# ip ospf cost 390
```

Another parameter related to the OSPF cost metric is the *reference bandwidth*, which is used to calculate interface cost, also referred to as the link cost.

The bandwidth value calculation of each interface uses the equation 100,000,000 / bandwidth. 100,000,000, or $10^8$, is known as the reference bandwidth.

A problem exists with links of higher speeds, such as Gigabit Ethernet and 10 Gigabit Ethernet links. Using the default reference bandwidth of 100,000,000 results in interfaces with bandwidth values of 100 Mbps and higher all having the same OSPF cost of 1.

To obtain more accurate cost calculations, it might be necessary to adjust the reference bandwidth value. The reference bandwidth is modified using the OSPF command **auto-cost reference-bandwidth**.

When this command is necessary, use it on all routers so that the OSPF routing metric remains consistent. The new reference bandwidth is specified in terms of megabits per second. To set the reference bandwidth to 10 Gigabit speed, use the value of 10000.

 **Lab 6-4: Configuring OSPF Parameters (6.2.3)**

In this lab, you configure OSPF link cost in a point-to-point topology to influence routing decisions. Refer to the hands-on lab in Part II of this *Learning Guide*. You may perform this lab now or wait until the end of the chapter.

## Verifying OSPF Operation

Once configured, OSPF has several commands available that verify proper operation.

When troubleshooting OSPF networks, use the **show ip ospf neighbor** command to verify that the router has formed an adjacency with its neighboring routers. Example 6-7 shows the output of this command for the R1 router in Figure 6-13. Notice the neighbor ID of R2 is loopback 0 on that router (10.10.5.5). This is the highest router ID, so it becomes the DR with a full adjacency. Router R3 with the lowest router ID is a DROther and is in 2-way state.

**Example 6-7  R1 show ip ospf neighbor Command Output**

```
R1(config)# show ip ospf neighbor
Neighbor ID    Pri    State         Dead Time    Address        Interface
10.10.5.5      1      FULL/DR       00:00:37     192.168.1.2    FastEthernet0/0
10.10.1.6      1      2WAY/DROther  00:00:22     192.168.1.3    FastEthernet0/0
```

Information shown in Example 6-7 includes the following:

- **Neighbor ID**: The router ID of the neighbor

- **Pri**: The priority of the router interface

- **State**: The state of the neighbor relationship

- **Dead time**: The amount of time remaining without receiving a hello packet before the router declares the neighbor dead

- **Address**: The IP address of the interface of the neighbor

- **Interface**: The interface of this router that formed the adjacency with the neighbor

**Figure 6-13   OSPF Neighbors**

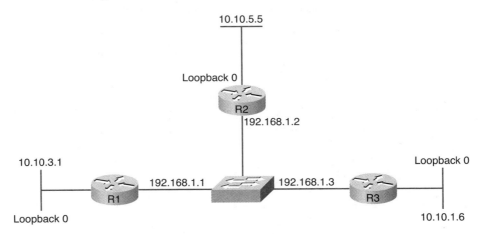

If the router ID of the neighboring router is not displayed, or if it does not show a state of full, the two routers have not formed an OSPF adjacency. If a router is a DROther, adjacency occurs if the state is full or 2-way. If this is a multiaccess Ethernet network, DR and BDR labels display after FULL/ in the State column.

Two routers may not form an OSPF adjacency in the following instances:

- The subnet masks do not match, causing the routers to be on separate networks.
- OSPF hello or dead timers do not match.
- OSPF network types do not match.
- There is a missing or incorrect OSPF network command.

Other **show** commands are also useful in verifying OSPF operation. See the OSPF topology diagram in Figure 6-14 and the following examples.

**Figure 6-14   OSPF show Commands Topology**

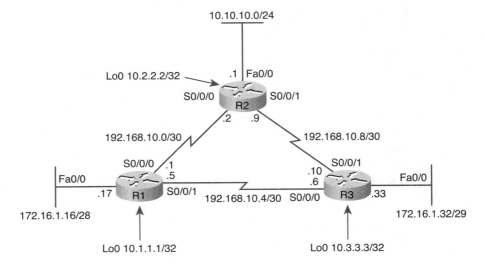

Example 6-8 displays the output from the **show ip protocols** command on R1. This command displays information such as the router ID, the networks that OSPF is advertising, and the IP addresses of adjacent neighbors.

**Example 6-8  R1 show ip protocols Command Output**

```
R1# show ip protocols
Routing Protocol is "ospf 1"
  Outgoing update filter list for all interfaces is not set
  Incoming update filter list for all interfaces is not set
  Router ID 10.1.1.1
  Number of areas in this router is 1. 1 normal 0 stub 0 nssa
  Maximum path: 4
  Routing for Networks:
    172.16.1.16 0.0.0.15 area 0
    192.168.10.0 0.0.0.3 area 0
    192.168.10.4 0.0.0.3 area 0
  Routing Information Sources:
    Gateway         Distance      Last Update
    10.2.2.2          110         00:11:43
    10.3.3.3          110         00:11:43
  Distance: (default is 110)
```

Example 6-9 displays the output from the **show ip ospf** command on R1. This command displays the router ID and details about the OSPF process, timers, and area information. It also shows the last time the SPF algorithm executed.

**Example 6-9  R1 show ip ospf Command Output**

```
R1# show ip ospf
<output omitted>
Routing Process "ospf 1" with ID 10.1.1.1
Start time: 00:00:19.540, Time elapsed: 11:31:15:776
Supports only single TOS (TOS0) routes
Supports opaque LSA
Supports Link-Local Signaling (LLS)
Supports area transit capability
Router is not originating router-LSAs with maximum metric
Initial SPF schedule delay 5000 msecs
Minimum hold time between two consecutive SPFs 10000 msecs
Maximum wait time between two consecutive SPFs 10000 msecs
Incremental-SPF disabled
Minimum LSA interval 5 secs
Minimum LSA arrival 1000 msecs
Area BACKBONE0
    Number of interfaces in this area is 3
Area has no authentication
SPF algorithm last executed 11:30:31.628 ago
SPF algorithm executed 5 times
```

Example 6-10 displays the output from the **show ip ospf interface** command on R1. This command displays information such as router ID, network type, cost, and timer settings.

**Example 6-10   R1 show ip ospf interface Command Output**

```
R1# show ip ospf interface
Serial0/0/1 is up, line protocol is up
  Internet Address 192.168.10.5/30, Area 0
  Process ID 1, Router ID 10.1.1.1, Network Type POINT_TO_POINT, Cost: 64
  Transmit Delay is 1 sec, State POINT_TO_POINT,
  Timer intervals configured, Hello 10, Dead 40, Wait 40, Retransmit 5
  Neighbor Count is 1, Adjacent neighbor count is 1
    Adjacent with neighbor 10.3.3.3
  Suppress hello for 0 neighbor(s)

Serial0/0/0 is up, line protocol is up
  Internet Address 192.168.10.1/30, Area 0
  Process ID 1, Router ID 10.1.1.1, Network Type POINT_TO_POINT, Cost: 64
  Transmit Delay is 1 sec, State POINT_TO_POINT,
  Timer intervals configured, Hello 10, Dead 40, Wait 40, Retransmit 5
  Neighbor Count is 1, Adjacent neighbor count is 1
    Adjacent with neighbor 10.2.2.2
  Suppress hello for 0 neighbor(s)

FastEthernet0/0 is up, line protocol is up
  Internet Address 172.16.1.17/28, Area 0
  Process ID 1, Router ID 10.1.1.1, Network Type BROADCAST, Cost: 1
  Transmit Delay is 1 sec, State DR, Priority 1
  Designated Router (ID) 10.1.1.1, Interface address 172.16.1.17
  No backup designated router on this network
  Timer intervals configured, Hello 10, Dead 40, Wait 40, Retransmit 5
  Neighbor Count is 0, Adjacent neighbor count is 0
  Suppress hello for 0 neighbor(s)
```

Example 6-11 displays the output from the **show ip route** command on R1. This command verifies that each router is sending and receiving routes via OSPF.

**Example 6-11   R1 show ip route Command Output**

```
R1# show ip route
Codes: C - connected, S - static, I - IGRP, R - RIP, M - mobile, B - BGP
       D - EIGRP, EX - EIGRP external, O - OSPF, IA - OSPF inter area
       N1 - OSPF NSSA external type 1, N2 - OSPF NSSA external type 2
       E1 - OSPF external type 1, E2 - OSPF external type 2, E - EGP
       i - IS-IS, L1 - IS-IS level-1, L2 - IS-IS level-2, ia - IS-IS inter area
       * - candidate default, U - per-user static route, o - ODR
       P - periodic downloaded static route

Gateway of last resort is not set
     10.0.0.0/8 is variably subnetted, 2 subnets, 2 masks
C       10.1.1.1/32 is directly connected, Loopback0
```

```
O        10.10.10.0/24 [110/65] via 192.168.10.2, 00:01:02, Serial0/0/0
      172.16.0.0/16 is variably subnetted, 2 subnets, 2 masks
C        172.16.1.16/28 is directly connected, FastEthernet0/0
O        172.16.1.32/29 [110/65] via 192.168.10.6, 00:01:12, Serial0/0/1
      192.168.10.0/30 is subnetted, 3 subnets
C        192.168.10.0 is directly connected, Serial0/0/0
C        192.168.10.4 is directly connected, Serial0/0/1
O        192.168.10.8 [110/128] via 192.168.10.6, 00:01:12, Serial0/0/1
                     [110/128] via 192.168.10.2, 00:01:02, Serial0/0/0
```

**Interactive Activity 6-6: Analyzing show ip route Output from an OSPF Router (6.2.4)**

In this activity, you use the **show ip route** output from an OSPF router to answer questions. Use file d3ia-624 on the CD-ROM that accompanies this book to perform this interactive activity.

**Lab 6-5: Configuring and Verifying Point-to-Point and Multiaccess OSPF (6.2.4)**

In this lab, you configure and verify point-to-point and multiaccess OSPF networks, including tuning parameters. Refer to the hands-on lab in Part II of this *Learning Guide*. You may perform this lab now or wait until the end of the chapter.

# Using Multiple Routing Protocols

This section discusses issues associated with the use of more than one protocol in the enterprise. Issues and limitations of OSPF are presented, as is the process for configuring OSPF default routes and summarization.

## Configuring and Propagating a Default Route

Most networks connect to other networks through the Internet. OSPF provides routing information about networks within an autonomous system. OSPF must also provide information about reaching networks outside of the autonomous system.

Sometimes administrators configure static routes on certain routers to provide information that is not received via a routing protocol. Configuring static routes on all routers in a large network is cumbersome. An easier method is to configure a default route that points to the Internet connection for a network.

With OSPF, an administrator configures this route on an Autonomous System Boundary Router (ASBR). The ASBR is also often called the Autonomous System Border Router. The ASBR connects the OSPF network to an outside network. As soon as the default route is entered in the routing table of the ASBR, it can be configured to advertise that pathway to the rest of the OSPF network. This process informs every router within the autonomous system of the default route and spares the administrator the work of configuring static routes on every router in the network. Figure 6-15 shows the ASBR router with a default route to the ISP. This route can be sent to all the other routers in the OSPF autonomous system so that it does not need to be configured on each one.

**Figure 6-15    Enterprise Autonomous System and Default Route Propagation**

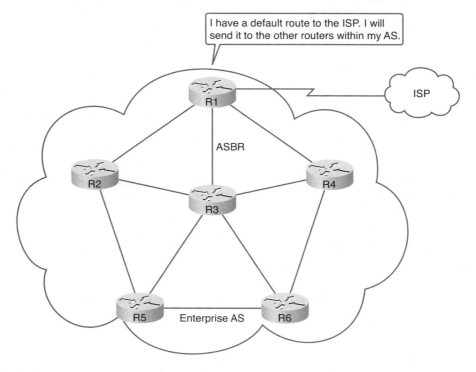

To configure a router to distribute a default route into the OSPF network, follow these two steps:

**Step 1.**    Configure the ASBR with a default route:

```
R1(config)# ip route 0.0.0.0 0.0.0.0 serial 0/0/0
```

The default static route statement can specify an interface or the next hop IP address.

**Step 2.**    Configure the ASBR to propagate the default route to other routers. By default, OSPF does not inject the default route into its advertisements even when the route exists in its routing table:

```
R1(config)# router ospf 1
R1(config-router)# default-information originate
```

The routing tables of the other routers in the OSPF domain should now have a gateway of last resort and an entry to the 0.0.0.0 /0 network in their routing tables. The default route injects into the OSPF domain so that it appears as an *external type route (E2)* in the routing tables of the other routers.

Figure 6-16 shows a sample topology where a default route needs to be configured on R1 and propagated to R2. Example 6-12 and Example 6-13 show the R1 and R2 **show ip route** output before a default route is configured on R1 and propagated to R2. R1 and R2 have nowhere to forward unknown traffic.

**Figure 6-16    Sample Topology for Default Route Configuration**

**Example 6-12    R1 show ip route Command Output Before Default Route Is Configured**

```
R1# show ip route
<output omitted>

Gateway of last resort is not set
     192.168.10.0/30 is subnetted, 1 subnets
C       192.168.10.0 is directly connected, Serial0/0/0
O    10.10.10.0/24 [110/782] via 192.168.10.2, 00:01:02, Serial0/0/0
C       209.165.200.224 is directly connected, Serial0/0/1
```

**Example 6-13    R2 show ip route Command Output Before Default Route Is Configured on R1**

```
R2# show ip route
<output omitted>
Gateway of last resort is not set
     192.168.10.0/30 is subnetted, 1 subnets
C       192.168.10.0 is directly connected, Serial0/0/0
     10.10.10.0/24 is subnetted, 1 subnets
C       10.10.10.0 is directly connected, FastEthernet0/0
```

Example 6-14 and Example 6-15 show the R1 and R2 **show ip route** output after a default route is configured on R1 and propagated to R2. R1 now has a static route to the Internet, and the gateway of last resort is set to 0.0.0.0. R1 is configured to send the default route to other OSPF routers. R2 receives the default routing information from R1 and now has an OSPF E2 (external type 2) route in its routing table, and its gateway of last resort is now set to 192.168.10.1, the IP address of the R1 S0/0/0 interface. R1 now forwards unknown traffic out its S0/0/1 interface toward the ISP, and R2 now forwards unknown traffic out its S0/0/0 interface toward R1. R1 will then forward it to the ISP.

**Example 6-14    R1 show ip route Command Output After Default Route Is Configured**

```
R1# show ip route
<output omitted>
Gateway of last resort is 0.0.0.0 to network 0.0.0.0
     192.168.10.0/30 is subnetted, 1 subnets
C       192.168.10.0 is directly connected, Serial0/0/0
O    10.10.10.0/24 [110/782] via 192.168.10.2, 00:01:02, Serial0/0/0
C       209.165.200.224 is directly connected, Serial0/0/1
S*   0.0.0.0/0 is directly connected, Serial0/0/1
```

**Example 6-15    R2 show ip route Command Output After Default Route Is Configured and Propagated from R1**

```
R2# show ip route
<output omitted>
Gateway of last resort is 192.168.10.1 to network 0.0.0.0
     192.168.10.0/30 is subnetted, 1 subnets
C       192.168.10.0 is directly connected, Serial0/0/0
     10.10.10.0/24 is subnetted, 1 subnets
C       10.10.10.0 is directly connected, FastEthernet0/0
O*E2    0.0.0.0/0 [110/1] via 192.168.10.1, 00:00:34, Serial0/0/0
```

**Lab 6-6: Configuring and Propagating an OSPF Default Route (6.3.1)**

In this lab, you configure an OSPF default route and propagate it to other routers in the OSPF area through the routing protocol. Refer to the hands-on lab in Part II of this *Learning Guide*. You may perform this lab now or wait until the end of the chapter.

## Configuring OSPF Summarization

With OSPF, route summarization of contiguous networks can be done inside an area (intra-area), between adjacent areas (inter-area), or between autonomous systems. Most commonly, summarization is performed on an ABR. To facilitate OSPF summarization, group IP addresses in a network area. For example, in a single OSPF area, allocate four contiguous network segments, such as the following:

- 192.168.0.0/24

- 192.168.1.0/24

- 192.168.2.0/24

- 192.168.3.0/24

It is possible to summarize and advertise the four networks as one supernet of 192.168.0.0 /22, as shown in Figure 6-17. Doing this reduces the number of networks that advertise throughout the OSPF domain. It also reduces memory requirements and the number of entries in the router updates.

**Figure 6-17    OSPF Route Summarization**

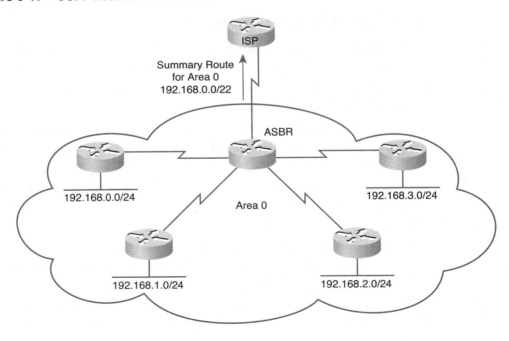

In addition, summary routes reduce the issue of flapping routes. By default, every time a route flaps, a link-state update is propagated throughout the entire domain. This updating can create a lot of traffic and processing overhead.

When a router is using a summary route, it uses a single, supernet address to represent several routes. Only one of the routes included within the summary must actually be up for the router to advertise the summary route. If one or more of the routes is flapping, the router continues to advertise the more stable summary route only. It does not forward updates about the individual routes. Any packets forwarded to the flapping route while the route is down are just dropped at the summarizing router.

To configure an OSPF ASBR router to summarize these networks, enter the following command in router configuration mode:

```
area 0 range 192.168.0.0 255.255.252.0
```

Specify the area in which the networks are summarized and the starting network number and summary mask.

> **Note**
>
> Interarea route summarization is configured on ABRs and applies to routes from within the autonomous system. To take advantage of summarization, network numbers in areas should be assigned in a contiguous way to be able to combine these addresses into one range. Summary routes between autonomous systems are configured on the ASBR.

 **Lab 6-7: Configuring OSPF Summarization (6.3.2)**

In this lab, you configure OSPF summarization to reduce the size of routing updates. Refer to the hands-on lab in Part II of this *Learning Guide*. You may perform this lab now or wait until the end of the chapter.

## OSPF Issues and Limitations

OSPF is a scalable routing protocol. It can converge quickly and operate within very large networks. There are, however, some issues to consider when using it.

OSPF must maintain multiple databases and therefore requires more router memory and CPU capabilities than distance vector routing protocols.

The Dijkstra algorithm requires CPU cycles to calculate the best path. If the OSPF network is complex and unstable, the algorithm consumes significant resources when recalculating frequently. Routers running OSPF are typically more powerful and more expensive.

To avoid excessive use of router resources, use a strict hierarchical design to divide the network into smaller areas. All areas must maintain connectivity to Area 0. If not, they might lose connectivity to other areas.

OSPF can be challenging to configure if the network is large and the design is complex. In addition, interpreting the information contained in the OSPF databases and routing tables requires a good understanding of the technology.

Despite the issues and limitations of OSPF, it is still the most widely used link-state routing protocol within an enterprise. The following summarizes the main advantages and disadvantages of OSPF.

Advantages of OSPF include the following:

- Uses bandwidth as a metric.
- Converges quickly using triggered updates.

- Limits routing loops with consistent view of network topology.

- Routing decisions based on latest information.

- Minimizes link-state database for fewer SPF calculations.

- Maps the topology of an area on each router.

- Supports classless interdomain routing (CIDR) and variable-length subnet masking (VLSM).

- Hierarchical use of areas provides design flexibility.

Disadvantages of OSPF include the following:

- Requires more router memory and processing power

- Requires more complex and expensive implementation

- Requires an administrator who understands the protocol

- Floods the network initially with LSAs, noticeably degrading network performance

## Using Multiple Protocols in the Enterprise

For various reasons, organizations might choose different routing protocols. For example, a network administrator may choose different routing protocols for different sections of a network, based on *legacy* equipment or available resources. Also, two companies that merge may have configured their networks using different routing protocols and still need to communicate with each other.

When multiple routing protocols exist on a single router, a router can learn of a destination from multiple sources. There must be a predictable method for the router to choose which route to view as the most desirable pathway and place it in the routing table. Figure 6-18 shows a RIP network and an OSPF network interconnected by two border routers. These routers must run both the OSPF and RIP routing protocols.

In cases where the metrics of one protocol do not match up with the metrics of another protocol, such as with RIP and OSPF, a process called route redistribution can be used. The metrics of the distributed protocol are manipulated to create protocol compatibility.

When a router learns of a single network from multiple sources, it uses the *administrative distance (AD)* to determine which route it prefers. The Cisco IOS assigns all routing information methods an AD.

If a router learns of a particular subnet by way of RIP and OSPF, the OSPF-learned route is the one that it chooses for the routing table. Its AD is lower and, therefore, more desirable. The code at the beginning of the routing table entry indicates the source of the route, or how it was learned. Each code associates with a specific AD.

Table 6-2 shows route sources sorted by AD. The ones most commonly encountered in the enterprise network are connected and static routes and those learned via internal routing protocols EIGRP, OSPF, and RIP. External BGP routes are found on border routers and ISP routers.

**Figure 6-18    Multiple Routing Protocols Between Organizations**

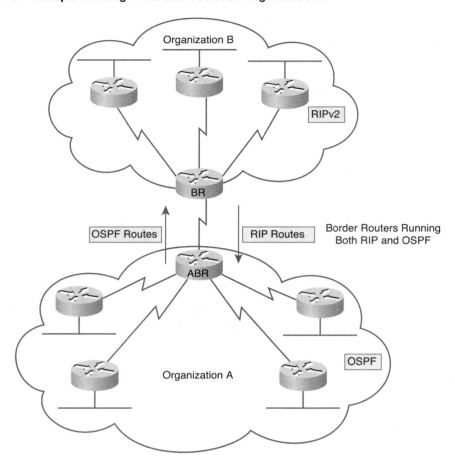

**Table 6-2    Route Sources, Administrative Distance, and Metrics**

| Route Source | Administrative Distance | Default Metric(s) |
| --- | --- | --- |
| Connected | 0 | 0 |
| Static | 1 | 0 |
| EIGRP summary route | 5 | N/A |
| External BGP | 20 | Value assigned by admin |
| Internal EIGRP | 90 | Bandwidth, delay |
| IGRP | 100 | Bandwidth, delay |
| OSPF | 110 | Link cost (bandwidth) |
| IS-IS | 115 | Link cost (bandwidth) |
| RIP | 120 | Hop count |
| External EIGRP | 170 | N/A |
| Internal BGP | 200 | Value assigned by admin |

**Interactive Activity 6-7: Determining the Router Source, AD, and Metric in a Routing Table (6.3.4.3)**

In this activity, you analyze the routing table and determine the route source, the AD, and the metric. Use file d3ia-6343 on the CD-ROM that accompanies this book to perform this interactive activity.

If two networks have the same base address and subnet mask, a router views them as identical. It considers a summarized network and an individual network that is part of that summary as different networks.

The summarized network 192.168.0.0/22 and the individual network 192.168.1.0 /24 are different entries, even though the summarization includes the individual network. When this situation occurs, both networks are placed in the routing table. The decision of which route to use falls to the entry with the closest, or longest, prefix match.

As an example, a router receives a packet with a destination IP address of 172.16.0.10. Three possible routes match this packet: 172.16.0.0/12, 172.16.0.0/18, and 172.16.0.0/26. Of the three routes, 172.16.0.0/26 has the longest match. For any of these routes to be considered a match, there must be at least the number of matching bits indicated by the subnet mask of the route.

Table 6-3 shows three examples where an incoming packet is compared bit by bit to possible route/mask combinations. In each case, the route with the longest number of matching bits is highlighted to show which route and interface would be selected by the router to forward the packet.

**Table 6-3    Route Sources, Administrative Distance, and Metrics**

| Destination IP Address and Possible Routes | Best Route Matching Bits |
|---|---|
| **Example 1** | |
| Dest IP    192.168.1.15 | 11000000.10101000.00000001.00001111 |
| Route 1    O 192.168.0.0/22 [110/65] via 192.168.0.1, Serial 0/0/0 | 11000000.10101000.00000000.00000000 |
| Route 2    O 192.168.1.0/24 [110/65] via 192.168.1.1, Serial 0/0/1 | 11000000.10101000.00000001.00000000 |
| **Example 2** | |
| Dest IP    192.168.3.23 | 11000000.10101000.00000011.00010111 |
| Route 1    O 192.168.0.0/22 [110/65] via 192.168.0.1, Serial 0/0/0 | 11000000.10101000.00000000.00000000 |
| Route 2    O 192.168.1.0/24 [110/65] via 192.168.1.1, Serial 0/0/1 | 11000000.10101000.00000001.00000000 |
| **Example 3** | |
| Dest IP    172.168.0.10 | 10101100.00010000.00000000.00001010 |
| Route 1    O 172.16.0.0/12 [110/65] via 172.16.1.1, Serial 0/0/0 | 10101100.00010000.00000000.00000000 |
| Route 2    O 172.16.0.0/18 [110/65] via 172.16.1.1, Serial 0/0/1 | 10101100.00010000.00000000.00000000 |
| Route 3    O 192.168.1.0/26 [110/65] via 192.168.1.1, Serial 0/1/0 | 10101100.00010000.00000000.00000000 |

**Interactive Activity 6-8: Selecting the Route (6.3.4.5)**

In this activity, you select one route that the packet would take to each destination network. Use file d3ia-6345 on the CD-ROM that accompanies this book to perform this interactive activity.

**Interactive Activity 6-9: Critical Thinking—Analyzing a Routing Table (6.4.2)**

In this activity, you work through a practice scenario in which you analyze the routing table displayed by the **show ip route** command and answer questions about the output. Use file d3ia-642 on the CD-ROM that accompanies this book to perform this interactive activity.

# Summary

OSPF is a classless interior link-state routing protocol used in enterprise networks. It offers scalability and route summarization, and it isolates routing issues and uses bandwidth to generate the cost metric.

An OSPF autonomous system design starts with the backbone area of Area 0. All the other areas created are adjacent to Area 0, and routers within an area advertise information about the status of links to their neighbors using LSAs. An ASBR connects the entire OSPF autonomous system to another autonomous system. To ensure the security of OSPF updates when LSAs are sent, use authentication between routers. The most secure method of authentication is MD5.

OSPF routers use their router ID to elect a DR and BDR on multiaccess network, whereas no DR or BDR is needed on point-to-point links. A network administrator can dictate which routers become the DR and the BDR by setting the priority or router ID on the routers.

The OSPF **network** command uses a combination of network address and wildcard mask. It specifies the interface address or range of addresses enabled for OSPF. The **bandwidth** interface command and the **ip ospf cost** interface command ensure that OSPF uses an actual cost to determine the best route.

Several **show** commands verify OSPF operation, including **show ip protocols**, **show ip ospf**, or **show ip ospf interface**, **show ip route**, and **show ip ospf neighbor**.

An administrator configures a default route on an ASBR and then configures it to advertise the default route into the rest of the OSPF network. Interarea route summarization is configured on ABRs and applies to routes from within the autonomous system. Summary routes between autonomous systems are configured on the ASBR.

OSPF requires more router memory and CPU resources, which means more powerful and more expensive routers.

Route redistribution allows routes from one routing protocol or static routes to be imported into another routing protocol. AD and longest prefix match determines the preferred route to a network.

# Activities and Labs

This summary outlines the activities and labs you can perform to help reinforce important concepts described in this chapter. You can find the activity files on the CD-ROM accompanying this book. The complete hands-on labs appear in Part II.

**Interactive activities on the CD-ROM:**

Interactive Activity 6-1: Identifying the Characteristics of RIP and OSPF (6.1.1)

Interactive Activity 6-2: Identifying the Path Through an OSPF Network (6.1.2)

Interactive Activity 6-3: Determining OSPF Router ID and Designated Router (6.1.3)

Interactive Activity 6-4: Matching OSPF Terms and Descriptions (6.1.4)

Interactive Activity 6-5: Determining the Subnet Mask and Wildcard Mask for OSPF. (6.2.1)

Interactive Activity 6-6: Analyzing **show ip route** Output from an OSPF Router (6.2.4)

Interactive Activity 6-7: Determining the Router Source, AD, and Metric in a Routing Table (6.3.4.3)

Interactive Activity 6-8: Selecting the Route (6.3.4.5)

Interactive Activity 6-9: Critical Thinking—Analyzing a Routing Table (6.4.2)

**Labs in Part II of this book:**

Lab 6-1: Configuring and Verifying Single-Area OSPF (6.2.1)

Lab 6-2: Configuring OSPF Authentication (6.2.2)

Lab 6-3: Controlling a DR/BDR Election (6.2.3.2)

Lab 6-4: Configuring OSPF Parameters (6.2.3.5)

Lab 6-5 Part A: Configuring and Verifying Point-to-Point and Multiaccess OSPF (6.2.4)

Lab 6-5 Part B: Configuring and Verifying Multiaccess OSPF (6.2.4)

Lab 6-6: Configuring and Propagating an OSPF Default Route (6.3.1)

Lab 6-7: Configuring OSPF Summarization (6.3.2)

# Check Your Understanding

Complete all the review questions listed here to check your understanding of the topics and concepts in this chapter. Appendix A, "Check Your Understanding and Challenge Questions Answer Key," lists the answers.

1. What attribute is associated with link-state routing protocols?

   A. Hop count

   B. Poison reverse

   C. Low processor overhead

   D. Shortest path first calculations

2. Based on Figure 6-19, if OSPF is configured in the network using the costs shown in the table, which path will a packet take from H1 to H2?

**Figure 6-19   Network Topology for Question 2**

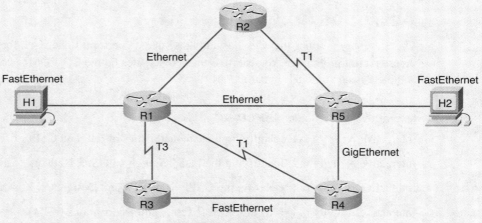

| Interface Link Type | Configured OSPF Cost |
|---|---|
| GigabitEthernet | 1 |
| FastEthernet | 10 |
| T3 | 20 |
| Ethernet | 100 |
| T1 | 800 |

A. R1-R5

B. R1-R2-R5

C. R1-R4-R5

D. R1-R3-R4-R5

3. The router learned three different routes to the subnet 192.168.1.0 as follows (partial output from **show ip route** command). What action will the router take to forward a packet to the destination of 192.168.1.143?

```
O 192.168.1.0 /24 (110/65) via 192.168.2.2, 00:00:05, Serial 0/0/0
R 192.168.1.0 /24 (120/1) via 192.168.3.2, 00:00:05, FastEthernet 0/0
D 192.168.1.0 /24 (90/1765) via 192.168.4.2, 00:00:05, Serial 0/0/1
```

A. The packet will be dropped by the router.

B. The packet will be load-balanced across the three routes.

C. The packet will be forwarded to the next hop of 192.168.4.2.

D. The packet will exit the router through the FastEthernet 0/0 interface.

4. Refer to the following output, which shows partial output from the **show running-config** command on RouterA. With all interfaces on RouterA active, the network administrator modifies the configuration of the router by issuing the command **no router-id 18.20.20.172**. The configuration is then saved, and the router restarted. What will be the router ID for RouterA when OSPF is reestablished?

```
RouterA# show running-config
interface Loopback0
 ip address 192.168.30.1 255.255.255.0
interface Loopback1
 ip address 192.168.70.18 255.255.255.252
interface FastEthernet0/0
 ip address 10.190.102.1 255.255.255.0
interface FastEthernet0/1
 ip address 192.168.102.1 255.255.255.0
interface Serial0/0/0
 ip address 172.20.20.18 255.255.255.252
router ospf 100
 router-id 18.20.20.172
```

A. 10.190.102.1

B. 172.20.20.18

C. 192.168.30.1

D. 192.168.70.18

E. 192.168.102.1

5. RouterA, RouterB, and RouterC in Figure 6-20 are running OSPF on their Ethernet interfaces. RouterD was just added to the network. Routers are configured with the loopback interfaces (Lo0) that are shown in the figure. What happens to the OSPF DR/BDR after RouterD is added to the network?

**Figure 6-20    Network Topology for Question 5**

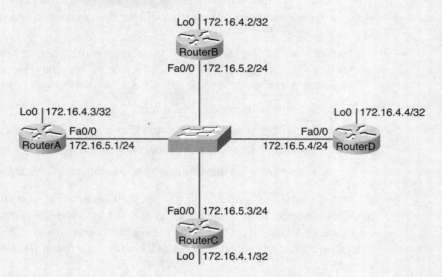

A. RouterB takes over as DR, and RouterD becomes the BDR.

B. RouterD becomes the BDR, and RouterA remains the DR.

C. RouterD becomes the DR, and RouterA remains the BDR.

D. RouterC acts as the DR until the election process is complete.

E. RouterD becomes the DR, and RouterB remains the BDR.

F. There is no change in the DR or BDR until either the current DR or BDR goes down.

6. Based on Figure 6-21, what network commands will Configure router A to properly advertise the OSPF routes?

**Figure 6-21    Network Topology for Question 6**

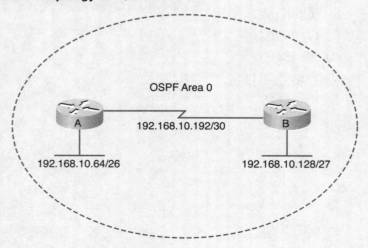

   A. **network 192.168.10.0 0.0.0.63 area 0**

      **network 192.168.10.128 0.0.0.63 area 0**

   B. **network 192.168.10.64 0.0.0.63 area 0**

      **network 192.168.10.192 0.0.0.3 area 0**

   C. **network 192.168.10.0 255.255.255.252 area 0**

      **network 192.168.10.128 255.255.255.252 area 0**

   D. **network 192.168.10.64 255.255.255.252 area 0**

      **network 192.168.10.192 255.255.255.252 area 0**

**7.** Which two statements are true regarding the cost calculation for a link in OSPF?

   A. It can be set with the **ip ospf cost** command.

   B. It is set to 1544 by default for all OSPF interfaces.

   C. The configured loopback addresses map to link costs.

   D. It may be calculated using the formula *Reference bandwidth / Bandwidth*.

   E. It is calculated proportionally to observed throughput capacity of the router.

**8.** See Figure 6-22 and the following command output. The OSPF routing protocol is configured for the routers, but Router A is not receiving any OSPF routes from the other routers. Based on the information in the exhibit, what is the problem with the Router A configuration?

**Figure 6-22    Network Topology for Question 8**

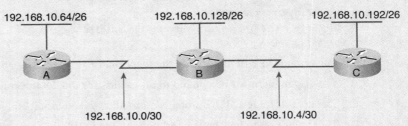

```
R1# show ip protocols
Routing Protocol is "ospf 1"
  Outgoing update filter list for all interfaces is not set
  Incoming update filter list for all interfaces is not set
  Router ID 192.168.10.65
  Number of areas in this router is 1. 1 normal 0 stub 0 nssa
  Maximum path: 4
  Routing for Networks:
    192.168.10.64 0.0.0.63 area 0
    192.168.10.128 0.0.0.63 area 0
  Routing Information Sources:
    Gateway         Distance      Last Update
    192.168.10.65        110       00:11:43
  Distance: (default is 110)
```

   A. None of the interfaces are enabled.

   B. OSPF has an improper process ID.

   C. One of the **network** statements is wrong.

   D. Auto summarization needs to be disabled.

9. See Figure 6-23 and the following configuration commands. A network administrator is implementing OSPF between headquarters and multiple branch offices. All branch offices are connected to the Internet through the headquarters router. What effect will the commands entered on the headquarters router have?

**Figure 6-23   Network Topology for Question 9**

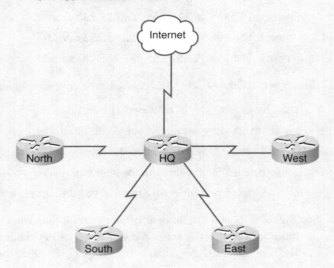

```
HQ(config)# ip route 0.0.0.0 0.0.0.0 serial 0/0/1
HQ(config)# router ospf 1
HQ(config-router)# default-information originate
HQ(config-router)# end
```

A. The command will affect only the local router.

B. The command must be applied to all routers for the default route to be propagated.

C. The default route will be propagated to all routers participating in the same OSPF area.

D. The default route will be learned only by the OSPF adjacent neighbors.

10. For what two reasons would a network administrator choose to enable MD5 authentication and encryption for OSPF exchanges?

A. To prevent routing information from being falsified

B. To reduce OSPF information from being captured

C. To keep routing information from being captured and deciphered

D. To encrypt routing tables to prevent unauthorized viewing

E. To ensure that OSPF routing information takes priority over RIP or EIGRP updates

11. Creating a route on an ABR with a shorter mask to aggregate and advertise multiple networks is called _____.

12. The main area that other OSPF areas connect to in a multiarea OSPF network is called

_____.

# Challenge Questions and Activities

These questions require a deeper application of the concepts covered in this chapter. You can find the answers in Appendix A.

1. You want to create a summary route on an ASBR to advertise the following 16 internal networks as one network to your ISP:

- 192.168.0.0/24

- 192.168.1.0/24

- 192.168.2.0/24

- 192.168.3.0/24

- 192.168.4.0/24

- 192.168.5.0/24

- 192.168.6.0/24

- 192.168.7.0/24

- 192.168.8.0/24

- 192.168.9.0/24

- 192.168.10.0/24

- 192.168.11.0/24

- 192.168.12.0/24

- 192.168.13.0/24

- 192.168.14.0/24

- 192.168.15.0/24

What is the command you would use? It is possible to summarize and advertise the 16 networks as one supernet of 192.168.4.0 /20 (4 bits = $2^4$, which covers 16 networks). Doing this reduces the number of networks that are advertised to the ISP from 16 to 1.

To configure an OSPF ASBR router to summarize these networks, issue the following command in OSPF router configuration mode:

**area 0 range 192.168.0.0 255.255.240.0**

2. OSPF/IS-IS Routing Protocol Investigation Interview Activity (optional)

In this activity, you talk with your instructor or a network administrator at your institution, where you work, or at another organization. Use the following form to ask administrators a few questions to learn more about organizations they know of that use OSPF or IS-IS as their main routing protocol.

Person's name: _____

Position/title: _____

Organization name: _____

Do they use OSPF or IS-IS? _____

Why did they choose OSPF or IS-IS? _____

What other routing protocols do they use? _____

Did they convert from another routing protocol (such as RIP or IGRP)? _____

How many routers do they have total in their network? _____

If multiarea OSPF, how many areas? _____

Do they also use static routing, and if so, how much? _____

What is the main benefit they receive from running this protocol? _____

_____

What is the biggest challenge of running this protocol? _____

# CHAPTER 7

# Implementing Enterprise WAN Links

## Objectives

Upon completion of this chapter, you should be able to answer the following questions:

- What WAN connectivity options are available?

- What are the relative advantages and limitations of the various WAN connectivity options?

- What advantages does PPP have over HDLC?

- What steps are required to configure a PPP link between two devices?

- How does CHAP differ from PAP authentication?

- What happens to data on a Frame Relay network that exceeds the CIR?

- How does a Frame Relay network handle congestion?

## Key Terms

This chapter uses the following key terms. You can find the definitions in the Glossary.

Connecting remote sites by an enterprise WAN allows users to access network resources and information. As information transverses the WAN, the Layer 2 encapsulation adapts to match the technology. The Layer 2 encapsulation can change several times as the information moves between source and destination. Many different WAN technologies exist, each offering distinct advantages and possessing certain limitations. One popular WAN technology that uses packet switching is Frame Relay.

Part II of this book includes the corresponding labs for this chapter.

## Connecting the Enterprise WAN

As companies grow, they often expand from a single location to multiple remote locations. These locations may be in different cities or even different countries. This expansion requires that the business network expand from a LAN to a WAN, as shown in Figure 7-1.

**Figure 7-1    Enterprise WAN**

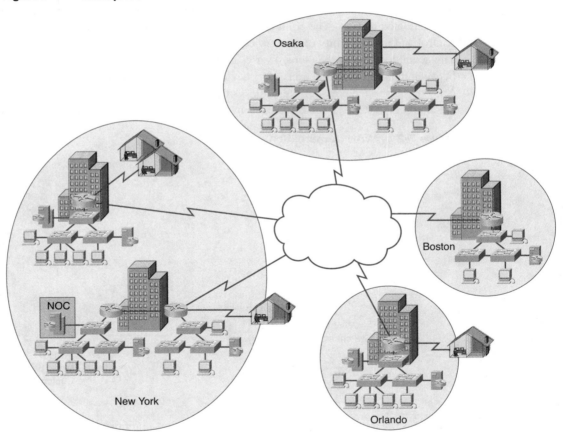

## WAN Devices and Technology

Within a LAN, a network administrator has physical control over all cabling, devices, and services. Although some larger companies maintain their own WAN, most organizations purchase WAN services from a service provider. The company or individual loses control of the packets as they enter the service provider's network for delivery. Service providers charge for the use of their network resources. Service providers allow users to share resources among remote locations without incurring the expense of building and maintaining their own network.

Control of network resources is not the only difference between a LAN and a WAN. The technologies also differ. The most common LAN technology is Ethernet. WAN technologies are serial transmissions. Serial transmissions enable reliable, long-range communications but at slower speeds than LAN technology.

When implementing a WAN, the WAN technology used determines the type of devices required by an organization. For example, a router used as a gateway to connect to the WAN translates the data into a format acceptable to the service provider network. A translation device, such as a modem, prepares the data for transmission across the service provider network. Preparing the data for transmission on the WAN using digital lines requires a CSU and a data service unit (DSU). These two devices are often combined into a single piece of equipment called the CSU/DSU. This device can be integrated into a router on an interface card. When using an analog connection, a modem is necessary.

When a business subscribes to WAN services through an ISP, the service provider owns and maintains most of the equipment. In certain environments, the subscriber may own and maintain some of the connection equipment. The point at which the control and responsibility of the customer ends and the control and responsibility of the service provider begins is known as the demarcation point (demarc). The actual location of the demarc varies around the world. For example, the demarc might exist between the router and the translating device or between the translating device and the *central office (CO)* of the service provider. Regardless of ownership, service providers use the term customer premises equipment (CPE) to describe equipment located at the customer site, as shown in Figure 7-2.

**Figure 7-2    WAN Demarcation**

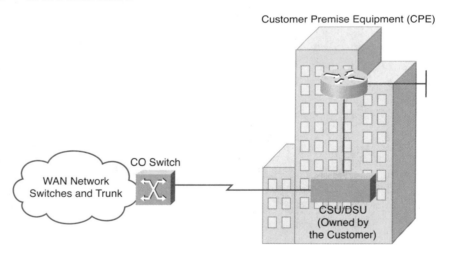

The CO is the location where the service provider stores equipment and accepts customer connections. The physical line from the CPE connects into a router or WAN switch at the CO using copper or fiber cabling. This connection is called the *local loop*, or *last mile*. From the customer perspective, it is the *first mile*, because it is the first part of the medium leading from the location of the customer.

The CSU/DSU or modem controls the rate at which data moves onto the local loop. It also provides the *clocking signal* to the router. The CSU/DSU is *data communications equipment (DCE)*. The router, which is responsible for passing the data to the DCE, is *data terminal equipment (DTE)*. The DTE/DCE interface uses various physical layer protocols, such as X.21 and V.35. These protocols establish the codes and electrical parameters that the router and the CSU/DSU use to communicate with each other. Figure 7-3 shows some of the available physical layer protocols that are described in Table 7-1.

**Figure 7-3    Physical Layer Protocols**

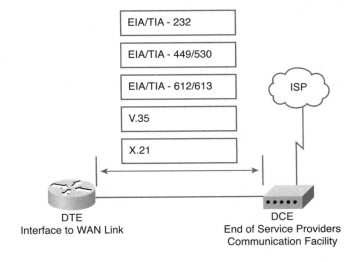

**Table 7-1    Physical Layer Protocols**

| Protocol | Description |
| --- | --- |
| EIA/TIA-232 | Allows signal speeds of up to 64 kbps on a 25-pin D connector over short distances |
| | Formerly known as RS-232 |
| | Same as ITU-T V.24 specification |
| EIA/TIA-449/530 | Faster (up to 2 Mbps) version of EIA/TIA-232 |
| | Uses a 36-pin D connector and is capable of longer cable runs |
| | Also known as RS-422 and RS-423 |
| EIA/TIA-612/613 | Provides access to services at up to 52 Mbps on a 60-pin D connector |
| V.35 | An ITU-T standard for synchronous communications between a network access device and a packet network at speeds up to 48 kbps |
| | Uses a 34-pin rectangular connector |
| X.21 | An ITU-T standard for synchronous digital communications |
| | Uses a 15-pin D connector |

Technology continuously develops and improves signaling standards that enable an increased data-communication speed. When choosing a WAN technology, it is important to consider the link speed. The first digital networks created for WAN implementations provided support for a 64-kbps connection across a leased line. The term *digital signal level 0 (DS0)* refers to this standard. As technology improved, service providers supplied subscribers with specific increments of the DS0 channel. For example, in North America, a *digital signal level 1 (DS1)* standard, also called a T1 line, defines a single line that supports 24 DS0s, plus an 8-kbps overhead channel. This standard enables speeds of up to 1.544 Mbps. A T3 line uses a *digital signal level 3 (DS3)* standard, which supports 28 DS1s and speeds of up to 44.736 Mbps.

Other parts of the world use different standards. For example, Europe offers lines such as E1s, which support 32 DS0s for a speed of up to 2.048 Mbps, and E3s, which support 16 E1s for a speed of up to 34.064 Mbps. Table 7-2 lists some of the more common line types along with the signaling standard they use and their data-carrying capacity.

**Table 7-2    WAN Line Characteristics**

| Line Type | Signal Standard | Bit Rate |
| --- | --- | --- |
| 56 | DS0 | 56 kbps |
| 64 | DS0 | 64 kbps |
| T1 | DS1 | 1.544 Mbps |
| E1 | ZM | 2.048 Mbps |
| J1 | Y1 | 2.048 Mbps |
| E3 | M3 | 34.064 Mbps |
| T3 | DS3 | 44.736 Mbps |
| OC-1 | SONET | 51.84 Mbps |
| OC-3 | SONET | 155.54 Mbps |
| OC-9 | SONET | 466.56 Mbps |
| OC-12 | SONET | 622.08 Mbps |
| OC-18 | SONET | 933.12 Mbps |
| OC-24 | SONET | 1444.16 Mbps |
| OC-36 | SONET | 1866.24 Mbps |
| OC-48 | SONET | 2488.32 Mbps |

**Interactive Activity 7-1: Matching WAN Terminology (7.1.1)**

In this activity, you match the WAN term to the appropriate definition. Use file d3ia-711 on the CD-ROM that accompanies this book to perform this interactive activity.

## WAN Standards

Designing a network based on specific standards ensures that all the different devices and technologies found in a WAN environment work together. WAN standards describe the Layer 1 and Layer 2 characteristics of data transportation. Layer 2 WAN standards include parameters such as physical addressing, flow control, and encapsulation type, and how the information moves across the WAN link. The type of WAN technology used determines the specific Layer 2 standards used. Examples of Layer 2 WAN protocols are shown in Figure 7-4 and include the following:

- Link Access Procedure for Frame Relay (LAPF)

- High-Level Data Link Control (HDLC)

- PPP

**Figure 7-4    WAN Data Link Layer Standards**

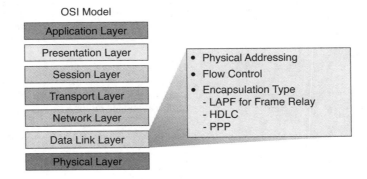

Several organizations are responsible for managing both the physical layer and data link layer WAN standards, including the following:

- ITU-T

- ISO

- IETF

- EIA

- TIA

**Interactive Activity 7-2: Matching WAN Standards to the OSI Model (7.1.2)**

In this activity, you determine whether the standard is a Layer 1 or Layer 2 standard. Use file d3ia-712 on the CD-ROM that accompanies this book to perform this interactive activity.

## Accessing the WAN

WAN links use either digital or analog technology. With analog connections, the data is encoded, or *modulated*, onto a *carrier wave*. The modulated signal then carries the information across the medium to the remote site. At the remote site, the signal is demodulated and the receiver extracts the information. A modem encodes the information onto that carrier wave before transmission and then decodes it at the receiving end, as shown in Figure 7-5. The modem gets its name from its task of modulation and demodulation of the carrier signal. Modems enable remote sites to communicate through the *plain old telephone system (POTS)*. They also enable end users to connect to service provider networks through digital subscriber line (DSL) or cable connections.

**Figure 7-5    Modems in Data Communications**

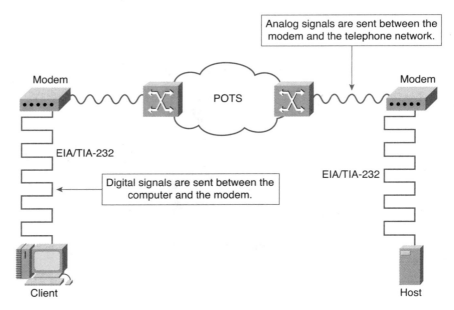

Companies often purchase connectivity using dedicated links between their location and the ISP. These services are often provided using leased lines for which the companies pay a regular service charge to use. These lines carry large amounts of data. For example, a T1 link carries 1.544 Mbps of traffic, and an E1 link carries 2.048 Mbps of traffic. Often, this bandwidth is larger than the amount that the organization actually requires. If the end user does not require the full bandwidth available on a T1 or an E1 connection, the user can purchase only a portion of the available bandwidth. A T1 can be split into 24 DS0s of 64 kbps each. Each of these can then be assigned to a customer. In this case, the customer is ordering part of a T1, or a *fractional T1*. E1 connections can be treated in a similar manner. Customers can be assigned a portion of an E1 connection, or *fractional E1*. Figure 7-6 shows the use of fractional T1 and E1 connections.

High-bandwidth connections are split up into several DS0s. The ISP assigns each DS0 to a different conversation or end user. Organizations purchase one or more DS0 channels depending on their requirements. A DS0 is not a separate physical entity but rather a *time slice* of the physical bandwidth on one wire. Each fractional connection enables full use of the media by the organization for part of the total time. There are two techniques by which information from multiple channels can be allocated bandwidth on a single cable based on time: *time-division multiplexing (TDM)* and *statistical time-division multiplexing (STDM)*.

## TDM

TDM allocates bandwidth based on preassigned time slots. Each of these time slices is assigned to individual conversations. Each time slice represents a period during which a conversation has complete use of the physical media. Bandwidth is allocated to each channel or time slot regardless of whether the station using the channel has data to transmit. Therefore, with standard TDM, if a sender has nothing to say, its time slice goes unused, wasting valuable bandwidth.

**Figure 7-6    Fractional T1 and Fractional E1 Data Connections**

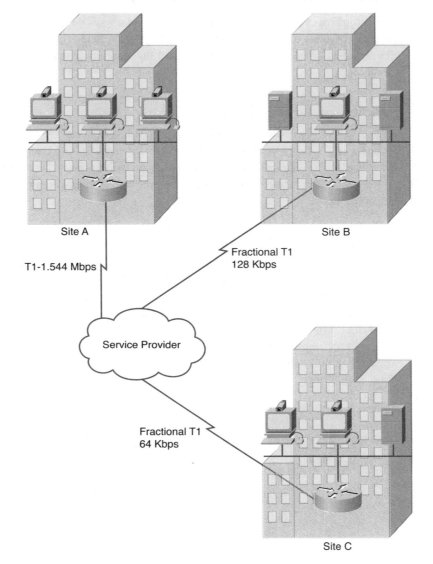

## STDM

STDM is similar to TDM except that it keeps track of conversations that require extra bandwidth. It then dynamically reassigns unused time slices on an as-needed basis. In this way, STDM minimizes wasted bandwidth. STDM requires an intelligent device that can keep track of the conversations and determine which requires extra bandwidth.

**Interactive Activity 7-3: Determining How TDM and STDM Handle a Data Stream (7.1.3)**

In this activity, you determine how a data stream is treated by TDM and STDM. Use file d3ia-713 on the CD-ROM that accompanies this book to perform this interactive activity.

# Packet and Circuit Switching

An enterprise connects to WAN services in various ways depending on their requirements. Some techniques provide a dedicated connection to the WAN, whereas others share the connection bandwidth. The connection technology may be a leased-line, circuit-switched, packet-switched, or cell-switched technology.

## Dedicated Leased Line

A *leased line* is a dedicated point-to-point serial link between two routers. This enables a one-to-one connection for the basic function of data delivery across a link. Each link requires a separate physical interface and a separate CSU/DSU. As an organization grows to multiple locations, supporting a dedicated leased line between each location becomes very expensive, and other techniques become more economical.

## Circuit Switching

*Circuit switching*, as shown in Figure 7-7, establishes an end-to-end circuit between nodes before forwarding any data. A standard telephone call uses this type of connection. While the circuit is in place, it provides dedicated bandwidth between the two points. Completion of the conversation releases the circuit for reuse. No other organizations can use the circuit until it is released. This method provides a level of security not available in packet-switching or cell-switching technology. With circuit switching, the service provider assigns links to different connections as the need arises. Costs are incurred for the link only when the connection is active. The cost for circuit switching varies based on usage time and distance. It can become quite expensive if the circuit is used on a regular basis.

**Figure 7-7    Circuit Switching**

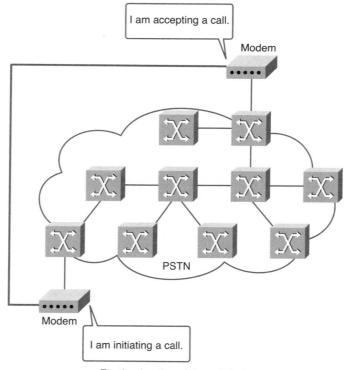

For the duration of the call the line is dedicated to the sender and receiver.

## Packet Switching

*Packet switching* uses bandwidth more efficiently than other types of data switching. The data is first segmented into packets, and an identifier is placed on each packet. The data is then released into the service provider network. The service provider accepts the data and switches the packet from one node to another until the packet reaches its final destination, as shown in Figure 7-8. The circuit, or pathway, between the source and destination is often a preconfigured link, but it is not an exclusive link. The service provider switches packets from multiple organizations over the same physical links. The link between nodes is established as required, but there is no end-to-end physical connectivity between source and destination. Frame Relay is an example of packet-switching technology.

**Figure 7-8    Packet Switching**

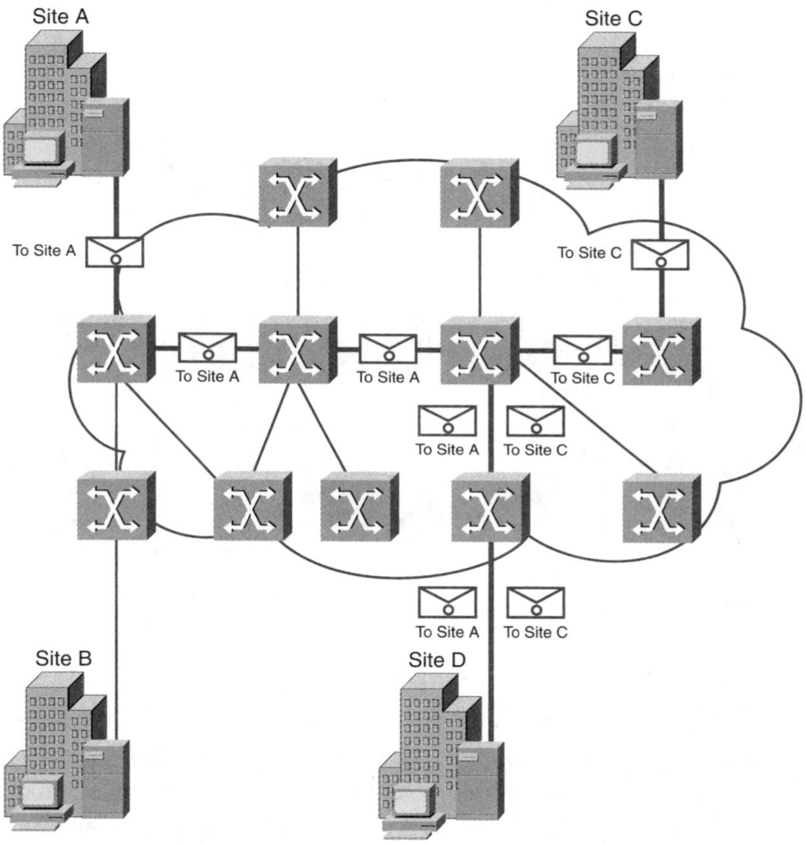

Traffic from two virtual circuits share the same links.

## Cell Switching

*Cell switching* is a variation of packet switching. It is capable of transferring voice, video, and data through private and public networks at speeds in excess of 155 Mbps. An example of cell switching is *Asynchronous Transfer Mode (ATM)*. ATM uses fixed length, 53-byte cells that have 48 bytes of data and a 5-byte header. The small, uniform size of the cells allows them to be switched quickly and efficiently between nodes. An advantage of ATM is that it prevents small messages from being held up behind larger messages. However, for networks handling mainly *segmented data*, ATM introduces a large amount of overhead and actually slows network performance. This is because each cell only carries 48 bytes of data and has a 5-byte header regardless of the payload. In packet-switched technology such as Frame Relay, the much larger frames require less overhead.

When using packet-switching technology, the service provider establishes *virtual circuits (VC)*. Virtual circuits share the link between devices with traffic from other sources. As a result, the medium is not private during the duration of a connection. As shown in Figure 7-9, there are two types of virtual circuits: switched and permanent.

**Figure 7-9    Virtual Circuits**

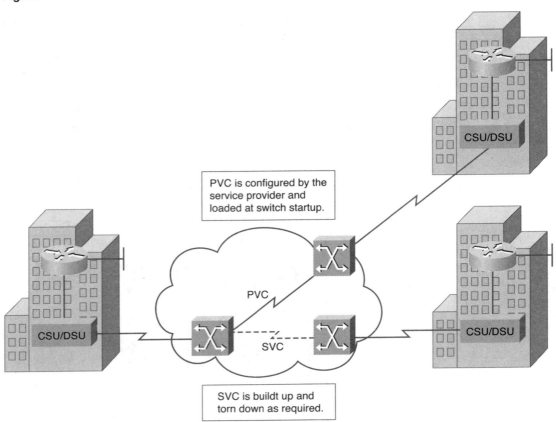

## Switched Virtual Circuit

A *switched virtual circuit (SVC)* is dynamically established between two points when a device requests a transmission. The circuit is set up on demand and torn down when transmission is complete, such as after a file has been downloaded. When establishing an SVC, call setup information must be sent before transmitting any data. Call clearing information tears down the connection after it is no longer required. Building up and tearing down the connection for every conversation introduces delays in the network.

## Permanent Virtual Circuit

A *permanent virtual circuit (PVC)* provides a permanent path to forward data between two points. The service provider must preconfigure the PVCs, and they are very seldom broken or disconnected. This eliminates the need for call setup and clearing for each conversation. PVCs speed the flow of information across the WAN and provide the ISP with much greater control over the data-flow patterns and management of their network. PVCs are more popular than SVCs and usually service sites with high-volume, constant flows of traffic. Frame Relay typically uses PVCs.

**Interactive Activity 7-4: Selecting the Appropriate WAN Technology (7.1.4)**

In this activity, you identify the best WAN connection technology to support the given scenario. Use file d3ia-714 on the CD-ROM that accompanies this book to perform this interactive activity.

## Last-Mile and Long-Range WAN Technologies

ISPs use several different WAN technologies to connect their subscribers. The connection type used on the local loop, or last mile, might not be the same as the WAN connection type used within the ISP network or between various ISPs. Some common last-mile technologies are shown in Figure 7-10 and include the following:

- Analog dialup
- ISDN
- Leased line
- Cable
- Digital subscriber line (DSL)
- Frame Relay
- Wireless

**Figure 7-10    Local Loop Technologies**

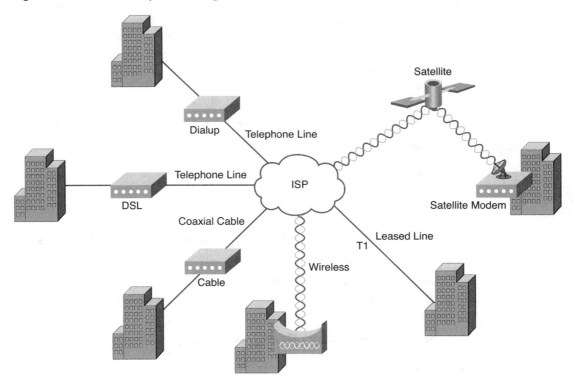

Each of these technologies provides advantages and disadvantages for the customer. Not all technologies are available in all locations. Regardless of the connection technology used, when a service provider receives data, it must forward this data to other remote sites for final delivery to the recipient. These remote sites either connect directly to the service provider network or may be connected to a different service provider. If the source and destination are not connected to the same service provider, the service provider passes the data from service provider to service provider and then finally to the recipient.

Long-range communications are usually those connections between service providers or between branch offices in very large companies. Many different WAN technologies exist that allow the service provider to reliably forward data over great distances. Some of these include ATM, satellite, Frame Relay, and leased lines.

Enterprises are becoming larger and more dispersed. Applications used across the enterprise are demanding more bandwidth, and of a higher quality, free from noise and other defects. Many enterprises require networks that support diverse applications, including VoIP, streaming audio and video, and reliable, high-speed data communications. This requires technologies that support high-speed and high-bandwidth transfer of data over even greater distances.

*Synchronous Optical Network (SONET)* and *Synchronous Digital Hierarchy (SDH)* are standards that allow the movement of large amounts of data over great distances through fiber-optic cables. Both SONET and SDH encapsulate earlier digital transmission standards and support either ATM or Packet over SONET/SDH (POS) networking. SDH and SONET are used for moving both voice and data.

One of the newer developments for extremely long-range communications is *dense wavelength-division multiplexing (DWDM)*. DWDM assigns incoming optical signals to specific frequencies or wavelengths of light. It is also capable of amplifying these wavelengths to boost the signal strength. DWDM can multiplex more than 80 different wavelengths or channels of data onto a single piece of fiber. Each channel is capable of carrying a multiplexed signal at 2.5 Gbps. Demultiplexed data at the receiving end allows a single piece of fiber to carry many different formats at the same time and at different data rates. For example, DWDM can carry IP, SONET, and ATM data concurrently.

**Interactive Activity 7-5: Describing WAN Technologies (7.1.5)**

In this activity, you match the WAN technology to its description. Use file d3ia-715 on the CD-ROM that accompanies this book to perform this interactive activity.

# Comparing Common WAN Encapsulations

Encapsulation occurs before data travels across a WAN. The encapsulation conforms to a specific format based on the technology used on the network. Before converting data into bits for transmission across the media, Layer 2 encapsulation adds addressing and control information.

## Ethernet and WAN Encapsulations

Layer 2 encapsulation adds header information specific to the type of physical network transmission. Within a LAN environment, Ethernet is the most common technology. The data link layer encapsulates the packet into Ethernet frames. The frame headers contain information such as the source and destination MAC addresses, and specific Ethernet controls, such as the frame size and timing information. Similarly, the encapsulation of frames destined for transmission across a WAN link match the technology in use on the link. For example, if using Frame Relay on the link, the type of encapsulation required is Frame Relay specific.

The type of data link layer encapsulation is separate from the type of network layer encapsulation. As data moves across a network, the Layer 2 encapsulation may change continuously, whereas the network layer encapsulation will not. If this packet must move across the WAN on its way to the final destination, the Layer 2 encapsulation changes to match the technology in use at that specific point in the WAN.

Packets exit the LAN by way of the default gateway router. The router strips off the Ethernet frame and then re-encapsulates that data into the correct frame type for the WAN link. Conversion of frames received on the WAN interface into the Ethernet frame format occurs before placement on the local network. The router acts as a media converter by adapting the Layer 2 frame format to a format appropriate to the interface, as shown in Figure 7-11.

**Figure 7-11    Layer 2 Network Encapsulation**

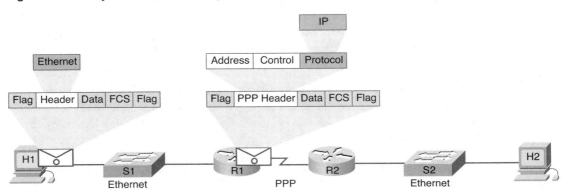

The encapsulation type must match on both ends of a point-to-point connection. Table 7-3 describes the fields in a data link layer encapsulation.

**Table 7-3    WAN Line Characteristics**

| Field | Description |
| --- | --- |
| Flag | Marks the beginning and end of each frame |
| Address | Depends on the encapsulation type |
| | Not required if the WAN link is point-to-point |
| Control | Used to indicate the type of frame |
| Protocol | Used to specify the type of encapsulated network layer protocol |
| | Not present in all WAN encapsulations |
| Data | Used as Layer 3 data and IP datagram |
| Frame Check Sequence (FCS) | Provides a mechanism to verify that the frame was not damaged in transit |

**Interactive Activity 7-6: Matching Layer 2 Encapsulation Terminology (7.2.1)**

In this activity, you match the Layer 2 encapsulation term to its definition. Use file d3ia-721 on the CD-ROM that accompanies this book to perform this interactive activity.

# HDLC and PPP

Many different Layer 2 serial line encapsulations are encountered on WANs. Two of the most common are HDLC and PPP.

## HDLC

*High-Level Data Link Control (HDLC)* is a standard *bit-oriented* data link layer encapsulation. HDLC uses synchronous serial transmission, which provides error-free communication between two points. HDLC defines a Layer 2 framing structure that allows for flow control and error control using acknowledgments and a windowing scheme. Each frame has the same format, whether it is a data frame or a control frame. The standard HDLC frame does not contain a field that identifies the type of protocol carried by the frame. For that reason, standards-based HDLC cannot handle multiple protocols across a single link.

Cisco HDLC incorporates an extra field, known as the Type field, which allows multiple network layer protocols to share the same link. Cisco HDLC is the default data link layer encapsulation type on Cisco serial links and should be used only when interconnecting Cisco devices. Figure 7-12 compares a standards-based HDLC frame with the Cisco proprietary one.

**Figure 7-12    Cisco HDLC and Standards-Based HDLC**

Open Standard HDLC Frame

| Flag | Address | Control | Information | FCS | Flag |
|---|---|---|---|---|---|
| 8 Bits | 8 Bits | 8 or 16 Bits | Variable Length, 0 or More Bits, Multiples of 8 | 16 or 32 Bits | 8 Bits |

Cisco HDLC Frame

| Flag | Address | Control | Type (Protocol Code) | Information | FCS | Flag |
|---|---|---|---|---|---|---|
| 8 Bits | 8 Bits | 16 Bits | 16 Bits | Variable Length, 0 or More Bits, Multiples of 8 | 16 Bits | 8 Bits |

## PPP

*Point-to-Point Protocol (PPP)*, like HDLC, is a data link layer encapsulation for serial links. It uses a layered architecture to encapsulate and carry multiprotocol datagrams over a point-to-point link. Because PPP is standards based, it enables communication between equipment of different vendors. PPP is supported on the following interface types:

- Asynchronous serial
- Synchronous serial
- High-Speed Serial Interface (HSSI)
- ISDN

As shown in Figure 7-13, PPP has two subprotocols:

■ Link Control Protocol

■ Network Control Protocol

**Figure 7-13    PPP Subprotocols**

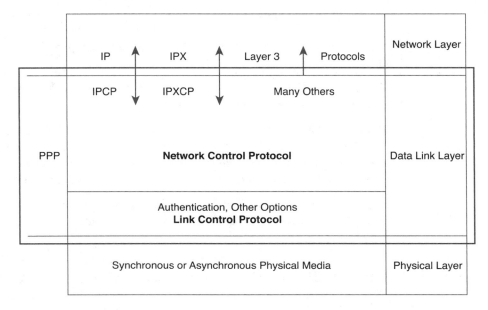

PPP uses the *Link Control Protocol (LCP)* to establish, maintain, test, and terminate the point-to-point link. In addition, LCP negotiates and configures control options on the WAN link, as shown in Figure 7-14.

**Figure 7-14    LCP-Negotiated Options**

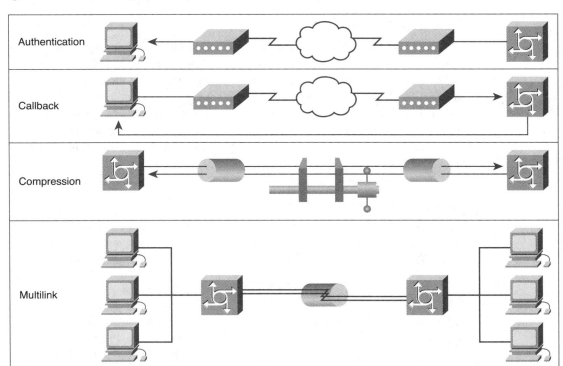

The following list describes each option:

- **Authentication**: Authentication options require that the calling side of the link enter information to ensure that the caller has the permission to make the call. Peer routers exchange authentication messages. Two authentication choices are Password Authentication Protocol (PAP) and Challenge Handshake Authentication Protocol (CHAP).

- **Compression**: Compression options increase the effective throughput on PPP connections by reducing the amount of data in the frame that travels across the link. The protocol decompresses the frame at its destination. Two compression protocols available in Cisco routers are Stacker and Predictor.

- **Multilink**: Cisco IOS Release 11.1 and later supports multilink PPP. This alternative provides load balancing over the PPP router interfaces.

- **PPP callback**: Cisco IOS Release 11.1 offers callback over PPP. With this LCP option, a Cisco router can act as a callback client or as a callback server. The client makes the initial call, requests that it be called back, and terminates its initial call. The callback router answers the initial call and makes the return call to the client based on information configured in its memory.

LCP is responsible for the handling of carried packet sizes, the detection of common misconfigurations, and the determination of link quality. If the LCP determines that the link is of sufficient quality, it brings up the NCPs.

PPP uses the *Network Control Protocol (NCP)* component to encapsulate multiple network layer protocols so that they operate on the same communications link. Every network layer protocol carried on the PPP link requires a separate NCP. For example, IP uses the IP Control Protocol (IPCP), and IPX uses the IPX Control Protocol (IPXCP). NCPs include fields containing codes that indicate the network layer protocol.

PPP sessions progress through three phases: link establishment, authentication (optional), and NCP negotiation.

## Link-Establishment Phase

PPP sends LCP frames to configure and test the data link. LCP frames contain a configuration option field that negotiates options such as maximum transmission unit (MTU), compression, and link authentication. If a configuration option is missing, it assumes the default value. Link authentication and link-quality determination tests are optional parameters within the link-establishment phase. A link-quality determination test determines whether the link quality is good enough to bring up network layer protocols. Optional parameters, such as these, must be complete before the receipt of a configuration acknowledgment frame. Receipt of the configuration acknowledgment frame completes the link-establishment phase.

## Authentication Phase (Optional)

The authentication phase provides password protection to identify connecting routers. Authentication occurs after the two routers agree to the set parameters but before the NCP negotiation phase can begin. This phase is optional and requires additional configuration to complete.

## NCP Negotiation Phase

After the LCPs have determined that the link is of sufficient quality to carry Layer 3 data and the authentication phase, if configured, has completed successfully, PPP sends NCP packets to select and configure one or more network layer protocols. If LCP closes the link, it informs the network layer protocols so that they can take appropriate action. When established, the PPP link remains active until the LCP or NCP frames close the link or until an activity timer expires. A user can also terminate the link.

**Interactive Activity 7-7: Identifying PPP Components and Phases (7.2.2)**

In this activity, you identify the correct location of the various PPP components. Use file d3ia-722 on the CD-ROM that accompanies this book to perform this interactive activity.

## Configuring PPP

On Cisco routers, HDLC is the default encapsulation on serial links. The **encapsulation ppp** interface configuration command changes the encapsulation to PPP. The **encapsulation hdlc** interface configuration command changes the encapsulation back to HDLC.

After PPP has been enabled, you can configure optional features such as compression and load balancing. To enable compression on a PPP link, issue the following command:

```
compress [predictor | stac]
```

Compressing data sent across the network can improve network performance. *Predictor* and *Stacker* are software compression techniques that vary in the way compression is handled. Stacker compression is more CPU intensive and less memory intensive. Predictor is more memory intensive and less CPU intensive. For this reason, Stacker is used if the bottleneck is due to line bandwidth issues, and Predictor is used if the bottleneck is due to excessive load on the router.

Compression should be used only if network performance issues exist. Enabling compression increases router processing times and overhead. Also, do not use compression if the majority of traffic crossing the network is already compressed files. Compressing an already compressed file often increases the size of the file.

PPP multilink allows for multiple WAN links to be aggregated into one logical channel for the transport of traffic. It enables the load balancing of traffic from different links and allows some level of redundancy in case of a line failure on a single link. To enable multilink on a router interface, use the following command:

```
ppp multilink
```

Many different commands are used to verify and troubleshoot HDLC and PPP encapsulation. Examples of some of the more common commands follow.

The following command displays the encapsulation and the states of LCP:

```
show interfaces serial
```

Example 7-1 shows sample output from this command.

**Example 7-1  Output from show interfaces serial Command**

```
R1# show interfaces serial 0/0/0
Serial0/0/0 is up, line protocol is up
  Hardware is PowerQUICC Serial
  Internet address is 192.168.2.1/24
  MTU 1500 bytes, BW 128 Kbit, DLY 20000 usec,
     reliability 255/255, txload 1/255, rxload 1/255
```

```
Encapsulation PPP, LCP Open
 Open: IPCP, CCP, CDPCP, loopback not set
 Keepalive set (10 sec)
 Last input 00:00:02, output 00:00:02, output hang never
 Last clearing of "show interface" counters 00:01:45
 Input queue: 0/75/0/0 (size/max/drops/flushes); Total output drops: 0
 Queueing strategy: weighted fair
 Output queue: 0/1000/64/0 (size/max total/threshold/drops)
       Conversations  0/1/32 (active/max active/max total)
       Reserved Conversations 0/0 (allocated/max allocated)
       Available Bandwidth 96 kilobits/sec
 5 minute input rate 0 bits/sec, 0 packets/sec
 5 minute output rate 0 bits/sec, 0 packets/sec
       39 packets input, 1971 bytes, 0 no buffer
       Received 0 broadcasts, 0 runts, 0 giants, 0 throttles
       0 input errors, 0 CRC, 0 frame, 0 overrun, 0 ignored, 0 abort
       40 packets output, 1993 bytes, 0 underruns
       0 output errors, 0 collisions, 0 interface resets
       0 output buffer failures, 0 output buffers swapped out
       0 carrier transitions
       DCD=up  DSR=up  DTR=up  RTS=up  CTS=up
```

The following command indicates the state of the interface channels and whether a cable is attached to the interface:

`show controllers`

Example 7-2 shows a sample output from this command.

**Example 7-2  Output from show controllers Command**

```
R1# show controllers serial 0/0/0
Interface Serial0/0/0
Hardware is PowerQUICC MPC860
DCE V.35, clock rate 64000
idb at 0x8247BCD0, driver data structure at 0x82485364
SCC Registers:
General [GSMR]=0x2:0x00000030, Protocol-specific [PSMR]=0x8
Events [SCCE]=0x0000, Mask [SCCM]=0x001F, Status [SCCS]=0x06
Transmit on Demand [TODR]=0x0, Data Sync [DSR]=0x7E7E

<output omitted >

buffer size 1524

PowerQUICC SCC specific errors:
0 input aborts on receiving flag sequence
0 throttles, 0 enables
0 overruns
0 transmitter underruns
0 transmitter CTS losts
```

The following command verifies the incrementation of keepalive packets:

```
debug serial interface
```

If packets are not incrementing, a possible timing problem exists on the interface card or in the network. Example 7-3 shows a sample output from this command.

**Example 7-3  Output from debug serial interface Command**

```
*Mar  1 08:21:34.317: Serial0/0/0: HDLC myseq 18, mineseen 18*, yourseen 20, line up
*Mar  1 08:21:44.317: Serial0/0/0: HDLC myseq 19, mineseen 19*, yourseen 21, line up
*Mar  1 08:21:54.317: Serial0/0/0: HDLC myseq 20, mineseen 20*, yourseen 22, line up
*Mar  1 08:22:04.318: Serial0/0/0: HDLC myseq 21, mineseen 20*, yourseen 23, line up
*Mar  1 08:22:14.318: Serial0/0/0: HDLC myseq 22, mineseen 22*, yourseen 24, line up
*Mar  1 08:22:24.319: Serial0/0/0: HDLC myseq 23, mineseen 23*, yourseen 25, line up
*Mar  1 08:22:24.319: Serial0/0/0: HDLC myseq 24, mineseen 24*, yourseen 26, line up
*Mar  1 08:22:24.319: Serial0/0/0: HDLC myseq 25, mineseen 24*, yourseen 27, line up
*Mar  1 08:22:24.319: Serial0/0/0: HDLC myseq 26, mineseen 24*, yourseen 28, line down
*Mar  1 08:22:24.319: Serial0/0/0: HDLC myseq 20, mineseen 20*, yourseen 21, line up
*Mar  1 08:22:24.319: Serial0/0/0: HDLC myseq 21, mineseen 21*, yourseen 22, line up
*Mar  1 08:22:24.319: Serial0/0/0: HDLC myseq 22, mineseen 22*, yourseen 23, line up
*Mar  1 08:22:24.319: Serial0/0/0: HDLC myseq 23, mineseen 23*, yourseen 24, line up
```

The following command provides information about the various stages of the PPP process, including negotiation and authentication:

```
debug ppp
```

Example 7-4 shows a sample output from this command.

**Example 7-4  Output from debug ppp negotiation Command**

```
R1# debug ppp negotiation
PPP protocol negotiation debugging is on
*Mar  1 08:24:08.201: Se0/0/0 PPP: Outbound cdp packet dropped
R1#
*Mar  1 08:24:10.200: %LINK-3-UPDOWN: Interface Serial0/0/0, changed state to up
*Mar  1 08:24:10.200: Se0/0/0 PPP: Using default call direction
*Mar  1 08:24:10.200: Se0/0/0 PPP: Treating connection as a dedicated line
*Mar  1 08:24:10.200: Se0/0/0 PPP: Session handle[EE000004] Session id[4]
*Mar  1 08:24:10.200: Se0/0/0 PPP: Phase is ESTABLISHING, Active Open
*Mar  1 08:24:10.200: Se0/0/0 LCP: O CONFREQ [Closed] id 4 len 10
*Mar  1 08:24:10.200: Se0/0/0 LCP:    MagicNumber 0x112C0700 (0x0506112C0700)
*Mar  1 08:24:10.208: Se0/0/0 LCP: I CONFREQ [REQsent] id 4 len 10
*Mar  1 08:24:10.208: Se0/0/0 LCP:    MagicNumber 0x112C0687 (0x0506112C0687)
*Mar  1 08:24:10.208: Se0/0/0 LCP: O CONFACK [REQsent] id 4 len 10
*Mar  1 08:24:10.208: Se0/0/0 LCP:    MagicNumber 0x112C0687 (0x0506112C0687)
*Mar  1 08:24:10.208: Se0/0/0 LCP: I CONFACK [ACKsent] id 4 len 10
*Mar  1 08:24:10.212: Se0/0/0 LCP:    MagicNumber 0x112C0700 (0x0506112C0700)
*Mar  1 08:24:10.212: Se0/0/0 LCP: State is Open
*Mar  1 08:24:10.212: Se0/0/0 PPP: Phase is FORWARDING, Attempting Forward
*Mar  1 08:24:10.212: Se0/0/0 PPP: Phase is ESTABLISHING, Finish LCP
*Mar  1 08:24:10.212: Se0/0/0 PPP: Phase is UP
*Mar  1 08:24:10.216: Se0/0/0 IPCP: O CONFREQ [Closed] id 1 len 10
```

```
*Mar  1 08:24:10.216: Se0/0/0 IPCP:    Address 192.168.2.1 (0x0306C0A80201)
*Mar  1 08:24:10.216: Se0/0/0 CCP: O CONFREQ [Closed] id 1 len 10
*Mar  1 08:24:10.216: Se0/0/0 CCP:    LZSDCP history 1 check mode SEQ process UNCOMPRESSSED
  (0x170600010201)
*Mar  1 08:24:10.216: Se0/0/0 CDPCP: O CONFREQ [Closed] id 1 len 4
*Mar  1 08:24:10.216: Se0/0/0 PPP: Process pending ncp packets
*Mar  1 08:24:10.220: Se0/0/0 IPCP: I CONFREQ [REQsent] id 1 len 10
*Mar  1 08:24:10.220: Se0/0/0 IPCP:    Address 192.168.2.2 (0x0306C0A80202)
*Mar  1 08:24:10.220: Se0/0/0 IPCP: O CONFACK [REQsent] id 1 len 10
*Mar  1 08:24:10.220: Se0/0/0 IPCP:    Address 192.168.2.2 (0x0306C0A80202)
*Mar  1 08:24:10.220: Se0/0/0 CCP: I CONFREQ [REQsent] id 1 len 10
*Mar  1 08:24:10.220: Se0/0/0 CCP:    LZSDCP history 1 check mode SEQ process UNCOMPRESSSED
  (0x170600010201)
*Mar  1 08:24:10.224: Se0/0/0 CCP: O CONFACK [REQsent] id 1 len 10
*Mar  1 08:24:10.224: Se0/0/0 CCP:    LZSDCP history 1 check mode SEQ process UNCOMPRESSSED
  (0x170600010201)
*Mar  1 08:24:10.224: Se0/0/0 CDPCP: I CONFREQ [REQsent] id 1 len 4
*Mar  1 08:24:10.224: Se0/0/0 CDPCP: O CONFACK [REQsent] id 1 len 4
*Mar  1 08:24:10.224: Se0/0/0 IPCP: I CONFACK [ACKsent] id 1 len 10
*Mar  1 08:24:10.228: Se0/0/0 IPCP:    Address 192.168.2.1 (0x0306C0A80201)
*Mar  1 08:24:10.228: Se0/0/0 IPCP: State is Open
*Mar  1 08:24:10.228: Se0/0/0 CCP: I CONFACK [ACKsent] id 1 len 10
*Mar  1 08:24:10.228: Se0/0/0 CCP:    LZSDCP history 1 check mode SEQ process UNCOMPRESSSED
  (0x170600010201)
*Mar  1 08:24:10.228: Se0/0/0 CCP: State is Open
*Mar  1 08:24:10.232: Se0/0/0 CDPCP: I CONFACK [ACKsent] id 1 len 4
*Mar  1 08:24:10.232: Se0/0/0 CDPCP: State is Open
*Mar  1 08:24:10.232: Se0/0/0 IPCP: Install route to 192.168.2.2
*Mar  1 08:24:10.244: %SYS-5-CONFIG_I: Configured from console by console
*Mar  1 08:24:11.214: %LINEPROTO-5-UPDOWN: Line protocol on Interface Serial0/0, changed
  state to up
```

**Lab 7-1: Configuring and Verifying a PPP Link (7.2.3)**

In this lab, you configure and verify a PPP link between two routers. Refer to the lab in Part II of this Learning Guide. You may perform this lab now or wait until the end of the chapter.

# PPP Authentication

Authentication on a PPP link is optional. If configured, authentication occurs after establishment of the link but before the network layer protocol configuration phase begins. Two possible types of authentication on a PPP link are *Password Authentication Protocol (PAP)* and *Challenge Handshake Authentication Protocol (CHAP)*.

## Password Authentication Protocol

PAP provides a simple method for a remote device to establish its identity. PAP uses a two-way handshake to send its username and password. The called device looks up the username of the calling device and confirms that the sent password matches what it has stored in its database. If the two passwords match, authentication is successful, as shown in Figure 7-15. PAP sends the username/password pair across the link repeatedly in clear text until acknowledgment of the authentication or termination of the connection. This authentication method does not protect the username and password from being stolen using a packet sniffer.

**Figure 7-15    Password Authentication Protocol**

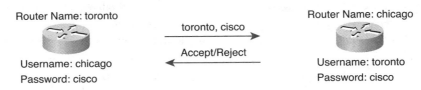

Router Name: toronto

toronto, cisco →
← Accept/Reject

Router Name: chicago

Username: chicago
Password: cisco

Username: toronto
Password: cisco

In addition, the remote node is in control of the frequency and timing of the login attempts. Once authenticated, no further verification of the remote device occurs. Without ongoing verification, the link is vulnerable to *hijacking* of the authenticated connection and the possibility of a hacker gaining illegal authorized access to the router using a *replay attack*.

A hijack attack is when an attacker gains control of an already established communication session. This allows the hijacker to view, and alter, all traffic moving across the communications channel. If the attacker alters the information as it flows across the communications channel, the attack is referred to as a man-in-the-middle attack.

A replay attack results when a valid data stream is intercepted and retransmitted. The retransmitted stream may contain malicious code with the intent of compromising the recipient machine.

## Challenge Handshake Authentication Protocol

CHAP is a more secure authentication process than PAP. CHAP does not send the password across the link. Authentication occurs both during initial link establishment and repeatedly during the time the link is active. The called device is in control of the frequency and timing of the authentication, making a hijack attack extremely unlikely.

CHAP uses a three-way handshake, as shown in Figure 7-16.

**Figure 7-16    Challenge Handshake Authentication Protocol**

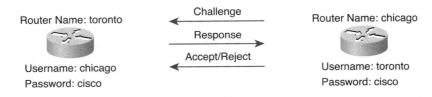

Router Name: toronto

← Challenge
Response →
← Accept/Reject

Router Name: chicago

Username: chicago
Password: cisco

Username: toronto
Password: cisco

The following list outlines the CHAP handshake authentication process:

1. PPP establishes the link phase.

2. The local router sends a *challenge message* to the remote router. This is usually a randomly generated binary string.

3. The remote router uses the challenge, a *shared secret* password, and an encryption algorithm to generate a one-way hash. A one-way hash is an encrypted string that cannot be decrypted.

4. The remote router sends back the one-way hash to the local router.

5. The local router checks the response against its own calculation, using the challenge and the same shared secret. If values match, the local router acknowledges authentication. If the values do not match, the local router immediately terminates the connection.

CHAP provides protection against playback attack through a variable challenge value. Because the challenge is unique and random, the resulting hash value is also unique and random. The use of repeated challenges limits the time of exposure to any single attack. The local router or a third-party *authentication server* is in control of the frequency and timing of the challenges.

**Interactive Activity 7-8: Identifying CHAP and PAP Characteristics (7.2.4)**

In this activity, you identify the characteristics of CHAP and PAP authentication. Use file d3ia-724 on the CD-ROM that accompanies this book to perform this interactive activity.

## Configuring PAP and CHAP

The first step in configuring either CHAP or PAP authentication on a link is to create an account for the device at the opposite end of the link. To do this, use the following global configuration command:

```
username name password password
```

In this command, the username is the name of the device at the other end of the link, and the password is the password or shared secret to enable the remote device to authenticate. This command creates a local database that contains the username and password of the remote device. The username must match the hostname of the remote router exactly and is case sensitive.

Once the user account is established, authentication can be turned on with the interface configuration command:

```
ppp authentication {chap | chap pap | pap chap | pap}
```

This command specifies the type of authentication on each interface, such as PAP or CHAP. If more than one type is specified (for example, **chap pap**), the router attempts the first type listed and will attempt the second only if the remote router suggests it. If authentication fails with the first authentication technique, the second technique is not attempted.

For CHAP authentication, no other configuration commands are required. However, in Cisco IOS Release 11.1 or later, PAP is disabled on the interface by default. This means that the router will not send its own username and password combination just because PAP authentication is enabled. To have PAP send its username and password, an additional configuration command is required on IOS Release 11.1 or later:

```
ppp pap sent-username name password password
```

This interface configuration command specifies the local username and password combination that should be sent to the remote router. This must match what the remote router has configured in the local username and password database.

Example 7-5 shows PAP configuration, and Example 7-6 shows CHAP configuration for the network shown in Figure 7-17. Two-way authentication is normally configured with each end of the link, authenticating the device on the opposite end.

**Example 7-5  PAP Configuration**

```
hostname Left
username Right password sameone
!
interface serial 0/0/0
```

```
ip address 128.0.1.1 255.255.255.0encapsulation ppp
ppp authentication PAP
ppp pap sent-username Left password sameone

hostname Right
username Left password sameone
!
interface serial 0/0/0
ip address 128.0.1.2 255.255.255.0
encapsulation ppp
ppp authentication PAP
ppp pap sent-username Right password sameone
```

**Example 7-6  CHAP Configuration**

```
hostname Left
username Right password sameone
!
interface serial 0/0/0
ip address 128.0.1.1 255.255.255.0
encapsulation ppp
ppp authentication CHAP

hostname Right
username Left password sameone
!
interface serial 0/0/0
ip address 128.0.1.2 255.255.255.0
encapsulation ppp
ppp authentication CHAP
```

**Figure 7-17    Sample Network**

Use debug commands on both routers to display the exchange sequence as it occurs. The command to debug the PPP process is as follows:

```
debug ppp{authentication | packet | error | negotiation | chap }
```

In this command, the options dictate what output will be displayed:

- **authentication**: Displays the authentication exchange sequence

- **packet**: Displays PPP packets sent and received

- **negotiation**: Displays packets transmitted during PPP startup, where PPP options are negotiated

- **error**: Displays protocol errors and statistics associated with PPP connection and negotiation

- **chap**: Displays CHAP packet exchanges

Excessive debugging can have a very serious impact on network performance. To turn off PPP debugging, use the **no** form of the command. To turn off all debugging, use **undebug all**.

Example 7-7 and Example 7-8 show a successful and an unsuccessful authentication process, respectively.

**Example 7-7  Successful PPP Authentication**

```
*Mar  1 09:09:05.899: %LINK-3-UPDOWN: Interface Serial0/0/0, changed state to up
 *Mar  1 09:09:05.899: Se0/0/0 PPP: Using default call direction
 *Mar  1 09:09:05.899: Se0/0/0 PPP: Treating connection as a dedicated line
 *Mar  1 09:09:05.899: Se0/0/0 PPP: Session handle[53000003] Session id[2]
 *Mar  1 09:09:05.899: Se0/0/0 PPP: Authorization required
 *Mar  1 09:09:05.911: Se0/0/0 CHAP: O CHALLENGE id 1 len 23 from "R1"
 *Mar  1 09:09:05.915: Se0/0/0 CHAP: I CHALLENGE id 1 len 23 from "R2"
 *Mar  1 09:09:05.919: Se0/0/0 CHAP: Using hostname from unknown source
 *Mar  1 09:09:05.919: Se0/0/0 CHAP: Using password from AAA
 *Mar  1 09:09:05.919: Se0/0/0 CHAP: O RESPONSE id 1 len 23 from "R1"
 *Mar  1 09:09:05.923: Se0/0/0 CHAP: I RESPONSE id 1 len 23 from "R2"
 *Mar  1 09:09:05.927: Se0/0/0 PPP: Sent CHAP LOGIN Request
 *Mar  1 09:09:05.927: Se0/0/0 PPP: Received LOGIN Response PASS
 *Mar  1 09:09:05.931: Se0/0/0 PPP: Sent LCP AUTHOR Request
 *Mar  1 09:09:05.931: Se0/0/0 PPP: Sent IPCP AUTHOR Request
 *Mar  1 09:09:05.931: Se0/0/0 LCP: Received AAA AUTHOR Response PASS
 *Mar  1 09:09:05.931: Se0/0/0 IPCP: Received AAA AUTHOR Response PASS
 *Mar  1 09:09:05.935: Se0/0/0 CHAP: O SUCCESS id 1 len 4
 *Mar  1 09:09:05.935: Se0/0/0 CHAP: I SUCCESS id 1 len 4
 *Mar  1 09:09:05.935: Se0/0/0 PPP: Sent CDPCP AUTHOR Request
 *Mar  1 09:09:05.939: Se0/0/0 CDPCP: Received AAA AUTHOR Response PASS
 *Mar  1 09:09:05.939: Se0/0/0 PPP: Sent IPCP AUTHOR Request
 *Mar  1 09:09:06.937: %LINEPROTO-5-UPDOWN: Line protocol on Interface Serial0/0/0, changed
state to up
```

**Example 7-8  Unsuccessful PPP Authentication**

```
 *Mar  1 09:16:42.736: Se0/0/0 PPP: Authorization required
 *Mar  1 09:16:42.748: Se0/0/0 CHAP: O CHALLENGE id 2 len 23 from "R1"
 *Mar  1 09:16:42.752: Se0/0/0 CHAP: I CHALLENGE id 2 len 23 from "R2"
 *Mar  1 09:16:42.756: Se0/0/0 CHAP: Using hostname from unknown source
 *Mar  1 09:16:42.756: Se0/0/0 CHAP: Using password from AAA
 *Mar  1 09:16:42.756: Se0/0/0 CHAP: O RESPONSE id 2 len 23 from "R1"
 *Mar  1 09:16:42.760: Se0/0/0 CHAP: I RESPONSE id 2 len 23 from "R2"
 *Mar  1 09:16:42.760: Se0/0/0 PPP: Sent CHAP LOGIN Request
 *Mar  1 09:16:42.764: Se0/0/0 PPP: Received LOGIN Response FAIL
 *Mar  1 09:16:42.764: Se0/0/0 CHAP: O FAILURE id 2 len 25 msg is "Authentication failed"
```

**Lab 7-2: Configuring and Verifying CHAP and PAP Authentication (7.2.5)**

In this lab, you configure and verify CHAP and PAP authentication on a PPP link. Refer to the lab in Part II of this Learning Guide. You may perform this lab now or wait until the end of the chapter.

# Using Frame Relay

HDLC and PPP are two common serial line encapsulations, but they are not the only options available. Frame Relay is a common technology for linking a remote network to an ISP. In addition, some large organizations use Frame Relay technology as the principle technology for their WAN environment.

## Overview of Frame Relay

Frame Relay is a common Layer 2 WAN encapsulation. Frame Relay networks are multiaccess networks similar to Ethernet except that they do not forward broadcast traffic. Thus, Frame Relay is a nonbroadcast multiaccess (NBMA) network.

Frame Relay uses packet-switching technology with variable-length packets. It also makes use of STDM for optimum use of the available bandwidth. The router, or DTE device, normally connects to the service provider via a leased line. It connects via a Frame Relay switch, or DCE device, to the nearest point of presence of the service provider. This connection is referred to as an access link. The remote router at the destination end of the network is also a DTE device. The connection between the two DTE devices is a virtual circuit (VC).

The virtual circuit is typically established using PVCs that the service provider preconfigures. Most service providers discourage or even disallow the use of SVCs in a Frame Relay network. Figure 7-18 shows a typical Frame Relay network.

**Figure 7-18    Frame Relay Network**

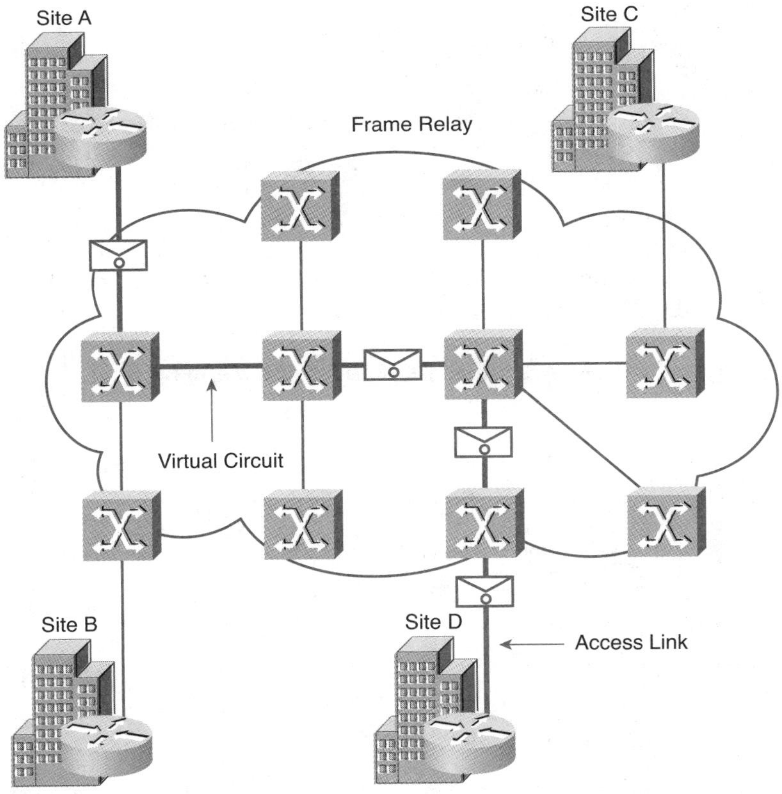

# Frame Relay Functionality

To function properly, Frame Relay must have a way to associate a specific VC with a destination Layer 3 network. It also requires a complete and accurate knowledge of the status of network VCs to reduce the chance that information is sent to a destination circuit that is no longer functioning. Inverse Address Resolution Protocol (IARP) and Local Management Interface (LMI) are mechanisms within Frame Relay to help ensure that information can be reliably sent to remote networks.

## Inverse ARP

In an NBMA network, each virtual circuit requires a Layer 2 address for identification. In Frame Relay, this address is the *data-link connection identifier (DLCI)*. The DLCI identifies the VC that data uses to reach a particular destination. The DLCI is stored in the Address field of every frame transmitted. The DLCI usually has only local significance and may be different at each end of a VC.

The Layer 2 DLCI is associated with the Layer 3 address of the device at the other end of the VC. Mapping the DLCI to a remote IP address can occur manually or dynamically using a process known as *Inverse ARP*. The Inverse ARP process requires many steps to successfully map the local DLCI to the remote IP address. These steps follow and are shown in Figures 7-19 through 7-22:

1. The local device announces its presence by sending its Layer 3 address out on the VC, as shown in Figure 7-19.

**Figure 7-19    Inverse ARP: Initial Announcement**

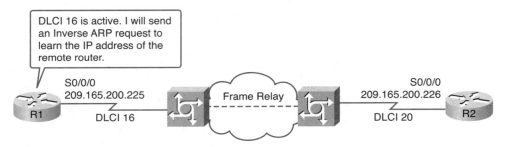

2. The remote device receives this information and maps the Layer 3 IP address to the local Layer 2 DLCI, as shown in Figure 7-20.

**Figure 7-20    Inverse ARP: Remote Device Mapping**

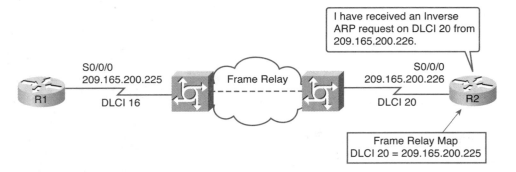

3. The remote device announces its IP address on the VC, as shown in Figure 7-21.

4. The local device maps the Layer 3 address of the remote device to the local DLCI on which it received the information, as shown in Figure 7-22.

**Figure 7-21    Inverse ARP: Remote Device Announcement**

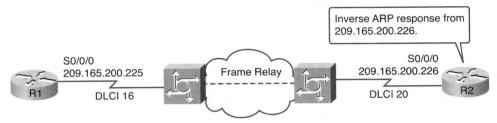

**Figure 7-22    Inverse ARP: Local Device Mapping**

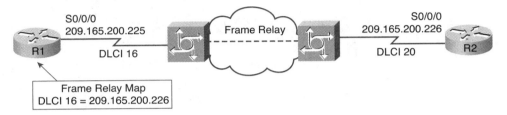

## Local Management Interface

*Local Management Interface (LMI)* is a signaling standard between the DTE and the Frame Relay switch. LMI is responsible for managing the connection and maintaining the status between devices. LMI messages provide communication and synchronization between the network and the user device. They periodically report the existence of new PVCs and the deletion of existing PVCs. They also provide information about PVC integrity. VC status messages prevent data being sent to PVCs that no longer exist. This is illustrated in Figure 7-23.

LMI provides VC connection status information that appears in the Frame Relay map table:

- **Active state**: The connection is active and routers can exchange data.

- **Inactive state**: The local connection to the Frame Relay switch is working, but the remote connection to the Frame Relay switch is not.

- **Deleted state**: No LMI is being received from the Frame Relay switch, or there is no service between the CPE router and Frame Relay switch.

When an end user subscribes to a Frame Relay service, the user negotiates certain service parameters with the provider. One parameter is the *committed information rate (CIR)*. The CIR is the minimum bandwidth rate guaranteed by the provider for data on a VC. The service provider calculates the CIR as the average amount of data transmitted over a period of time. The calculated time interval is the *committed time (Tc)*. The number of committed bits within the Tc is the *committed burst (Bc)*. The cost of the Frame Relay service depends on the speed of the link and the CIR. The CIR defines the minimum rate provided; however, if there is no congestion on the links, the service provider boosts or bursts the bandwidth up to a second agreed-upon bandwidth.

The *excess information rate (EIR)* is the average rate above the CIR that a VC can support when no network congestion exists. Any extra bits above the committed burst, up to the maximum speed of the access link, is known as the *excess burst (Be)*. Frames transmitted above the speed of the CIR are uncommitted, but they are forwarded if the network supports it. These extra fames are marked as *discard eligible (DE)*. If congestion occurs, the provider first drops frames with the DE bit set. Users often pay for a lower CIR, counting on the fact that the service provider supplies higher bandwidth and bursts their traffic when there is no congestion.

**Figure 7-23    LMI Functionality**

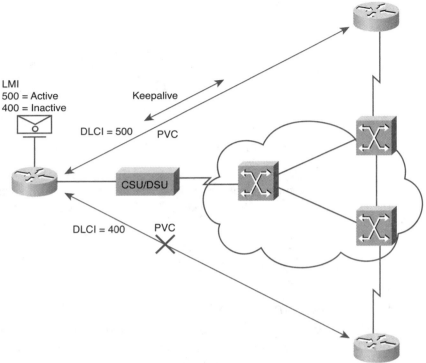

The *forward explicit congestion notification (FECN)* is a single-bit field that can be set to a value of 1 by a switch. It indicates to an end DTE device that the network is congested ahead. The *backward explicit congestion notification (BECN)* is a single-bit field that, when set to a value of 1 by a switch, indicates that the network is congested in the opposite direction. FECN and BECN allow higher-layer protocols to react intelligently to these congestion indicators. For example, the sending device uses BECNs to slow its transmission rate. This is shown in Figure 7-24.

**Figure 7-24    Congestion on a Frame Relay Circuit**

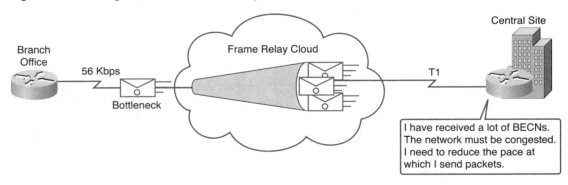

**Interactive Activity 7-9: Matching Frame Relay Terminology (7.3.2)**

In this activity, you match the Frame Relay term to its definition. Use file d3ia-732 on the CD-ROM that accompanies this book to perform this interactive activity.

# Summary

A WAN uses many different technologies to connect remote users. Each technology offers distinct advantages but also has some serious limitations. The choice of WAN technology depends on both the end-user requirements and the technology available in the geographical location.

WAN technologies are either last mile or long range in nature. Last-mile technologies connect the end user to the ISP, and long-range technologies normally interconnect ISPs.

Analog WAN technologies require the use of a modem to encode or modulate the digital signal onto the analog carrier wave. Digital technologies use a CSU/DSU to prepare the data for transmission on the WAN link.

WAN technologies can be classified as either leased line, circuit switching, or packet and cell switching. Leased-line connections provide a dedicated circuit and are normally used for access circuits to a service provider or when data security and dedicated bandwidth are required. Circuit-switching technology creates a physical end-to-end connection between source and destination before any information is sent. Packet- and cell-switching technologies create virtual circuits through the service provider network to connect end devices. There is no physical end-to-end connectivity between end devices in a packet or cell-switched network. Virtual circuits may either be permanent (PVC) or created when required and torn down when no longer required (SVC).

HDLC is the default serial line encapsulation on Cisco routers. Cisco HDLC includes an extra type field, making it incompatible with the HDLC used by other vendors. PPP is a standards-based encapsulation that supports many advanced features and can be used to interconnect equipment from different vendors.

PPP uses LCP to set options and test the quality of the link. One option that can be configured is authentication. If the link quality is sufficient, LCP starts an NCP for every Layer 3 protocol carried across the link. If the LCP terminate the link, it first notifies the NCP to shut down the Layer 3 protocols.

PPP supports both PAP and CHAP authentication. With PAP, the username and password are sent once at the beginning of the conversation. CHAP never sends the password across the link in clear text. It periodically challenges the remote device to provide a response. If the response fails, the connection is terminated. CHAP should be used whenever possible.

Frame Relay is a packet-switched technology that uses either SVCs or PVCs to connect to a remote device. The Frame Relay network uses many different parameters to determine the cost of a link and to ensure reliable delivery. BECNs and FECNs are used to identify congestion on the link to allow measures to be taken to reduce the congestion.

# Activities and Labs

This summary outlines the activities and labs you can perform to help reinforce important concepts described in this chapter. You can find the activity files on the CD-ROM accompanying this book. The complete hands-on labs appear in Part II.

**Interactive activities on the CD-ROM:**

Interactive Activity 7-1: Matching WAN Terminology (7.1.1)

Interactive Activity 7-2: Matching WAN Standards to the OSI Model (7.1.2)

Interactive Activity 7-3: Determining How TDM and STDM Handle a Data Stream (7.1.3)

Interactive Activity 7-4: Selecting the Appropriate WAN Technology (7.1.4)

Interactive Activity 7-5: Describing WAN Technologies (7.1.5)

Interactive Activity 7-6: Matching Layer 2 Encapsulation Terminology (7.2.1)

Interactive Activity 7-7: Identifying PPP Components and Phases (7.2.2)

Interactive Activity 7-8: Identifying CHAP and PAP Characteristics (7.2.4)

Interactive Activity 7-9: Matching Frame Relay Terminology (7.3.2)

**Hands-on labs in Part II of this book:**

Lab 7-1: Configuring and Verifying a PPP Link (7.2.3)

Lab 7-2: Configuring and Verifying PAP and CHAP Authentication (7.2.5)

# Check Your Understanding

Complete all the review questions listed here to check your understanding of the topics and concepts in this chapter. Appendix A, "Check Your Understanding and Challenge Questions Answer Key" lists the answers.

1. What is the most common Layer 2 LAN encapsulation?

   A. Ethernet

   B. Frame Relay

   C. HDLC

   D. PPP

2. Which organizations are responsible for the creation of WAN standards? (Choose all that apply.)

   A. ITU-T

   B. ISO

   C. Internet Engineering Task Force (IETF)

   D. EIA

   E. TIA

3. How does STDM differ from TDM?

4. Which technology is used for long-range WAN connections? (Choose all that apply.)

   A. Cable

   B. DSL

   C. DWDM

   D. Ethernet

   E. SONET

5. Which WAN technology forms a physical end-to-end connection between sender and receiver before transmitting any data?

   A. Cell Switching

   B. Circuit Switching

   C. Packet Switching

   D. PVC

   E. SVC

6. Why is HDLC not a good protocol to use when connecting routers from different vendors?

7. What is the role of LCP in PPP?

8. A PPP link is configured on the Toronto and Sydney routers with the following commands:

   ```
   Toronto(config-if)# ppp authentication chap pap
   Sydney(config-if)# ppp authentication chap pap
   ```

   What will happen if CHAP authentication fails?

9. What is the role of the Frame Relay LMI?

10. In a Frame Relay network, what happens to data that exceeds the CIR?

## Challenge Questions and Activities

These questions require a deeper application of the concepts covered in this chapter. You can find the answers in Appendix A.

1. A junior networking technician has configured a new PPP link between the head office router and the new remote office. Unfortunately, the link fails to activate, and he has asked for your assistance in determining and correcting the problem. The relevant parts of the configuration files follow. What is wrong with the configuration, and how would you correct the issue?

   Head Office Router

   ```
   hostname Main
   username Main password cisco
   !
   int serial 0/0/0
   ip address 128.0.1.1
   255.255.255.0
   encapsulation ppp
   ppp authentication CHAP
   ```

   Remote Office Router

   ```
   hostname Remote
   username Remote password Cisco
   !
   int serial 0/0/0
   ip address 128.0.1.2
   255.255.255.0
   encapsulation ppp
   ppp authentication PAP
   ```

   There are three configuration errors. The username accounts must be for the opposite router, not the router that they are configured on. The password is case sensitive and must be the same on both ends. The third configuration mistake is that one end of the link is configured for CHAP authentication, and the other end is configured for PAP. All three of these must be corrected before the link will come up.

2. AnyCompany currently has dedicated leased lines between all three branch offices and the head office. They have just acquired a new manufacturing division that has offices in four other countries. The cost of obtaining leased-line connections to these sites is extremely high, and the company management has asked you to suggest an alternative technology. What would you suggest and why?

Leased-line connections require a dedicated interface and a separate CSU/DSU for each line. The lines themselves are extremely expensive to obtain and maintain making their use in large organizations cost prohibitive. An alternative packet-switching technology such as Frame Relay would be an excellent choice for this organization. Each office could maintain a leased line connect to their nearest ISP, and multiple PVCs could be established through the ISPs network to connect each of the offices. Each site would require only a single leased-line connection, meaning one interface and one CSU/DSU.

# CHAPTER 8

# Filtering Traffic Using Access Control Lists

## Objectives

Upon completion of this chapter, you should be able to answer the following questions:

- What is traffic filtering?

- How do access control lists (ACL) filter traffic at router interfaces?

- What is an ACL wildcard mask, and how is it used?

- How are ACLs configured and implemented?

- How can ACL activity be logged?

- What are ACL best practices?

## Key Terms

This chapter uses the following key terms. You can find the definitions in the Glossary.

Enterprise networks need security to ensure that only authorized users access network resources. Traffic filtering tools such as access control lists (ACL) are an important component of enterprise network security. ACLs permit and deny specific types of inbound and outbound network traffic. Network engineers and technicians plan, configure, and verify ACLs on routers and other networking devices.

Part II of this book includes the corresponding labs for this chapter.

# Using Access Control Lists

Traffic filtering using ACLs is an important part of network management and control. This section describes the concepts of traffic filtering and ACLs. Types of ACLS and their usage and ACL processing are discussed.

## Traffic Filtering

Security within an enterprise network is extremely critical. It is important to prevent access by unauthorized users and protect the network from various attacks, such as denial-of-service (DoS) attacks. Unauthorized users can modify, destroy, or steal sensitive data on servers. DoS attacks prevent valid users from accessing facilities. Both of these situations cause a business to lose time and money.

The function of traffic filtering for network access is similar to the card-reader security systems that a company might use to control access to various buildings on a campus in an enterprise environment. An employee of the company might be able to enter one building or floor in a building but not another depending on his or her clearance level. A nonemployee might be prevented from entering any building on campus. In the same way, ACLs placed at specific locations in a network can control which traffic is allowed to enter and exit from a given area.

Through *traffic filtering*, an administrator controls traffic in various segments of the network. Filtering is the process of analyzing the contents of a packet to determine whether the packet should be allowed or blocked. Just as with a physical filter, certain elements are permitted to pass, and others are blocked or filtered.

Packet filtering can be simple or complex, denying or permitting traffic based on the following criteria:

- Source IP address
- Destination IP address
- MAC address
- Protocol
- Application type

Packet filtering can be compared to junk e-mail filtering. Many e-mail applications enable the user to adjust the configuration to automatically delete e-mail from a particular source address. Packet filtering can be done in the same way by configuring a router to identify and remove unwanted traffic. Much the same way that you might look at the caller ID on your phone and decide not to answer it, a packet filter can look at a source address and deny it.

Traffic filtering improves network performance. By denying unwanted or restricted traffic close to its source, the traffic does not travel across a network and consume valuable resources. Figure 8-1 illustrates the concept of traffic filtering, whereby some types of traffic and traffic from certain sources are permitted and others are blocked.

**Figure 8-1    Filtering Different Types of Traffic**

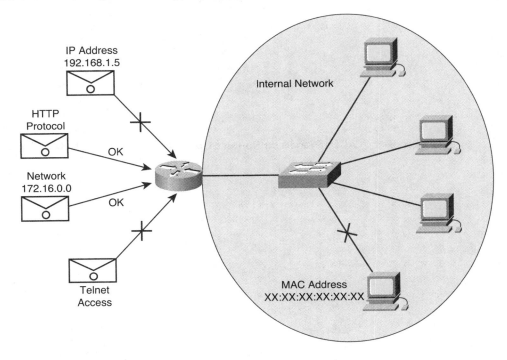

Devices most commonly used to provide traffic filtering include the following:

- Firewalls built in to integrated routers

- Dedicated security appliances

- Servers

Some devices filter traffic that originates only from the internal network. More sophisticated security devices recognize and filter known types of attacks from external sources. Figure 8-2 shows several different network devices that have firewall capabilities and can provide traffic filtering.

Enterprise routers recognize harmful traffic and prevent it from accessing and damaging the network. Nearly all routers filter traffic based on the source and destination IP addresses of packets. They also filter on specific applications and on protocols such as IP, TCP, HTTP, FTP, and Telnet.

## Access Control Lists

One of the most common methods of traffic filtering is the use of ACLs. ACLs can be used to manage and filter traffic that enters a network and traffic that exits a network. Figure 8-3 shows the placement of ACLs on router interfaces to filter traffic.

**Figure 8-2    Networking Devices That Provide Traffic Filtering**

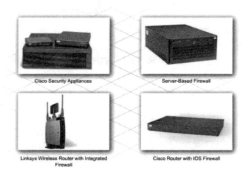

**Figure 8-3    ACLs Placed on Routers Control Traffic Between Networks**

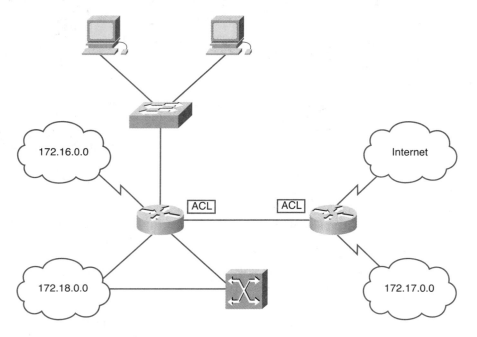

An ACL ranges in size from one statement that allows or denies traffic from one source, to hundreds of statements that allow or deny packets from multiple sources. The primary use of ACLs is to identify the types of packets to accept or deny.

ACLs identify traffic for multiple uses, such as the following:

- Specifying internal hosts for Network Address Translation (NAT)

- Identifying or classifying traffic for advanced features such as quality of service (QoS) and queuing

- Restricting the contents of routing updates

- Limiting debug output

- Controlling virtual terminal access to routers

The following potential problems can result from using ACLs:

- The additional load on the router to check all packets means less time to actually forward packets.

- Poorly designed ACLs place an even greater load on the router and might disrupt network usage.

- Improperly placed ACLs block traffic that should be allowed and permit traffic that should be blocked.

- ACLs can also introduce problems in troubleshooting.

Cisco IOS permits the creation of three types of ACLs: standard, extended, and named. Table 8-1 shows the three types of ACLs, an example of how each is created, and the effects of the configuration command or statement.

**Table 8-1    Types of IOS Access Lists**

| Type of ACL | Sample ACL Command/Statement | Purpose of Statement |
|---|---|---|
| Standard | Router(config)# **access-list 1 permit host 172.16.2.88** | Permits a specific IP address |
| Extended | Router(config)# **access-list 100 deny tcp 172.16.2.0 0.0.0.255 any eq telnet** | Denies access to the 172.16.2.0/24 subnet to any other host attempting to use Telnet |
| Named | Router(config)# **ip access-list standard permit-ip**<br>Router(config-std-nacl)# **permit host 192.168.5.47** | Creates a standard ACL named permit-ip<br><br>(After first command puts the router into NACL sub-command mode)<br><br>Allows access to IP address 192.168.5.47 |

## Types and Usage of ACLs

When creating ACLs, a network administrator has several options. The complexity of the design guidelines determines the type of ACL required.

This section describes the three types of ACLs.

## Standard ACLs

The *standard ACL* is the simplest of the three types. When you create a standard IP ACL, the ACL filters based on the source IP address of a packet. Standard ACLs permit or deny based on the entire Layer 3 IP and cannot filter based on Layer 4 or higher protocols that run over IP. So, if a host device is denied by a standard ACL, all services from that host are denied. This type of ACL is useful for allowing all services from a specific user, or LAN, access through a router while denying other IP addresses access. Standard ACLs are identified by the number assigned to them. For access lists permitting or denying IP traffic, the identification number can range from 1 to 99 and from 1300 to 1999.

## Extended ACLs

*Extended ACLs* filter not only on the source IP address but also on the destination IP address, protocol, and port numbers. Extended ACLs are used more frequently than standard ACLs because they are more specific and provide greater control. The range of numbers for extended ACLs is from 100 to 199 and from 2000 to 2699.

## Named ACLs

*Named ACLs (NACL)* are either standard or extended format that are referenced by a descriptive name rather than a number. When configuring NACLs, the router IOS uses an NACL subcommand mode.

**Interactive Activity 8-1: Types and Usage of ACLs (8.1.3)**

In this activity, you indicate whether the characteristic describes a standard, extended, or named ACL. Use file d3ia-813 on the CD-ROM that accompanies this book to perform this interactive activity.

# ACL Processing

ACLs consist of one or more statements. Each statement either permits or denies traffic based on specified parameters. Traffic is compared to each statement in the ACL sequentially until a match is found or until there are no more statements.

The last statement of an ACL is always an *implicit deny*. This statement is automatically inserted at the end of each ACL; it is not entered as part of the ACL by an administrator. In addition, it does not display with ACL **show** commands. The implicit **deny** blocks all traffic. This feature prevents the accidental entry of unwanted traffic.

After you create an ACL, you must apply it to an interface for it to become effective. In addition, if an ACL is applied to an interface without first creating it, all traffic is denied.

An ACL targets traffic that is either inbound or outbound through the interface. If a packet matches a *permit* statement, it is allowed to enter or exit the router. If it matches a *deny* statement, it is dropped and goes no further. An ACL that does not have at least one **permit** statement blocks all traffic. This is because at the end of every ACL is an implicit **deny**. Therefore, an ACL will deny all traffic not specifically permitted.

In Figures 8-4 and 8-5, the following ACL is applied to the router S0/0/0 interface in the inbound direction. The first statement permits packets from the host with IP address 192.168.1.1. The **deny** statement is implied:

```
access-list 1 permit host 192.168.1.1
```

Is the same as

```
access-list 1 permit host 192.168.1.1
access-list 1 deny any (implied)
```

In Figure 8-4, when a packet from host 192.168.1.1 reaches the router, the first **permit** statement matches the source IP address in the packet, and the ACL permits the packet to pass though the router. In Figure 8-5, when a packet from host 192.168.1.5 reaches the router, the first **permit** statement does not match the source IP address in the packet, and the implied **deny any** statement at the end of the ACL blocks the packet, not allowing it to pass through the router.

**Figure 8-4    Access List Statement Permits Specific Traffic**

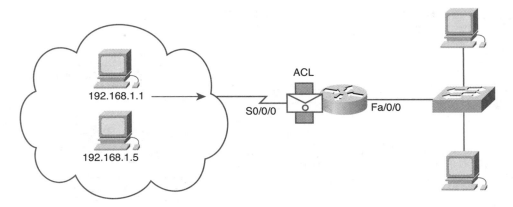

**Figure 8-5    Access List Implicit Deny Blocks All Other Traffic**

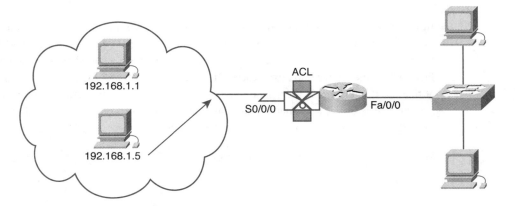

An administrator applies an ACL to a router interface either inbound or outbound. The inbound or outbound direction is always from the perspective of the router. Traffic coming in an interface from the outside is inbound, and traffic leaving or going out an interface is outbound.

When a packet arrives at an interface, the router checks the following parameters:

- Is there an ACL associated with the interface?

- Is the ACL inbound or outbound?

- Does the traffic match the criteria for permitting or denying?

An ACL applied outbound to an interface has no effect on traffic inbound on that same interface.

Each interface of a router can have one ACL per direction for each network protocol. For IP, one interface can have one ACL inbound and one ACL outbound at the same time.

ACLs applied to an interface add latency to the traffic. Even one long ACL can affect router performance.

In Figure 8-6, the router has an ACL applied to the S0/0/0 interface inbound. When any IP packet from the 192.168.1.0/24 network reaches that interface, the router must examine it. If there is a match and the packet is to be permitted, it is switched to the outbound interface. If there is a match and the packet is to be denied, it is dropped at the S0/0/0 interface.

**Figure 8-6    Inbound ACL Placement**

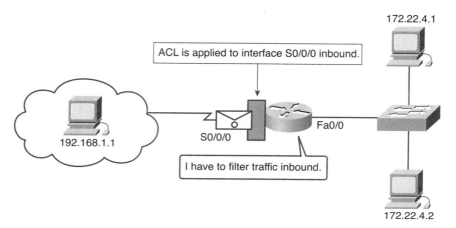

In Figure 8-7, the router has an ACL applied to the Fa0/0 interface outbound and no ACL on the S0/0/0 interface. When any IP packet from the 192.168.1.0/24 network destined for the 172.22.4.0 network reaches the S0/0/0 interface, the router immediately switches it to the Fa0/0 outbound interface, where the router must examine it. If there is a match and the packet is to be denied, it is dropped at the Fa0/0 interface. If there is a match and the packet is to be permitted, it is allowed to pass to the switch. If it is possible to match and deny packets at the S0/0/0 interface rather than the Fa0/0 interface, the router does not have to switch the packet first.

**Figure 8-7    Outbound ACL Placement**

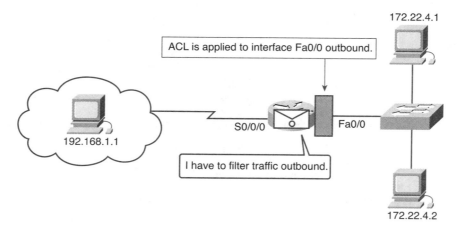

**Interactive Activity 8-2: ACL Processing (8.1.4)**

In this activity, you determine whether the packet will be permitted or denied based on source IP address. Use file d3ia-814 on the CD-ROM that accompanies this book to perform this interactive activity.

# Using a Wildcard Mask

The ACL wildcard mask is used to control which IP address or group of addresses is matched and ultimately permitted or denied. This section describes the purpose of the ACL wildcard mask, its structure, and how to determine the wildcard mask for a particular requirement. It also analyzes various wildcard masks and their effects on traffic filtering.

## ACL Wildcard Mask Purpose and Structure

Simple ACLs specify only one permitted or denied address. Blocking multiple addresses or ranges of addresses requires using either multiple statements or a wildcard mask. Using an IP network address with a wildcard mask allows much more flexibility. A wildcard mask can block a range of addresses, a subnet, or a whole network with one statement.

A wildcard mask uses 0s to indicate the portion of an IP address that must match exactly and 1s to indicate the portion of the IP address that does not have to match a specific number. As an example, the 0s in the following wildcard mask allow all traffic from the 10.1.1.0/24 network. A packet from host 10.1.1.1 would match this ACL, as would one from host 10.1.1.253. This wildcard mask looks at the first 24 bits (the 0s) of an incoming address and ignores the last 8 bits (the 1s).

**Decimal IP address**:        10  .  1  .  1  .  1

**Binary IP address**:    00001010.00000001.00000001.00000001

**Wildcard mask**:        00000000.00000000.00000000.11111111

A wildcard mask of 0.0.0.0 requires an exact match on all 32 bits of the IP address. This mask equates to the use of the host parameter. The following examples show combinations of an ACL IP address and wildcard mask that permits a single host or a range of hosts for full-octet network boundaries. A wildcard mask is always paired with a base comparison address. The combination of the wildcard mask and the comparison address determines which bits of an incoming packet are analyzed by the ACL statement:

- **Wildcard mask that permits a single host**

    172.16.22.87        0.0.0.0

- **Wildcard mask that permits all hosts for a /24 network**

    192.168.1.0        0.0.0.255

- **Wildcard mask that permits all hosts for a /16 network**

    172.20.0.0        0.0.255.255

- **Wildcard mask that permits all hosts for a /8 network**

    10.0.0.0        0.255.255.255

The wildcard mask used with ACLs functions like the one used in the OSPF routing protocol. However, the purpose of each mask is different. With the OSPF routing protocol, the wildcard mask specifies a host or range of network addresses to advertise for routing purposes. With ACL statements, the wildcard mask specifies a host or range of addresses to be permitted or denied.

When creating an ACL statement, the IP address and wildcard mask become the comparison fields. All packets that enter or exit an interface are compared to each statement of the ACL to determine whether there is a match. The wildcard mask determines how many bits of the incoming IP address match the comparison address.

As an example, the following statement permits all hosts from the 192.168.1.0 network and blocks all others:

```
access-list 1 permit 192.168.1.0 0.0.0.255
```

The comparison address is network 192.168.1.0, and the wildcard mask is 0.0.0.255. The wildcard mask specifies that only the first 3 octets must match. Therefore, if the first 24 bits of the incoming packet match the first 24 bits of the comparison address, the packet is permitted. Any packet with a source IP address in the range of 192.168.1.1 to 192.168.1.255 matches the example comparison address and mask combination. All other packets are denied by the ACL implicit **deny any** statement.

To determine whether a packet matches the ACL statement, use the following steps while referring to Table 8-2:

**Step 1.** Convert the decimal comparison address to binary.

**Step 2.** Convert the decimal wildcard mask to binary.

**Step 3.** Compare the wildcard mask match bits (first 24 0s) with comparison address bits to determine the bits that must match.

**Step 4.** Convert the incoming address to binary.

Compare the first 24 bits from an incoming address to the first 24 bits of the comparison address (bits that must match from the comparison address). If they match, the packet is either permitted or denied based on the action specified in the ACL statement. In this case, the 192.168.1.27 packet is permitted, based on the previous ACL statement.

Table 8-2 shows the steps as they are applied.

**Table 8-2    Using the Wildcard Mask to Match Incoming Packets**

| Step | Decimal Equivalent | Binary Equivalent |
| --- | --- | --- |
| 1. Comparison address | 192.168.1.0 | 11000000.10101000.00000001.00000000 |
| 2. Wildcard mask | 0.0.0.255 | 00000000.00000000.00000000.11111111 |
| 3. Comparison address bits to match | 192.168.1.x | 11000000.10101000.00000001.*XXXXXXXX* |
| 4. Incoming packet address | 192.168.1.27 | 11000000.10101000.00000001.00011011 |

### Interactive Activity 8-3: ACL Wildcard Mask Purpose and Structure (8.2.1)

In this activity, you determine the wildcard mask based on the ACL statement objective. Use file d3ia-821 on the CD-ROM that accompanies this book to perform this interactive activity.

## Analyzing the Effects of the Wildcard Mask

When creating an ACL, you can use two special keywords in place of a wildcard mask: **host** and **any**.

To filter a single, specific host, use either the wildcard mask 0.0.0.0 after the IP address or the **host** keyword before the IP address:

```
R1(config)# access-list 9 deny 192.168.15.99 0.0.0.0
```

Is the same as

```
R1(config)# access-list 9 deny host 192.168.15.99
```

To filter all hosts, use the all-1s wildcard mask of 255.255.255.255. When using a wildcard mask of 255.255.255.255, all bits are considered matches, and therefore the IP address is typically represented as 0.0.0.0. Another way to filter all hosts is to use the **any** keyword:

```
R1(config)# access-list 9 permit 0.0.0.0 255.255.255.255
```

Is the same as

```
R1(config)# access-list 9 permit any
```

Consider the following example that denies a specific host and permits all others:

```
R1(config)# access-list 9 deny host 192.168.15.99
R1(config)# access-list 9 permit any
```

The **permit any** command permits all traffic not specifically denied in the ACL. When this is configured, no packets will reach the implicit **deny any** at the end of the ACL. In Figure 8-8, when the previous ACL is applied to the router Fa0/0 interface inbound, it denies only host 192.168.15.99 but allows all others.

**Figure 8-8    ACL Denies a Specific Host and Permits All Others**

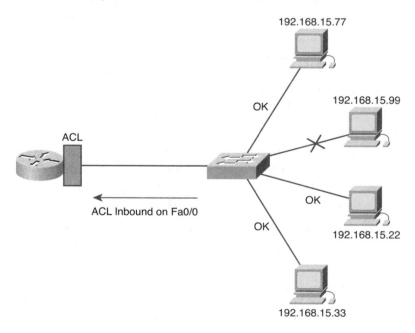

In an enterprise network with a hierarchical IP addressing scheme, it is often necessary to filter subnet traffic.

If 3 bits are used for subnetting the 192.168.77.0 network, the subnet mask is 255.255.255.224. Subtracting the subnet mask from the all-255s mask results in a wildcard mask of 0.0.0.31. To permit the hosts on the 192.168.77.32 subnet, the ACL statement is as follows:

```
access-list 44 permit 192.168.77.32 0.0.0.31
```

The first 27 bits of each packet match the first 27 bits of the comparison address. The overall range of addresses that this statement permits is from 192.168.77.33 to 192.168.77.63, which is the range of all addresses on the 192.168.77.32 subnet.

Table 8-3 shows how the wildcard mask can be derived from the last octet of the subnet mask. The first 3 octets of the subnet mask are all 255s. A subnet octet of 255 (eight 1s) always converts to a wildcard octet of 0 (eight 0s), so the first three wildcard octets are all decimal zero (0). The last non-255 subnet octet is 224. Using the table, you can determine that the wildcard equivalent of 224 is 31. You can check that this is correct by adding the two to see whether they equal 255 (224 + 31 = 255). The wildcard mask is normally the complement of the subnet mask. Zero bits in the wildcard mask are the match bits. One bits are nonmatch bits, meaning the incoming packet address does not have to match these bits. To match subnet address 192.168.77.32 255.255.255.224, you need a base comparison address and wildcard mask of 192.168.77.32 0.0.0.31.

**Table 8-3    Converting a Subnet Mask to a Wildcard Mask**

| Bit Value | 128 | 64 | 32 | 16 | 8 | 4 | 2 | 1 | Decimal Value |
|-----------|-----|----|----|----|----|----|----|----|---------------|
| All 1s | 1 | 1 | 1 | 1 | 1 | 1 | 1 | 1 | 255 |
| Subnet mask | 1 | 1 | 1 | 0 | 0 | 0 | 0 | 0 | 244 |
| Wildcard mask | 0 | 0 | 0 | 1 | 1 | 1 | 1 | 1 | 31 |

**Tip**

By looking at the fourth octet portion of the wildcard mask, you can determine how many hosts are covered by the mask. The mask is always one more than the number of valid host addresses on the subnet. A mask of .31 defines 30 hosts, and the subnet numbers with this subnet mask increment by 32 (.0, .32, .64, and so on).

A network that is a full Class A, B, or C has a subnet mask and a wildcard mask that divide evenly at an octet boundary, which results in every octet having a value of 0 (00000000) or 255 (11111111). Subnets that do not break on an octet boundary produce a different wildcard mask value. An octet boundary is a place between the first and second, second and third, or third and fourth octets.

For example, a default Class A subnet falls between bit positions 8 and 9. This breaks at the end of one octet and the beginning of the next, said to be at the boundary of the next octet. An example is 10.1.0.0 with a wildcard mask of 0.0.255.255.

Creating accurate wildcard masks for ACL statements provides the control required to fine-tune traffic flow. Filtering different subnet traffic is the most difficult concept for beginners.

The 192.168.77.0 network, with a subnet mask of 255.255.255.192 or /26, creates the following four subnets:

192.168.77.0/26

192.168.77.64/26

192.168.77.128/26

192.168.77.192/26

To create an ACL to filter any of these four subnets, subtract the subnet mask 255.255.255.192 from the all-255s mask, resulting in a wildcard mask of 0.0.0.63. To permit traffic from the first two of these subnets, you can use two ACL statements:

```
access-list 55 permit 192.168.77.0 0.0.0.63
access-list 55 permit 192.168.77.64 0.0.0.63
```

The first two networks also summarize to 192.168.77.0/25. Subtracting the summarized subnet mask of 255.255.255.128 from the all-255s mask results in a wildcard mask of 0.0.0.127. Using this mask groups these two subnets into one ACL statement rather than two:

```
access-list 55 permit 192.168.77.0 0.0.0.127
```

Figure 8-9 shows all four of the 192.168.77.0/26 subnets, with the first two being permitted and the last two being blocked by the implied **deny any** statement. Two subnets can be referenced by either one or two ACL statements, as described previously.

**Figure 8-9    Matching Multiple Subnets with ACL Statements**

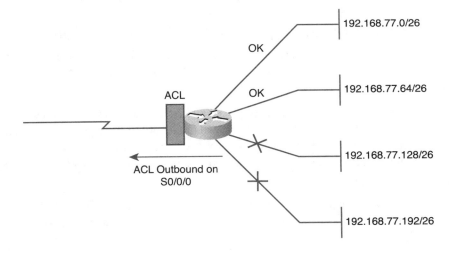

**Interactive Activity 8-4: Analyzing the Effects of the Wildcard Mask (8.2.2)**

In this activity, you determine whether the IP packet is permitted or denied by analyzing the comparison address and wildcard mask. Use file d3ia-822 on the CD-ROM that accompanies this book to perform this interactive activity.

# Configuring Access Control Lists

The configuration and placement of ACLs is a valuable skill for a network technician, as is the selection of the type of ACL to be used. This section describes the basic ACL configuration process and provides guidance for the placement of standard and extended ACLs. In addition, specific instructions are provided for configuring numbered and named ACLS.

## Placing Standard and Extended ACLs

Properly designed ACLs positively impact network performance and availability. Plan the creation and placement of ACLs to maximize this effect.

Planning involves the following steps:

**Step 1.**   Determine the traffic-filtering requirements.

**Step 2.**   Decide which type of ACL best suits the requirements.

**Step 3.**   Determine the router and the interface on which to apply the ACL.

**Step 4.**   Determine in which direction to filter traffic.

### Step 1: Determine Traffic-Filtering Requirements

Gather traffic-filtering requirements from *stakeholders* from within each department of an enterprise. These requirements differ from enterprise to enterprise and are based on customer needs, traffic types, traffic loads, and security concerns.

### Step 2: Decide Type of ACL to Suit Requirements

The decision to use a standard ACL or an extended ACL depends on the filtering requirements of the situation. The choice of ACL type can affect the flexibility of the ACL, the router performance, and network link bandwidth.

Standard ACLs are simple to create and implement. However, standard ACLs filter based only on the source address and filter all traffic without regard to the type or the destination of the traffic. With routes to multiple networks, a standard ACL placed too close to the source might unintentionally block traffic that should be permitted, Therefore, it is important to place standard ACLs as close to the destination as possible.

Examine Figure 8-10. The requirements are to prevent traffic from the 192.168.1.0 network from entering the 192.168.4.0 network but allow it to reach the other networks.

The standard ACL to be used is this:

```
access-list 9 deny 192.168.1.0 0.0.0.255
access-list 9 permit any
```

The ACL placed on the R1 Fa0/0 interface in the inbound direction is not at a good location. Putting the ACL here succeeds in preventing traffic from the 192.168.1.0 network from getting to the 192.168.4.0 network, but it also prevents it from reaching the 192.168.2.0 and the 192.168.3.0 networks, which does not meet the requirement. Placing the ACL on this interface inbound would have the same effect as shutting down the interface.

**Figure 8-10    Standard ACL Placement**

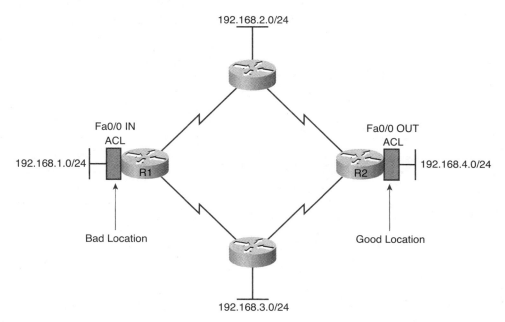

Figure 8-10 also shows placing a standard ACL on the Fa0/0 interface of R2 as close to the destination as possible. This is a better location because it denies 192.168.1.0 network traffic access to the 192.168.4.0 network but still allows it to reach the other networks. Unfortunately, the traffic must travel all the way across the network before it is blocked, using up WAN bandwidth. This is not necessarily bad. If there is no need to filter application traffic and you have decent bandwidth, a standard access list may be appropriate. Although they can be used for security, standard ACLS are often used for other purposes, such as specifying the range of addresses to be translated with NAT or to limit debug output.

When filtering requirements are more complex, use an extended ACL. Extended ACLs offer more control than standard ACLs. They filter on source and destination addresses. They also filter by looking at the network layer protocol, transport layer protocol, and port numbers if required. This increased filtering detail allows a network administrator to create ACLs that meet the specific needs of a security plan.

Place an extended ACL close to the source address. By looking at both the source and destination address, the ACL blocks packets intended for a specific destination network before they leave the source router. The packets are filtered before they cross the network, which helps conserve bandwidth.

In Figure 8-11, the requirements are the same, but an extended ACL is to be used:

```
access-list 109 deny ip 192.168.1.0 0.0.0.255  192.168.4.0 0.0.0.255
access-list 109 permit ip any any
```

This extended ACL is placed on the R1 Fa0/0 interface in the inbound direction. Whereas this was not a good location for a standard ACL, it is a good location for an extended one because the destination network can be specified. The ACL blocks the traffic from the 192.168.1.0 network and prevents it from getting to the 192.168.4.0 network, but it still allows it to reach the other networks. In addition, the traffic is prevented from traveling across the network before it is blocked, because the destination address could be specified at the source router.

**Figure 8-11    Extended ACL Placement**

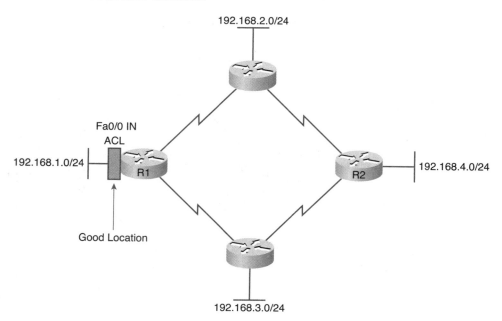

## Step 3: Determine Router and Interface for ACL

Place ACLs on routers in either the access or distribution layer. A network administrator must have control of these routers and be able to implement a security policy. A network administrator who does not have access to a router cannot configure an ACL on it.

Selection of the appropriate interface depends on the filtering requirements, the ACL type, and the location of the designated router. It is best to filter traffic before it advances onto a lower-bandwidth serial link. The interface selection is usually obvious after the router has been chosen.

## Step 4: Determine Direction to Filter Traffic

When determining the direction in which to apply an ACL, visualize the traffic flow from the perspective of the router.

Inbound traffic is traffic coming into a router interface from outside. The router compares the incoming packet to the ACL before looking up the destination network in the routing table. Packets discarded at this point save the overhead of routing lookups. This makes the inbound ACL more efficient for the router than an outbound ACL.

Outbound traffic is inside the router and leaves through an interface. For an outbound packet, the router has already done a routing table lookup and has switched the packet to the correct interface. The packet is compared to the ACL just before leaving the router.

Figure 8-12 shows another network topology. The requirements are to prevent traffic from the 192.168.1.0/24 network from entering the 192.168.2.0/24 network but allow it to reach other networks.

To satisfy these requirements, answer the four basic questions:

1. What kind of ACL? Extended

2. On which router? R1

3. On what interface? Fa0/0

4. In what direction? Inbound

The extended ACL statements are these:

```
access-list 101 deny ip 192.168.1.0  0.0.0.255  192.168.2.0 0.0.0.255
access-list 101 permit ip any any
```

**Figure 8-12    Determining ACL Type and Placement**

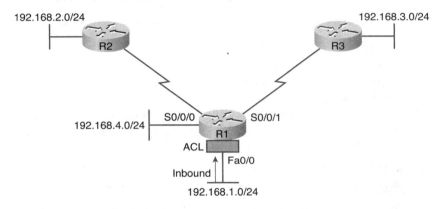

**Interactive Activity 8-5: Placing Standard and Extended ACLs (8.3.1)**

In this activity, you determine the correct router, interface, and direction for placement of the ACL. Use file d3ia-831 on the CD-ROM that accompanies this book to perform this interactive activity.

## Basic ACL Configuration Process

After capturing the requirements, planning the ACL, and determining the location, configure the ACL.

Each ACL requires a unique identifier. This identifier can be either a number or a descriptive name.

In numbered ACLs, the number identifies the type of ACL created:

- Standard IP ACLs have numbers in the ranges from 1 to 99 and from 1300 to 1999.

- Extended IP ACLs have numbers in the ranges from 100 to 199 and from 2000 to 2699.

**Note**

It is also possible to create AppleTalk and IPX protocol ACLs, although they do not apply to IP-only networks. IP networks and ACLs are by far the most common because IP is the protocol of the Internet. The IPX and AppleTalk protocols are infrequently used in modern networks, and this course does not address ACLs for use with these protocols.

The limit for any one router interface is one ACL per protocol (IP, IPX, and so on) per direction. If a router is running IP exclusively, each interface handles a maximum of two ACLs: one inbound and one outbound. Because each ACL compares every packet passing through an interface, ACLs add to latency.

The following guidelines and statements apply to ACL creation and processing:

- Configure only one ACL per protocol, per direction.

- Apply standard ACLs closest to the destination.

- Apply extended ACLs closest to the source.

- Use the correct number range for the type of list.

- Determine the inbound or outbound direction looking at the port from inside the router.

- Statements are processed sequentially from the top of the list to the bottom.

- Deny packets if no match is found.

- Enter the access list statements in order from specific to general.

- Configure an ACL with at least one **permit** statement; otherwise, all traffic will be denied.

**Note**

Also note the following points about ACLs:

- Rejected packets cause an IP access list to send an ICMP host unreachable message to the sender and discard the packet.
- Outbound filters do not affect traffic that originates from the local router.
- An implicit **deny any** is at the end of all access lists but does not appear in the listing.

Configuring an ACL requires two steps: creation and application. This section describes ACL creation. The next section, "Configuring Numbered Standard ACLs," describes ACL application.

Enter global configuration mode. Using the **access-list** command, enter the ACL statements. Enter all statements with the same ACL number until the ACL is complete.

The syntax for the standard ACL statement is as follows:

```
access-list [access-list-number] [deny|permit] [source address] [source-wildcard][log]
```

Because every packet is compared to every ACL statement until a match is found, the order that statements are placed within the ACL can affect the latency introduced. Therefore, order the statements so that the more common conditions appear in the ACL before the less common ones. For example, statements that find a match for the highest amount of traffic should be placed toward the beginning of the ACL.

Keep in mind, however, that when a match is found, the packet is no longer compared to any other statements within the ACL. This means that if one line permits a packet, but a line further down the ACL denies it, the packet is permitted. For this reason, plan the ACL so that the more specific requirements appear before more general ones. In other words, deny a specific host of a network before permitting the remainder of the entire network.

Document the function of each section or statement of the ACL using the **remark** command:

```
access-list [list number] remark [text]
```

To delete an ACL, use the following command:

```
no access-list [list number]
```

It is not possible to delete a single line from a standard or extended numbered ACL using the basic ACL creation method. Instead, the ACL as a whole is deleted and must be replaced in its entirety. However, using the NACL process with numbered ACLs does allow you to remove and add ACL statements.

Examine Figure 8-13. The standard ACL that follows is applied to Fa0/0 on R2. A **remark** statement at the beginning describes the purpose of the ACL. Remarks do not display when the **show access-lists** command is used, but they do appear in the output of the **show running-config** command.

**Figure 8-13    Reference Topology for ACL Commands**

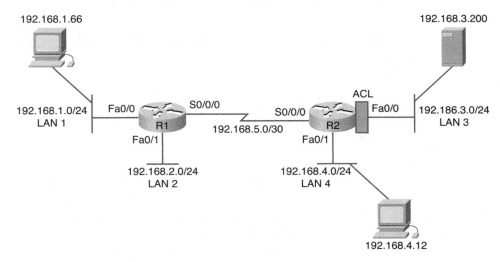

This ACL places a specific **deny** statement first, followed by another specific **permit** statement. A more general **permit** statement then follows. In the **deny** or **permit** statement for a specific host, a wildcard mask is not needed. The keyword **host** may be used but is not required. In the general statement, the wildcard mask must be used to specify the range of 192.168.4.1 through 192.168.4.255:

```
R2(config)# access-list 3 remark Access to departmental server
R2(config)# access-list 3 deny host 192.168.4.12
R2(config)# access-list 3 permit 192.168.1.66
R2(config)# access-list 3 permit 192.168.4.0  0.0.0.255
```

## Configuring Numbered Standard ACLs

An ACL does not filter traffic until it has been applied, or assigned, to an interface.

Assign an ACL to one or more interfaces, specifying either inbound traffic or outbound traffic. Apply a standard ACL as close to the destination as possible. The syntax of the command to apply an ACL to an interface is as follows:

```
R2(config-if)# ip access-group access list number [in | out]
```

The following commands place access list 3 on the R2 Fa0/0 interface filtering outbound traffic:

```
R2(config)# interface fastethernet 0/0
R2(config-if)# ip access-group 3 out
```

The default direction for an ACL applied to an interface is out. Even though out is the default, it is important to specify the direction to avoid confusion and to ensure that traffic filters in the correct direction.

To remove an ACL from an interface while leaving the ACL intact, use the **no ip access-group** **interface** command. When the ACL has been removed from the interface, the ACL will no longer filter traffic.

Several ACL commands evaluate the proper syntax, order of statements, and placement on interfaces. See the network topology in Figure 8-13 and the command output shown in the following examples.

The **show ip interface** displays IP interface information and indicates any assigned ACLs. Example 8-1 show the ACL-related output of the **show ip interface** command. This command enables you to see whether there is an ACL configured on an interface and the direction in which it is applied.

**Example 8-1  R2 show ip interface fa0/0 Command Output**

```
R2# show ip interface fa0/0
FastEthernet0/0 is up, line protocol is up
<output omitted>
Internet address is 192.168.3.1 /24
Broadcast address is 255.255.255.255
MTU is 1500 bytes
Outgoing access list is 3
Inbound access list is not set
```

The **show access-lists** command displays the contents of all ACLs on the router. It also displays the number of matches for each **permit** or **deny** statement since application of the ACL. To see a specific list, add the ACL name or number as an option for this command.

Example 8-2 shows the output of the **show access-lists** command. This command enables you to see all ACLs configured on a router, their type (standard or extended), and the statements in each one. Note that each statement is followed by the number of matches in parentheses. This is a simple form of logging and monitoring ACL results.

**Example 8-2  R2 show access-lists Command Output**

```
R2# show access-lists
Standard IP access list 3
10 permit 192.168.1.66
20 deny   192.168.1.0, wildcard bits 0.0.0.255 (8 matches)
30 permit 192.168.2.0, wildcard bits 0.0.0.255 (12 matches)
40 deny   192.168.4.0, wildcard bits 0.0.0.255 (6 matches)
```

The **show running-config** displays all configured ACLs on a router, even if they might not be currently applied to an interface. Example 8-3 shows the output of the **show running-config** command. This command enables you to see all ACLs configured on a router, whether or not they have been applied to an interface, and the direction and the statements in each ACL.

**Example 8-3  R2 show running-config Command Output**

```
R2# show running-config
<output omitted>
Current configuration : 840 bytes
version 12.4
!
hostname R2
!
```

```
interface FastEthernet0/0
 ip address 192.168.3.1 255.255.255.0
 ip access-group 3 out
 duplex auto
 speed auto
!
Access-list 3 remark This is a standard ACL
Access-list 3 permit 192.168.1.66
Access-list 3 deny 192.168.1.0 0.0.0.255
Access-list 3 permit 192.168.2.0 0.0.0.255
Access-list 3 deny 192.168.4.0 0.0.0.255
```

If you are using numbered ACLs, statements entered after the initial creation of the ACL are added to the end. This order might not yield the desired results. To resolve this issue, you may remove the original ACL and re-create it.

It is often recommended to create ACLs in a text editor, such as the Notepad application that comes with Windows. This allows the ACL to be easily edited and pasted into the router configuration. However, keep in mind when copying and pasting the ACL that it is important to remove the currently applied ACL first; otherwise, all statements will be pasted to the end.

**Interactive Activity 8-6: Configuring Numbered Standard ACLs (8.3.3)**

In this activity, you determine the proper sequence for the ACL configuration statement to meet the objectives. Use file d3ia-833 on the CD-ROM that accompanies this book to perform this interactive activity.

**Lab 8-1: Configuring and Verifying Standard ACLs (8.3.3)**

In this lab, you configure and verify a standard ACL. Refer to the hands-on lab in Part II of this *Learning Guide*. You may perform this lab now or wait until the end of the chapter.

# Configuring Numbered Extended ACLs

Extended ACLs provide a greater range of control than standard ACLs. The extended ACL permits or denies access based on source IP address, destination IP address, protocol type, and port numbers. Because extended ACLs can be very specific, they tend to grow in size quickly. The more statements that an ACL contains, the more difficult it is to manage.

Extended ACLs use an ACL number in the ranges 100 to 199 and 2000 to 2699. The same rules that apply to standard ACLs also apply to extended ACLs:

- Configure multiple statements in one ACL.

- Assign the same ACL number to each statement.

- Use the **host** or **any** keywords to represent IP addresses.

A key difference in the extended ACL syntax is the requirement to specify a protocol after the **permit** or **deny** condition. This protocol can be IP, indicating all IP traffic, or it can indicate filtering on a specific IP protocol such as TCP, UDP, ICMP, and OSPF. A typical extended ACL statement is shown here:

```
R2(config)# access-list 105 permit tcp 192.168.5.0 0.0.0.255  host 172.16.5.254 eq http
```

The main components are identified as follows:

- **ACL number**: Identifies an ACL with a unique number. Standard ACLs use numbers in the ranges 1 to 99 and 1300 to 1999. Extended ACLs use numbers in the ranges 100 to 199 and 2000 to 2699. In the preceding statement, the ACL number is 105.

- **Action**: Identifies whether a packet is to be permitted or denied. In the preceding statement, the action is permit.

- **Protocol**: Identifies Layer 3 and 4 protocols. In this case, the protocol is TCP (Transmission Control Protocol). Other common options include the following:

  **eigrp**: Cisco's Enhanced Interior Gateway Routing Protocol

  **esp**: Encapsulation Security Payload

  **gre**: Cisco's generic routing encapsulation tunneling

  **icmp**: Internet Control Message Protocol

  **igmp**: Internet Gateway Message Protocol

  **ip**: Any Internet Protocol

  **ipinip**: IP in IP tunneling

  **ospf**: Open Shortest Path First (OSPF) Protocol

  **pcp**: Payload Compression Protocol

  **udp**: User Datagram Protocol

- **Source IP address**: Identifies the IP address or range of addresses to which packet source addresses will be compared. This value can be

  An individual host address

  A range of host addresses

  The host parameter

  The any parameter

  The source IP address is this case is 192.168.5.0.

- **Wildcard mask**: Optional for source or destination address. Depends on the source or destination address specified. Required for a range of addresses. The wildcard mask in this case is 0.0.0.255.

- **Destination IP address**: Identifies the IP address or range of addresses to which packet destination addresses will be compared. This value can be

  An individual host address

  A range of host addresses

The host parameter

The any parameter

The destination IP address in the preceding statement is 172.16.5.254.

- **Matching condition**: Determines whether certain fields must match the application equally, greater than, less than, and so on. The matching condition in the statement shown previously is **eq**.

- **TCP application**: Identifies the application either by port number or acronym (for example, port 80 or HTTP). In this case, HTTP is shown as the TCP application.

There are often many different ways to meet a set of requirements. For example, a company has a server with the address of 192.168.3.75. It has the following requirements:

- Allow access to hosts on the 192.168.2.0 LAN.

- Allow access to host 192.168.1.66.

- Deny access to hosts on 192.168.4.0 LAN.

- Permit access to everyone else in the enterprise.

At least two possible solutions satisfy these requirements. When planning the ACL, try to minimize statements where possible. Ways to minimize statements and reduce the processing load of the router include the following:

- Match high-volume traffic and deny blocked traffic early in the ACL. This approach ensures that packets do not compare to later statements.

- Consolidate multiple **permit** and **deny** statements into a single statement using ranges.

- Consider denying a particular group rather than permitting a larger, opposite group.

Referring to the topology in Figure 8-14, Example 8-4 and Example 8-5 both deny hosts from the 192.168.4.0 network access to host 192.168.3.75 and permit other traffic, but the 8-5 example does it with fewer statements.

**Example 8-4  ACL Configuration Option 1**

```
R2(config)# access-list 103 permit ip 192.168.2.0 host 192.168.3.75
R2(config)# access-list 103 permit ip 192.168.1.66 host 192.168.3.75
R2(config)# access-list 103 deny ip 192.168.4.0 0.0.0.255 host 192.168.3.75
R2(config)# access-list 103 permit ip any any

R2(config)# interface fa0/0
R2(config-if)# ip access-group 103 out
```

**Example 8-5  ACL Configuration Option 2**

```
R2(config)# access-list 103 deny ip 192.168.4.0 0.0.0.255 host 192.168.3.75
R2(config)# access-list 103 permit ip any any

R2(config)# interface fa0/0
R2(config-if)# ip access-group 103 out
```

Note that this ACL could also be placed on the R2 Fa0/1 interface to block the 192.168.4.0 traffic destined for the server. This would prevent the router from having to switch the packets to the Fa0/0 interface.

**Figure 8-14    Reference Topology for ACL Options**

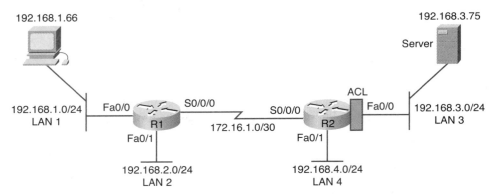

**Interactive Activity 8-7: Configuring Numbered Extended ACLs (8.3.4)**

In this activity, based on the ACL, you determine whether packet will be permitted or denied. Use file d3ia-834 on the CD-ROM that accompanies this book to perform this interactive activity.

**Lab 8-2: Planning, Configuring, and Verifying Standard ACLs (8.3.4)**

In this lab, you plan, configure, and verify an extended ACL. Refer to the hands-on lab in Part II of this *Learning Guide*. You may perform this lab now or wait until the end of the chapter.

## Configuring Named ACLs

Cisco IOS Releases 11.2 and higher can create named ACLs (NACL). In an NACL, a descriptive name replaces the numeric ranges required for standard and extended ACLs. NACLs offer all the functionality and advantages of standard and extended ACLs; only the syntax for creating them differs.

The name given to an ACL is unique. Using capital letters in the name makes it easier to recognize in router command output and troubleshooting.

Create an NACL with the following command:

```
ip access-list {standard | extended} name
```

After you issue this command, the router switches to NACL configuration subcommand mode. After the initial naming command, enter all **permit** and **deny** statements, one at a time. NACLs use standard or extended ACL command syntax starting with the **permit** or **deny** statement.

Apply an NACL to an interface in the same manner as applying a standard or extended ACL.

The commands that help with evaluating NACLs for proper syntax, order of statements, and placement on interfaces are the same as the commands for standard ACLs.

Example 8-6 shows the basic configuration commands for creating an NACL and applying it to an interface. Note that the prompt changes to R1(config-ext-nacl).

**Example 8-6  NACL Configuration Commands**

```
R1(config)# ip access-list extended SALES-ONLY
R1(config-ext-nacl)# permit ip 192.168.1.66 0.0.0.0 any
R1(config-ext-nacl)# permit ip 192.168.1.77 0.0.0.0 any

R1(config)# interface fa0/0
R1(config-if)# ip access-group SALES-ONLY in
```

Editing ACLs with older versions of IOS make it necessary to

- Copy the ACL to a text editor.

- Remove the ACL from the router.

- Re-create and apply the edited version.

Unfortunately, this process allows all traffic to flow through the interface during the editing cycle, thereby leaving the network open to potential security breaches.

With current versions of the IOS, you can edit numbered and NACLs using the **ip access-list** command. ACLs display with the lines numbered as 10, 20, 30, and so forth. To see the line numbers, use the **show access-lists** command.

To edit an existing line

- Remove the line using the **no line number** command.

- Re-add the same line using its line number.

To insert a new line between existing lines 20 and 30:

- Issue the **new ACL** statement, starting with a number between the two existing lines, such as 25.

- Issue the **show access-lists** command to display the lines re-sorted and renumbered by 10s.

Example 8-7 shows the output of the **show access-lists** command for an NACL, which we want to make changes to.

**Example 8-7  R1 show access-lists Command Output**

```
R1# show access-lists
Extended IP access list SERVER-ACCESS
    10 permit ip 192.168.1.66 host 192.168.3.75
    20 permit ip 192.168.1.77 host 192.168.3.75
    30 deny ip 192.168.1.0 0.0.0.255 host 192.168.3.75
```

Example 8-8 shows the use of ACL editing to remove line 20 from the ACL and then adding a new line 20 to replace the one deleted.

**Example 8-8 Deleting and Changing ACL Statements**

```
R1(config)# ip access list extended SERVER-ACCESS
R1(config-ext-nacl)# no 20
R1(config-ext-nacl)# 20 permit ip 192.168.1.77 any
R1(config-ext-nacl)# end

R1# show access-lists
Extended IP access list SERVER-ACCESS
    10 permit ip 192.168.1.66 host 192.168.3.75
    20 permit ip 192.168.1.77 any
    30 deny ip 192.168.1.0 0.0.0.255 host 192.168.3.75
```

Example 8-9 shows the use of ACL editing to insert a new line 25 between existing lines 20 and 30. The **show access-lists** command displays the new lines in sequence.

**Example 8-9 Inserting New Lines in a NACL**

```
R1(config)# ip access list extended SERVER-ACCESS
R1(config-ext-nacl)# 25 deny ip host 192.168.1.88 any
R1(config-ext-nacl)# end

R1# show access-lists
Extended IP access list SERVER-ACCESS
    10 permit ip 192.168.1.66 host 192.168.3.75
    20 permit ip 192.168.1.77 any
    25 deny ip 192.168.1.88 any
    30 deny ip 192.168.1.0 0.0.0.255 host 192.168.3.75
```

### Configuring and Verifying Standard Named ACLs (8.3.5)

In this activity, you configure and verify a standard NACL. Use file d3-835.pka on the CD-ROM that accompanies this book to perform this interactive activity.

### Lab 8-3: Configuring and Verifying Extended Named ACLs (8.3.5)

In this lab, you configure and verify an extended NACL. Refer to the hands-on lab in Part II of this *Learning Guide.* You may perform this lab now or wait until the end of the chapter.

## Configure Router vty Access

Network administrators often need to configure a router located at a remote location. To log in to the remote router, they use a program such as Telnet or a Secure Shell (SSH) client. Telnet transmits usernames and passwords in plaintext, and therefore is not very secure. SSH transmits username and password information in an encrypted format.

When a network administrator connects to a remote router using Telnet, the router initiates an inbound session. Telnet and SSH are in-band network management tools and require IP and a network connection to the router.

The purpose of restricting vty access is to increase network security. Outside intruders may attempt to gain access to a router. If an ACL is not in place on the router virtual port, anyone who can determine the Telnet username and password can gain entry. If an ACL is applied to the router vty port that permits only specific IP addresses, anyone trying to telnet to the router from an IP address not permitted in the ACL is denied access. Keep in mind, however, that this can create issues if the administrator must connect to the router from different locations using different IP addresses.

In Figure 8-15, the network admin at 209.165.202.130 configures vty access to the router at 209.165.200.225. This prevents the hacker from getting into the router from another IP address.

**Figure 8-15    Using vty Passwords to Prevent Unauthorized Access to a Router**

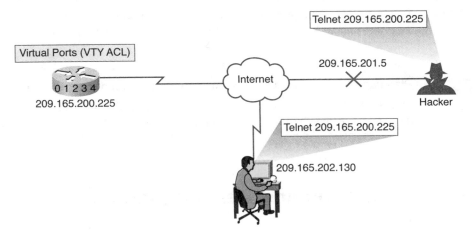

The process used to create the vty ACL is the same as for an interface. However, applying the ACL to a vty line uses a different command. Instead of using the **ip access-group** command, use the **access-class** command.

Follow these guidelines when configuring access lists on vty lines:

- Apply a numbered ACL, not an NACL, to the vty lines.

- Place identical restrictions on all vty lines, because it is not possible to control the line on which a user may connect.

The vty sessions are established between the Telnet client software and the destination router. The network administrator establishes a session with the destination router, enters a username and password, and makes configuration changes.

In Figure 8-16, the network administrator configures a simple standard ACL to allow her PC's IP address to have access to the router. She enables login through vty lines 0 through 4 and creates a password that will be required. She then applies the ACL to the vty lines using the **access-class** command. Example 8-10 shows the commands used to configure vty access to the router.

**Figure 8-16    Configuring vty Passwords**

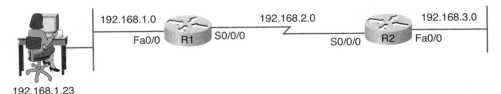

**Example 8-10    Configuring Router vty Access Control**

```
R1(config)# access-list 2 permit 192.168.1.23

R1(config)# line vty 0 4
R1(config-line)# login
R1(config-line)# password itsasecret
R1(config-line)# access-class 2 in
```

**Lab 8-4: Configuring and Verifying vty Restrictions (8.3.6)**

In this lab, you configure and verify router vty restrictions. Refer to the hands-on lab in Part II of this *Learning Guide*. You may perform this lab now or wait until the end of the chapter.

**Planning, Configuring, and Verifying Standard, Extended, and Named ACLs (8.3.6)**

In this activity, you plan, configure, and verify standard, extended, and named ACLs. Use file d3-836.pka on the CD-ROM that accompanies this book to perform this interactive activity.

# Permitting and Denying Specific Types of Traffic

You have learned about the structure and configuration of standard, extended, and named ACLs in previous sections. This section provides specific examples of how to control various types of traffic and how to apply ACLS to help protect an internal network from external attacks. Also covered are the effects of Network Address Translation (NAT) and Port Address Translation (PAT) on ACL placement and ACL use with inter-VLAN routing.

## Configuring ACLs for Application and Port Filtering

Extended ACLs filter on source and destination IP addresses. It is often desirable to filter on even more specific packet details. OSI Layer 3 network protocol, Layer 4 transport protocols, and application ports provide this capability. Protocols available to use for filtering include IP, TCP, UDP, and ICMP.

Extended ACLs also filter on destination port numbers. These port numbers describe the application or service required by the packet. Each application has a registered port number assigned. The router must investigate the Ethernet frame to extract all the IP addresses and port number information required for comparison with ACLs.

In addition to entering port numbers, it is necessary to specify a condition before the statement is matched. The abbreviations most commonly used are as follows:

- **eq** = Equals
- **gt** = Greater than
- **lt** = Less than

Consider the following example:

```
R1(config)# access-list 122 permit tcp 192.168.1.0 0.0.0.255 host 192.168.2.89 eq 80
```

This ACL statement permits traffic from 192.168.1.0 that is requesting HTTP access using port 80. If a user attempts to telnet or FTP into host 192.168.2.89, the user is denied because of the implicit **deny** statement assumed at the end of every ACL. In Figure 8-17, the ACL statement is mapped to the various components in an Ethernet frame that are used in defining the ACL statement. Although sophisticated ACLs can examine the Ethernet frame header MAC addresses, the primary components used are the parts of the IP packet within the Ethernet frame.

**Figure 8-17    Comparing an Extended ACL Statement to an Ethernet Frame and IP Packet**

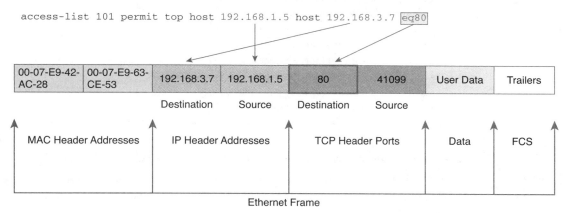

Filtering based on a particular application requires knowledge of the port number for that application. Applications are associated with both a port number and a name. An ACL can reference port 80 or WWW.

If neither the port number nor the name is known for an application, try these steps to locate that information:

**Step 1.**    Research one of the IP addressing registry sites on the web, such as http://www.iana.org/.

**Step 2.**    Refer to the software documentation.

**Step 3.**    Refer to the website of the application vendor.

**Step 4.**    Use a packet sniffer and capture data from the application.

**Step 5.**    Use the **?** option in the **access-list** command. The list includes well-known port names and numbers for TCP.

Some applications use more than one port number. For example, FTP data transmits using port 20, but the session control that makes FTP possible uses port 21. To deny all FTP traffic, deny both ports.

To accommodate multiple port numbers, Cisco IOS ACLs filter a range of ports. Use the **gt**, **lt**, or **range** operators in the ACL statement to accomplish this. For example, two FTP ACL statements can filter into one with the following command:

```
R1(config)# access-list 181 deny tcp any 192.168.77.0 0.0.0.255 range 20 21
```

In Example 8-11, the help function is used to determine what applications can be filtered on using extended ACLs. If e-mail is to be filtered, the POP3 and SMTP applications can be used. Notice that the application keyword is shown (for example, SMTP) and the port number (for example, 25), which can also be used in ACL statements.

**Example 8-11    Using the IOS Help (?) Function to Determine Application Options and Port Numbers**

```
ISP(config)# access-list 101 permit tcp host 192.168.1.1 host 192.168.2.89 eq ?
  <0-65535>    Port number
  bgp          Border Gateway Protocol (179)
  domain       Domain Name Service (53)
  echo         Echo (7)
  ftp          File Transfer Protocol (21)
  ftp-data     FTP data connections (20)
  ident        Ident Protocol (113)
  irc          Internet Relay Chat (194)
  pop3         Post Office Protocol v3 (110)
  smtp         Simple Mail Transport Protocol (25)
  telnet       Telnet (23)
  www          World Wide Web (HTTP, 80)
```

Packet Tracer
☐ Activity

**Configuring and Verifying Extended ACLs to Filter on Port Numbers (8.4.1)**

In this activity, you configure and verify extended ACLs that filter on port numbers. Use file d3-841.pka on the CD-ROM that accompanies this book to perform this interactive activity.

## Configuring ACLs to Support Established Traffic

ACLs are often created to protect an internal network from outside sources. However, while protecting the internal network, it should still allow internal users access to all resources. When internal users access external resources, those requested resources must pass through the ACL. For example, should an internal user want to establish a connection with an external web server, the ACL must permit the requested HTML packets. Because of the ACL's use of implicit **deny**, resources must be specifically permitted by the ACL. Individual **permit** statements for all possible requested resources can result in a long ACL and leave security holes.

To resolve this issue, it is possible to create a single statement that permits internal users to establish a TCP session with external resources. When the TCP three-way handshake is accomplished and the connection is established, all packets sent between the two devices are permitted. To accomplish this, use the keyword **established**, as follows:

```
access-list 101 permit tcp any any established
```

If you use this statement, all external TCP packets are permitted under the condition that they are responses to internal requests. Permitting the incoming responses to established communications is a form of stateful packet inspection (SPI).

In addition to established traffic, it might be necessary for an internal user to ping external devices. It is not desirable, however, to allow external users to ping or trace a device on the inside network. In this case, a statement using the keywords **echo-reply** and **unreachable** can be written to permit ping responses and unreachable messages. A ping originating from external sources, however, is denied unless specifically permitted in another statement. Figure 8-18 shows the topology used in Example 8-12 for ACL configuration to permit established traffic, ping replies, and unreachable messages into the internal network.

**Figure 8-18    Reference Topology for the Established Parameter**

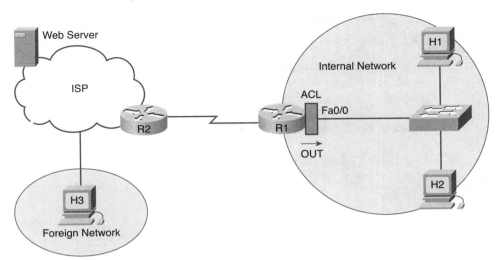

**Example 8-12    Configuring Network Access Control**

```
R1(config)# access-list 101 permit tcp any any established
R1(config)# access-list 101 permit icmp any any echo-reply
R1(config)# access-list 101 permit icmp any any unreachable
R1(config)# access-list 101 deny any any

R1(config)# interface fa0/0
R1(config-if)# ip access-group 101 out.
```

**Interactive Activity 8-8: Configuring ACLs to Support Established Traffic (8.4.2)**

In this activity, you determine whether the packet will be allowed or blocked based on source and destination address, packet type, and the ACLs. Use file d3ia-842 on the CD-ROM that accompanies this book to perform this interactive activity.

# Effects of NAT and PAT on ACL Placement

Implementing NAT and PAT might create a problem when planning ACLs. Network administrators need to account for the address translation when creating and applying ACLs to interfaces where NAT occurs.

When using NAT with ACLs, it is important to know how they interact in the router.

If the packet comes inbound into a NAT outside interface, the router

- Applies the inbound ACL
- Translates the destination address from outside to inside, or global to local
- Routes the packet

If the packet goes outbound through a NAT outside interface, the router

- Translates the source address from inside to outside, or local to global

- Applies outbound ACL

Plan the ACL so that it filters either the private or public addresses, depending on the relationship with NAT. If traffic is inbound or outbound on a NAT outside interface, the addresses to filter are the public ones. Figure 8-19 illustrates the interaction of ACLs and NAT.

**Figure 8-19   Interaction of ACLs and NAT**

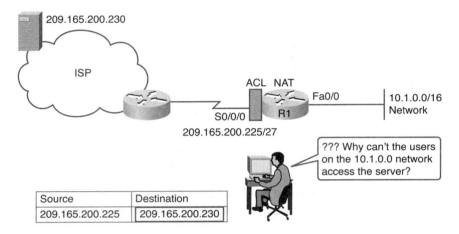

In Example 8-13, an ACL has been created to permit the internal users on the private 10.1.0.0 network access to the server 209.165.200.230. The ACL is placed on the S0/0/0 interface in the outbound direction. The problem is that the ACL permits the 10.1.0.0 addresses but not the NAT-translated 209.165.200.225 address of the router's S0/0/0 interface. For the ACL to work, it needs to specify the external interface IP address, as shown in Example 8-14.

**Example 8-13   Configuring ACLs with NAT: Incorrect**

```
R1(config)# access-list 101 permit ip 10.1.0.0 0.0.255.255 host 209.165.200.230


R1(config)# interface s0/0/0
R1(config-if)# ip access-group 101 out
```

**Example 8-14   Configuring ACLs with NAT: Correct**

```
R1(config)# access-list 101 permit ip 209.165.200.225  0.0.255.255 host 209.165.200.230


R1(config)# interface s0/0/0
R1(config-if)# ip access-group 101 out
```

 **Lab 8-5: Configuring an ACL with NAT (8.4.3)**

In this lab, you configure an ACL with NAT. Refer to the hands-on lab in Part II of this *Learning Guide*. You may perform this lab now or wait until the end of the chapter.

## Analyzing Network ACLs and Placement

Network administrators evaluate the effect of every statement in an ACL before implementation. An improperly designed ACL can immediately cause problems when it is applied to an interface. These problems range from a false sense of security to an unnecessary load on a router or even a nonfunctioning network.

Administrators need to examine the ACL, one line at a time, and answer the following questions:

- What service does the statement deny?
- What is the source, and what is the destination?
- What port numbers are denied?
- What would happen if the ACL were moved to another interface?
- What would happen if the ACL were to filter traffic in a different direction?
- Is NAT an issue?

When evaluating an extended ACL, it is important to remember these key points:

- The keyword **tcp** permits or denies protocols such as FTP, HTTP, and Telnet that use TCP as their transport protocol.
- The key phrase **permit ip** is used to permit all types of IP traffic, including any TCP, UDP, and ICMP and any other protocols and applications that use IP as the Layer 3 network protocol.

Table 8-4 shows the statements within each of the four ACLs placed in Figure 8-20 and what they accomplish.

**Table 8-4    ACLs and Their Functions**

| ACL | Function |
|---|---|
| **Main: Extended ACL 111, Interface Fa0/0 IN** | |
| access-list 111 permit ip host 192.168.5.57 any | Allows the Payroll server access to anywhere |
| access-list 111 permit udp 192.168.5.0 0.0.0.255 any eq 53 | Allows all users on this network access to remote DNS |
| access-list 111 permit tcp 192.168.5.0 0.0.0.255 any eq 80 | Allows all users on this network access to web services |
| **HQ: Extended ACL 100, Interface Fa0/0 IN** | |
| access-list 100 permit ip 192.168.1.0 0.0.0.15 any | Allows Net Admin and Server Farm full access |
| access-list 100 deny tcp 192.168.1.0 0.0.0.255 eq 23 | Denies user PCs Telnet access |
| access-list 100 permit ip any any | Allows all other traffic |

*continues*

**Table 8-4   ACLs and Their Functions**   *continued*

| ACL | Function |
|---|---|
| **HQ: Extended ACL 105, Interface S0/0/0 IN** | |
| **access-list 105 permit icmp any any echo-reply** | Allows pings from inside to return from the Internet |
| **access-list 105 permit icmp any any unreachable** | Allows error messages to return from the Internet |
| **access-list 105 permit tcp any any established** | Allows established TCP sessions from the Internet |
| **Sales: Extended ACL 122, Interface Fa0/0 IN** | |
| **access-list 122 deny ip 192.168.3.0 0.0.0.255 host 192.168.5.57** | Denies access from this network to Payroll server |
| **access-list 122 permit udp 192.168.3.0 0.0.0.255 any range 20 21** | Allows all users on this network access to FTP data and FTP |
| **access-list 111 permit udp 192.168.3.0 0.0.0.255 any eq 53** | Allows all users on this network access to remote DNS |
| **access-list 122 permit tcp 192.168.3.0 0.0.0.255 any eq 80** | Allows all users on this network access to web services |

**Figure 8-20   Analyzing ACLs and Their Function**

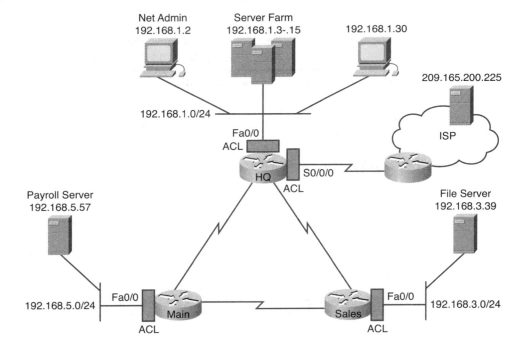

**Interactive Activity 8-9: Analyzing Network ACLs and Placement (8.4.4)**

In this activity, you create an extended ACL based on the requirements and the network topology shown. Use file d3ia-844 on the CD-ROM that accompanies this book to perform this interactive activity.

## Configuring ACLs with Inter-VLAN Routing

When routing between VLANs in a network, it is sometimes necessary to control traffic from one VLAN to another using ACLs. Apply ACLs directly to VLAN interfaces or subinterfaces on a router just as with physical interfaces.

Enterprise networks typically have servers on a different VLAN than user groups. In such cases, access to the server VLAN requires filtering.

All rules and guidelines for creation and application are the same for ACLs on subinterfaces as they are for physical interfaces. Figure 8-21 shows two VLANs defined on switch S1 with Router R1 routing between them as though they were physically separate network segments.

**Figure 8-21   VLANs Create Logical Subnets on a Switch**

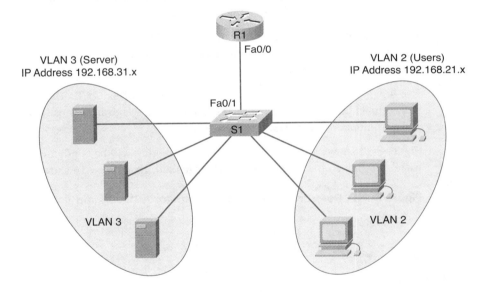

**Lab 8-6: Configuring and Verifying ACLs to Filter Inter-VLAN Traffic (8.4.5)**

In this lab, you configure and verify ACLs to filter inter-VLAN traffic. Refer to the hands-on lab in Part II of this *Learning Guide*. You may perform this lab now or wait until the end of the chapter.

**Configuring and Verifying Extended ACLs with a DMZ (8.4.5)**

In this activity, you configure and verify an extended ACL that creates a DMZ and protects the corporate network. Use file d3-845.pka on the CD-ROM that accompanies this book to perform this interactive activity.

# ACL Logging and Best Practices

ACLs can prove valuable in controlling various types of traffic in and out of a network or to specific resources. The use of console logging and syslog servers provide more detailed information as to what traffic is being permitted or denied.

This section describes ACL logging and the use of syslog servers to record the ACL activity. In addition, it provides a summary of ACL best practices.

## Using Logging to Verify ACL Functionality

After writing an ACL and applying it to an interface, a network administrator evaluates the number of matches. When the fields of an incoming packet are equal to all ACL comparison fields, this is a match. Viewing the number of matches helps to identify whether the ACL statements are having the desired effect.

By default, an ACL statement captures the number of matches and displays them at the end of each statement. View the matches using the **show access-list** command.

The basic match counts displayed with the **show access-list** command provide the number of ACL statements matched and the number of packets processed. The output does not indicate the source or destination of the packet or the protocols in use.

For additional detail on packets permitted or denied, activate a process called *logging*. Logging activates for individual ACL statements. To activate this feature, add the **log** option to the end of each ACL statement to be tracked.

Use logging for a short time, just to complete testing of the ACL. The process of logging events places an additional load on the router. Table 8-5 shows examples of source and destination addresses and port numbers for network applications.

Figure 8-22 shows a topology on which ACL logging will be configured. Example 8-15 shows that basic ACL match tracking, which is on by default. Example 8-16 shows the use of console logging.

**Figure 8-22    Reference Topology Diagram for ACL Logging**

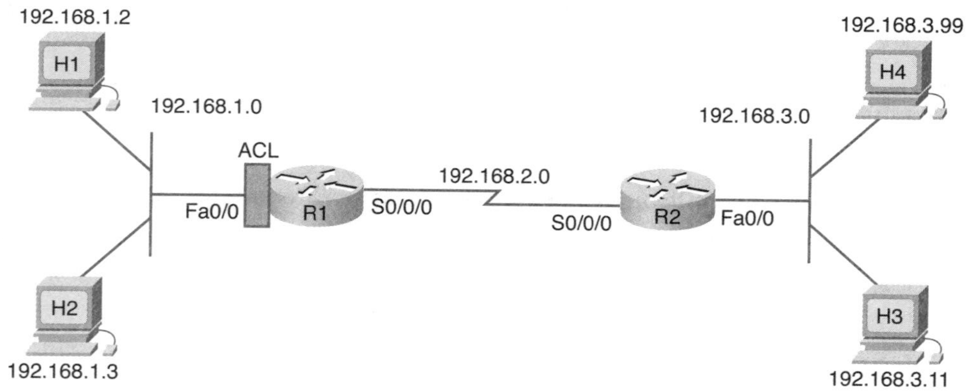

**Example 8-15    Default ACL Match Tracking**

```
R1(config)# access-list 123 deny tcp host 192.168.1.2 host 192.168.3.11 eq 23
R1(config)# access-list 123 permit ip host 192.168.1.2 0.0.0.255 any
R1(config)# int fa0/0
R1(config-if)# ip access-group 123 in
R1(config-if)# end

R1# show access-list 123
Extended IP access list 123
        10 deny tcp host 192.168.1.2 host 192.168.3.11 eq telnet (1 matches)
        20 permit ip host 192.168.1.2 0.0.0.255 any (1 matches)
```

**Example 8-16    Console Logging Activated for ACL Tracking**

```
R1(config)# no access-list 123
R1(config)# access-list 123 deny tcp host 192.168.1.2 host 192.168.3.11 eq 23 log
R1(config)# access-list 123 permit ip host 192.168.1.2 0.0.0.255 any log
R1(config)# access-list 123 deny ip any any log
R1(config)# end
R1#
*Sep 9 20:02:53.067: %SEC-6-IPACCESSLOGP: list 123 denied tcp 192.168.1.2(1141)
  192.168.3.11(23), 1 packet
R1#
*Sep 9 20:02:11.979: %SEC-6-IPACCESSLOGP: list 123 permitted udp 192.168.1.2(2138)
  192.168.3.99(53), 1 packet
R1#
*Sep 9 20:03:48.279: %SEC-6-IPACCESSLOGP: list 123 permitted icmp  192.168.1.3
  192.168.3.11 (8/0), 1 packet
```

Table 8-5 shows the three packets that generated the log messages seen in Example 8-16 with source address, destination addresses, and port numbers:

- The first packet is an attempted Telnet from host 192.168.1.2 to host 192.168.3.11 (destination TCP port 23), which is denied by the first statement in the ACL.

- The second packet is a DNS request from host 192.168.1.2 to DNS server 192.168.3.99 (UDP port 53), which is permitted by the second statement in the ACL.

- The third packet is a ping from host 192.168.1.3 to host 192.168.3.11 (ICMP type 8/0 or echo request), which is permitted by the second statement in the ACL.

**Table 8-5    Packets That Generated ACL Log Activity**

| Source | Destination | Protocol | Destination Port Number | Application Name |
|---|---|---|---|---|
| 192.168.1.2 | 192.168.3.11 | TCP | 23 | Telnet |
| 192.168.1.2 | 192.168.3.99 | UDP | 53 | DNS |
| 192.168.1.3 | 192.168.3.11 | ICMP | Type/code 8/0 | ICMP echo request |

Logging to the console uses router memory, which is a limited resource. Instead, configure a router to send logging messages to an external server. These messages, called *syslog* messages, allow the user to view them both in real time or at a later date.

The message types include seven message severity levels. The levels range from 0, representing an emergency or an unusable system, to level 7, representing informational messages such as debugging. Table 8-6 shows various logging severity levels and examples of the types of generated messages associated with them.

**Table 8-6    Logging Severity Levels**

| Severity Level | Name | Description |
| --- | --- | --- |
| 0 | Emergencies | System is unusable. |
| 1 | Alerts | Immediate action needed. |
| 2 | Critical | Critical conditions. |
| 3 | Errors | Error conditions. |
| 4 | Warnings | Warning conditions. |
| 5 | Notifications | Normal but significant conditions. |
| 6 | Informational | Informational messages. |
| 7 | Debugging | Debugging messages. |

ACL logging generates an informational message that contains the following information:

- ACL number
- Packet permitted or denied
- Source and destination addresses
- Number of packets

The message generates for the first packet that matches and then at 5-minute intervals.

To turn off logging, use the **no logging console** command.

To turn off all debugging, use the **undebug all** command.

To turn off specific debugging, such as IP packets, use the **no debug ip packet** command.

**Lab 8-7: Configuring ACLs and Verifying with Console Logging (8.5.1)**

In this lab, you configure ACLs and verify using the **show access-lists** command and console logging. Refer to the hands-on lab in Part II of this *Learning Guide*. You may perform this lab now or wait until the end of the chapter.

## Analyzing Router Logs

Syslog messages can include different types of information as specified by the network administrator.

Types of reported events include the status of

- Router interfaces
- Protocols in use
- Bandwidth usage
- ACL messages
- Configuration events

**Tip**

It is advisable to include the option to notify a network administrator by e-mail, pager, or cell phone when a critical event occurs.

Other configurable options include the following:

- Providing notification of new messages received
- Sorting and grouping messages
- Filtering messages by severity
- Removing all or selected messages

Syslog software is available from many resources. The level of reporting and ease of use vary with the price, but there are also several free programs available on the Internet.

Syslog is a protocol supported by all network equipment, including switches, routers, firewalls, storage systems, modems, wireless devices, and UNIX hosts.

To use a syslog server, install the software on a Windows, Linux, UNIX, or MAC OS server, and configure the router to send logged events to the syslog server.

The **logging 192.168.3.11** command is a sample of the command that specifies the IP address of the host where the syslog server is installed.

When troubleshooting a problem, always set the service timestamps for logging. Be sure the router date and time are set correctly so that log files display the proper timestamp.

Use the **show clock** command to check the date and time setting:

```
R1# show clock
*00:03:45.213 UTC Mon Mar 1 2007
```

To set the clock, first set the time zone. Base the time zone on *Greenwich mean time (GMT)*, and then set the clock. The time zone is the three-letter abbreviation for the time zone name (in this case, central standard time, CST, in the United States). The number following the time zone is the number of hours offset from GMT, also known as ***coordinated universal time (UTC)*** (from –23 to 23). Note that the **clock set** command is not used in configuration mode.

To set the time zone, use the following command:

```
R1(config)# clock timezone CST -6
```

To set the clock, use the following command:

```
R1# clock set 10:25:00 Sep 10 2007
```

**Lab 8-8: Configuring ACLs and Recording Activity to a Syslog Server (8.5.2)**

In this lab, you configure ACLs and download a syslog server to record ACL activity. Refer to the hands-on lab in Part II of this *Learning Guide*. You may perform this lab now or wait until the end of the chapter.

## ACL Best Practices

ACLs are a very powerful filtering tool. They are active immediately after application onto an interface.

It is much better to spend extra time planning and troubleshooting before applying an ACL than trying to troubleshoot after applying the ACL. Always test basic connectivity before applying ACLs. If pinging a host is unsuccessful because of a bad cable or an IP configuration problem, the ACL can compound the problem and make it harder to troubleshoot.

When logging, add the **deny any** statement (standard ACLs) or **deny ip any any** (extended ACLs) to the end of the ACL. This statement allows tracking the number of matches for packets denied.

Use the **reload in 30** command when working with remote routers and testing ACL functionality. If a mistake in an ACL blocks access to the router, remote connectivity might be denied. When you use this command, the router reloads in 30 minutes and reverts to the startup configuration. When satisfied with how the ACL is functioning, copy the running configuration to the startup configuration.

It is best to create and edit ACLs in a text editor such as Notepad.

**Interactive Activity 8-10: Critical Thinking—Analyzing ACL Statements (8.6.2)**

In this practice scenario, you are given a network topology and must answer questions on ACL statements and placement. Use file d3ia-862 on the CD-ROM that accompanies this book to perform this interactive activity.

# Summary

Traffic filtering is the process of analyzing the contents of a packet to determine whether the packet should be allowed or blocked. ACLs enable management of traffic and secure access to and from a network and its resources.

There are three types of ACLs: standard, extended, and named.

ACLs filter traffic based on source and destination IP address, application, and protocol. They are applied to a router interface to examine packets that are inbound or outbound.

Using a wildcard mask provides flexibility and can block a range of addresses or whole networks with one statement. The wildcard mask compares the incoming address to a comparison address to determine which bits match. To determine the wildcard mask, subtract the decimal subnet mask for an address or range from the all -255s mask (255.255.255.255).

There is an implied **deny any** statement at the end of the ACL. The keyword **any** refers to all hosts, and the keyword **host** refers to an individual IP address.

Standard ACLs filter on source IP address and are placed as close to the destination as possible. Extended ACLs can filter on source and destination addresses, and on protocol and port number, and should be placed as close to the source as possible. Extended ACLs filter a range of ports using the **gt**, **lt**, and **range** operators. NACLs offer all the functionality and advantages of standard and extended ACLs.

Decide placement of ACLs based on the type of ACL and requirements. Each interface supports one ACL per direction per protocol. Create an ACL using a unique identifier and apply either inbound or outbound on an interface using the **ip access-group** command. Apply ACLs directly to VLAN logical interfaces just as with physical interfaces. Network administrators also need to account for NAT when creating and applying ACLs to interfaces.

The **show ip interface**, **show access-lists**, and **show running-config** commands enable a network administrator to view all ACLs that have been configured on a router.

ACLs restrict vty access to increase network security. The **access-class** command is used to apply a vty ACL.

Using the **established** parameter permits external traffic that is a response to a request.

There are different ways to approach writing ACLs: Permit specific traffic first, and then deny general traffic, or deny specific traffic first, and then permit general traffic. The order in which the statements are written impacts how well the router performs.

By default, an ACL statement performs basic logging by capturing the number of matches and displays them at the end of each statement matched. The ACL **log** option provides additional detail about packets permitted or denied. To activate logging, add the **log** option to the end of each ACL statement. Also, add the **deny any log** (standard ACLs) or the **deny ip any any log** (extended ACLs) to monitor the number of packets that are not matched by previous ACL statements. Use caution when logging, because the process places an additional load on the router. In addition to displaying on the console screen, the log contents can be sent to an external syslog server. Always set the service timestamps for logging, and be sure the router date and time are set correctly so that log files display the proper timestamp.

# Activities and Labs

This summary outlines the activities and labs you can perform to help reinforce important concepts described in this chapter. You can find the activity and Packet Tracer files on the CD-ROM accompanying this book. The complete hands-on labs appear in Part II.

**Interactive activities on the CD-ROM:**

Interactive Activity 8-1: Types and Usage of ACLs (8.1.3)

Interactive Activity 8-2: ACL Processing (8.1.4)

Interactive Activity 8-3: ACL Wildcard Mask Purpose and Structure (8.2.1)

Interactive Activity 8-4: Analyzing the Effects of the Wildcard Mask (8.2.2)

Interactive Activity 8-5: Placing Standard and Extended ACLs (8.3.1)

Interactive Activity 8-6: Configuring Numbered Standard ACLs (8.3.3)

Interactive Activity 8-7: Configuring Numbered Extended ACLs (8.3.4)

Interactive Activity 8-8: Configuring ACLs to Support Established Traffic (8.4.2)

Interactive Activity 8-9: Analyzing Network ACLs and Placement (8.4.4)

Interactive Activity 8-10: Critical Thinking—Analyzing ACL Statements (8.6.2)

**Packet Tracer activities on the CD-ROM:**

Configuring and Verifying Standard Named ACLs (8.3.5)

Planning, Configuring, and Verifying Standard, Extended, and Named ACLs (8.3.6)

Configuring and Verifying Extended ACLs to Filter on Port Numbers (8.4.1)

Configuring and Verifying Extended ACLs with a DMZ (8.4.5)

**Labs in Part II of this book:**

Lab 8-1: Configuring and Verifying Standard ACLs (8.3.3)

Lab 8-2: Planning, Configuring, and Verifying Standard ACLs (8.3.4)

Lab 8-3: Configuring and Verifying Extended Named ACLs (8.3.5)

Lab 8-4: Configuring and Verifying vty Restrictions (8.3.6)

Lab 8-5: Configuring an ACL with NAT (8.4.3)

Lab 8-6: Configuring and Verifying ACLs to Filter Inter-VLAN Traffic (8.4.5)

Lab 8-7: Configuring ACLs and Verifying with Console Logging (8.5.1)

Lab 8-8: Configuring ACLs and Recording Activity to a Syslog Server (8.5.2)

# Check Your Understanding

Complete all the review questions listed here to check your understanding of the topics and concepts in this chapter. Appendix A, "Check Your Understanding and Challenge Questions Answer Key," lists the answers.

1. An administrator has been asked to explain ACLs to a trainee. What are some of the suggested uses for ACLs that the trainee should learn? (Choose three.)

    A. Limit network traffic and increase performance.

    B. Notify downstream devices in the event of increased traffic or congestion.

    C. Determine whether interfaces are active or shut down during peak usage.

    D. Provide traffic flow control.

    E. Provide a basic level of security for network access.

    F. Open additional links when paths become saturated.

2. What statements are true regarding the meaning of the ACL wildcard mask 0.0.0.15? (Choose two.)

    A. The first 28 bits of a supplied IP address will be ignored.

    B. The last 4 bits of a supplied IP address will be ignored.

    C. The first 32 bits of a supplied IP address will be matched.

    D. The first 28 bits of a supplied IP address will be matched.

    E. The last 5 bits of a supplied IP address will be ignored.

    F. The last 4 bits of a supplied IP address will be matched.

3. What IP address and wildcard mask pair will test for addresses of a subnet containing only a host configured with an IP address of 192.168.12.6 and subnet mask of 255.255.255.248?

    A. 192.168.12.0 0.0.0.7

    B. 192.168.12.0 0.0.0.8

    C. 192.168.12.6 0.0.0.15

    D. 192.168.12.6 0.0.0.255

4. After an ACL has been created, it must be applied in the proper location to have the desired effect. What rules should be observed when applying ACLs? (Choose two.)

    A. Standard ACLs should be applied as close to the source as possible.

    B. Outbound filters do not affect traffic that originates within the local router.

    C. The inbound and outbound interface should be referenced as if looking from the outside of a router.

    D. Extended ACLs should be applied closest to the source.

    E. All ACL statements are processed for each packet through the interface.

5. A network administrator is writing a standard ACL that will deny any traffic from the 172.16.0.0/16 network, but permit all other traffic. Which two commands should be used?

    A. Router(config)# **access-list 95 deny any**

    B. Router(config)# **access-list 95 deny 172.16.0.0 0.0.255.255**

    C. Router(config)# **access-list 95 deny 172.16.0.0 255.255.0.0**

    D. Router(config)# **access-list 95 permit any**

    E. Router(config)# **access-list 95 host 172.16.0.0**

    F. Router(config)# **access-list 95 172.16.0.0 255.255.255.255**

6. What can you conclude from the following **show-running config** output? (Choose two.)

    ```
    R1# show running-config
    <output omitted>
    Current configuration : 840 bytes
    version 12.4
    !
    interface Serial0/0/1
     ip address 192.168.1.1 255.255.255.0
     ip access-group 99 in
     no fair-queue
     clock rate 64000
    !
    ip classless
    no ip http server
    !
    Access-list 99 deny 10.213.177.76
    Access-list 99 permit any
    ```

    A. This is an extended IP access list.

    B. The keyword **host** is implied in the command line **access-list 99 deny 10.213.177.76**.

    C. The wildcard mask must be configured for this access list to function properly.

    D. Host 10.213.177.100 will be allowed access to the Serial 0/1 interface.

    E. This ACL will not limit any traffic through this router.

7. Refer to the topology in Figure 8-23. The new security policy for the company allows all IP traffic from the Engineering LAN to the Internet, whereas only web traffic from the Marketing LAN is allowed to the Internet. Which ACL can be applied in the outbound direction of Serial 0/0/1 on the Marketing router to implement the new security policy?

**Figure 8-23    Question 7 Topology**

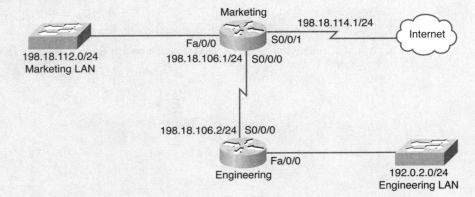

A. **access-list 197 permit ip 192.0.2.0 0.0.0.255 any**

   **access-list 197 permit ip 198.18.112.0 0.0.0.255 any eq www**

B. **access-list 165 permit ip 192.0.2.0 0.0.0.255 any**

   **access-list 165 permit tcp 198.18.112.0 0.0.0.255 any eq www**

   **access-list 165 permit ip any any**

C. **access-list 137 permit ip 192.0.2.0 0.0.0.255 any**

   **access-list 137 permit tcp 198.18.112.0 0.0.0.255 any eq www**

D. **access-list 98 permit TCP 192.0.2.0 0.0.0.255 any**

   **access-list 98 permit ip 192.18.112.0 0.0.0.255 any eq www**

8. In the following output, which two statements are correct based on the set of the commands shown?

```
R1(config)# ip access-list extended Server1Access
R1(config-ext-nacl)# deny ip 10.128.114.0 0.0.0.255 any
R1(config-ext-nacl)# deny tcp 192.168.85.0 0.0.0.255 host 172.25.0.26 eq 23
R1(config-ext-nacl)# permit ip any any

R1(config)# interface fa0/0
R1(config-if)# ip access-group Server1Acces out
```

A. Host 10.128.114.76 will be able to establish a Telnet session with host 172.25.0.26.

B. Host 10.128.114.76 will not be able to establish an FTP session with available hosts on the 172.25.0.0/16 network.

C. Host 192.168.85.76 will be able to establish a Telnet session with host 172.25.0.26.

D. Host 192.168.85.76 will be able to establish an FTP session with available hosts on the 172.25.0.0 network.

E. Host 172.25.0.26 will not be able to establish a Telnet session with available hosts on the 192.168.85.0/24 network.

9. A network engineer wants to ensure that only users of the network management host can access the vty lines of R1. Pair the command on the left to the correct prompt on the right as it would be entered in the router. Not all options are used.

| Command | Prompt |
| --- | --- |
| **line vty 0 4** | R1(config)# |
| **access-class 1 in** | R1(config)# |
| **ip access-group 1 in** | R1(config-line)# |
| **access-list 1 deny any** | |
| **access-list 1 deny ip any any** | |
| **access-list 1 permit host 10.0.0.1** | |

**10.** Which two statements are true about IP ACLs?

   A. ACLs control host access to a network or to another host.

   B. Standard ACLs can restrict access to specific applications and ports.

   C. ACLs provide a basic level of security for network access.

   D. ACLs can permit or deny traffic based on the MAC address originating on the router.

   E. ACLs can be applied to only one interface.

**11.** Refer to Figure 8-24 and access list 101. ACL 101 is applied as an inbound ACL on interface Serial 0 of router RTA and should permit Telnet access to the 172.16.28.3 host. However, Telnet access fails when host 10.10.10.3 attempts to connect to host 172.16.28.3. What could be the cause?

```
access-list 101 permit tcp 10.10.10.0 0.0.0.255 any eq 21
access-list 101 deny ip any any
```

**Figure 8-24   Question 11 Topology**

172.16.28.3/24                                                                    10.10.10.3

   A. The line **access-list 101 permit tcp any any established** should be added before the **permit** statement.

   B. The line **access-list 101 permit tcp any any established** should be added after the **permit** statement.

   C. The port number is incorrect for the access list **permit** statement.

   D. The access list should be on the outbound interface of FastEthernet 0.

**12.** A network administrator is interested in tracking all packets that do not match any statement in a standard ACL. What must the network administrator do to allow tracking?

   A. Enter the command **debug ACL deny** from global configuration mode.

   B. Add **permit ip any log** to the end of the ACL statements.

   C. Enter the **syslog** command in global configuration mode.

   D. Nothing. Logging of denied packets happens automatically.

   E. Enter the **deny ip any log** to the end of the ACL statements.

**13.** A network administrator wants to use an ACL to permit traffic from the 172.16.2.0/24 network on Router R1 from reaching a specific host on the 192.168.5.0/24 network but allow access to all other hosts on the 192.168.5.0/24 network on Router R2. Routers R1 and R2 are connected by a serial WAN link. The administrator does not have access to the R2 router that the 192.168.5.0/24 network is on. What kind of ACL must the administrator use?

**14.** Which of the following are considered best practices for working with ACLs? (Choose three.)

A. Test basic connectivity before applying ACLs.

B. Make changes to ACLs on remote routers, and copy the running configuration to the startup configuration before testing the ACL.

C. When logging, add the **deny any** statement to the end of a standard ACL.

D. It is best to create and edit ACLs in a text editor such as Notepad.

E. Apply extended ACLs closest to the destination, because they can permit or deny traffic based on a destination address.

## Challenge Questions and Activities

These questions require a deeper application of the concepts covered in this chapter. You can find the answers in Appendix A.

**1.** Refer to Figure 8-25. You are a network administrator and want to create a standard ACL to accomplish the following:

■ Permit all traffic from remote network 192.168.125.0/24 on Router R2 to reach local hosts on the Router R1 10.1.1.0/24 LAN.

■ Deny traffic from remote 172.20.10.0/24 network on R2 access to the Router R1 10.1.1.0/24 LAN.

■ Deny network 10.1.2.0/24 on Router R1 access to local hosts on the Router R1 10.1.1.0/24 network.

You have administrative control over both routers. What is the best router/interface and direction configuration so that the ACL satisfies the requirements and minimizes the number of ACLs?

**Figure 8-25    Challenge Question 1 Topology**

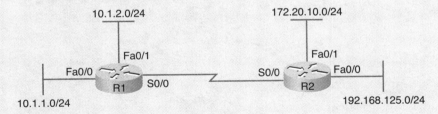

A. The R1 S0/0 interface outbound

B. The R1 Fa0/0 interface outbound

C. The R1 S0/0 interface inbound

D. The R2 S0/0 interface inbound

E. The R2 Fa0/0 and Fa0/1 interfaces inbound

F. The R2 S0/0 interface outbound

2. Write the standard ACL statements that would accomplish the goals described in Question 1 and apply them to the correct router interface in the correct direction. Be sure to include the correct router prompt.

3. Refer to Figure 8-25. You are a network administrator and want to create an extended ACL to accomplish the following:

   ■ Permit traffic from remote network 192.168.125.0/24 on Router R2 to reach local hosts on the Router R1 10.1.1.0/24 LAN.

   ■ Deny traffic from remote 172.20.10.0/24 network on R2 access to the Router R1 10.1.1.0/24 LAN.

   Where is the best location to place the ACL to minimize WAN bandwidth usage? You have administrative control over both routers.

   A. The R1 S0/0 interface inbound

   B. The R1 Fa0/0 interface outbound

   C. The R2 S0/0 interface inbound

   D. The R2 S0/0 interface outbound

   E. The R2 Fa0/0 interface inbound

4. Write the extended ACL statements that would accomplish the goals described in Question 3, and apply them to the correct router interface in the correct direction. In addition, allow administrator host 172.20.10.99 on the 172.20.10.0/24 network to telnet and FTP (data and control) to the 10.1.1.0/24 network. Be sure to include the correct router prompt.

5. Activity: Real-World ACLs

   Try to identify examples of access lists that we use every day (for example, a bouncer at the door of a bar asking "Are you old enough?"). Develop examples where another entity (for example, bouncer = router) makes the decision. The user (traffic) does not make the decision of go / no go.

# CHAPTER 9

# Troubleshooting an Enterprise Network

## Objectives

Upon completion of this chapter, you should be able to answer the following questions:

- What is uptime, and why is it important?

- What is a failure domain, and why is it important?

- What types of issues can cause a network to fail?

- How would you isolate and correct common switching problems?

- How would you isolate and correct common routing problems?

- How would you isolate and correct common WAN link issues?

- How would you isolate and correct common ACL problems?

## Key Terms

This chapter uses the following key terms. You can find the definitions in the Glossary.

*proactive maintenance*   *page 330*

*baseline*   *page 330*

*Simple Network Management Protocol (SNMP)*   *page 331*

*Management Information Base (MIB)*   *page 331*

*network management system (NMS)*   *page 332*

*network monitoring plan*   *page 332*

*transceivers*   *page 338*

*rogue switch*   *page 344*

*Serial Line Address Resolution Protocol (SLARP)*   *page 369*

Enterprise networks can have problems that range from poor performance to unreachable resources. Network monitoring, proactive maintenance, effective troubleshooting processes, and an awareness of failure domains can help to minimize network downtime. Network problems can involve a variety of technologies, including LAN switching, routing protocols, WAN links, and access control lists (ACL).

Part II of this book includes the corresponding labs for this chapter.

# Understanding the Impact of Network Failure

Most enterprises rely on their networks to provide consistent and reliable access to shared resources. Network uptime is the time that the network is available and functioning as expected. Network downtime is any time that the network is not performing as required. A reduction in the performance level of the network might negatively impact the business.

Without a reliable network, many organizations lose access to customer databases and accounting records that employees need to perform their daily activities. Network outages also prevent customers from placing orders or obtaining the information they require. Downtime results in lost productivity, customer frustration, and often the loss of customers to competitors.

## Enterprise Network Requirements

Many different metrics are used to determine the cost of downtime to an enterprise. The actual cost to a company varies depending on the day, date, and time. Large enterprises generally span many different time zones and have employees, customers, and suppliers accessing their network around the clock. For these organizations, any downtime is extremely costly. Many factors cause network downtime, including the following:

- Weather and natural disasters
- Security breaches
- Man-made disasters
- Power surges and failures
- Virus attacks
- Equipment failure
- Misconfiguration of devices
- Lack of resources such as system memory and CPU cycles

A well-planned network design and implementation are crucial for meeting uptime requirements. To ensure the proper and efficient flow of traffic, a good design includes redundancy of all critical components and data paths. Redundancy in network design should eliminate any single point of failure. Complete redundancy of all network components and links can be extremely costly. Most networks are designed to provide redundancy to key areas of the network, but they might not provide redundancy in areas where downtime is more tolerable.

The three-layer hierarchical network design model, as shown in Figure 9-1, separates the functionality of the various networking devices and links. This separation ensures efficient network performance. In addition, the use of enterprise-class equipment provides a high degree of reliability.

**Figure 9-1    Three-Layer Hierarchical Network Design Model**

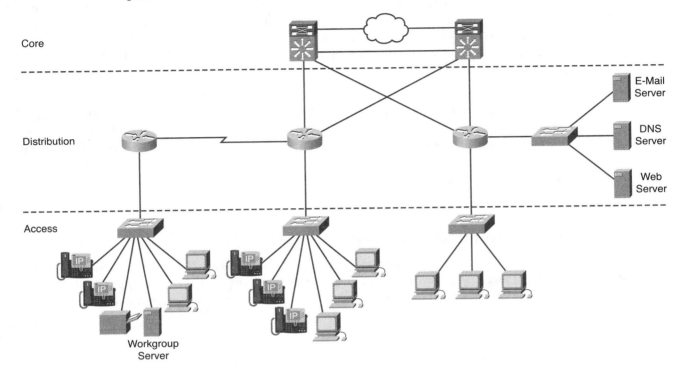

Even with proper network design, some downtime is inevitable. Keeping downtime to a minimum and ensuring rapid recovery requires additional considerations. To guarantee service levels, an enterprise should have service level agreements (SLA) with key service providers and suppliers. An SLA clearly documents network expectations in terms of level of service. These expectations include the acceptable level of downtime and the recovery period, should downtime occur. SLAs often specify the penalty associated with any loss of service.

Outages are not only associated with loss of service from ISPs. Quite often, the problem stems from the failure of a key piece of equipment that is part of the local network. Minimizing this type of downtime requires warrantees on all critical pieces of equipment. Warrantees provide for rapid replacement of mission-critical components.

Business continuity plans provide a detailed plan of action in case of unexpected man-made or natural disasters such as power failures or earthquakes. Business continuity plans provide the details on how the business continues or resumes operations, with minimal disruption to its clients, after the disaster. They clearly specify how the network reestablishes functionality in the event of a catastrophic failure.

Over the past several years, there has been a shift from recovery to continuity. Once it was sufficient to have a plan in place that would ensure that access to network resources could be reestablished within a certain period of time. The acceptable time varied depending on the organization; but quite often, a network outage could last several days. This is no longer acceptable. With the increased dependence of organizations on their networked resources, downtime is no longer an acceptable option for many organizations.

One way to ensure functionality is to have a redundant backup site at another location, in case of failure at the primary site. For large organizations, these backup sites are located at a different geographic site, often in another country, to ensure that the disaster in one area does not affect the backup site. All data and key resources are mirrored to the backup site, and failure of the primary site triggers an automatic switchover to the backup facilities. Often, this switchover is done in a manner that goes unnoticed by customers and vendors.

## Monitoring and Proactive Maintenance

No organization wants to rely on a backup site for business continuity. Organizations spend large amounts of money to ensure that their primary network remains functional. One way of ensuring uptime is to monitor current network functionality and perform *proactive maintenance*.

### Network Monitoring

The purpose of network monitoring is to watch network performance in comparison to a predetermined *baseline*. Any observed deviations from this baseline indicate potential problems with the network and require investigation. As soon as the network administrator determines the cause of degraded performance, corrective actions can be taken to prevent a serious network outage.

Several tools are available for monitoring network performance levels and gathering data. These include network utilities, packet sniffers, and SNMP monitoring tools. Each of these groups of tools has different capabilities and provides different types of information. Using these tools in combination provides comprehensive information on current network performance.

It is best practice to determine the baseline network performance levels when the network is first installed and then again after any major changes or upgrades occur. Network administrators perform baseline testing of the network under normal load levels, using the protocols and applications normally encountered on the network.

Many complex tools and procedures exist to determine performance baselines. Some programs perform many different tests with different types of traffic. The tests determine the network performance under very accurately defined loads and conditions. Others, such as a simple ping (as shown in Example 9-1), are less accurate but often provide sufficient information to alert the administrator to a problem. If the time required for a ping to the same site increases substantially, a network problem such as congestion may be occurring.

**Example 9-1  Using ping To Detect Network Problems**

```
!January 4


C:\> ping 10.66.254.159


Pinging 10.66.254.159 with 32 bytes of data:
Reply from 10.66.254.159: bytes=32 time=1ms TTL-128
Reply from 10.66.254.159: bytes=32 time=1ms TTL-128
Reply from 10.66.254.159: bytes=32 time=1ms TTL-128
Reply from 10.66.254.159: bytes=32 time=1ms TTL-128


Ping statistics for 10.66.254.159:
      Packets: Sent = 4, Received = 4, Lost = 0 (0% loss),
Approximate round trip times in milli-seconds:
    Minimum = 1ms, Maximum = 1ms, Average = 1ms



!March 18


C:\> ping 10.66.254.159


Pinging 10.66.254.159 with 32 bytes of data:
Reply from 10.66.254.159: bytes=32 time=6ms TTL-128
Reply from 10.66.254.159: bytes=32 time=5ms TTL-128
Reply from 10.66.254.159: bytes=32 time=7ms TTL-128
Reply from 10.66.254.159: bytes=32 time=6ms TTL-128


Ping statistics for 10.66.254.159:
      Packets: Sent = 4, Received = 4, Lost = 0 (0% loss),
Approximate round trip times in milli-seconds:
    Minimum = 5ms, Maximum = 7ms, Average = 6ms
```

Simple network utilities, such as ping and tracert, provide information on the performance of the network or network link. Performing these commands at multiple times shows the difference in time required for a packet to travel between two locations. Using these commands, however, does not provide a reason for the difference in times, only an indication that something has occurred that is affecting the network performance and warrants further investigation.

Packet sniffing tools monitor the types of traffic on various parts of the network. These tools indicate whether there is an excessive amount of a particular traffic type or whether traffic is on the network that should be filtered out. They examine the contents of the packets, which provides a quick way of locating the source of this traffic. These tools may also be able to remedy the situation before network congestion becomes critical. For example, traffic sniffing can detect whether a type of traffic or a particular transaction occurring on the network is unexpected. This detection might stop a potential denial-of-service (DoS) attack before it affects network performance.

*Simple Network Management Protocol (SNMP)* allows monitoring of individual devices on the network. SNMP-compliant devices use agents to monitor a number of predefined parameters for specific conditions. These agents collect information and store it in a database known as the *Management Information Base (MIB)*. SNMP polls devices at regular intervals to collect information about managed parameters. SNMP also traps certain events that exceed a predefined threshold or condition.

For example, SNMP can monitor a router interface for errors. The network administrator defines a specific level of acceptable errors for that interface. If the errors exceed the threshold level, SNMP traps the condition and sends it to a *network management system (NMS)*. The NMS alerts the network administrator. Some SNMP systems trigger events, such as the automatic reconfiguration of a device, to eliminate the problem. Most enterprise class network management systems use SNMP. Figure 9-2 shows an example of the various components used in SNMP.

**Figure 9-2    SNMP Components**

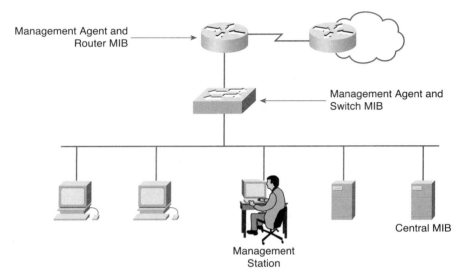

A number of freeware and commercial proactive network monitoring tools exist. These tools monitor traffic type, traffic load, server configurations, traffic patterns, and a multitude of other conditions. A *network monitoring plan* and the use of proper tools help a network administrator evaluate the health of the network and detect any problem situations.

## Proactive Maintenance

A network administrator performs proactive maintenance on a regular basis to verify and service equipment. By doing this, the administrator can detect weaknesses before a critical error occurs that could bring down the network. Like regular servicing on a car, proactive maintenance extends the life of a network device.

Network monitoring tools, techniques, and programs rely on the availability of a complete set of accurate and current network documentation, including physical and logical topology diagrams, configuration files of all network devices, and a baseline performance level for the network.

Packet Tracer
☐ Activity

**Creating a Baseline (9.1.2)**

In this activity, you create a performance and configuration baseline for a supplied network. Use file d3-912.pka on the CD-ROM that accompanies this book to perform this activity using Packet Tracer.

## Troubleshooting and the Failure Domain

The objective of any troubleshooting effort is to return functionality quickly and with little disruption to the end users. Achieving this objective often means postponing an extensive or prolonged process for determining the cause of a problem in favor of quickly reestablishing functionality. In some situations, putting a temporary solution into place allows investigation and correction of the problem under a less-critical time constraint. Temporary solutions should be used only to restore network functionality while the cause of the problem is investigated and a more permanent solution devised.

Redundancy is a key design element for enterprise networks. In a redundant environment, if one link goes down, traffic diversion to the redundant link occurs immediately. This temporary solution allows the network to maintain functionality and gives the administrator time to diagnose and correct the problem with the failed link. If problems occur with a specific device or configuration, having backup copies of the configuration files or spare devices allows quick restoration of connectivity.

Quick solutions are not always possible or appropriate. The security of the network and the resources that it houses must always be the highest priority. If a quick fix compromises this security, it is important to take the time to investigate a more appropriate alternative solution.

The business continuity plan should include information on any security threats or concerns, including such items as the following:

- Documentation of potential problems

- Description of the appropriate course of action in the event of problems

- Details of the security policy of the company

- Details of the security risks of the actions

When designing an enterprise network, it is important to limit the size of all failure domains. The failure domain is the area of the network impacted by the failure or misconfiguration of a network device. The actual size of the domain depends on the device and the type of failure or misconfiguration. When troubleshooting a network, one of the first steps is to determine the scope of the issue and isolate the issue to a specific failure domain.

If both a Layer 2 switch and a border router fail at the same time, they affect different failure domains. The failure of a Layer 2 switch on a LAN segment affects only users in the broadcast domain. It has no effect on other regions of the network. Failure of a border router, however, prevents all users in the company from connecting to network resources outside of their local network. Figure 9-3 shows an example of the extent of the failure domains for different devices.

The router in the example has a larger impact on the network because it has a larger failure domain. Under normal circumstances, troubleshoot resources with the larger failure domains first. In some circumstances, the size of the failure domain is not the deciding factor in troubleshooting priority. For example, if a business-critical server is connected to a failed switch, correction of this issue may take precedence over the border router.

**Interactive Activity 9-1: Determining the Size of a Failure Domain (9.1.3)**

In this activity, you determine the size of the failure domain associated with various devices. Use file d3ia-913 on the CD-ROM that accompanies this book to perform this interactive activity.

**Figure 9-3    Failure Domains**

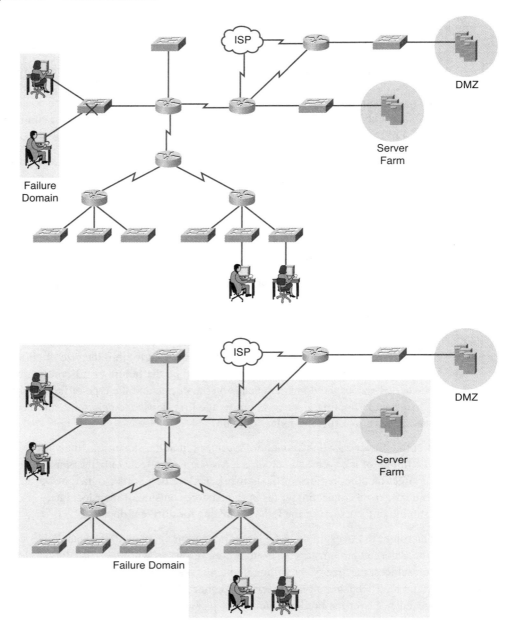

## Troubleshooting Process

When a problem occurs on an enterprise network, troubleshooting that problem quickly and efficiently is important to avoid extended periods of downtime. Many different structured and unstructured problem-solving techniques are available to the network technician. These techniques have been discussed in detail earlier in the course "CCNA Discovery Networking for Home and Small Businesses" and its accompanying *Learning Guide*. The troubleshooting techniques include the following:

- Top down

- Bottom up

- Divide and conquer

- Trial and error

- Substitution

Most experienced network technicians rely on the knowledge gained from past experience and start the troubleshooting process using a trial-and-error approach. Correcting the problem in this manner saves a great deal of time. Unfortunately, less-experienced technicians cannot rely solely on previous experience. In addition, many times the trial-and-error approach does not provide a solution. Both of these cases require application of one of the more structured approaches to troubleshooting.

When a situation requires a more structured approach, most network personnel use a layered process based on the OSI or TCP/IP models. The technician uses previous experience to determine whether the issue is associated with the lower layers of the OSI model or the upper layers. The layer dictates whether a top-down or bottom-up approach is appropriate. Table 9-1 lists some of the more common problems encountered at each layer of the OSI model.

**Table 9-1    Common Network Problems and Their Associated OSI Model Layer**

| Layer | Common Problems |
|---|---|
| Application | If resources are unreachable or unusable and the physical, data link, network, and transport layers are functional, the problem is associated with this layer. |
| Presentation | Responsible for data representation.<br><br>Includes compression and encryption.<br><br>If data is being reliably transmitted across the network but is unreadable on the receiving end, suspect the presentation layer.<br><br>Verify that any encryption keys match and are properly configured. |
| Session | Responsible for establishing, maintaining, and terminating end-to-end communication sessions between applications.<br><br>Related to synchronization and flow control.<br><br>An application server failing during a communication session could generate problems at the session layer. |
| Transport | Uses port numbers to identify the type of traffic being carried in the conversation.<br><br>Misconfigured ACLs are a common problem at this layer. |
| Network | Involved with logical addressing and best path determination.<br><br>Layer 3 addressing and routing problems are associated with this layer.<br><br>The most common problems are improperly configured addresses and improper routing information.<br><br>Misconfigured ACLs are an issue at the network layer. |
| Data link | Concerned mainly with the encapsulation of data.<br><br>Mismatched encapsulation is one of the most common issues at this layer.<br><br>Includes improper conversion of Layer 2 encapsulation as the frames move across the network. Improperly configured switch ports and Layer 2 addressing issues are also common.<br><br>Misconfigured ACLs can generate problems at Layer 2. |

*continues*

**Table 9-1**     **Common Network Problems and Their Associated OSI Model Layer**    *continued*

| Layer | Common Problems |
|---|---|
| Physical | Concerned with physical connectivity. |
| | Common issues include damaged or improper cabling, physical damage to ports, and power issues. |
| | In wireless networks, antennas are physical layer devices, as is the RF medium. |
| | Any loss in signal strength or interference is considered a Layer 1 problem. |

When approaching a problem situation, follow the generic problem-solving model, regardless of the type of troubleshooting technique used.

**How To**

**Step 1.**    Define the problem.

**Step 2.**    Gather facts.

**Step 3.**    Deduce possibilities and alternatives.

**Step 4.**    Design plan of action.

**Step 5.**    Implement solution.

**Step 6.**    Analyze results.

If the first pass through this procedure does not determine and correct the problem, repeat the process as necessary. Before repeating the process, be certain to undo any changes made during the previous pass. Be sure to document the initial symptoms and all attempts at finding and correcting the cause. This documentation serves as a valuable resource should the same or similar problem occur again. It is important to document even failed attempts, to save time during future troubleshooting activities.

**Interactive Activity 9-2: Determining the OSI Layer Associated with a Problem (9.1.4)**

In this activity, you determine the OSI layer most likely associated with a given problem. Use file d3ia-914 on the CD-ROM that accompanies this book to perform this interactive activity.

# Troubleshooting Switching and Connectivity Issues

Switches are currently the most commonly used access layer networking device. Workstations, printers, and servers connect into the network through switches. Faults with the switch hardware or configuration prevent connection between these local and remote devices.

## Troubleshooting Basic Switching

The most common problems with switches occur at the physical layer. If a switch is installed in an unprotected environment, it can suffer damage such as dislodged or damaged data or power cables. Ensure that switches are placed in a physically secure area.

If an end device cannot connect to the network and the link LED is not illuminated, or the link or the switch port is defective or shut down, perform the following steps:

**Step 1.**    Ensure that the power LED is illuminated.

**Step 2.**    Ensure that the correct type of cable connects the end device to the switch.

**Step 3.**    Reseat the cables at both the workstation and the switch end.

**Step 4.**    Check the configuration to ensure that the port is in a no-shutdown state.

If a connectivity problem exists, and if the link LED is illuminated, the switch configuration is the most likely problem. If a switch port fails or malfunctions, the easiest way to test it is to move the physical connection to another port and see whether this corrects the problem.

Ensure that switch port security has not disabled the port. Use the following commands to view how security is configured on individual switch ports.

```
show running-config
show port-security interface interface_id
```

If the switch security settings are disabling the port, review the security policy to see whether altering the security is acceptable. Never make a change in the switch port security settings without first verifying that such a change falls within the organization's security policy.

Switches function at Layer 2 and keep a record of the MAC address of all connected devices. If the MAC address in this table is not correct, the switch forwards information to the wrong port and communication does not occur. The **show mac-address-table** command displays the MAC address of the device connected to each switch port. To clear the dynamic entries in the table, use the **clear mac-address-table dynamic** command. The switch then repopulates the MAC address table with updated information. Example 9-2 shows a sample MAC address table.

**Example 9-2  Viewing the MAC Address Table**

```
S2# show mac-address-table
Mac Address Table
-------------------------------------------------------------


Vlan    Mac Address      Type      Ports
----    -----------      ----      -----
All     000.d.6563.bd00  STATIC    CPU
All     0100.0ccc.cccc   STATIC    CPU
All     0100.0ccc.cccd   STATIC    CPU
All     0100.0cdd.dddd   STATIC    CPU
   1    000d.29a0.88e0   DYNAMIC   Fa0/2
   1    000d.6563.0582   DYNAMIC   Fa0/2
   1    0010.a4fa.b23e   DYNAMIC   Fa0/6
   1    00b0.d04d.01f7   DYNAMIC   Fa0/4
 101    000d.29a0.88e0   DYNAMIC   Fa0/2
 101    000d.6563.0582   DYNAMIC   Fa0/2
 102    000d.29a0.88e0   DYNAMIC   Fa0/2
 102    000d.6563.0582   DYNAMIC   Fa0/2
 103    000d.29a0.88e0   DYNAMIC   Fa0/2
 103    000d.6563.0582   DYNAMIC   Fa0/2
Total Mac Addresses for this criterion: 14
```

Although automatically detected on many devices, mismatched speed or duplex settings can prevent the link between the switch and end device from functioning. Some switches do not properly detect the speed and duplex of the connected device. If this is the suspected problem, lock down the values on the switch port to match the host device using the interface **speed** and **duplex** commands. The **show interface** *interface_id* command displays both the speed and duplex settings of the port. This command produces an output similar to that shown in Example 9-3.

**Example 9-3  Viewing the Switch Port Speed and Duplex Settings**

```
S1# show interface fa 0/6
FastEthernet0/6 is up, line protocol is up (connected)
 Hardware is Fast Ethernet, address is 000d.6563.bd06 (bia 000d.6563.bd06)
 MTU 1500 bytes, BW 100000 Kbit, DLY 1000 usec,
  reliability 255/255, txload 1/255, rxload 1/255
 Encapsulation ARPA, loopback not set
 Keepalive set (10 sec)
 Full-duplex, 100Mb/s
 input flow-control is off, output flow-control is off
 ARP type: ARPA, ARP Timeout 04:00:00
 Last input never, output 00:00:01, output hang never
 Last clearing of "show interface" counters never
 Input queue: 0/75/0/0 (size/max/drops/flushes); Total output drops: 0
 Queueing strategy: fifo
 Output queue :0/40 (size/max)
 5 minute input rate 0 bits/sec, 0 packets/sec
 5 minute output rate 0 bits/sec, 0 packets/sec
  1201 packets input, 200969 bytes, 0 no buffer
  Received 1142 broadcasts, 0 runts, 0 giants, 0 throttles
  0 input errors, 0 CRC, 0 frame, 0 overrun, 0 ignored
  0 watchdog, 9 multicast, 0 pause input
  0 input packets with dribble condition detected
  131267 packets output, 10715646 bytes, 0 underruns
  0 output errors, 0 collisions, 2 interface resets
  0 babbles, 0 late collision, 0 deferred
  0 lost carrier, 0 no carrier, 0 PAUSE output
  0 output buffer failures, 0 output buffers swapped out
```

Switching loops are another potential source of connectivity issues. Spanning Tree Protocol (STP) normally prevents bridging loops and broadcast storms by shutting down redundant paths in a switched network. If STP bases its decisions on inaccurate information, loops may occur. A loop develops when the switch does not receive bridge protocol data units (BPDU) or is unable to process them. This could be due to miconfigurations, defective *transceivers*, hardware and cabling issues, or overloaded processors.

Overloaded processors disrupt STP and prevent the switch from processing the BPDUs. A port that is flapping causes multiple transitions to occur. Multiple transitions can overload the processors. This should be a rare occurrence in a properly configured network. To remedy this type of problem, remove as many of the redundant links as possible.

There are many indicators that a switching loop is present in a network, including the following:

- Loss of connectivity to, from, and through affected network regions

- High CPU utilization on routers connected to affected segments

- High link utilization up to 100 percent

- High switch backplane utilization as compared to the baseline utilization

- Syslog messages indicating packet looping, constant address relearning, or MAC address flapping messages

- Increasing number of output drops on many interfaces

Another troubleshooting issue is suboptimal switching. Left to default values, STP does not always identify the best root bridge or root ports. Changing the priority value on a switch can force the selection of the root bridge. The root bridge should normally be at the center of the network to provide for optimum switching.

Although STP is a fairly automated process on Cisco switches, if it is suspect, use the **show spanning-tree** command to gather information about the STP configuration. To view the STP state of a single port, use the **show spanning-tree interface** *interface_id* command. Example 9-4 shows the output of the **show spanning-tree command** for the two switches in the network shown in Figure 9-4.

**Example 9-4  Spanning Tree**

```
S1# show spanning-tree


VLAN0001
  Spanning tree enabled protocol ieee
  Root ID    Priority    32769
             Address     000d.6563.0580
             Cost        19
             Port        2 (FastEthernet0/2)
             Hello Time   2 sec  Max Age 20 sec  Forward Delay 15 sec
  Bridge ID  Priority    32769  (priority 32768 sys-id-ext 1)
             Address     000d.6563.bd00
             Hello Time   2 sec  Max Age 20 sec  Forward Delay 15 sec
             Aging Time 300
Interface          Role Sts Cost      Prio.Nbr Type
---------------- ---- --- --------- -------- --------------------------------
Fa0/2              Root FWD 19        128.2    P2p
Fa0/4              Desg FWD 19        128.4    P2p
Fa0/6              Desg FWD 19        128.6    Shr
S2# show spanning-tree


VLAN0001
  Spanning tree enabled protocol ieee
  Root ID    Priority    32769
             Address     000d.6563.0580
             This bridge is the root
             Hello Time   2 sec  Max Age 20 sec  Forward Delay 15 sec

  Bridge ID  Priority    32769  (priority 32768 sys-id-ext 1)
```

```
                Address      000d.6563.0580
                Hello Time    2 sec  Max Age 20 sec  Forward Delay 15 sec
                Aging Time 300

Interface         Role Sts Cost      Prio.Nbr Type
---------------- ---- --- --------- -------- --------------------------------
Fa0/1             Desg FWD 19        128.1    P2p
Fa0/2             Desg FWD 19        128.2    P2p
```

**Figure 9-4    Sample Network**

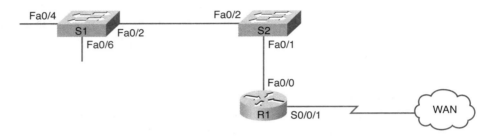

**Troubleshooting Host Connectivity (9.2.1)**

In this activity, you troubleshoot and resolve host connectivity issues. Use file d3-921 on the CD-ROM that accompanies this book to perform this activity using Packet Tracer.

# Troubleshooting VLAN Configuration Issues

Another common problem is the misconfiguration of VLANs or the misconfiguration of inter-VLAN routing. If the physical layer is functioning correctly and communication is still not occurring between end devices, check the VLAN configuration.

If the nonfunctioning ports are in the same VLAN, the hosts must have IP addresses on the same network or subnet to communicate. If the nonfunctioning ports are in different VLANs, communication is possible only with the aid of a Layer 3 device, such as a router.

As shown in Example 9-5, the **show vlan** command can be used to provide information on the VLAN configuration of a switch. If information is required on a specific VLAN, use the command **show vlan id** *vlan_number* to display the ports assigned to each VLAN. The **show vlan brief** command provides a listing of which ports are assigned to which VLANs. Examples 9-6 and 9-7 shows sample output from these commands.

**Example 9-5  show vlan Command Output**

```
S2# show vlan
VLAN    Name                          Status    Ports
----  ------------------------------- --------- -------------------------------
1     default                         active    Fa0/3, Fa0/4, Fa0/17, Fa0/18
                                                Fa0/19, Fa0/20, Fa0/21, Fa0/22
                                                Fa0/23, Fa0/24
```

```
101    VLAN0101                          active    Fa0/5, Fa0/7, Fa0/8
102    VLAN0102                          active    Fa0/9, Fa0/10, Fa0/11, Fa0/12
103    VLAN0103                          active    Fa0/13, Fa0/14, Fa0/15, Fa0/16
1002   fddi-default                      active
1003   token-ring-default                active
1004   fddinet-default                   active
1005   trnet-default                     active
VLAN Type   SAID       MTU   Parent RingNo BridgeNo Stp  BrdgMode Trans1 Trans2
---- ----- ---------- ----- ------ ------ -------- ---- -------- ------ ------
1    enet  100001     1500  -      -      -        -    -        0      0
101  enet  100101     1500  -      -      -        -    -        0      0
102  enet  100102     1500  -      -      -        -    -        0      0
103  enet  100103     1500  -      -      -        -    -        0      0
1002 fddi  101002     1500  -      -      -        -    -        0      0
1003 tr    101003     1500  -      -      -        -    -        0      0
1004 fdnet 101004     1500  -      -      -        ieee -        0      0
1005 trnet 101005     1500  -      -      -        ibm  -        0      0
Remote SPAN VLANs
------------------------------------------------------------------------------

Primary Secondary Type      Ports
------- --------- ----------------- ---------------------------------------------
```

**Example 9-6  show vlan id Command Output**

```
S2# show vlan id 101
VLAN Name          Status Ports
---- ------------------------------ --------- --------------------------------
101 VLAN0101        active Fa0/5, Fa0/7, Fa0/8
VLAN Type  SAID       MTU   Parent RingNo BridgeNo Stp  BrdgMode Trans1 Trans2
---- ----- ---------- ----- ------ ------ -------- ---- -------- ------ ------
101  enet  100101     1500  -      -      -        -    -        0      0
Remote SPAN VLAN
----------------
Disabled
Primary Secondary Type      Ports
------- --------- ----------------- ---------------------------------------------
```

**Example 9-7  show vlan brief Command Output**

```
S2# show vlan brief

VLAN  Name                          Status    Ports
----  ----------------------------- --------- ------------------------------
1     default                       active    Fa0/3, Fa0/4, Fa0/17, Fa0/18
                                               Fa0/19, Fa0/20, Fa0/21, Fa0/22
                                               Fa0/23, Fa0/24
101   VLAN0101                      active    Fa0/5, Fa0/7, Fa0/8
102   VLAN0102                      active    Fa0/9, Fa0/10, Fa0/11, Fa0/12
103   VLAN0103                      active    Fa0/13, Fa0/14, Fa0/15, Fa0/16
1002  fddi-default                  active
```

```
1003 token-ring-default             active
1004 fddinet-default                active
1005 trnet-default                  active


    ------------------------------------------------
```

If inter-VLAN routing is required, either trunking must be configured on both the router and the switch port or a router port must be connected to a switch port in each VLAN. If trunking is configured, verify the following configurations:

- Both the switch port and the router interface are configured with trunking.
- Both the switch and router interface are configured with the same encapsulation.

Newer switches default to 802.1Q, but some Cisco switches support both 802.1Q and the Cisco proprietary Inter-Switch Link (ISL) format. IEEE 802.1Q should be used whenever possible because it is the de facto standard. The 802.1Q and ISL formats are not compatible.

When troubleshooting inter-VLAN issues, use the **show ip interface brief** command to ensure that there is no IP address on the physical interface of the router and that the interface is active.

The network associated with each VLAN should be visible in the routing table. If not, recheck all physical connections and trunk configuration on both ends of the link. If the router is not directly connected to the VLAN subnets, check the configuration of the routing protocol to verify that there is a route to each of the VLANs. The **show ip route** command displays the output of the routing table. All subnets should be visible in the table. Example 9-8 and Example 9-9 provide sample output of these commands as they relate to R1 in Figure 9-4.

**Example 9-8  Verifying Inter-VLAN Routing Using the show ip interface brief Command**

```
R1# show ip interface brief
Interface            IP-Address     OK?   Method   Status                Protocol
FastEthernet0/0      unassigned     YES   manual   up                    up
FastEthernet0/0.100  10.20.100.1    YES   manual   up                    up
FastEthernet0/0.101  10.20.101.1    YES   manual   up                    up
FastEthernet0/0.102  10.20.102.1    YES   manual   up                    up
FastEthernet0/0.103  10.20.103.1    YES   manual   up                    up
Serial0/0/0          unassigned     YES   manual   down                  down
FastEthernet0/1      unassigned     YES   unset    administratively down down
Serial0/0/1          10.20.30.1     YES   manual   up                    up
```

**Example 9-9  Verifying Inter-VLAN Routing Using the show ip route Command**

```
R1# show ip route
Codes: C - connected, S - static, I - IGRP, R - RIP, M - mobile, B - BGP
   D - EIGRP, EX - EIGRP external, O - OSPF, IA - OSPF inter area
   N1 - OSPF NSSA external type 1, N2 - OSPF NSSA external type 2
   E1 - OSPF external type 1, E2 - OSPF external type 2, E - EGP
   i - IS-IS, L1 - IS-IS level-1, L2 - IS-IS level-2, ia - IS-IS inter area
   * - candidate default, U - per-user static route, o - ODR
   P - periodic downloaded static route
```

```
Gateway of last resort is not set
  10.0.0.0/8 is variably subnetted, 6 subnets, 2 masks
C  10.20.30.0/24 is directly connected, Serial0/0/1
C  10.20.30.2/32 is directly connected, Serial0/0/1
C  10.20.102.0/24 is directly connected, FastEthernet0/0.102
C  10.20.103.0/24 is directly connected, FastEthernet0/0.103
C  10.20.100.0/24 is directly connected, FastEthernet0/0.100
C  10.20.101.0/24 is directly connected, FastEthernet0/0.101
```

When configuring VLANs, it is important to understand how switches configure access and trunk ports and the concept of native and management VLANs.

## Access or Trunk Port

Each switch port is either an access port or a trunk port. On some switch models, other switch port modes are available, and the switch automatically configures the port to the appropriate status. It is sometimes advisable to lock the port into either access or trunk status to avoid potential problems with this detection process.

## Native and Management VLANs

The native VLAN and management VLAN are VLAN1 by default. Untagged frames sent across a trunk are assigned to the native VLAN of the trunk line. If the native VLAN assignment is changed on a device, each end of the 802.1Q trunk should be configured with the same native VLAN number. If one end of the trunk is configured for native VLAN10 and the other end is configured for native VLAN14, a frame sent from VLAN10 on one side is received on VLAN14 on the other. VLAN10 "leaks" into VLAN14. This can create unexpected connectivity issues and increase latency. For smoother, quicker transitions, verify that the native VLAN assignment is the same on all devices throughout the network.

### Troubleshooting Inter-VLAN Routing Issues (9.2.2)

In this activity, you troubleshoot and resolve issues related to inter-VLAN routing. Use file d3-922.pka on the CD-ROM that accompanies this book to perform this activity using Packet Tracer.

# Troubleshooting VTP

VLAN Trunking Protocol (VTP) simplifies the distribution of VLAN information to multiple switches in a domain. Switches that participate in VTP operate in one of three modes: server, client, or transparent. Only the server adds, deletes, and modifies VLAN information. When troubleshooting VTP on a network, check the following items:

- All participating devices have the same VTP domain name.
- Two VTP servers exist in every domain, in case one fails.
- All servers have the same information.
- The revision numbers are the same on all devices.
- All devices use the same VTP version.

To display the VTP version in use on a device, the VTP domain name, the VTP mode, and the VTP revision number, issue the **show vtp status** command. Two versions of VTP exist and are not compatible. To modify the VTP version number, use the **vtp version** [**1** | **2**] command. Example 9-10 shows the VTP configuration information for the two switches in Figure 9-4.

**Example 9-10    Switch VTP Configurations**

```
S1# show vtp status
VTP Version      : 2
Configuration Revision   : 5
Maximum VLANs supported locally : 64
Number of existing VLANs  : 8
VTP Operating Mode    : Client
VTP Domain Name      : Toronto
VTP Pruning Mode     : Disabled
VTP V2 Mode      : Disabled
VTP Traps Generation   : Disabled
MD5 digest       : 0x32 0x77 0x7A 0x1E 0xA3 0x68 0xAD 0x30
Configuration last modified by 10.20.100.2 at 9-17-07 20:26:40
S2# show vtp status
VTP Version       : 2
Configuration Revision   : 5
Maximum VLANs supported locally : 64
Number of existing VLANs  : 8
VTP Operating Mode    : Server
VTP Domain Name      : Toronto
VTP Pruning Mode     : Disabled
VTP V2 Mode      : Disabled
VTP Traps Generation   : Disabled
MD5 digest       : 0x32 0x77 0x7A 0x1E 0xA3 0x68 0xAD 0x30
Configuration last modified by 10.20.100.2 at 9-17-07 20:26:40
Local updater ID is 10.20.100.2 on interface Vl1 (lowest numbered VLAN interface found)
```

VTP clients and servers use the VTP revision number to decide whether they should update their VLAN information. If the revision number of the update is higher than the revision number currently in use, the client and server use the information to update the configuration. Always check the VTP revision information and mode on any switch before allowing it to join the network. The revision number is stored in NVRAM, and erasing the startup configuration on the switch does not reset this value. To reset the revision number, either set the switch mode to transparent or change the VTP domain name.

Revision numbers are also a problem if a *rogue switch* joins the domain and modifies VLAN information. To prevent this situation, it is important to configure a password on the VTP domain. To set a VTP password for the domain, use the global configuration command **vtp password** *password*.

When configured, the authentication password must be the same on all devices in the VTP domain. If updates are not propagating to a new switch in the VTP domain, suspect the password. The **show vtp password** command will display the VTP password currently configured on a device.

Packet Tracer
☐ Activity

**Troubleshooting VTP Issues (9.2.3)**

In this activity, you troubleshoot and correct VTP issues. Use file d3-923.pka on the CD-ROM that accompanies this book to perform this activity using Packet Tracer.

# Troubleshooting Routing Issues

Many different routing protocols exist, and each behaves differently on a network. All routers running a routing protocol exchange information. All routers build routing tables, which they use to forward information to remote networks. Many tools exist for troubleshooting routing issues. These include IOS **show** commands, **debug** commands, and TCP/IP utilities such as ping, traceroute, and Telnet.

The **show** commands display a snapshot of a configuration or of a particular component. The **show** commands are important tools for understanding the status of a router, detecting neighboring routers, isolating problems in the network, and monitoring the network in general. The **debug** commands are dynamic and provide real-time information about traffic movement and the interaction of protocols. Use TCP/IP utilities such as ping for verifying connectivity.

## RIP Issues

Routing Information Protocol (RIP) is one of the simplest routing protocols available. You can use a combination of **show** and **debug** commands to troubleshoot RIP routing issues.

Many **show** commands are available to help troubleshoot RIP routing issues. These are listed in Table 9-2.

**Table 9-2    Common show Commands for Troubleshooting RIP**

| Command | Purpose |
| --- | --- |
| **show ip protocols** | Displays the parameters and current state of the active routing protocol process |
| **show running-config** | Displays the configuration information currently active on the router |
| **show interfaces** | Displays statistics for all interfaces configured on the router or access server |
| **show ip interface** | Displays the usability status of interfaces configured for IP |
| **show ip route** | Displays the current state of the routing table |

Figure 9-5 shows a sample RIP network, and Example 9-11 through Example 9-15 provide sample outputs from each command for the network.

**Figure 9-5    Sample RIP Network**

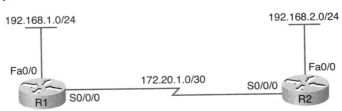

Example 9-11 shows the output from the **show ip protocols** command. This command should be used to determine the version of RIP that the interfaces are sending and listening for, along with the networks participating in the RIP process. This information will help detect whether the wrong version of RIP is configured on an interface or whether the wrong networks have been configured.

**Example 9-11    Sample show ip protocols Command Output**

```
R1# show ip protocols
Routing Protocol is "rip"
 Outgoing update filter list for all interfaces is not set
 Incoming update filter list for all interfaces is not set
 Sending updates every 30 seconds, next due in 22 seconds
 Invalid after 180 seconds, hold down 180, flushed after 240
 Redistributing: rip
 Default version control: send version 2, receive version 2
 Interface  Send Recv Triggered RIP Key-chain
 Serial0/0/0  2 2
 Automatic network summarization is in effect
 Maximum path: 4
 Routing for Networks:
 172.20.0.0
 192.168.1.0
 Passive Interface(s):
 FastEthernet0/0
 Routing Information Sources:
 Gateway  Distance Last Update
 172.20.1.2  120 00:00:15
 Distance: (default is 120)
```

In Example 9-12, the **show running-config** command shows the configuration information for each of the interfaces and the RIP configuration. This information will help determine whether RIP has been misconfigured or whether addressing information has been incorrectly configured.

**Example 9-12    Sample show running-config Command Output**

```
R1# show running-config
Building configuration...
< output omitted>
Current configuration : 1120 bytes
!
version 12.4
!
hostname R1
!
enable secret 5 $1$kbVM$rqp03lY42AhaHURL9BXTl0
enable password cisco
!
interface FastEthernet0/0
 description LAN gateway for 192.168.1.0
 ip address 192.168.1.1 255.255.255.0
 duplex auto
```

```
 speed auto
!
interface FastEthernet0/1
 no ip address
 shutdown
 duplex auto
 speed auto
!
interface Serial0/0/0
 description WAN link to R2
 ip address 172.20.1.1 255.255.255.252
 no fair-queue
!
interface Serial0/0/1
 no ip address
 shutdown
!
interface Vlan1
 no ip address
!
router rip
 version 2
 passive-interface FastEthernet0/0
 network 172.20.0.0
 network 192.168.1.0
!
banner motd # Unauthorized use prohibited#
!
line con 0
 password cisco
 login
line aux 0
line vty 0 4
 password cisco
 login
!
end
```

The **show interfaces** command displays the status of all interfaces, as shown in Example 9-13.

**Example 9-13    Sample show interfaces Command Output**

```
R1# show interfaces
<output omitted>
FastEthernet0/0 is up, line protocol is up
  Hardware is Gt96k FE, address is 001b.5325.256e (bia 001b.5325.256e)
  Description: LAN gateway for 192.168.1.0
  Internet address is 192.168.1.1/24
  MTU 1500 bytes, BW 100000 Kbit, DLY 100 usec,
  reliability 255/255, txload 1/255, rxload 1/255
  Encapsulation ARPA, loopback not set
```

```
    Keepalive set (10 sec)
   Auto-duplex, Auto Speed, 100BaseTX/FX

Serial0/0/0 is up, line protocol is up
 Hardware is GT96K Serial
 Description: WAN link to R2
 Internet address is 172.20.1.1/30
 MTU 1500 bytes, BW 1544 Kbit, DLY 20000 usec,
 reliability 255/255, txload 1/255, rxload 1/255
 Encapsulation HDLC, loopback not set
 Keepalive set (10 sec)
```

In Example 9-14, the **show ip interface** command provides information on the IP configuration of interfaces. This information helps to verify that the correct network addresses have been configured and that these interfaces are active.

**Example 9-14    Sample show ip interface Command Output**

```
R1# show ip interface
<output omitted>
FastEthernet0/0 is up, line protocol is up
 Internet address is 192.168.1.1/24
 Broadcast address is 255.255.255.255
 Address determined by setup command
 MTU is 1500 bytes
 Helper address is not set
 Directed broadcast forwarding is disabled
 Multicast reserved groups joined: 224.0.0.9

Serial0/0/0 is up, line protocol is up
 Internet address is 172.20.1.1/30
 Broadcast address is 255.255.255.255
 Address determined by setup command
 MTU is 1500 bytes
 Helper address is not set
 Directed broadcast forwarding is disabled
 Multicast res18erved groups joined: 224.0.0.9
```

In Example 9-15, the **show ip route** command provides information on routes to remote networks known to the router, along with information on how these routes were learned.

**Example 9-15    Sample show ip route Command Output**

```
R1# show ip route
Codes: C - connected, S - static, R - RIP, M - mobile, B - BGP
 D - EIGRP, EX - EIGRP external, O - OSPF, IA - OSPF inter area
 N1 - OSPF NSSA external type 1, N2 - OSPF NSSA external type 2
 E1 - OSPF external type 1, E2 - OSPF external type 2
 i - IS-IS, su - IS-IS summary, L1 - IS-IS level-1, L2 - IS-IS level-2
```

```
   ia - IS-IS inter area, * - candidate default, U - per-user static route
   o - ODR, P - periodic downloaded static route

Gateway of last resort is not set

 172.20.0.0/30 is subnetted, 1 subnets
C 172.20.1.0 is directly connected, Serial0/0/0
C 192.168.1.0/24 is directly connected, FastEthernet0/0
R 192.168.2.0/24 [120/1] via 172.20.1.2, 00:00:04, Serial0/0/0
```

The **debug ip rip** command enables you to observe RIP updates as they move in real time. A sample debug output is provided in Example 9-16 for the network shown earlier in Figure 9-5. Before using the **debug** command, narrow the problems to a likely subset of causes. Use **debug** commands to isolate problems, not to monitor normal network operation.

**Example 9-16    Debugging RIP**

```
R1# debug ip rip
RIP protocol debugging is on
R1#
*Sep 12 21:08:51.959: RIP: build update entries
*Sep 12 21:08:51.959: 192.168.1.0/24 via 0.0.0.0, metric 1, tag 0
*Sep 12 21:09:16.399: RIP: received v2 update from 172.20.1.2 on Serial0/0/0
*Sep 12 21:09:16.399: 192.168.2.0/24 via 0.0.0.0 in 1 hops
*Sep 12 21:09:18.575: RIP: sending v2 update to 224.0.0.9 via Serial0/0/0 (172.2
0.1.1)
```

RIP is a fairly basic and simple protocol to configure. However, some common issues can arise when configuring RIP routers. Compatibility issues exist between RIPv1 and RIPv2. If the RIP routes are not being advertised, check for the following problems:

- Layer 1 or Layer 2 connectivity issues

- Using VLSM subnetting but using RIPv1

- RIPv1 and RIPv2 routing configurations mismatched

- Network statements missing or incorrect

- Interface IP addressing incorrect

- Outgoing interface is down

- Advertised network interface is down

- Passive interface misconfigurations

In addition to the issues identified here, it is always important is remember that RIP has a hop count limit of 15 hops. This limitation alone can be a problem in a large enterprise network.

When testing with the **show ip route** command, it is a good idea to clear the routing tables using the **clear ip route** * command. When this command is issued, dynamic routes are removed from the routing table and are rebuilt as new routing updates are received.

Example 9-17 shows the output from some diagnostic commands for the network shown earlier in Figure 9-5. In this example, R1 is configured to work only with RIPv2, but R2 is sending only RIPv1 updates, which are discarded by the router.

**Example 9-17   Misconfigured RIP Routing**

```
R1# show ip protocol
Routing Protocol is "rip"
<output omitted>
Default version control: send version 2, receive version 2
 Interface  Send Recv Triggered RIP Key-chain
 Serial0/0/0  2 2

R2# show ip protocol
Routing Protocol is "rip"
<output omitted>

Default version control: send version 1, receive any version
 Interface  Send Recv Triggered RIP Key-chain
 Serial0/0/0  1 1 2

R1# debug ip rip
RIP protocol debugging is on
R1#
*Sep 12 22:09:08.147: RIP: sending v2 update to 224.0.0.9 via Serial0/0/0 (172.2
0.1.1)
*Sep 12 22:09:08.147: RIP: build update entries
*Sep 12 22:09:08.147: 192.168.1.0/24 via 0.0.0.0, metric 1, tag 0
*Sep 12 22:09:08.223: RIP: ignored v1 packet from 172.20.1.2 (illegal version)

R1# show ip route
Codes: <omitted>
Gateway of last resort is not set
 172.20.0.0/30 is subnetted, 1 subnets
C 172.20.1.0 is directly connected, Serial0/0/0
C 192.168.1.0/24 is directly connected, FastEthernet0/0
```

### Troubleshooting RIPv2 Routing Issues (9.3.1)

In this activity, you troubleshoot and resolve routing issues related to RIP. Use file d3-931.pka on the CD-ROM that accompanies this book to perform this activity using Packet Tracer.

### Lab 9-1: Troubleshooting RIPv2 Routing issues (9.3.1)

In this lab, you configure, observe, and troubleshoot the RIP routing process. Refer to the lab in Part II of this *Learning Guide*. You may perform this lab now or wait until the end of the chapter.

# EIGRP Issues

A number of IOS **show** commands and **debug** commands are the same for troubleshooting Enhanced Interior Gateway Routing Protocol (EIGRP) routing issues as they are for RIP. Table 9-3 lists some of the additional commands useful for troubleshooting EIGRP.

**Table 9-3    Common Commands for Troubleshooting EIGRP**

| Command | Purpose |
| --- | --- |
| **show ip eigrp neighbors** | Displays neighbor IP addresses and the interface on which they were learned |
| **show ip eigrp topology** | Displays the topology table of known networks with successor routes, status codes, feasible distance, and interface |
| **show ip eigrp traffic** | Displays EIGRP traffic statistics for the autonomous system configured, including hello packets sent/received, updates, and so on |
| **debug eigrp packets** | Displays real-time EIGRP packet exchanges between neighbors |
| **debug ip eigrp** | Displays real-time EIGRP events, such as link status changes and routing table updates |

Example 9-18 through Example 9-25 show the output of some of the commands that enable you to troubleshoot and verify EIGRP problems. These outputs relate to the network shown in Figure 9-6.

**Figure 9-6    Sample EIGRP Network**

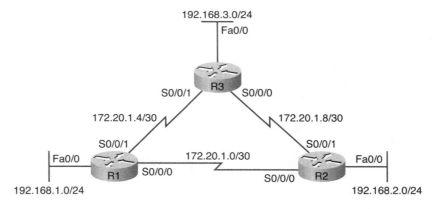

In Example 9-18, the **show running-config** command provides a convenient method to verify the basic configuration of the router, including the EIGRP configuration.

**Example 9-18    Sample Output from the show running-config Command**

```
R1# show running-config
Building configuration...
<output omitted>

Current configuration : 1210 bytes
!
version 12.4
```

```
!
hostname R1
!
enable secret 5 $1$Fox4$4J.8UbaGn1FjsPorIMWob1
enable password cisco
!
interface FastEthernet0/0
 description LAN gateway for 192.168.1.0 net
 ip address 192.168.1.1 255.255.255.0
 duplex auto
 speed auto
!
interface FastEthernet0/1
 no ip address
 shutdown
 duplex auto
 speed auto
!
interface Serial0/0/0
 description WAN link to R2
 ip address 172.20.1.1 255.255.255.252
 no fair-queue
!
interface Serial0/0/1
 description WAN link to R3
 ip address 172.20.1.5 255.255.255.252
!
interface Vlan1
 no ip address
!
router eigrp 101
 network 172.20.1.0 0.0.0.3
 network 172.20.1.4 0.0.0.3
 network 192.168.1.0
 no auto-summary
!
banner motd ^CUnauthorized use prohibited^C
!
line con 0
 password cisco
 login
line aux 0
 password cisco
 login
line vty 0 4
 password cisco
 login
end
```

To verify the addressing information on an interface and to confirm that the interface is activated, use the **show ip interface** command, as shown in Example 9-19.

**Example 9-19    Sample Output from the show ip interface Command**

```
R1# show ip interface
<output omitted>
FastEthernet0/0 is up, line protocol is up
 Internet address is 192.168.1.1/24
 Broadcast address is 255.255.255.255
 Address determined by non-volatile memory
 MTU is 1500 bytes
 Helper address is not set
 Directed broadcast forwarding is disabled
 Multicast reserved groups joined: 224.0.0.10

FastEthernet0/1 is administratively down, line protocol is down
 Internet protocol processing disabled

Serial0/0/0 is up, line protocol is up
 Internet address is 172.20.1.1/30
 Broadcast address is 255.255.255.255
 Address determined by non-volatile memory
 MTU is 1500 bytes
 Helper address is not set
 Directed broadcast forwarding is disabled
 Multicast reserved groups joined: 224.0.0.10

Serial0/0/1 is up, line protocol is up
 Internet address is 172.20.1.5/30
 Broadcast address is 255.255.255.255
 Address determined by non-volatile memory
 MTU is 1500 bytes
 Helper address is not set
 Directed broadcast forwarding is disabled
 Multicast reserved groups joined: 224.0.0.10
```

Use the **show ip route** command to verify that routes learned by EIGRP have populated the routing table, as shown in Example 9-20. If routes are not appearing in the routing table, you should suspect some sort of misconfiguration.

**Example 9-20    Sample Output from the show ip route Command**

```
R1# show ip route
Codes: C - connected, S - static, R - RIP, M - mobile, B – BGP
 D - EIGRP, EX - EIGRP external, O - OSPF, IA - OSPF inter area
 N1 - OSPF NSSA external type 1, N2 - OSPF NSSA external type 2
 E1 - OSPF external type 1, E2 - OSPF external type 2
 i - IS-IS, su - IS-IS summary, L1 - IS-IS level-1, L2 - IS-IS level-2
 ia - IS-IS inter area, * - candidate default, U - per-user static route
 o - ODR, P - periodic downloaded static route
```

```
Gateway of last resort is not set

 172.20.0.0/30 is subnetted, 3 subnets
D 172.20.1.8 [90/2681856] via 172.20.1.6, 00:11:56, Serial0/0/1
   [90/2681856] via 172.20.1.2, 00:11:56, Serial0/0/0
C 172.20.1.0 is directly connected, Serial0/0/0
C 172.20.1.4 is directly connected, Serial0/0/1
C 192.168.1.0/24 is directly connected, FastEthernet0/0
D 192.168.2.0/24 [90/2172416] via 172.20.1.2, 00:11:53, Serial0/0/0
D 192.168.3.0/24 [90/2172416] via 172.20.1.6, 00:11:53, Serial0/0/1
R1#
```

As shown in Example 9-21, the **show ip protocols** command enables you to determine the EIGRP process running on the router and the configuration settings of this process. Remember that the EIGRP AS must be the same on all routers.

**Example 9-21   Sample Output from the show ip protocols Command**

```
R1# show ip protocols
Routing Protocol is "eigrp 101"
 Outgoing update filter list for all interfaces is not set
 Incoming update filter list for all interfaces is not set
 Default networks flagged in outgoing updates
 Default networks accepted from incoming updates
 EIGRP metric weight K1=1, K2=0, K3=1, K4=0, K5=0
 EIGRP maximum hopcount 100
 EIGRP maximum metric variance 1
 Redistributing: eigrp 101
 EIGRP NSF-aware route hold timer is 240s
 Automatic network summarization is not in effect
 Maximum path: 4
 Routing for Networks:
 172.20.1.0/30
 172.20.1.4/30
 192.168.1.0
 Routing Information Sources:
 Gateway  Distance Last Update
 (this router)  90 00:19:18
 172.20.1.2  90 00:08:45
 172.20.1.6  90 00:10:15
 Distance: internal 90 external 170
```

To view EIGRP neighbors, use the **show ip eigrp neighbors** command. If a router does not see a neighbor, it will not receive routing updates from that device. This failure to see a neighbor is normally caused by a difference in configuration between the routers.

**Example 9-22     Sample Output from the show ip eigrp neighbors Command**

```
R1# show ip eigrp neighbors
IP-EIGRP neighbors for process 101
H Address     Interface Hold     Uptime     SRTT   RTO    Q    Seq
                        (sec)    (ms)       Cnt          Num
1 172.20.1.2  Se0/0/0   10       00:13:59   1      200    0    18
0 172.20.1.6  Se0/0/1   12       00:15:29   1      200    0    21
```

The **show ip eigrp topology** command displays how the device views the network.

**Example 9-23     Sample Output from the show ip eigrp topology Command**

```
R1# show ip eigrp topology
IP-EIGRP Topology Table for AS(101)/ID(192.168.1.1)

Codes: P - Passive, A - Active, U - Update, Q - Query, R - Reply,
 r - reply Status, s - sia Status

P 192.168.1.0/24, 1 successors, FD is 28160
 via Connected, FastEthernet0/0
P 192.168.2.0/24, 1 successors, FD is 2172416
 via 172.20.1.2 (2172416/28160), Serial0/0/0
P 192.168.3.0/24, 1 successors, FD is 2172416
 via 172.20.1.6 (2172416/28160), Serial0/0/1
P 172.20.1.8/30, 2 successors, FD is 2681856
 via 172.20.1.2 (2681856/2169856), Serial0/0/0
 via 172.20.1.6 (2681856/2169856), Serial0/0/1
P 172.20.1.0/30, 1 successors, FD is 2169856
 via Connected, Serial0/0/0
P 172.20.1.4/30, 1 successors, FD is 2169856
 via Connected, Serial0/0/1
```

To keep its routing tables current, a router must be able to communicate with neighboring devices. The **show ip eigrp traffic** command provides a summary of the traffic statistics for an autonomous system, as shown in Example 9-24.

**Example 9-24     Sample Output from the show ip eigrp traffic Command**

```
R1# show ip eigrp traffic
IP-EIGRP Traffic Statistics for AS 101
 Hellos sent/received: 1102/469
 Updates sent/received: 10/19
 Queries sent/received: 0/5
 Replies sent/received: 5/0
 Acks sent/received: 20/11
 Input queue high water mark 2, 0 drops
 SIA-Queries sent/received: 0/0
 SIA-Replies sent/received: 0/0
 Hello Process ID: 177
 PDM Process ID: 176
```

You can observe the movement of EIGRP packets on the network in real time using the **debug eigrp packet** command, as shown in Example 9-25. Remember that debugging puts an enormous load on the router and should be used with extreme caution to prevent degrading network performance.

**Example 9-25    Sample Output from the debug eigrp packet Command**

```
R1# debug eigrp packet
EIGRP Packets debugging is on
 (UPDATE, REQUEST, QUERY, REPLY, HELLO, IPXSAP, PROBE, ACK, STUB, SIAQUERY,
  SIAREPLY)
*Sep 13 20:19:01.431: EIGRP: Sending HELLO on FastEthernet0/0
*Sep 13 20:19:01.431: AS 101, Flags 0x0, Seq 0/0 idbQ 0/0 iidbQ un/rely 0/0
*Sep 13 20:19:03.115: EIGRP: Sending HELLO on Serial0/0/1
*Sep 13 20:19:03.115: AS 101, Flags 0x0, Seq 0/0 idbQ 0/0 iidbQ un/rely 0/0
*Sep 13 20:19:03.555: EIGRP: Sending HELLO on Serial0/0/0
*Sep 13 20:19:03.555: AS 101, Flags 0x0, Seq 0/0 idbQ 0/0 iidbQ un/rely 0/0
*Sep 13 20:19:05.583: EIGRP: Received HELLO on Serial0/0/1 nbr 172.20.1.6
*Sep 13 20:19:05.583: AS 101, Flags 0x0, Seq 0/0 idbQ 0/0 iidbQ un/rely 0/0
  peerQ un/rely 0/0
*Sep 13 20:19:05.627: EIGRP: Received HELLO on Serial0/0/0 nbr 172.20.1.2
*Sep 13 20:19:05.627: AS 101, Flags 0x0, Seq 0/0 idbQ 0/0 iidbQ un/rely 0/0
  peerQ un/rely 0/0
```

Example 9-26 shows the output of the **debug ip eigrp** command resulting from the disconnection of R2 from the network.

**Example 9-26    Sample debug Output When R2 (S0/0/0) Is Disconnected**

```
R1# debug ip eigrp IP-EIGRP Route Events debugging is on
R1#
*Sep 13 20:36:30.483: %LINK-3-UPDOWN: Interface Serial0/0/0, changed state to
  down
*Sep 13 20:36:30.487: %DUAL-5-NBRCHANGE: IP-EIGRP(0) 101: Neighbor 172.20.1.2
  (Serial0/0/0) is down: interface down
*Sep 13 20:36:30.491: IP-EIGRP(Default-IP-Routing-Table:101): route installed
  for 172.20.1.8 ()
*Sep 13 20:36:30.503: IP-EIGRP(Default-IP-Routing-Table:101): 172.20.1.0/30
  - not in IP routing table
*Sep 13 20:36:30.503: IP-EIGRP(Default-IP-Routing-Table:101): Int 172.20.1.0/30
metric 4294967295 - 0 4294967295
*Sep 13 20:36:30.503: IP-EIGRP(Default-IP-Routing-Table:101): 192.168.2.0/24
  - not in IP routing table
*Sep 13 20:36:30.503: IP-EIGRP(Default-IP-Routing-Table:101): Int 192.168.2.0/24
 metric 4294967295 - 1657856 4294967295
*Sep 13 20:36:30.515: IP-EIGRP(Default-IP-Routing-Table:101): Processing
  incoming QUERY packet
*Sep 13 20:36:30.515: IP-EIGRP(Default-IP-Routing-Table:101): Int 172.20.1.0/30
M 4294967295 - 0 4294967295 SM 4294967295 - 0 4294967295
*Sep 13 20:36:30.523: IP-EIGRP(Default-IP-Routing-Table:101): Processing
  incoming REPLY packet
*Sep 13 20:36:30.523: IP-EIGRP(Default-IP-Routing-Table:101): Int 192.168.2.0/24
```

```
  M 2684416 - 1657856 1026560 SM 2172416 - 1657856 514560
*Sep 13 20:36:30.523: IP-EIGRP(Default-IP-Routing-Table:101): route installed
  for 192.168.2.0 ()
*Sep 13 20:36:30.535: IP-EIGRP(Default-IP-Routing-Table:101): 172.20.1.0/30 -
  not in IP routing table
*Sep 13 20:36:30.535: IP-EIGRP(Default-IP-Routing-Table:101): Int 172.20.1.0/30
metric 4294967295 - 0 4294967295
*Sep 13 20:36:30.559: IP-EIGRP(Default-IP-Routing-Table:101): Processing
  incoming REPLY packet
*Sep 13 20:36:30.559: IP-EIGRP(Default-IP-Routing-Table:101): Int 172.20.1.0/30
  M 4294967295 - 0 4294967295 SM 4294967295 - 0 4294967295
*Sep 13 20:36:31.483: %LINEPROTO-5-UPDOWN: Line protocol on Interface Serial0/0/0,
  changed state to down
```

Certain issues commonly occur when configuring EIGRP. Possible reasons why EIGRP might not be working include the following:

- Layer 1 or Layer 2 connectivity issues exist.

- An interface has incorrect addressing or subnet mask.

- AS numbers on EIGRP routers are mismatched.

- The wrong network or incorrect wildcard mask is specified in the routing process.

- The link might be congested or down.

- The outgoing interface is down.

- The interface for an advertised network is down.

If auto summarization is enabled on routers with discontiguous subnets, routes might not be advertised correctly.

Example 9-27 shows the output of the **show ip route** and the **show ip eigrp neighbors** commands for the network shown earlier in Figure 9-6. Notice that in this example the routing information is not being exchanged as a result of the misconfiguration of autonomous system numbers.

**Example 9-27   Diagnosing Misconfigured Autonomous System Numbers**

```
R1# show ip route
<output omitted>
 172.20.0.0/30 is subnetted, 3 subnets
D 172.20.1.8 [90/2681856] via 172.20.1.6, 00:01:35, Serial0/0/1
C 172.20.1.0 is directly connected, Serial0/0/0
C 172.20.1.4 is directly connected, Serial0/0/1
C 192.168.1.0/24 is directly connected, FastEthernet0/0
D 192.168.3.0/24 [90/2172416] via 172.20.1.6, 01:37:16, Serial0/0/1

R1# show ip eigrp neighbors
IP-EIGRP neighbors for process 101
H Address   Interface Hold Uptime SRTT RTO Q Seq
       (sec) (ms)  Cnt Num
0 172.20.1.6  Se0/0/1  11 01:44:51 1 200 0 67
```

```
R2# show ip route
<output omitted>
 172.20.0.0/30 is subnetted, 2 subnets
C 172.20.1.8 is directly connected, Serial0/0/1
C 172.20.1.0 is directly connected, Serial0/0/0
C 192.168.2.0/24 is directly connected, FastEthernet0/0

R2# # show ip eigrp neighbors
IP-EIGRP neighbors for process 11
```

**Troubleshooting Common EIGRP Issues (9.3.2)**

In this activity, you troubleshoot and resolve routing issues related to EIGRP. Use file d3-932.pka on the CD-ROM that accompanies this book to perform this activity using Packet Tracer.

# OSPF Issues

The majority of problems encountered with Open Shortest Path First (OSPF) Protocol relate to the formation of adjacencies and the synchronization of the link-state databases. For OSPF to function properly, a number of conditions must be met, including the following:

- Neighbors must be part of the same OSPF area.
- Interfaces for neighbors must have compatible IP addresses and subnet masks.
- Routers in an area should have the same OSPF hello interval and dead interval.
- The routers must advertise the correct networks for interfaces to participate in the OSPF process.
- The appropriate wildcard masks must be used to advertise the correct IP address ranges.
- Authentication must be correctly configured on routers for communication to occur.

In addition to the standard **show** and **debug** commands, there are a number of commands specific to troubleshooting OSPF issues. Table 9-4 lists these.

**Table 9-4     Common Commands for Troubleshooting OSPF**

| Command | Purpose |
|---------|---------|
| **show ip ospf** | Displays information about OSPF routing process, areas, number of interfaces, authentication, and how often SPF algorithm executes. SPF executions indicate a change in the topology, such as a router being added or a network link going down. |
| **show ip ospf neighbor** | Displays neighbor ID, IP addresses of the neighbor interfaces, and interface on which they were learned. Useful for troubleshooting adjacency problems. |
| **show ip ospf interface** | Displays router ID, network type, link cost, state, interface priority, designated router ID, timer intervals configured, and neighbor adjacency information. |
| **debug ip ospf events** | Displays real-time OSPF exchanges between neighbors, such as adjacencies, flooding information, designated router selection, and SPF calculation. |
| **debug ip ospf packet** | Displays information about each OSPF packet received. |

Sample output as it relates to the network in Figure 9-7 is provided in Example 9-28 through Example 9-32.

**Figure 9-7     Sample OSPF Network**

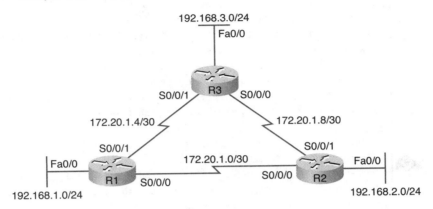

Example 9-28 shows the **show ip ospf** command output.

**Example 9-28     Sample Output from the show ip ospf Command**

```
R1# show ip ospf
<output omitted>
Routing Process "ospf 1" with ID 192.168.1.1
 Start time: 00:08:40.340, Time elapsed: 00:17:56.552
 Number of areas in this router is 1. 1 normal 0 stub 0 nssa
 Number of areas transit capable is 0
 External flood list length 0
 Area BACKBONE(0)
 Number of interfaces in this area is 3
 Area has no authentication
 SPF algorithm last executed 00:08:48.240 ago
 SPF algorithm executed 6 times
```

Example 9-29 shows the **show ip ospf neighbor** command output.

**Example 9-29     Sample Output from the show ip ospf neighbor Command**

```
R1# show ip ospf neighbor
Neighbor ID Pri State  Dead Time Address  Interface
192.168.3.1 0 FULL/ - 00:00:31 172.20.1.6 Serial0/0/1
192.168.2.1 0 FULL/ - 00:00:37 172.20.1.2 Serial0/0/0
```

Example 9-30 shows the **show ip ospf interface** command output.

**Example 9-30    Sample Output from the show ip ospf interface Command**

```
R1# show ip ospf interface
<output omitted>
FastEthernet0/0 is up, line protocol is up
  Internet Address 192.168.1.1/24, Area 0
  Process ID 1, Router ID 192.168.1.1, Network Type BROADCAST, Cost: 1
  Transmit Delay is 1 sec, State DR, Priority 1
  Designated Router (ID) 192.168.1.1, Interface address 192.168.1.1
  No backup designated router on this network
  Timer intervals configured, Hello 10, Dead 40, Wait 40, Retransmit 5
  Neighbor Count is 0, Adjacent neighbor count is 0

Serial0/0/1 is up, line protocol is up
  Internet Address 172.20.1.5/30, Area 0
  Process ID 1, Router ID 192.168.1.1, Network Type POINT_TO_POINT, Cost: 64
  Timer intervals configured, Hello 10, Dead 40, Wait 40, Retransmit 5
  Neighbor Count is 1, Adjacent neighbor count is 1
  Adjacent with neighbor 192.168.3.1

Serial0/0/0 is up, line protocol is up
  Internet Address 172.20.1.1/30, Area 0
  Process ID 1, Router ID 192.168.1.1, Network Type POINT_TO_POINT, Cost: 64
  Timer intervals configured, Hello 10, Dead 40, Wait 40, Retransmit 5
  Neighbor Count is 1, Adjacent neighbor count is 1
  Adjacent with neighbor 192.168.2.1
```

Example 9-31 shows output from the **debug ip ospf events** command.

**Example 9-31    Sample Output from the debug ip ospf events Command**

```
R1# debug ip ospf events
OSPF events debugging is on
R1#
*Sep 14 17:22:58.631: OSPF: Send hello to 224.0.0.5 area 0 on FastEthernet0/0
  from 192.168.1.1
*Sep 14 17:22:58.631: OSPF: Send hello to 224.0.0.5 area 0 on Serial0/0/0 from
  172.20.1.1
*Sep 14 17:23:00.351: OSPF: Send hello to 224.0.0.5 area 0 on Serial0/0/1 from
  172.20.1.5
*Sep 14 17:23:00.655: OSPF: Rcv hello from 192.168.3.1 area 0 from Serial0/0/1
  172.20.1.6
*Sep 14 17:23:06.479: OSPF: Rcv hello from 192.168.2.1 area 0 from Serial0/0/0
  172.20.1.2
```

Example 9-32 shows output from the **debug ip ospf packet** command.

**Example 9-32    Sample Output from the debug ip ospf packet Command**

```
R1# debug ip ospf packet
OSPF packet debugging is on
R1#
*Sep 14 17:26:36.475: OSPF: rcv. v:2 t:1 l:48 rid:192.168.2.1
 aid:0.0.0.0 chk:674B aut:0 auk: from Serial0/0/0
*Sep 14 17:26:40.651: OSPF: rcv. v:2 t:1 l:48 rid:192.168.3.1
 aid:0.0.0.0 chk:664B aut:0 auk: from Serial0/0/1
*Sep 14 17:26:46.475: OSPF: rcv. v:2 t:1 l:48 rid:192.168.2.1
 aid:0.0.0.0 chk:674B aut:0 auk: from Serial0/0/0
*Sep 14 17:26:50.651: OSPF: rcv. v:2 t:1 l:48 rid:192.168.3.1
 aid:0.0.0.0 chk:664B aut:0 auk: from Serial0/0/1
```

**Interactive Activity 9-3: OSPF Configuration (9.3.3)**

In this activity, you determine whether a given statement is true or false based on the OSPF configuration. Use file d3ia-933 on the CD-ROM that accompanies this book to perform this interactive activity.

**Lab 9-2: Troubleshooting OSPF Routing Issues (9.3.3)**

In this lab, you troubleshoot and correct OSPF routing issues. Refer to the lab in Part II of this *Learning Guide*. You may perform this lab now or wait until the end of the chapter.

## Route Redistribution Issues

Configuring a static default route on an edge router provides a gateway of last resort for packets destined for IP addresses outside the network. Although this configuration provides a solution for the edge router, it does not provide a way out of the internal network for other internal routers. One solution is to configure a default route on each internal router that points to the next hop or edge router. However, this method does not scale well with large networks. A better solution uses the routing protocol to propagate the default route on the edge router to other internal routers. All routing protocols, including RIP, EIGRP, and OSPF, provide mechanisms to accomplish this.

With each routing protocol, use the **ip route 0.0.0.0 0.0.0.0 S0/0/0** command to configure a default quad-zero static route on the edge router. Note that the interface designation might differ depending on the network. Next, configure the edge router to send or propagate its default route to the other routers. With RIP and OSPF, enter router configuration mode and use the command **default-information originate**. EIGRP redistributes default routes directly; the **redistribute static** command can also be used. Failure to properly implement default route redistribution prevents users who are connected to internal routers from accessing external networks.

Figure 9-8 shows the sample OSPF network used in Example 9-33, Example 9-34, and Example 9-35, which show the process for route redistribution using RIP, EIGRP, and OSPF, respectively.

**Figure 9-8    Sample OSPF Network**

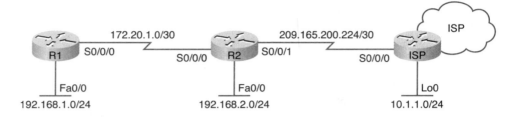

**Example 9-33    Route Redistribution Using RIP**

```
R2# show running-config
Building configuration...
<output omitted>
Current configuration : 1343 bytes
!
version 12.4
!
hostname R2
!
enable secret 5 $1$d8Kw$l5xQCPVfaWQKEmHAzXx5l0
enable password cisco
!
interface FastEthernet0/0
 description LAN gateway for 192.168.2.0 net
 ip address 192.168.2.1 255.255.255.0
 duplex auto
 speed auto

!
interface FastEthernet0/1
 no ip address
 shutdown
 duplex auto
 speed auto
!
interface Serial0/0/0
 description WAN link to R1
 ip address 172.20.1.2 255.255.255.252
 no fair-queue
 clock rate 2000000
!
interface Serial0/0/1
 description WAN link to ISP
 ip address 209.165.200.225 255.255.255.252
 no fair-queue
!
router rip
 version 2
 passive-interface FastEthernet0/0
 network 172.20.0.0
```

```
 network 192.168.2.0
 default-information originate
 no auto-summary
!
ip route 0.0.0.0 0.0.0.0 209.165.200.226
!
banner motd ^CUnauthorized use prohibited^C
!
line con 0
 password cisco
 login
line aux 0
 password cisco
 login
line vty 0 4
 password cisco
 login
end
```

```
R2# show ip route
Codes: C - connected, S - static, R - RIP, M - mobile, B - BGP
 D - EIGRP, EX - EIGRP external, O - OSPF, IA - OSPF inter area
 N1 - OSPF NSSA external type 1, N2 - OSPF NSSA external type 2
 E1 - OSPF external type 1, E2 - OSPF external type 2
 i - IS-IS, su - IS-IS summary, L1 - IS-IS level-1, L2 - IS-IS level-2
 ia - IS-IS inter area, * - candidate default, U - per-user static route
 o - ODR, P - periodic downloaded static route
Gateway of last resort is 209.165.200.226 to network 0.0.0.0

 172.20.0.0/30 is subnetted, 1 subnets
C 172.20.1.0 is directly connected, Serial0/0/0
 209.165.200.0/30 is subnetted, 1 subnets
C 209.165.200.224 is directly connected, Serial0/0/1
R 192.168.1.0/24 [120/1] via 172.20.1.1, 00:00:28, Serial0/0/0
C 192.168.2.0/24 is directly connected, FastEthernet0/0
S* 0.0.0.0/0 [1/0] via 209.165.200.226
```

**Example 9-34    Route Redistribution Using EIGRP**

```
R2# show running-config
Building configuration...
<output omitted>
Current configuration : 1299 bytes
!
version 12.4
!
hostname R2
!
enable secret 5 $1$0qLI$seW2r817/b5gl.SHfk07g0
enable password cisco
!
interface FastEthernet0/0
```

```
  description LAN gateway for 192.168.2.0 net
  ip address 192.168.2.1 255.255.255.0
  duplex auto
  speed auto
 !
 interface FastEthernet0/1
  no ip address
  shutdown
  duplex auto
  speed auto
 !
 interface Serial0/0/0
  description WAN link to R1
  ip address 172.20.1.2 255.255.255.252
  no fair-queue
  clock rate 2000000
 !
 interface Serial0/0/1
  description WAN link to ISP
  ip address 209.165.200.225 255.255.255.252
  no fair-queue
 !
 router eigrp 1
  redistribute static
  network 172.20.1.0 0.0.0.3
  network 192.168.2.0
  no auto-summary
 !
 ip route 0.0.0.0 0.0.0.0 209.165.200.226
 !
 banner motd ^CUnauthorized use prohibited^C
 !
 line con 0
  password cisco
  login
 line aux 0
  password cisco
  login
 line vty 0 4
  password cisco
  login
 end
```

```
R1# show ip route
Codes: C - connected, S - static, R - RIP, M - mobile, B - BGP
  D - EIGRP, EX - EIGRP external, O - OSPF, IA - OSPF inter area
  N1 - OSPF NSSA external type 1, N2 - OSPF NSSA external type 2
  E1 - OSPF external type 1, E2 - OSPF external type 2
  i - IS-IS, su - IS-IS summary, L1 - IS-IS level-1, L2 - IS-IS level-2
  ia - IS-IS inter area, * - candidate default, U - per-user static route
  o - ODR, P - periodic downloaded static route
Gateway of last resort is 209.165.200.226 to network 0.0.0.0

  172.20.0.0/30 is subnetted, 1 subnets
```

```
C 172.20.1.0 is directly connected, Serial0/0/0
 209.165.200.0/30 is subnetted, 1 subnets
C 209.165.200.224 is directly connected, Serial0/0/1
D 192.168.1.0/24 [90/2172416] via 172.20.1.1, 00:15:36, Serial0/0/0
C 192.168.2.0/24 is directly connected, FastEthernet0/0
S* 0.0.0.0/0 [1/0] via 209.165.200.226
```

**Example 9-35    Route Redistribution Using OSPF**

```
R2# show running-config
Building configuration...
<output omitted>
Current configuration : 1338 bytes
!
version 12.4
!
hostname R2
!
enable secret 5 $1$VsE7$k1kZvjFFqPFmuwkojLO/u0
enable password cisco
!
interface FastEthernet0/0
 description LAN gateway for 192.168.2.0 net
 ip address 192.168.2.1 255.255.255.0
 duplex auto
 speed auto
!
interface FastEthernet0/1
 no ip address
 shutdown
 duplex auto
 speed auto
!
interface Serial0/0/0
 description WAN link to R1
 ip address 172.20.1.2 255.255.255.252
 no fair-queue
 clock rate 2000000
!
interface Serial0/0/1
 description WAN link to ISP
 ip address 209.165.200.225 255.255.255.252
 no fair-queue
!
interface Vlan1
 no ip address
!
router ospf 1
 log-adjacency-changes
 network 172.20.1.0 0.0.0.3 area 0
 network 192.168.2.0 0.0.0.255 area 0
```

```
  default-information originate
!
ip route 0.0.0.0 0.0.0.0 209.165.200.226
!
banner motd ^CUnauthorized use prohibited^C
!
line con 0
 password cisco
 login
line aux 0
 password cisco
 login
line vty 0 4
 password cisco
 login
end
```

```
R2# # show ip route
Codes: C - connected, S - static, R - RIP, M - mobile, B - BGP
  D - EIGRP, EX - EIGRP external, O - OSPF, IA - OSPF inter area
  N1 - OSPF NSSA external type 1, N2 - OSPF NSSA external type 2
  E1 - OSPF external type 1, E2 - OSPF external type 2
  i - IS-IS, su - IS-IS summary, L1 - IS-IS level-1, L2 - IS-IS level-2
  ia - IS-IS inter area, * - candidate default, U - per-user static route
  o - ODR, P - periodic downloaded static route
Gateway of last resort is 209.165.200.226 to network 0.0.0.0

  172.20.0.0/30 is subnetted, 1 subnets
C 172.20.1.0 is directly connected, Serial0/0/0
  209.165.200.0/30 is subnetted, 1 subnets
C 209.165.200.224 is directly connected, Serial0/0/1
O 192.168.1.0/24 [110/65] via 172.20.1.1, 00:07:29, Serial0/0/0
C 192.168.2.0/24 is directly connected, FastEthernet0/0
S* 0.0.0.0/0 [1/0] via 209.165.200.226
```

### Lab 9-3: Troubleshooting EIGRP Default Route Redistribution (9.3.4)

In this lab, you troubleshoot and correct EIGRP route redistribution issues. Refer to the lab in Part II of this *Learning Guide*. You may perform this lab now or wait until the end of the chapter.

### Lab 9-4: Troubleshooting OSPF Default Route Redistribution (9.3.4)

In this lab, you troubleshoot and correct OSPF route redistribution issues. Refer to the lab in Part II of this *Learning Guide*. You may perform this lab now or wait until the end of the chapter.

# Troubleshooting WAN Configurations

When configuring WAN interfaces, a number of potential problem areas can surface. Some of these problems are unavoidable if the network administrator has control over only one end of the link and the ISP controls the other end. In this case, the network administrator uses the configuration information provided by the ISP to ensure connectivity.

## Troubleshooting WAN Connectivity

At the physical layer, the most common problems involve clocking, cable types, and loose or faulty connectors. Serial line connections link a DCE device to a DTE device. Two different types of cables exist for connecting devices: DTE and DCE. Usually the DCE device at the service provider provides the clocking signal.

Visually check each cable for loose connections or faulty connectors. If a cable cannot be correctly connected, swap the current cable with one known to work. To display the type of cable and the detection and status of DTE, DCE, and clocking, use the **show controllers** *serial_port* command. Figure 9-9 shows the sample network used in the Example 9-36 output.

**Figure 9-9    Sample OSPF Network**

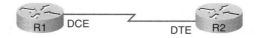

**Example 9-36    show controllers Command Output**

```
R1# show controllers s0/1
Interface Serial0/1
Hardware is PowerQUICC MPC860
DCE V.35, clock rate 56000
idb at 0x828A8C98, driver data structure at 0x828ABA9C
SCC Registers:
General [GSMR]=0x2:0x00000030, Protocol-specific [PSMR]=0x8
Events [SCCE]=0x0300, Mask [SCCM]=0x001F, Status [SCCS]=0x06
Transmit on Demand [TODR]=0x0, Data Sync [DSR]=0x7E7E
Interrupt Registers:
<output omitted>
buffer size 1524
PowerQUICC SCC specific errors:
0 input aborts on receiving flag sequence
0 throttles, 0 enables
0 overruns
0 transmitter underruns
0 transmitter CTS losts
0 aborted short frames
R2# show controllers s0/1
Interface Serial0/1
Hardware is PowerQUICC MPC860
DTE V.35 TX and RX clocks detected.
idb at 0x828A2B94, driver data structure at 0x828A5998
SCC Registers:
General [GSMR]=0x2:0x00000030, Protocol-specific [PSMR]=0x8
Events [SCCE]=0x0300, Mask [SCCM]=0x001F, Status [SCCS]=0x06
Transmit on Demand [TODR]=0x0, Data Sync [DSR]=0x7E7E
Interrupt Registers:
Config [CICR]=0x00367F80, Pending [CIPR]=0x00008044
Mask [CIMR]=0x48204002, In-srv [CISR]=0x00000000
Command register [CR]=0x6C0
Port A [PADIR]=0x013C, [PAPAR]=0xFFFF
  [PAODR]=0x0010, [PADAT]=0x4AFF
< Output omitted >
```

```
buffer size 1524
PowerQUICC SCC specific errors:
0 input aborts on receiving flag sequence
0 throttles, 0 enables
0 overruns
0 transmitter underruns
3 transmitter CTS losts
22 aborted short frames
```

For a serial link to come up, the encapsulation format on both ends of the link must match. The default serial line encapsulation used on Cisco routers is High-Level Data Link Control (HDLC). Because Cisco HDLC and open standard HDLC are not compatible, do not use the Cisco default encapsulation when connecting to a non-Cisco device. Some Layer 2 encapsulations have more than one form. For example, Cisco routers support both the proprietary Cisco Frame Relay format and the industry-standard IETF format. These formats are not compatible. The default format on Cisco devices is Cisco Frame Relay format. Example 9-37 shows the output of the **show interfaces** *serial_port* command and indicates the encapsulation format in use.

**Example 9-37    show interfaces Command Output**

```
R1# show interfaces s0/1
Serial0/1 is up, line protocol is up
 Hardware is PowerQUICC Serial
 Internet address is 10.20.30.1/24
 MTU 1500 bytes, BW 128 Kbit, DLY 20000 usec,
 reliability 255/255, txload 1/255, rxload 1/255
 Encapsulation PPP, loopback not set
 LCP Open
 Open: IPCP, CDPCP
 Last input 00:00:01, output 00:00:01, output hang never
 Last clearing of "show interface" counters 00:59:07
 Input queue: 0/75/0/0 (size/max/drops/flushes); Total output drops: 0
 Queueing strategy: weighted fair
 Output queue: 0/1000/64/0 (size/max total/threshold/drops)
 Conversations 0/1/32 (active/max active/max total)
 Reserved Conversations 0/0 (allocated/max allocated)
 Available Bandwidth 96 kilobits/sec
 5 minute input rate 0 bits/sec, 0 packets/sec
 5 minute output rate 0 bits/sec, 0 packets/sec
 2486 packets input, 62975 bytes, 0 no buffer
 Received 0 broadcasts, 0 runts, 0 giants, 0 throttles
 1 input errors, 0 CRC, 0 frame, 0 overrun, 0 ignored, 0 abort
 2395 packets output, 63160 bytes, 0 underruns
 0 output errors, 0 collisions, 443 interface resets
 0 output buffer failures, 0 output buffers swapped out
 872 carrier transitions
 DCD=up DSR=up DTR=up RTS=up CTS=up
R2# show interface s0/1
Serial0/1 is up, line protocol is up
 Hardware is PowerQUICC Serial
 Internet address is 10.20.30.2/24
```

```
MTU 1500 bytes, BW 128 Kbit, DLY 20000 usec,
reliability 255/255, txload 1/255, rxload 1/255
Encapsulation PPP, loopback not set
LCP Open
Open: IPCP, CDPCP
Last input 00:00:10, output 00:00:10, output hang never
Last clearing of "show interface" counters 1d16h
Input queue: 0/75/0/0 (size/max/drops/flushes); Total output drops: 0
Queueing strategy: weighted fair
Output queue: 0/1000/64/0 (size/max total/threshold/drops)
Conversations 0/2/32 (active/max active/max total)
Reserved Conversations 0/0 (allocated/max allocated)
Available Bandwidth 96 kilobits/sec
5 minute input rate 0 bits/sec, 0 packets/sec
5 minute output rate 0 bits/sec, 0 packets/sec
35931 packets input, 1866175 bytes, 0 no buffer
Received 0 broadcasts, 0 runts, 0 giants, 0 throttles
110 input errors, 0 CRC, 105 frame, 0 overrun, 2 ignored, 0 abort
30781 packets output, 1265772 bytes, 0 underruns
2 output errors, 0 collisions, 227 interface resets
0 output buffer failures, 0 output buffers swapped out
444 carrier transitions
DCD=up DSR=up DTR=up RTS=up CTS=up
```

Layer 3 configurations can also prevent data from moving across a serial link. Although it is not necessary to use an IP address on a serial link, if one is used, both ends of the link must be on the same network or subnet. A process known as *Serial Line Address Resolution Protocol (SLARP)* assigns an address to the endpoint of a serial link if the other end is already configured. SLARP assumes that each serial line is a separate IP subnet, and that one end of the line is host number 1 and the other end is host number 2. As long as one end of the serial link is configured, SLARP automatically configures an IP address for the other end. The IP address configured on an interface and the status of the port and line protocol are viewable with the **show ip interface brief** command.

Before Layer 3 information moves across the link, both the interface and the protocol must be up. If the interface is down, there is a problem with the interface itself. If the interface is up but the line protocol is down, check that the proper cable is connected and is firmly attached to the port. If this step still does not correct the problem, replace the cable. If the status of an interface is administratively down, the most probable cause is that the **no shutdown** command was not entered on the interface. Interfaces are shut down by default.

The PPP process involves both the Link Control Protocol (LCP) and Network Control Protocol (NCP) phases. LCP establishes the link and verifies that it is of sufficient quality to bring up the Layer 3 protocols. NCP allows Layer 3 traffic to move across the link. There is an optional authentication field between the LCP and NCP phases. Each phase has to complete successfully before the other begins.

When troubleshooting PPP connectivity, verify the following information:

- The LCP phase is complete.

- Authentication has passed, if configured.

- The NCP phase is complete.

The **show interfaces** command enables you to see the status of both the LCP and the NCP. To display PPP packets transmitted during the startup phase where PPP options are negotiated, use **debug ppp negotiation**. The **debug ppp packet** displays real-time PPP packet flow. Example 9-38 shows output of the **show interfaces** command for a simple PPP link.

**Example 9-38    PPP Authentication Diagnostic show interfaces Command**

```
R1# show interfaces s0/1
Serial0/1 is up, line protocol is up
 Hardware is PowerQUICC Serial
 Internet address is 10.20.30.1/24
 MTU 1500 bytes, BW 128 Kbit, DLY 20000 usec,
 reliability 255/255, txload 1/255, rxload 1/255
 Encapsulation PPP, loopback not set
 LCP Open
 Open: IPCP, CDPCP
 Last input 00:00:01, output 00:00:01, output hang never
 Last clearing of "show interface" counters 00:59:07
 Input queue: 0/75/0/0 (size/max/drops/flushes); Total output drops: 0
 Queueing strategy: weighted fair
 Output queue: 0/1000/64/0 (size/max total/threshold/drops)
 Conversations 0/1/32 (active/max active/max total)
 Reserved Conversations 0/0 (allocated/max allocated)
 Available Bandwidth 96 kilobits/sec
 5 minute input rate 0 bits/sec, 0 packets/sec
 5 minute output rate 0 bits/sec, 0 packets/sec
 2486 packets input, 62975 bytes, 0 no buffer
 Received 0 broadcasts, 0 runts, 0 giants, 0 throttles
 1 input errors, 0 CRC, 0 frame, 0 overrun, 0 ignored, 0 abort
 2395 packets output, 63160 bytes, 0 underruns
 0 output errors, 0 collisions, 443 interface resets
 0 output buffer failures, 0 output buffers swapped out
 872 carrier transitions
 DCD=up DSR=up DTR=up RTS=up CTS=up
```

Example 9-39 shows output from the **debug ppp negotiation** command.

**Example 9-39    Debugging the PPP Negotiation Process**

```
R1# debug ppp negotiation
PPP protocol negotiation debugging is on

1d05h: Se0/1 PPP: Outbound cdp packet dropped, line protocol not up
1d05h: Se0/1 PPP: Outbound cdp packet dropped, line protocol not up
1d05h: Se0/1 PPP: Outbound cdp packet dropped, line protocol not up
1d05h: %SYS-5-CONFIG_I: Configured from console by console
1d05h: Se0/1 LCP: I CONFREQ [Closed] id 31 len 15
1d05h: Se0/1 LCP: AuthProto CHAP (0x0305C22305)
1d05h: Se0/1 LCP: MagicNumber 0x1362F0CC (0x05061362F0CC)
1d05h: Se0/1 LCP: Lower layer not up, Fast Starting
1d05h: Se0/1 PPP: Treating connection as a dedicated line
```

```
1d05h: Se0/1 PPP: Phase is ESTABLISHING, Active Open
1d05h: Se0/1 LCP: O CONFREQ [Closed] id 251 len 15
1d05h: Se0/1 LCP: AuthProto CHAP (0x0305C22305)
1d05h: Se0/1 LCP: MagicNumber 0x136BD30A (0x0506136BD30A)
1d05h: Se0/1 LCP: O CONFACK [REQsent] id 31 len 15
1d05h: Se0/1 LCP: AuthProto CHAP (0x0305C22305)
1d05h: Se0/1 LCP: MagicNumber 0x1362F0CC (0x05061362F0CC)
1d05h: %LINK-3-UPDOWN: Interface Serial0/1, changed state to up
1d05h: Se0/1 LCP: I CONFACK [ACKsent] id 251 len 15
1d05h: Se0/1 LCP: AuthProto CHAP (0x0305C22305)
1d05h: Se0/1 LCP: MagicNumber 0x136BD30A (0x0506136BD30A)
1d05h: Se0/1 LCP: State is Open
1d05h: Se0/1 PPP: Phase is AUTHENTICATING, by both
1d05h: Se0/1 CHAP: O CHALLENGE id 146 len 28 from "R1"
1d05h: Se0/1 CHAP: I CHALLENGE id 148 len 27 from "R2"
1d05h: Se0/1 CHAP: Using hostname from configured hostname
1d05h: Se0/1 CHAP: Using password from AAA
1d05h: Se0/1 CHAP: O RESPONSE id 148 len 28 from "R1"
1d05h: Se0/1 CHAP: I RESPONSE id 146 len 27 from "R2"
1d05h: Se0/1 PPP: Phase is FORWARDING, Attempting Forward
1d05h: Se0/1 PPP: Phase is AUTHENTICATING, Unauthenticated User
1d05h: Se0/1 PPP: Phase is FORWARDING, Attempting Forward
1d05h: Se0/1 CHAP: I SUCCESS id 148 len 4
1d05h: Se0/1 PPP: Phase is AUTHENTICATING, Authenticated User
1d05h: Se0/1 CHAP: O SUCCESS id 146 len 4
1d05h: Se0/1 PPP: Phase is UP
1d05h: Se0/1 IPCP: O CONFREQ [Closed] id 5 len 10
1d05h: Se0/1 IPCP: Address 10.20.30.1 (0x03060A141E01)
1d05h: Se0/1 CDPCP: O CONFREQ [Closed] id 5 len 4
1d05h: Se0/1 IPCP: I CONFREQ [REQsent] id 5 len 10
1d05h: Se0/1 IPCP: Address 10.20.30.2 (0x03060A141E02)
1d05h: Se0/1 IPCP: O CONFACK [REQsent] id 5 len 10
1d05h: Se0/1 IPCP: Address 10.20.30.2 (0x03060A141E02)
1d05h: Se0/1 CDPCP: I CONFREQ [REQsent] id 5 len 4
1d05h: Se0/1 CDPCP: O CONFACK [REQsent] id 5 len 4
1d05h: Se0/1 IPCP: I CONFACK [ACKsent] id 5 len 10
1d05h: Se0/1 IPCP: Address 10.20.30.1 (0x03060A141E01)
1d05h: Se0/1 IPCP: State is Open
1d05h: Se0/1 CDPCP: I CONFACK [ACKsent] id 5 len 4
1d05h: Se0/1 CDPCP: State is Open
1d05h: Se0/1 IPCP: Install route to 10.20.30.2
1d05h: Se0/1 IPCP: Add link info for cef entry 10.20.30.2
1d05h: %LINEPROTO-5-UPDOWN: Line protocol on Interface Serial0/1, changed state to up
```

Example 9-40 shows sample output from the **debug ppp packet** command for a simple PPP link.

**Example 9-40    Debugging PPP Packets**

```
R1# debug ppp packet
PPP packet display debugging is on
R1#
1d05h: Se0/1 LCP: O ECHOREQ [Open] id 1 len 12 magic 0x136F1E39
```

```
1d05h: Se0/1 PPP: I pkt type 0xC021, datagramsize 16
1d05h: Se0/1 LCP: I ECHOREP [Open] id 1 len 12 magic 0x13663C01
1d05h: Se0/1 LCP: Received id 1, sent id 1, line up
1d05h: Se0/1 PPP: I pkt type 0xC021, datagramsize 16
1d05h: Se0/1 LCP: I ECHOREQ [Open] id 1 len 12 magic 0x13663C01
1d05h: Se0/1 LCP: O ECHOREP [Open] id 1 len 12 magic 0x136F1E39
1d05h: Se0/1 PPP: O pkt type 0x0021, datagramsize 116
1d05h: Se0/1 LCP: O ECHOREQ [Open] id 2 len 12 magic 0x136F1E39
1d05h: Se0/1 PPP: I pkt type 0xC021, datagramsize 16
1d05h: Se0/1 LCP: I ECHOREP [Open] id 2 len 12 magic 0x13663C01
1d05h: Se0/1 LCP: Received id 2, sent id 2, line up
1d05h: Se0/1 PPP: I pkt type 0xC021, datagramsize 16
1d05h: Se0/1 LCP: I ECHOREQ [Open] id 2 len 12 magic 0x13663C01
1d05h: Se0/1 LCP: O ECHOREP [Open] id 2 len 12 magic 0x136F1E39
1d05h: Se0/1 LCP: O ECHOREQ [Open] id 3 len 12 magic 0x136F1E39
1d05h: Se0/1 PPP: I pkt type 0xC021, datagramsize 16
1d05h: Se0/1 LCP: I ECHOREP [Open] id 3 len 12 magic 0x13663C01
1d05h: Se0/1 LCP: Received id 3, sent id 3, line up
1d05h: Se0/1 PPP: I pkt type 0xC021, datagramsize 16
1d05h: Se0/1 LCP: I ECHOREQ [Open] id 3 len 12 magic 0x13663C01
1d05h: Se0/1 LCP: O ECHOREP [Open] id 3 len 12 magic 0x136F1E39
```

**Troubleshooting WAN Connectivity (9.4.1)**

In this activity, you troubleshoot and correct issues relating to WAN connectivity. Use file d3-941.pka on the CD-ROM that accompanies this book to perform this activity using Packet Tracer.

# Troubleshooting WAN Authentication

PPP offers many advantages over the default HDLC serial line encapsulation. Among these features is the ability to use either Password Authentication Protocol (PAP) or Challenge Handshake Authentication Protocol (CHAP) to authenticate end devices. Authentication occurs as an optional phase after the establishment of the link with LCP but before the NCPs allow the movement of Layer 3 traffic.

If the LCP is not able to connect, negotiation of the optional parameters, including authentication, cannot occur. The absence of active NCPs indicates a failed authentication.

When troubleshooting PPP authentication, determine whether authentication is the problem by examining the status of the LCP and NCPs using the **show interface** command. If both the LCP and NCPs are open, authentication has been successful, and the problem is elsewhere. If the LCP is not open, the problem exists with the physical link between the source and destination. If the LCP is open and the NCPs are not, authentication is suspect.

Authentication can be either one way or two way. For enhanced security, use two-way, or mutual, authentication. Two-way authentication requires that each end device authenticate to the other. On both ends of the link, verify that a user account exists for the remote device and that the password is correct. If uncertain, remove the old user account statement and re-create it. The configuration on both ends of the link must specify the same type of authentication.

The most common problem with authentication is either forgetting to configure an account for the remote router or misconfiguring the username and password. By default, the username is the name of the remote router. Both the username and the password are case sensitive. If using PAP authentication on a current version of the IOS, you must activate it with the following command:

```
ppp pap sent-username username password password
```

Debugging the authentication process provides a quick method of determining what is wrong. To display packets involved in the authentication process as they are exchanged between end devices and thus debug the authentication process, use the **debug ppp authentication** command. Example 9-41 shows **debug** output for a proper configuration, no user account, and a wrong password.

**Example 9-41    Debugging the PPP Authentication Process**

```
CHAP configured correctly

03:03:35: %LINK-3-UPDOWN: Interface Serial0/1, changed state to up
03:03:35: Se0/1 PPP: Treating connection as a dedicated line
03:03:35: Se0/1 PPP: Authorization NOT required
03:03:35: Se0/1 CHAP: O CHALLENGE id 7 len 28 from "R1"
03:03:35: Se0/1 CHAP: I CHALLENGE id 9 len 27 from "R2"
03:03:35: Se0/1 CHAP: Using hostname from configured hostname
03:03:35: Se0/1 CHAP: Using password from AAA
03:03:35: Se0/1 CHAP: O RESPONSE id 9 len 28 from "R1"
03:03:35: Se0/1 CHAP: I RESPONSE id 7 len 27 from "R2"
03:03:35: Se0/1 PPP: Sent CHAP LOGIN Request to AAA
03:03:35: Se0/1 PPP: Received LOGIN Response from AAA = PASS
03:03:35: Se0/1 CHAP: O SUCCESS id 7 len 4
03:03:35: Se0/1 CHAP: I SUCCESS id 9 len 4
03:03:36: %LINEPROTO-5-UPDOWN: Line protocol on Interface Serial0/1, changed state to up


No User Account

03:21:41: Se0/1 PPP: Authorization NOT required
03:21:43: Se0/1 CHAP: O CHALLENGE id 65 len 28 from "R1"
03:21:43: Se0/1 CHAP: I CHALLENGE id 67 len 27 from "R2"
03:21:43: Se0/1 CHAP: Unable to authenticate for peer


Incorrect Password

03:17:47: Se0/1 PPP: Authorization NOT required
03:17:47: Se0/1 CHAP: O CHALLENGE id 15 len 28 from "R1"
03:17:47: Se0/1 CHAP: I CHALLENGE id 17 len 27 from "R2"
03:17:47: Se0/1 CHAP: Using hostname from configured hostname
03:17:47: Se0/1 CHAP: Using password from AAA
03:17:47: Se0/1 CHAP: O RESPONSE id 17 len 28 from "R1"
03:17:47: Se0/1 CHAP: I RESPONSE id 15 len 27 from "R2"
03:17:47: Se0/1 PPP: Sent CHAP LOGIN Request to AAA
03:17:47: Se0/1 PPP: Received LOGIN Response from AAA = FAIL
03:17:47: Se0/1 CHAP: O FAILURE id 15 len 26 msg is "Authentication failure"
```

**Troubleshooting PPP Authentication Using CHAP (9.4.2)**

In this activity, you troubleshoot and correct issues relating to PPP authentication. Use file d3-942.pka on the CD-ROM that accompanies this book to perform this activity using Packet Tracer.

**Lab 9-5: Troubleshooting WAN and PPP Connectivity (9.4.2)**

In this lab, you troubleshoot and correct WAN and PPP connectivity issues. Refer to the lab in Part II of this *Learning Guide*. You may perform this lab now or wait until the end of the chapter.

# Troubleshooting ACL Issues

ACLs add a level of complexity to troubleshooting network issues. Therefore, it is important to verify basic network connectivity before applying an ACL. When networks or hosts become unreachable and ACLs are in use, it is critical to determine whether the ACL is the problem.

## Determining If an ACL Is the Issue

To determine whether an ACL may be the cause of a network of host being inaccessible, ask the following questions:

- Is an ACL applied to the problem router or interface?
- Has it been applied recently?
- Did the issue exist before the ACL was applied?
- Is the ACL performing as expected?
- Is the problem with all hosts connected to the interface or only specific hosts?
- Is the problem with all protocols being forwarded or only specific protocols?
- Are the networks appearing in the routing table as expected?

One way to determine the answer to several of these questions is to enable logging. Logging shows the effect that ACLs are having on various packets. By default, the number of matches display with the **show access-list** command. To display details about packets permitted or denied, add the **log** keyword to the end of ACL statements, as shown in Example 9-42.

**Example 9-42    Sample ACL Logging**

```
R1(config)# access-list 123 deny tcp host 192.168.1.2 host 192.168.2.2 eq 23 log
R1(config)# access-list 123 permit ip 192.168.1.0 0.0.0.255 any log
R1(config)# access-list 123 deny ip any any log

R1(config)# int fa0/0
R1(config-if)# ip access-group 123 in

!Console Logging Messages

*Sep 17 20:02:53.067: %SEC-6-IPACCESSLOGP: list 123 denied tcp 192.168.1.2(1141)
 -> 192.168.2.2(23), 1 packet
R1#
*Sep 17 20:03:48.279: %SEC-6-IPACCESSLOGDP: list 123 permitted icmp 192.168.1.3
-> 192.168.2.2 (8/0), 1 packet
R1#
```

A number of commands help to determine whether ACLs are configured and applied correctly. To display all ACLs configured on the router, whether applied to an interface or not, use the **show access-lists** command. To clear the number of matches for each ACL statement, issue the **clear access-list counters** command.

The **debug ip packet** command displays the source and destination IP address for each packet received or sent by any interface on the router. This command includes packets that are denied by an ACL at the interface. Examples of traffic that create a debug message include RIP updates to or from a router interface and Telnet from an external source to an external destination blocked by an ACL on the interface. If the packets are just passing through and the ACL does not block a packet from this IP address, no debug message is generated.

**Interactive Activity 9-4: ACL Configuration (9.5.1)**

In this activity, you determine whether a given statement is true or false based on the ACL configuration. Use file d3ia-951 on the CD-ROM that accompanies this book to perform this interactive activity.

**Troubleshooting ACL Issues (9.5.1)**

In this activity, you verify and correct issues relating to ACLs. Use file d3-951.pka on the CD-ROM that accompanies this book to perform this activity using Packet Tracer.

## ACL Configuration and Placement Issues

Issues such as slow performance and unreachable network resources can result from an incorrectly configured ACL. In some cases, the ACL may permit or deny the intended traffic but can also have unintended effects on other traffic. If it appears that the ACL is the problem, there are several issues to check.

ACLs are processed from top to bottom. If the ACL statements are not in the most efficient order to permit the highest-volume traffic early in the ACL, simply rearranging the ACL can produce a substantial increase in performance. Check the logging results to determine whether a more efficient order is possible.

Another common problem is the implicit **deny** having unintended effects on other traffic. If so, use an explicit **deny ip any any log** command so that packets that do not match any of the previous ACL statements can be monitored.

In addition to determining whether the ACL is correctly configured, it is important to apply the ACL to the right router or interface, and in the appropriate direction. A correctly configured ACL incorrectly applied is one of the most common errors when creating ACLs. Standard ACLs filter only on the source IP address; therefore, place them as close to the destination as possible. Placing a standard ACL close to the source might unintentionally block traffic to networks that should be allowed. Placing the ACL close to the destination unfortunately allows traffic to flow across one or more network segments before being denied. This is a waste of valuable bandwidth.

Using an extended ACL resolves both of these issues. Packets destined for networks other than the one being blocked are unaffected. The routers along the potential path never see the denied packets, which helps to conserve bandwidth. Example 9-43 shows both an extended and a standard access list that can be used to prevent network 192.168.1.0 from entering the 192.168.4.0 network in Figure 9-10. The traffic is allowed into all other parts of the network.

**Figure 9-10   ACL Placement**

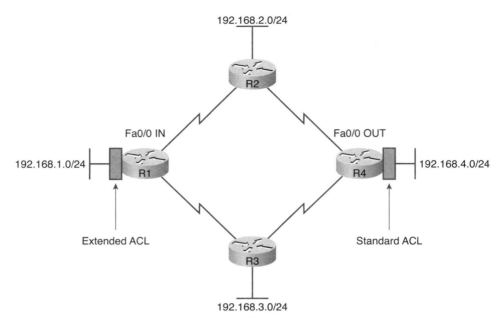

**Example 9-43   Standard and Extended ACLs**

```
Standard ACL
access-list 1 deny 192.168.1.0 0.0.0.255
access-list 1 permit any

Extended ACL
access-list 101 deny 192.168.1.0 0.0.0.255 192.168.4.0 0.0.0.255
access-list 101 permit ip any any
```

### Troubleshooting ACL Placement (9.5.2)

In this activity, you troubleshoot issues related to placement and direction of ACLs. Use file d3-952.pka on the CD-ROM that accompanies this book to perform this activity using Packet Tracer.

### Lab 9-6: Troubleshooting ACL Configuration and Placement (9.5.2)

In this lab, you troubleshoot and correct ACL configuration and placement issues. Refer to the lab in Part II of this *Learning Guide*. You may perform this lab now or wait until the end of the chapter.

### Interactive Activity 9-5: Critical Thinking (9.6.2)

In this activity, you answer questions based on a provided scenario. Use file d3ia-962 on the CD-ROM that accompanies this book to perform this interactive activity.

# Summary

Business enterprises continue to demand near 100 percent uptime from their networks. To achieve this level of performance, networks are designed in a manner that clearly defines the role and traffic types on each portion of the network. Adherence to the three-layer hierarchical design model accomplishes this goal.

In addition, the network administrator must incorporate proactive maintenance and network monitoring to anticipate and correct problems that could negatively impact network performance. Monitoring tools include simple utilities such as ping and tracert and extremely complicated tools that make use of SNMP.

The goal of troubleshooting is to quickly restore network functionality. When multiple problems exist, the one that has the largest failure domain is normally corrected first. This scenario might not always be the case if key network resources are affected. Backups of all key configuration files, devices, and links help ensure a quick recovery from problems. The business continuity plan outlines the method for ensuring that network resources remain accessible during natural and man-made disasters.

The most common problems with switches occur at the physical layer. Check all connections and cable and verify that link LEDs are illuminated before investigating configuration issues. VLANs are used to contain broadcast traffic and improve network performance. VTP provides a method for the management of large numbers of VLANs in an organization. When using VTP, ensure that all devices are using the same VTP version, a VTP domain is configured, and the same VTP password has been configured on all devices. If a new switch is being added into the network, ensure that its VTP revision number is not higher than the one currently being used on the network.

Many commands exist for troubleshooting routing issues. The most common RIP problems are mismatched network numbers or RIP versions. Misconfigured autonomous system numbers, incorrect wildcard masks, and auto-summarization issues with discontiguous subnets are the most common EIGRP routing issues. The majority of OSPF problems are related to the formation of adjacencies and the synchronization of link-state databases.

WAN configuration issues include mismatched encapsulations and incorrect authentication configurations. Both ends of a serial link must be using the same type of encapsulation. If using routers from different manufacturers, do not use HDLC because Cisco HDLC is not compatible with that from other vendors. WAN links should use authentication, and both the username and password are case sensitive. SLARP will automatically assign an IP address to the serial interface if the other end is already configured.

Before applying ACLs to a network, ensure that the network is functioning properly. The commands in an ACL are processed sequentially, and incorrect ordering can negatively impact network performance. Extended ACLs allow the ACL to be placed closer to the source because they contain both the source and destination addresses. Standard ACLs must be placed close to the destination because they are capable of filtering only on the source address. Always use ACL logging to understand which traffic is matching each line of the ACL.

# Activities and Labs

This summary outlines the activities and labs you can perform to help reinforce important concepts described in this chapter. You can find the activity and Packet Tracer files on the CD-ROM accompanying this book. The complete hands-on labs appear in Part II.

**Interactive activities on the CD-ROM:**

Interactive Activity 9-1: Determining the Size of a Failure Domain (9.1.3)

Interactive Activity 9-2: Determining the OSI Layer Associated with a Problem (9.1.4)

Interactive Activity 9-3: OSPF Configuration (9.3.3)

Interactive Activity 9-4: ACL Configuration (9.5.1)

Interactive Activity 9-5: Critical Thinking (9.6.2)

Packet Tracer
☐ Activity

**Packet Tracer activities on the CD-ROM:**

Creating a Baseline (9.1.2)

Troubleshooting Host Connectivity (9.2.1)

Troubleshooting Inter-VLAN Routing Issues (9.2.2)

Troubleshooting VTP Issues (9.2.3)

Troubleshooting RIPv2 Routing Issues (9.3.1)

Troubleshooting Common EIGRP Issues (9.3.2)

Troubleshooting WAN Connectivity (9.4.1)

Troubleshooting PPP Authentication Using CHAP (9.4.2)

Troubleshooting ACL Issues (9.5.1)

Troubleshooting ACL Placement (9.5.2)

**Hands-on labs in Part II of this book:**

Lab 9-1: Troubleshooting RIPv2 Routing Issues (9.3.1)

Lab 9-2: Troubleshooting OSPF Routing Issues (9.3.3)

Lab 9-3: Troubleshooting EIGRP Default Route Redistribution (9.3.4)

Lab 9-4: Troubleshooting OSPF Default Route Redistribution (9.3.4)

Lab 9-5: Troubleshooting WAN and PPP Connectivity (9.4.2)

Lab 9-6: Troubleshooting ACL Configuration and Placement (9.5.2)

# Check Your Understanding

Complete all the review questions listed here to check your understanding of the topics and concepts in this chapter. Appendix A, "Check Your Understanding and Challenge Questions Answer Key," lists the answers.

1. What could cause downtime in a network? (Choose all that apply.)

   A. Equipment failure

   B. Man-made disasters

   C. Natural disasters

   D. Security breaches

   E. Virus attacks

2.  What information is contained in an SLA? (Choose all that apply.)

    A.  Expected level of service

    B.  Cost of replacement network devices

    C.  Device configurations

    D.  Recovery period from any downtime

3.  What is a business continuity plan?

4.  What is the purpose of proactive maintenance? (Choose all that apply.)

    A.  Detection of problems before they occur

    B.  Rapid recovery from a network failure

    C.  Repair of failed network devices

    D.  Correction of problems before they occur

5.  What is the purpose of network monitoring?

6.  What is required for proper network monitoring? (Choose all that apply.)

    A.  Physical topology diagrams

    B.  Logical topology diagrams

    C.  Configuration files of all network devices

    D.  Baseline performance level

    E.  Device warrantee information

7.  What do SNMP-enabled devices use to monitor device parameters?

    A.  NMS

    B.  MIB

    C.  Agents

    D.  Polls

    E.  Traps

8.  What is the primary objective of troubleshooting?

    A.  Restore network functionality

    B.  Repair failed devices

    C.  Determine the cause of network failure

    D.  Replace failed network components

9.  What is a failure domain, and why is it important?

10. Which troubleshooting technique is often used by an experienced network technician?

    A.  Top down

    B.  Bottom up

    C.  Divide and conquer

    D.  Trial and error

    E.  Substitution

11. Which command will clear only the dynamic addresses in a switch's MAC address table?

    A. **clear mac-address-table**

    B. **clear mac-address-table dynamic**

    C. **clear mac-address-table** *MAC Address*

    D. **clear dynamic address** *MAC Address*

12. What factors could indicate that a switching loop might be present in a network? (Choose all that apply.)

    A. Loss of network connectivity

    B. High CPU utilization on routers

    C. High link utilization

    D. Increasing number of output drops on many interfaces

13. What is the native VLAN, and why should it be the same on all switches?

14. What is the default VTP configuration mode on Cisco switches?

    A. Client

    B. Server

    C. Transparent

    D. Disabled

15. When troubleshooting routing problems, when would you use **show** commands, and when would you use **debug** commands?

16. Which command will clear dynamic routes in the routing table?

    A. **clear ip route dynamic**

    B. **clear ip route ***

    C. **clear ip route**

    D. **clear routing-table dynamic**

17. Which command will show whether a WAN port is configured as DTE or DCE?

    A. **show clocking** *serial_port*

    B. **show controllers clocking** *serial_port*

    C. **show** *serial_port* **DCE**

    D. **show controllers** *serial_port*

18. What is the purpose of SLARP?

19. Where should ACLs be placed in a network?

# Challenge Questions and Activities

This question requires a deeper application of the concepts covered in this chapter. You can find the answers in Appendix A.

1. AnyCompany has just expanded into a new office building and has asked your team to configure the leased-line connection between the main office and the remote office. It has also been decided to deny WWW and Telnet traffic from the remote office but to permit all other traffic into the main office network.

   As the IT manager, you have asked one team to configure the remote office router with a WAN interface IP address of 192.168.1.11 and to have all outbound traffic use PAT and overload the IP address of the outbound interface. A second team has been asked to create an ACL on the main office router to permit only the desired traffic types. This team creates the following ACL and applies it inbound on the main office WAN interface:

   ```
   access-list 101 permit ip any any
   access-list 101 deny ip host 192.168.1.11 any eq www
   access-list 101 deny ip host 192.168.1.11 any eq telnet
   access-list 101 deny ip any any
   ```

   When you test the configuration from the remote site, you find that you are able to use Telnet to connect to an internal server at the main office site. You quickly "sniff" the traffic on the link and notice that all outbound traffic is using the IP address 192.168.1.2. When you confront each team, they claim that their configurations are correct. Which team has made a misconfiguration? What is the misconfiguration? How would you confirm and correct it?

# CHAPTER 10

# Putting It All Together

Businesses increasingly rely on their enterprise network infrastructure to provide mission-critical services. Outages in the enterprise network prevent the business from performing its normal activities, which can cause lost revenue and lost customers. To prevent disruption, enterprise networks must be properly designed and configured to maximize bandwidth utilization and improve overall network performance.

Nearly all modern networks, regardless of size, employ Ethernet switches to connect users and at least one router to connect the local network to an ISP or another remote location. As the number of users grows, an increased number of more sophisticated switches is normally required to accommodate increased wireless and wired connectivity requirements.

Enterprise networks require a large number of switches at the access layer to connect user workstations, servers, network printers, wireless access points, web cameras, IP phones, and other Ethernet/IP-based devices. Many of these networks also have multiple locations that are interconnected at the distribution layer and core layers using routers. Enterprise networks can have thousands of switch connections and hundreds of routers. Understanding how to deploy switching and routing technologies and how to configure these network devices is crucial to working in the enterprise network environment.

Throughout this course, you have learned about the enterprise network infrastructure, switching technologies, hierarchical IP addressing, routing protocols, and WAN technologies. In addition, you learned about traffic filtering to help improve network security and performance, using access control lists. This course has provided the skills and information necessary to understand the role of a network support technician in installing, configuring, and maintaining switches and routers in an enterprise environment.

# Summary Activity

By successfully completing this course, you have gained the knowledge and skills necessary to prepare you for a career as an entry-level network support technician in an enterprise network. The Packet Tracer Activities and the hands-on labs that culminate this course are designed to give you an opportunity to demonstrate your new abilities.

In the summary activities, use the knowledge and skills presented in this course to perform the following tasks:

- Analyze a network design and create a hierarchical addressing scheme using VLSM.
- Configure switches with multiple VLANs, VTP, and port security.
- Configure routers and switches to provide inter-VLAN routing.
- Configure multiple routers using OSPF, PAT, a default route, and route summarization.
- Configure WAN links using PPP and authentication.
- Configure ACLs to control network access and to secure routers.
- Verify network connectivity, device configuration, and functionality.

# Activities and Labs

This chapter does not include Interactive Activities or Packet Tracer Activities. However, Packet Tracer is used to complete the final summative project.

 **Labs in Part II of this book:**

Lab 10-1: Capstone Project—Putting It All Together (10.0.1)

# Check Your Understanding and Challenge Questions Answer Key

## Chapter 1

### Check Your Understanding

1.  D. Extranet

    D. LAN and WAN are component technologies used to create both intranets and extranets, which then form the enterprise network. An intranet allows only company employees to connect to secure databases. Extranets extend this service to trusted individuals such as customers.

2.  B. Distribution

    B. Filtering of traffic occurs at the distribution layer. The access layer provides a connection point for end users and devices, and the core layer provides a high-speed backbone.

3.  B. Enterprise Edge

    B. Intrusion prevention and intrusion detection must be located on an edge device as traffic passes from the service provider network to the company network.

4.  B. Building Distribution module

    B. The Building Access module contains both Layer 2 and Layer 3 switches to provide the correct port density for the environment. This module is responsible for the implementation of VLANs and trunk links to the Building Distribution module. The Building Distribution module uses Layer 3 devices to aggregate building access. Routing, access control, and quality of service (QoS) are all implemented by this module. Redundancy of devices and links are important design considerations. The Campus Core module provides high-speed connectivity between Building Distribution modules, data center server farms, and the Enterprise Edge.

5.  C. Chat

    C. Chat allows real-time communication between individuals. FTP is used to move files between computers, Telnet allows a terminal session to be opened on a remote machine, and e-mail does not function in real time.

6.  A. Departmental file sharing

    B. Printing

    C. Internal backup

    D. Intracampus voice

    All answers provided are correct. Some common traffic types that should remain local to users on the LAN include file sharing, printing, internal backup, mirroring, and intracampus voice. If these types of traffic are found on the WAN link, they consume bandwidth and pose a security concern.

7.  When using a VPN, a virtual tunnel is created by linking the source and destination addresses. All data flow between the source and destination is encrypted and encapsulated using a secure protocol. This secure packet is transmitted across the network. When it arrives at the receiving end, it is de-encapsulated and unencrypted.

8.  Voice and video applications require an uninterrupted stream of data to ensure high-quality conversations and images. The acknowledgment process in TCP introduces delays, which break these streams and degrade the quality of the application. Therefore, voice and video applications use UDP rather than TCP. Because UDP does not incorporate mechanisms for retransmitting lost packets, it minimizes delays.

9.  When traffic is detected in an area of the network where it is unexpected, that traffic can be filtered and the source of the traffic investigated.

10. A failure domain is the area of a network impacted when a key device or service experiences problems. The function of the device that initially fails determines the impact of a failure domain. By limiting the size of failure domains, any device or component failure will have minimal impact on the overall network. Smaller failure domains reduce the impact of a failure on company productivity. They also simplify the troubleshooting process, thereby shortening the downtime for all users.

## Challenge Questions and Activities

1.  If the company printers were located on a segment other than where the print requests are being generated, the traffic would have to move across the distribution layer, thus slowing network performance. An analysis of where the requests are coming from must be completed, and then the printers should be relocated onto these segments to keep the traffic localized.

2.  To allow the accounting department staff to work from home, the company must provide remote access to a secure database. The best solution is to implement a secure VPN and force the remote workers to VPN into the corporate network and authenticate before being granted access to the databases. Access by any other means could allow company financial data to be intercepted during transmission. This setup allows the employees to have access to all company network resources that they normally have access to when working in the office.

## Chapter 2

## Check Your Understanding

1.

| Term | Correct Description |
|---|---|
| POP | Physical link to outside networks at the enterprise edge |
| VPN | Allows remote workers to access the internal network securely |
| DoS | Maliciously prevents access to network resources by legitimate users |
| CPE | Equipment located at the customer facility |
| No term matches | A telecommunications room to which IDFs connect |
| No term matches | A method of providing electrical power to Ethernet end devices |
| DMZ | An area of the network accessible to external users and protected by firewalls |

2.  B.  The MAC addresses of the hosts connected to the switch ports

    B. The **show mac-address-table** command displays switch ports and the MAC addresses learned on each port. Frames with host destination MAC addresses will be forwarded out the port where the host is connected. Switch port MAC addresses are not normally shown, and the MAC address table is not related to IP addresses.

3.  A.  The amount of NVRAM, DRAM, and flash memory installed on the router

A. The **show version** command displays IOS version, ROM version, switch uptime, system image filename, boot method, number and type of interfaces installed, amount of RAM, NVRAM, and flash, and the config register. The output does show number and types of interfaces but not bandwidth, encapsulation, or I/O statistics. To determine the differences between the backup configuration and the current running configuration, the **show run** and **show start** commands would be used. The **show ip protocols** command would display the version of the routing protocols running on the router.

4.  B.  Create a logical topology map of the network and annotate it with the network application data.

B. A logical topology map of the network would be the best place to start; then add the desired network application data. The physical topology map is focused on actual device locations and cabling. Neither the blueprint nor the photograph is appropriate.

5.  B.  It is likely that someone attempted a DoS attack.

B. When hundreds of attempts come from a single IP address, it is likely to be a DoS attack. Although it is possible that the link to the website does not have enough capacity, this is not normal web-surfing activity. If the web server were turned off, there would be no logging activity in the server logs to trace.

6.  A.  Fiber-optic

A. Cabling between the buildings should always be fiber-optic, regardless of distance, to account for the electrical difference between buildings. Inter-building cabling can also be exposed to weather and lightning strikes, which fiber-optic can better withstand without damaging equipment connected to it. Coaxial cable, UTP, and STP are all copper cabling and are susceptible to EMI and RFI, whereas fiber-optic is not.

7.  A.  Wireless access points

C.  Web cameras

D.  IP phones

A, C, D. Power over Ethernet (PoE) is appropriate for end devices such as wireless APs, web cameras, and IP phones. Monitors and network switches are not end devices, and laptops are typically battery powered.

8.  A.  Defines broadcast domains (R)

B.  Connects IP phones and access points to the network (S)

C.  Enhances security with ACLs (R)

D.  Interconnects networks (R)

E.  Appears more commonly at the access layer (S)

F.  Connects hosts to the network (S)

G.  First FastEthernet interface designation is Fa0/0 (R)

H.  First FastEthernet interface designation is Fa0/1 (S)

Routers define broadcast domains and are frequently used to enhance security with ACLs. They interconnect networks, and the first FastEthernet interface designation is typically Fa0/0. Switches appear much more commonly at the access layer and are used to connect hosts such as PCs, servers, printers, IP phones, and access points to the network. So, you should have answered "R" for A, C, D, and G and "S" for B, E, F, and H.

**9.** B.   SSH

E.   Telnet

B, E. Telnet and SSH (which supports a secure form of Telnet) both require a functioning network connection and the IP protocol correctly configured. Although FTP can be used to access a Cisco router in-band, it is not normally used for device management. ARP resolves IP to MAC addresses, and SMTP is used for sending e-mail.

**10.** E. **show cdp neighbors detail**

E. Only the **show cdp neighbors detail** command can identify connected Cisco network devices. The **show tech-support** command is a valid command but is not suitable for this situation.

**11.** B.   **show ip route**

D.   **show ip protocols**

B, D. The **show ip route** and **show ip protocols** commands give the most information regarding the configuration of the RIP routing protocol and indicate which routes have been learned through RIP. The output from the **show version**, **show sessions**, and **show cdp neighbors** commands does not have routing-related information.

**12.** A. **show protocols**

A. The **show protocols** command lists all interfaces configured for IP along with their status (up/up and so on), their IP address, and the mask in slash (CIDR) format. The **show ip route command** provides some information on interfaces, but the focus is on routes. The **show running-config** command gives the IP address and subnet mask (in dot format) but no status information. The **show ip protocols** command gives information regarding the configuration of the routing protocol but not interface IPs and status. The output from the **show ip interfaces brief** command shows interface status in a brief format and IP address but does not show the subnet mask (/xx) of an interface.

**13.** A.   DMZ router (5)

B.   T1 circuit line (2)

C.   Internal switch (8)

D.   CSU/DSU (4)

E.   DMZ switch (6)

F.   Punchdown block (3)

G.   Internal router (7)

H.   Service provider (1)

I.   End-user PC (9)

**14.** A.   DoS

A. DoS, or denial of service, is a type of network threat or attack. Firewalls, access control lists (ACL), intrusion detection systems (IDS), intrusion prevention systems (IPS), demilitarized zones (DMZ), and Virtual Private Networks (VPN) are all forms of security.

## Challenge Questions and Activities

1. A number of potential problems can cause this. The R2 S0/0/0 interface could be down (perhaps the **no shutdown** command was not issued). The R2 S0/0/0 interface might not be configured for PPP encapsulation to match that of R1 S0/0/0 (the default is Cisco HDLC). The R2 S0/0/0 interface might have an incorrect IP address or subnet mask, which could prevent pings from working. The DCE cable might be connected to the R2 S0/0/0 interface, and the clock rate command should have been entered there. The clock rate command entered on R1 would be accepted without error but would have no effect. The network cable might not be connected to the interface properly. The R2 interface that R1 connects to might not be S0/0/0 (could be S0/0/1).

   In addition to checking physical cabling connections and DCE/DTE, the following **show** commands could help to isolate the problem:

   - **show protocols** (R2 to verify interface status and mask)
   - **show running-config** (R1 and R2 to verify interface configuration commands including encapsulation)
   - **show ip interfaces brief** (R2 to verify interface status)
   - **show interfaces** (R2 to verify interface IP address, mask, and encapsulation)
   - **show cdp neighbors detail** (R1 to verify device and interface connected to. Using the **detail** option also shows the IP address and mask assigned to the remote interface.)

2. Answers can vary.

# Chapter 3

## Check Your Understanding

1. A.  It floods the frame out all ports except the one on which it was received.

   A. If the destination address is not known, the frame will be flooded out all ports.

2. A.  Store-and-forward

   A. Most modern switches are fast enough to handle store-and-forward switching technology without introducing a significant level of latency into the network.

3. B.  Asymmetric

   B. Asymmetric switching would be the most appropriate because multiple hosts would require a higher bandwidth to simultaneously connect to the server farm. Cut-through and store-and-forward are switch technologies, and symmetric switching would be appropriate if the source and destination bandwidth requirements were the same.

**4.** A. Store-and-forward

B. Fragment-free

A and B. Store-and-forward switching reads the entire frame and checks the CRC before switching the frame. Fragment-free switching reads the first 64 bytes of a frame, ensuring that it is not a runt, before switching. Adaptive switching detects the number of error frames and alters its switching technology after a certain number of defective frames have been detected. This allows a certain number of runts to be switched before the switch begins to use fragment-free technology. Fast-forward switching begins to forward the frame as soon as the destination MAC address is read.

**5.** A. Disable Telnet and HTTP access

B. Disable unused ports

C. Enable port security

D. Restrict access to the physical switch

A, B, C, and D. All the listed items are security methods that should be implemented in a switched network.

**6.** A. MAC database instability

B. Broadcast storms

C. Multiple frame transmission

D. Increased availability

A, B, C, and D. All the listed items can be the result of a redundant link in a switched network. All negatively impact the network except increased availability.

**7.** B. STP

B. Spanning Tree Protocol (STP) is an open standard protocol used in a switched environment to create a loop-free logical topology. Switches exchange information using BPDUs. A VLAN is a collection of hosts on the same LAN, even though they are physically separated. VTP (VLAN Trunking Protocol) is used to manage VLAN configuration on an enterprise network.

**8.** D. RSTP

D. The only open standard listed is Rapid Spanning Tree Protocol (RSTP). The other three technologies are all Cisco proprietary.

**9.** A. Blocking

A. The port is immediately put into the blocking state to prevent the formation of a switch loop. When STP determines that a switching loop will not be created by activating the port, the switch transitions the port through listening, learning, and then forwarding.

**10.** A. Blocking

B. Listening

C. Learning

D. Forwarding

A, B, C, and D. The switch port continues to listen to BPDUs in all STP modes listed.

**11.** C.   VLAN

C. A VLAN is used to group separated hosts into communities of interest. Switches only group devices that can connect to that physical switch, meaning that they are not physically dispersed.

**12.** C.   Native VLAN

C. The native VLAN is used for untagged traffic.

**13.** The three types of VTP messages are summary advertisements, subset advertisements, and advertisement requests.

Catalyst switches issue summary advertisements every 5 minutes or whenever a change to the VLAN database occurs. Summary advertisements contain the current VTP domain name and the configuration revision number. If VLANs are added, deleted, or changed, the server increments the configuration revision number and issues a summary advertisement.

When a switch receives a summary advertisement packet, it compares the VTP domain name to its own VTP domain name. If the domain name is the same, the switch compares the configuration revision number to its own number. If it is lower or equal, the switch ignores the packet. If the revision number is higher, an advertisement request is sent.

A subset advertisement follows the summary advertisement. A subset advertisement contains a list of VLAN information. The subset advertisement contains the new VLAN information based on the summary advertisement. If several VLANs exist, they require more than one subset advertisement.

VTP clients use an advertisement request to ask for VLAN information. Advertisement requests are required if the switch has been reset or if the VTP domain name has been changed. The switch receives a VTP summary advertisement with a higher configuration revision number than its own.

**14.** Only one root bridge exists on each network, and it is elected based on the bridge ID (BID). The bridge priority value plus the MAC address creates the BID. Bridge priority has a default value of 32,768. If a switch has a MAC address of AA-11-BB-22-CC-33, the BID for that switch would be 32768: AA-11-BB-22-CC-33. The root bridge is based on the lowest BID value. Because switches typically use the same default priority value, the switch with the lowest MAC address becomes the root bridge.

**15.** The three VTP modes are server, client, and transparent.

By default, all Cisco switches are in VTP server mode. In this mode, the administrator can create, modify, and delete VLANs and VLAN configuration parameters for the entire domain. A VTP server saves VLAN configuration information in the switch NVRAM and sends out VTP messages on all trunk ports. It is good practice to have at least two switches configured as servers on a network to provide backup and redundancy.

A switch in VTP client mode does not create, modify, or delete VLAN information for the VTP domain. It accepts VTP messages from the VTP server and modifies its own database with this information. A VTP client sends VTP messages out all trunk ports.

A switch in VTP transparent mode ignores information in the VTP messages. It does not modify its database with information received from the VTP server but does forward VTP advertisements. A switch in VTP transparent mode will not send out an update that indicates a change in its own VLAN database. Therefore, all VLANs created on a switch in this mode remain local to the switch.

## Challenge Questions and Activities

1. Because the servers are now being concentrated into one area, it is important that the server farm be connected to the rest of the company network with a high-speed link. If the hosts in the company network normally connect at 100 Mbps, the link to the server farm must be capable of handling many simultaneous conversations. This would require more bandwidth than the individual hosts. In this situation, an asymmetric switch with one or two Gigabit connections would keep the costs down and still supply the high-speed connection to the server farm.

   In addition, the only way to prevent individual clients from having access to the server farm based on their IP address is to filter out their traffic with a router. Servers in the server farm should be placed in a specific VLAN and the regular network hosts in different VLANs. Traffic from a host VLAN would have to pass through the router to gain access to the server VLAN, and it is at this point that the traffic could be filtered.

2. The fact that a new switch was connected to the network at the same time that the VLAN configuration was altered indicates that the new switch was configured as a VTP server with a higher revision number than the one in the network. When the switch was connected to the network, it sent out a VTP message and updated the client machines with erroneous information. To prevent this from happening in the future, the junior administrator should be taught the correct way to add a switch to the network, ensuring that the VTP mode is set to client and the revision number has been reset. It is also a good idea to include VTP domain authentication to prevent rogue switches from being able to update the network switches.

# Chapter 4

## Check Your Understanding

1. B. 209.48.200.0/22

   B. The first two octets (16 bits) are the same for all four addresses. Looking at the third octet, the first 6 bits are the same, so the summary mask is 16 + 6 = 22. The summary address starts with the first network address and applies the summary mask: 209.48.200.0/22.

   Third octet:

   200 = 110010 | 00

   201 = 110010 | 01

   202 = 110010 | 10

   203 = 110010 | 11

2. C.   172.32.0.0

   C. The default mask for the Class B network 172.32.0.0 is 255.255.0.0, so the network portion of address 172.32.65.13 is the first two octets, or 172.32.

3. E.  /30

   E. A Class C network has 8 bits (/24) available to define IP addresses for hosts (256 addresses possible). Borrowing 3 bits from the 8 leaves 5 bits, creating eight subnets with 32 addresses each (30 usable) and a /27 mask. Subnetting one of the 32 address networks into eight smaller ones means borrowing another 3 bits, resulting in a /30 mask and eight networks of four host addresses (two usable) each.

4. C.  172.16.243.64

   C. A 26-bit mask leaves 6 bits, which can be used to define 62 hosts ($2^6 = 64 - 2 = 62$). This creates four subnets with 64 possible addresses on each subnet. The subnet numbers must increment by multiples of 64. The four valid subnet numbers (fourth octet) available with a /26 mask are as follows:

   X.Y.Z.0

   X.Y.Z.64

   X.Y.Z.128

   X.Y.Z.192

5. B.  IP address: 192.168.100.20; subnet mask: 255.255.255.240; default gateway: 192.168.100.17

   B. The Router 1 interface and the switch both have a mask of /28, or 255.255.255.240 dotted decimal. For host A to send packets to other parts of the network, it must have the same mask and be configured with the IP address of the Router 1 Ethernet interface as its default gateway (192.168.100.17). The only choice with the correct subnet mask and default gateway is B.

6. D.  PAT uses unique source port numbers to distinguish between translations.

   D. Answer A is incorrect because PAT uses overload at the end of the **ip nat** statement. Static NAT maps a single private address to a single public address, and dynamic NAT allows a host to receive various addresses from a pool of addresses. Only choice D is a true statement regarding PAT.

7. 
| Characteristic | NAT Technique |
|---|---|
| Provides one-to-one fixed mappings of local and global addresses | Static NAT |
| Assigns the translated addresses of IP hosts from a pool of public addresses | Dynamic NAT |
| Assigns unique source port numbers of an inside global address on a session-by-session basis | NAT overload (PAT) |
| Allows external hosts to establish sessions with an internal host | Static NAT |
| Defines translations on a host-to-host basis | Dynamic NAT |
| Can map multiple addresses to a single address of the external interface | NAT Overload (PAT) |

8. D.  209.13.24.3

   D. Address 209.13.24.3 is an inside global address. It is a registered address on the external interface of Router RTR2 and so is a public address to which the other internal private addresses will be translated. All the internal 10.x.x.x addresses are inside local addresses.

**9.** C.   NAT overloading configuration

C. The fact that different inside local addresses are being translated to the same inside global address and the inside IP addresses are followed by a port number (for example, 209.165.202.131:512) indicates NAT overload or PAT is in use.

**10.** C.   A subnet mask is used to identify the network portion of an IP address.

C. A subnet mask is necessary regardless of whether a default gateway is specified or whether bits are borrowed on a network. It separates the 32-bit address into network and host and is used to identify the network portion of an IP address.

**11.** B.   7

B. The range of addresses from 10.186.2.24 to 10.186.2.30 is seven addresses.

**12.** C.   192.168.200.64

C. The subnet mask of 255.255.255.224 leaves 5 bits for hosts or 30 hosts per subnet. All subnets shown as possible answers are valid subnets for this subnet mask. Applying the ANDing process to the IP address and subnet mask shows that host 192.168.200.75 is on the 192.168.200.64 subnet.

ANDing the fourth octet with 3 bits used for subnetting and address .75 shows the subnet is .64:

Subnet  IP address

[======][==========]

[ 64 ][ +8  +2+1 = 75]

[0 1 0 ][ 0 1 0 1 1]

**13.** B.   VLSM block: 128, mask: 255.255.255.128

B. A block of 128 addresses will be required (126 usable). This results in borrowing 1 bit for a /25 prefix, leaving 7 bits for hosts and additional subnetting. The dot subnet mask for a /25 prefix is 255.255.255.128.

**14.**

| Subnet Mask (Slash Format) | Subnet Mask (Dot Format) | Number of Host Bits | Number of Valid Host IP Addresses |
|---|---|---|---|
| /22 | 255.255.252.0 | 10 | 1022 ($2^{10} = 1024 - 2$) |
| /23 | 255.255.254.0 | 9 | 510 ($2^2 = 512 - 2$) |
| /24 | 255.255.255.0 | 8 | 254 ($2^8 = 256 - 2$) |
| /25 | 255.255.255.128 | 7 | 126 ($2^7 = 128 - 2$) |
| /26 | 255.255.255.192 | 6 | 62 ($2^6 = 64 - 2$) |
| /27 | 255.255.255.224 | 5 | 30 ($2^5 = 32 - 2$) |
| /28 | 255.255.255.240 | 4 | 14 ($2^4 = 16 - 2$) |
| /29 | 255.255.255.248 | 3 | 6 ($2^2 = 8 - 2$) |
| /30 | 255.255.255.252 | 2 | 2 ($2^2 = 4 - 2$) |

**15.** Classless interdomain routing (CIDR)

## Challenge Questions and Activities

| 1. Host 1 IP Address | Host 2 IP Address | Subnet Mask | Same Subnet? |
|---|---|---|---|
| 10.10.10.10<br>Net: 10.10.10.0 | 10.10.10.20<br>Net: 10.10.10.0 | 255.255.255.0 | Yes |
| 172.19.50.20<br>Net: 172.19.0.0 | 172.19.139.50<br>Net: 172.19.128.0 | 255.255.192.0 | No |
| 192.168.15.1<br>Net: 192.168.15.0 | 192.168.15.252<br>Net: 192.168.15.0 | 255.255.255.0 | Yes |
| 172.30.28.120<br>Net: 172.30.28.64 | 172.30.28.133<br>Net: 172.30.28.128 | 255.255.255.192 | No |
| 192.168.20.61<br>Net: 192.168.20.32 | 192.168.20.76<br>Net: 192.168.20.64 | 255.255.255.224 | No |

2. A. Dynamic NAT

   B. 15

   C. Inside global

   D. 172.31.232.1 through 172.31.232.255

   E. No hosts on the internal network would be able to communicate with the default gateway because it would be on a different network.

   F. False. This is an inside local address assigned to interface FastEthernet 0/0.

3. Answers can vary.

# Chapter 5

## Check Your Understanding

1. A. Redundancy

   B. QoS

   C. Packet filtering

   D. Hierarchical network design

   A, B, C, and D. Redundant links provide an alternative path in case a primary data path fails. Quality of service (QoS) is used to ensure critical data receives priority treatment. Packet filtering is implemented to deny certain types of packets, maximize available bandwidth, and protect the network from attacks. Networks should be designed in a hierarchical manner to support the flow of information and services in the organization.

**2.** D.  Full mesh

D.  The full-mesh design has every node directly connected to every other node in the network. This provides total redundancy, making it the most reliable. Unfortunately, it is also the most expensive to install and maintain.

**3.** The routing table attaches a number to each route that represents the trustworthiness or accuracy of the source of the routing information. This value is the administrative distance.

**4.** C.  D

C.  The letter D denotes that a route has been learned via EIGRP. The notation D EX identifies a route learned from a different autonomous system.

**5.** Limiting traffic to a single point of entrance/exit creates a stub network. In some enterprise networks, small branch offices have only one possible path to reach the rest of the network. In this situation, it is not necessary to burden the stub router with routing updates and increased overhead by running a dynamic routing protocol; therefore, static routing is beneficial.

**6.** D.  floating static route

D. A floating static route is a static route that has been entered with an administrative distance higher than the value assigned to the dynamic routing protocol in use on the network. When the primary link fails and the route learned from the dynamic process disappears from the routing table, the floating static link takes over. When the primary link is reestablished, the dynamic route takes over once again.

**7.** B.  Every 30 seconds.

B.  Both RIPv1 and RIPv2 send out their entire routing table every 30 seconds.

**8.** When a router starts up, each RIP-configured interface sends out a request message. This message requests that all RIP neighbors send their complete routing tables. RIP-enabled neighbors send a response message that includes known network entries. If a route entry is new, the receiving router installs the route in the routing table. The startup router then sends a triggered update out all RIP-enabled interfaces containing its own routing table. RIP neighbors are informed of any new routes.

**9.** A.  Ethernet0 will no longer send RIP routing updates, but will accept them.

A.  The passive-interface command prevents the interface from sending RIP updates.

**10.** C.  **show ip rip database**

C.  The command **show ip rip database** displays all routes known to RIP.

**11.** B.  Neighbor

C.  Topology

D.  Routing

B, C, and D. EIGRP maintains neighbor, topology, and routing tables.

**12.** B.  Hello

B.  The hello packet establishes neighbor relationships.

**13.** A.  Unicast

B.  Multicast

A and B. EIGRP uses both unicasts and multicasts depending on the role of the packet.

14. A.  Bandwidth

   B.  Delay

   A and B. EIGRP uses a composite metric value to determine the best path to a destination. This metric is determined from the bandwidth, delay, reliability, and load. By default, the k values associated with reliability and load are set to zero, simplifying the default metric to using bandwidth and delay.

15. As a routing protocol, EIGRP operates independently of the network layer. Cisco designed Reliable Transport Protocol (RTP) as a proprietary Layer 4 protocol. RTP guarantees delivery and receipt of EIGRP packets for all network layer protocols. Because large, complex networks may use a variety of network layer protocols, this protocol makes EIGRP flexible and scalable.

## Challenge Questions and Activities

1. RIPv1 is a classful routing protocol that does not support VLSM or CIDR. It also has a maximum hop count of 15 routers, meaning that any network further away than this is deemed unreachable. RIP does not scale well, and the slow convergence can often generate routing loops on large networks. RIPv2 has many of the same issues exhibited by RIPv1 and is not a viable solution for this large network.

   One possible solution is to implement EIGRP. This is possible because all routers are Cisco equipment. EIGRP has a much faster convergence time, thus minimizing the possibility of routing loops. It also uses small hello packets and bounded updates, unlike RIP, which broadcasts its entire routing table every 30 seconds. This would make more bandwidth available to data and should result in an improved performance.

2. The problem stems from the fact that RIPv1 automatically summarizes addresses at classful boundaries. To RIPv1, each remote office is on the same 10.0.0.0/8 network. Because there is a different network between these offices, a situation of discontiguous subnets has been generated. Because the company is using routers from different companies, EIGRP is not a possibility, so RIPv2 is the only solution at this point in time. RIPv2 supports classless routing, and auto summarization can be turned off, allowing each office to advertise the proper subnets.

# Chapter 6

## Check Your Understanding

1. D.  Shortest path first calculations

   D.  OSPF uses shortest path first (SPF) calculations to determine the best path. It uses more processor overhead, not less. Because each router has a complete view of the network, routing loops are minimized, and OSPF does not need to use split horizon or poison reverse. It uses cost, not hop count, to select a route.

2. D.  R1-R3-R4-R5

   D.  The path from R1-R3-R4-R5 has the most hops, but the sum of the link costs (path cost) is the lowest, at only 51. Note that this included the cost of the local FastEthernet interface for the router each host is attached to.

3. C.  The packet will be forwarded to the next hop of 192.168.4.2.

   C.  All three routes have the same network number and mask, but they are learned from different routing protocols. The EIGRP route (D) with the lowest AD of 90 is the preferred route, which has a next hop of 192.168.4.2.

4. D.   192.168.70.18

   D.   If the router ID is removed, the router will take on an ID based on the highest loopback interface IP address configured, which is Loopback1 with IP address 192.168.70.18.

5. F.   There is no change in the DR or BDR until either current DR or BDR goes down.

   F.   Bringing in a router with a higher ID does not replace the existing DR or BDR until one of them fails. Because RouterD has the highest loopback address, it could take over the role of the failed router.

6. B.   **network 192.168.10.64 0.0.0.63 area 0**

   **network 192.168.10.192 0.0.0.3 area 0**

   B.   Router A is connected to networks 192.168.10.64/26 and 192.168.10.192/30. The /26 mask is a 255.255.255.192 dot mask, which is a 0.0.0.63 wildcard mask. The /30 mask is a 255.255.255.252 dot mask, which is a 0.0.0.3 wildcard mask.

7. A.   It can be set with the **ip ospf cost** command.

   D.   It may be calculated using the formula *Reference bandwidth / Bandwidth*.

   A, D. The cost of an interface can be configured directly with the **ip ospf cost** command. It can also be set indirectly using the **bandwidth** command, and then OSPF uses the formula *Reference bandwidth / Bandwidth*.

8. C.   One of the **network** statements is wrong.

   C.   The topology shows Router A connected to networks 192.168.10.64/26 and 192.168.10.0/30. The output shows that the 192.168.10.64/26 network is being advertised correctly, but the 192.168.10.0/30 is not. The **network** statement in error is 192.168.10.128 0.0.0.63 Area 0.

9. C.   The default route will be propagated to all routers participating in the same OSPF area.

   C.   Configuring a 0.0.0.0 0.0.0.0 (called a quad-zero route) default route on HQ and using the **default-information originate** command will propagate it to the other OSPF routers.

10. A.   To prevent routing information from being falsified

    C.   To keep routing information from being captured and deciphered

    A, C. Authentication encrypts routing updates to prevent them from being captured and being falsified.

11. Supernetting, route summarization, or a summary route

12. Area 0 or the backbone area

## Challenge Questions and Activities

1. It is possible to summarize and advertise the 16 networks as one supernet of 192.168.4.0 /20 (4 bits = $2^4$, which covers 16 networks). Doing this reduces the number of networks that are advertised to the ISP from 16 to 1.

   To configure an OSPF ASBR router to summarize these networks, issue the following command in OSPF router configuration mode:

   **area 0 range 192.168.0.0 255.255.240.0**

2. Answers will vary.

# Chapter 7

## Check Your Understanding

1. A.  Ethernet

   A.  Ethernet is the most common Layer 2 LAN encapsulation. All others are serial line encapsulation technology normally found in a WAN environment.

2. A.  ITU-T

   B.  ISO

   C.  IETF

   D.  EIA

   E.  TIA

   A, B, C, D and E. All the listed organizations are involved in the creation of WAN standards.

3. STDM is similar to TDM except that it keeps track of conversations that require extra bandwidth. It then dynamically reassigns unused time slices on an as-needed basis. In this way, STDM minimizes wasted bandwidth.

4. C.  DWDM

   E.  SONET

   C and E. DWDM and SONET are normally used for long-range WAN connections such as that found between ISPs. Cable and DSL are last-mile technologies used to connect the end user to the ISP, and Ethernet is a LAN technology.

5. B.  Circuit Switching

   B.  Circuit Switching is the only technology that creates an end-to-end physical connection. PVCs are configured paths through a network but do not provide end-to-end physical connectivity.

6. Cisco HDLC incorporates an extra field, known as the Type field, which allows multiple network layer protocols to share the same link. This field is not found in standards-based HDLC, making the Cisco version of HDLC incompatible with the HDLC used by other vendors.

7. LCPs are responsible for establishing, testing, maintaining, and terminating links between devices. LCPs also configure optional parameters such as authentication and compression. LCP is responsible for the handling of carried packet sizes, the detection of common misconfigurations, and the determination of link quality. If the LCP determines that the link is of sufficient quality, it brings up the NCPs.

8. Because CHAP is listed as the first authentication protocol, it will try PAP only if the other router is unable to use CHAP authentication and suggests that PAP be used instead. Because CHAP failed, PAP will not be attempted, and the link will be terminated.

9. Local Management Interface (LMI) is a signaling standard between the DTE and the Frame Relay switch. LMI is responsible for managing the connection and maintaining the status between devices. LMI messages provide communication and synchronization between the network and the user device. They periodically report the existence of new PVCs and the deletion of existing PVCs. They also provide information about PVC integrity. VC status messages prevent data from being sent to PVCs that no longer exist.

10. Any data that exceeds the CIR will have the DE bit turned on. If congestion is encountered in the network and data must be dropped, this data is dropped first. If no congestion is encountered in the network and the bandwidth is available, the data is delivered.

## Challenge Questions and Activities

1. There are three configuration errors. The username accounts must be for the opposite router, not the router that they are configured on. The password is case sensitive and must be the same on both ends. The third configuration mistake is that one end of the link is configured for CHAP authentication, and the other end is configured for PAP. All three of these must be corrected before the link will come up.

2. Leased-line connections require a dedicated interface and a separate CSU/DSU for each line. The lines themselves are extremely expensive to obtain and maintain, making their use in large organizations cost prohibitive. An alternative packet-switching technology such as Frame Relay would be an excellent choice for this organization. Each office could maintain a leased line connect to their nearest ISP, and multiple PVCs could be established through the ISPs network to connect each of the offices. Each site would require only a single leased-line connection, meaning one interface and one CSU/DSU.

# Chapter 8

## Check Your Understanding

1. A.   Limit network traffic and increase performance.

   D.   Provide traffic flow control.

   E.   Provide a basic level of security for network access.

   A, D, E. ACLs can limit network traffic and provide traffic flow control, with the potential of increasing performance by preventing certain types of traffic from taking up network bandwidth. They also provide a basic level of security for network access. They do not notify other devices of congestion, control interfaces, or open links.

2. B.   The last 4 bits of a supplied IP address will be ignored.

   D.   The first 28 bits of a supplied IP address will be matched.

   B, D. The 32-bit mask 0.0.0.15 is made up of 28 zeros (0s) followed by 4 ones (1s). Thus, the first 28 bits of a supplied IP address will be matched, and the last 4 bits will be ignored.

3. A.   192.168.12.0 0.0.0.7

   A.   Applying the 255.255.255.248 mask to the host IP address of 192.168.12.6 results in a subnet network address of 192.168.12.0. The .248 mask in the last octet leaves 3 bits for hosts, so the subnet numbers increment in multiple of eight ($2^3 = 8$). Subtracting .248 from 255 leaves 7, so a wildcard mask of 0.0.0.7 specifies a subnet that ranges eight addresses from 192.168.12.0 to 192.168.12.7. Only six of these are usable ($2^3 = 8 - 2 = 6$).

4. B.   Outbound filters do not affect traffic that originates within the local router.

   D.   Extended ACLs should be applied closest to the source.

   B, D. Outbound filters do not affect traffic that originates within the local router. An outbound ACL that blocks a ping on an interface will not stop a ping from the router itself. Extended ACLs should be applied closest to the source, and standard ACLs should be applied as close to the destination as possible. The inbound and outbound interface should be referenced as if looking from the inside of a router. Ask this question: Is the packet coming into the router, or is it leaving the router? ACL statements will be processed until a match is made for each packet through the interface. The remaining ACL statement will have no effect on the packet.

5. B.   Router(config)# **access-list 95 deny 172.16.0.0 0.0.255.255**

   D.   Router(config)# **access-list 95 permit any**

   B, D. The **access-list 95 deny 172.16.0.0 0.0.255.255** statement blocks all hosts from the 172.16.0.0 network. The **access-list 95 permit any** statement allows all other hosts.

6. B.   The keyword **host** is implied in the command line **access-list 99 deny 10.213.177.76**.

   D.   Host 10.213.177.100 will be allowed access to the Serial 0/1 interface.

   B, D. The keyword **host** is not needed in the command line **access-list 99 deny 10.213.177.76** because this is a single IP address. Host 10.213.177.100 will be allowed access into the Serial 0/0/1 interface because it is not 10.213.177.76. Based on the ACL number (99), this is a standard IP ACL. A wildcard mask is not necessary when permitting/denying a single host or all hosts (any). This ACL will block any traffic from host 10.213.177.76.

7. C.   **access-list 137 permit ip 192.0.2.0 0.0.0.255 any**

   **access-list 137 permit tcp 198.18.112.0 0.0.0.255 any eq www**

   C.   The ACL statement **access-list 137 permit ip 192.0.2.0 0.0.0.255 any** allows all traffic from the Engineering LAN to access the Internet, and the statement **access-list 137 permit tcp 198.18.112.0 0.0.0.255 any eq www** allows only web traffic (could use **www**, **http**, or **80**) from the Marketing LAN.

8. B.   Host 10.128.114.76 will not be able to establish an FTP session with available hosts on the 172.25.0.0/16 network.

   D.   Host 192.168.85.76 will be able to establish an FTP session with available hosts on the 172.25.0.0 network.

   B, D. Host 10.128.114.76 will not be able to establish an FTP session because all hosts on the 10.128.114.76 are blocked to any destination. Host 192.168.85.76 will be able to establish an FTP session with available hosts on the 172.25.0.0 network because only Telnet (port 23) is blocked for 192.168.85.0 hosts.

9. Answer in correct sequence:
```
R1(config)# access-list 1 permit host 10.0.0.1
R1(config)# line vty 0 4
R1(config-line)# access-class 1 in
```

10. A.   ACLs control host access to a network or to another host.

    C.   ACLs provide a basic level of security for network access.

    A, C. ACLs control host access to a network or to another host and can provide a basic level of security for network access. Standard ACLs can restrict access based only on source address, not specific applications and ports. Router ACLs can permit or deny traffic based on the IP address, not MAC address. ACLs can be applied to as many interfaces as the router has.

11. C.   The port number is incorrect for the access list **permit** statement.

    C.   The **permit** statement allows any host on the 10.10.10.0/24 network to access any internal host as long as the application protocol is FTP (port 21). A Telnet (port 23) attempt will fail. The port specified should be 23, not 21.

12. E.   Enter the **deny ip any log** to the end of the ACL statements.

    E.   The network administrator must add the **deny ip any log** to the end of the ACL statements; any packet that does not match a statement in the ACL will be logged to the console. If the administrator is interested in just obtaining a count of packets that do not match any statement in the ACL, he can just add the **deny ip any** statement to the end of the ACL. You can display the number of matches for each ACL statement by using the **show access-lists** command.

13. Numbered extended or named extended. A standard ACL can filter only on source address. If traffic is to be denied access from hosts on a specific network to a specific host on a remote network, an extended ACL must be used (either numbered or named).

14. A.   Test basic connectivity before applying ACLs.

   C.   When logging, add the **deny any** statement to the end of a standard ACL.

   D.   It is best to create and edit ACLs in a text editor such as Notepad.

   A, C, and D. Always test basic connectivity before applying an ACL; otherwise, troubleshooting may be complicated. The **deny any** (**deny ip any any** for extended ACLs) statement at the end of a standard ACL allows the accumulation of statistics for packets that do not match the other ACL statements and can help identify "holes" in the ACL. The implied **deny any** statement will catch any missed packets; but unless the statement is explicitly added, the matches will not be tracked. It is best to create and edit ACLs, especially longer and more complex ones, in a text editor such as Notepad. This way the ACL can be modified more easily by deleting the existing ACL and re-adding it.

## Challenge Questions and Activities

1. B.   The R1 Fa0/0 interface outbound

   B.   The R1 LAN interface Fa0/0 outbound is best because a simple standard ACL placed here can permit or deny traffic from multiple networks and is closest to the destination LAN 10.1.1.0/24.

   (Choice A) Placing the ACL on the R1 S0/0 interface outbound would not block traffic destined for the 10.1.1.0/24 network.

   (Choice C) Placing the ACL on the R1 S0/0 interface inbound could control traffic from R2 but would not block traffic from the R1 10.1.2.0/24 network.

   (Choice D) Placing the ACL on the R2 S0/0 interface inbound would not block traffic destined for the 10.1.1.0/24 network.

   (Choice E) Placing the ACL on the R2 Fa0/0 and Fa0/1 interfaces inbound would require two ACLs and would not block the 10.1.2.0/24 network.

   (Choice F) Placing the ACL on the R2 S0/0 interface outbound could work, but it would control all traffic leaving the R2 router regardless of destination, because the standard ACL can filter based only on source address. If the ACL permitted source network 192.168.125.0/24 and denied 172.20.10.0/24, it would affect the traffic received by both networks on R1, not just 10.1.1.0/24.

2. 
```
R1(config)# access-list 55 permit 192.168.125.0 0.0.0.255
R1(config)# access-list 55 deny 172.20.10.0 0.0.0.255
R1(config)# access-list 55 deny 10.1.2.0 0.0.0.255
R1(config)# interface fastethernet 0/0
R1(config-if)# ip access-group 55 out
```

3. D.   The R2 S0/0 interface outbound

   D.   R2 S0/0 interface outbound is best because this is an extended ACL and you can control both source and destination, permitting 192.168.5.0/24 or denying traffic from 172.20.10.0/24. It is also closest to the source for these LANs.

   (Choice A) Placing the ACL on the R1 S0/0 interface inbound would work, but it allows traffic from the 172.20.10.0/24 network to travel across the WAN link before it is blocked, thus wasting bandwidth.

   (Choice B) Placing the ACL on the R1 Fa0/0 interface outbound would work, but it allows traffic from the 172.20.10.0/24 network to travel across the WAN link and forces the R1 router to switch the packets before finally being dropped, thus wasting bandwidth and placing an additional load on R1.

   (Choice C) Placing the ACL on the R2 S0/0 interface inbound would not block traffic destined for the 10.1.1.0/24 network.

   (Choice E) Placing the ACL on the R2 Fa0/0 interface inbound would work to allow the 192.168.5.0/24 network traffic, but it would not block the 172.20.10.0/24 traffic unless another ACL were placed on Fa0/1.

4. 
```
R2(config)# access-list 111 permit 192.168.125.0 0.0.0.255 10.1.1.0 0.0.0.255
R2(config)# access-list 111 permit host 172.20.10.99 10.1.1.0 0.0.0.255 eq 23
R2(config)# access-list 111 permit host 172.20.10.99 10.1.1.0 0.0.0.255 eq 20
R2(config)# access-list 111 permit host 172.20.10.99 10.1.1.0 0.0.0.255 eq 21
R2(config)# access-list 111 deny 172.20.10.0 0.0.0.255 10.1.1.0 0.0.0.255
R2(config)# interface serial 0/0
R2(config-if)# ip access-group 111 out
```

5. Answers will vary, but they could include the following:

   - The bouncer example
   - A list of invitees to a party
   - A receptionist controlling visitor access to the president of a company
   - An ID card scanner that allows access to a secured area of a building
   - An access list that controls which users can access server resources, such as files and folders

# Chapter 9

## Check Your Understanding

1. A.   Equipment failure

   B.   Man-made disasters

   C.   Natural disasters

   D.   Security breaches

   E.   Virus attacks

   A, B, C, D, and E. All the stated options can cause network downtime.

2. A.  Expected level of service

   D.  Recovery period from any downtime

   A, and D. An SLA clearly documents network expectations in terms of level of service. These expectations include the acceptable level of downtime and the recovery period, should downtime occur. SLAs often specify the penalty associated with any loss of service.

3. Business continuity plans provide a detailed plan of action in case of unexpected man-made or natural disasters such as power failures or earthquakes. Business continuity plans provide the details on how the business continues or resumes operations, with minimal disruption to its clients, after the disaster. They clearly specify how the network reestablishes functionality in the event of a catastrophic failure. One way to ensure functionality is to have a redundant backup site at another location, in case of failure at the primary site.

4. A.  Detection of problems before they occur

   D.  Correction of problems before they occur

   A and D. Proactive maintenance is designed to detect and correct potential problems before they can negatively impact network performance.

5. The purpose of network monitoring is to watch network performance in comparison to a predetermined baseline. Any observed deviations from this baseline indicate potential problems with the network and require investigation.

6. A.  Physical topology diagrams

   B.  Logical topology diagrams

   C.  Configuration files of all network devices

   D.  Baseline performance level

   A, B, C, and D. Warrantee information is not required for network monitoring.

7. C.  Agents

   C.  Agents monitor device parameters and send the information to an NMS when polled.

8. A.  Restore network functionality

   A.  The objective of any troubleshooting effort is to return functionality quickly and with little disruption to the end users.

9. The failure domain is the area of the network impacted by the failure or misconfiguration of a network device. The actual size of the domain depends on the device and the type of failure or misconfiguration. Larger failure domains usually result in increased downtime.

10. D.  Trial and error

    D.  An experienced troubleshooter will often start out with a trial-and-error technique. If this does not quickly solve the issue, an experienced troubleshooter will normally switch to a divide-and-conquer or a more structured approach.

11. B.  **clear mac-address-table dynamic**

    B.  The **clear mac-address-table dynamic** command will clear only the dynamic addresses in a switch's MAC address table.

12. A.  Loss of network connectivity

    B.  High CPU utilization on routers

    C.  High link utilization

    D.  Increasing number of output drops on many interfaces

    A, B, C, and D. All are signs that a switching loop might have developed.

13. Untagged frames sent across a trunk are assigned to the native VLAN of the trunk line. If the native VLAN assignment is changed on a device, each end of the 802.1Q trunk should be configured with the same native VLAN number. If one end of the trunk is configured for native VLAN10 and the other end is configured for native VLAN14, a frame sent from VLAN10 on one side is received on VLAN14 on the other. VLAN10 "leaks" into VLAN14. This can create unexpected connectivity issues and increase latency.

14. B.  Server

    B.  Server is the default VTP configuration mode on Cisco switches.

15. The **show** commands are important tools for understanding the status of a router, detecting neighboring routers, isolating problems in the network, and monitoring the network in general. The **debug** commands provide real-time information on the exchange of routing information between devices.

16. B.  **clear ip route ***

    B.  The **clear ip route *** command will clear dynamic routes in the routing table.

17. D.  **show controllers** *serial_port*

    D.  The **show controllers** *serial_port* command will show whether a WAN port is configured as DTE or DCE.

18. Serial Line Address Resolution Protocol (SLARP) assigns an address to the endpoint of a serial link if the other end is already configured. SLARP assumes that each serial line is a separate IP subnet, and that one end of the line is host number 1 and the other end is host number 2. As long as one end of the serial link is configured, SLARP automatically configures an IP address for the other end.

19. Standard ACLs filter only on the source IP address; therefore, they must be placed as close to the destination as possible. Placing the ACL close to the destination unfortunately allows traffic to flow across one or more network segments before being denied. This is a waste of valuable bandwidth. An extended ACL can filter both on the source and destination address and can therefore be placed close to the source.

## Challenge Questions and Activities

1. The first problem is that the outbound interface on the remote WAN interface has the wrong IP address assigned. Because all outbound traffic is using the same IP address, PAT is probably working properly. The address it is using indicates that SLARP might have automatically assigned the address to the interface. This should be confirmed using the **show interface** command on the remote office router. If this is found to be the problem, the device configuration should be changed to assign the correct IP address to the interface.

   The second issue is the inbound ACL on the main site router. ACLs are processed sequentially, and the first statement in this ACL allows all IP traffic. Also, the second and third line use the protocol IP rather than TCP. Logging should be used on all lines of this ACL to prove that all packets are matching the first statement and being permitted. To correct the problem, the list should be reordered and protocols corrected as follows:

   ```
   access-list 101 deny tcp host 192.168.1.11 any eq www
   access-list 101 deny tcp host 192.168.1.11 any eq telnet
   access-list 101 permit ip any any
   ```

   Logging should also be used on the corrected ACL to verify that it is functioning correctly. The list is correctly applied in the inbound direction.

## #

*802.1Q* IEEE standard that is designed to enable traffic (trunking) between VLANs. IEEE 802.1q uses an internal tagging mechanism that inserts a 4-byte tag field in the original Ethernet frame between the Source Address and Type/Length fields. Because the frame is altered, the trunking device recomputes the frame check sequence on the modified frame. 802.1Q is also referred to as dot1q.

## A

*access control list (ACL)* List kept by a network device, such as a router, to manage access to or from the router for a number of services. For example, an ACL can be used to prevent packets with a certain IP address or protocol from entering or leaving a particular interface on the router.

*access layer* Level of the hierarchical Cisco internetworking model that encompasses the hosts and devices that are the point of entry into the network. Access layer devices include switches, hubs, workstations, servers, IP phones, web cameras, and access points.

*access point (AP)* Access layer device that connects to a wired network and relays data between wireless and wired devices. An AP connects wireless communication devices to form a wireless network to allow roaming.

*access port* Pathway to a device that does not create loops in a switched network and always transitions to forwarding if a host is attached.

*active topology* RSTP network design that transitions ports to the forwarding state if they are not discarding or are blocked.

*adaptive cut-through switching* Type of switching in which the flow reverts to fast-forward mode when the number of errors drops below the threshold value to an acceptable level.

*adjacency* Relationship between neighboring routers for the purpose of exchanging routing information. Adjacency is based on the use of a common media segment.

*administrative distance* Used by Cisco routers to determine the trustworthiness of the routing source. For a Cisco router, an administrative distance is expressed as a numeric value between 0 and 255. The higher the value, the lower the trustworthiness rating. When two router sources (for example, routing protocols, static routes, connected routes) offer the same route to the Cisco router, the source with the lowest administrative distance is placed in the routing table.

*advertised distance (AD)* Distance that is broadcast by an upstream neighbor.

*advertisement request* VLAN information that a VTP client requires if the switch has been reset or the VTP domain name has been changed.

*aging time* Period of time in which an entry must be used before a switch deletes it from the MAC address table.

*application-specific integrated circuit (ASIC)* Circuit that gives precise instructions for the functionality of a device during Layer 3 switching.

*Area 0* The first area created at the top of an OSPF network hierarchy. An OSPF network must have at least one area, which is Area 0. As the network expands, other areas are created adjacent to Area 0. Area 0 is also known as the backbone area.

*Area Border Router (ABR)* Routing device that connects one or more OSPF areas to a backbone network. An ABR maintains routing tables for the backbone and the attached areas of an OSPF.

*area ID* Identification number of the OSPF area to which the network belongs.

*as-built* Diagram that shows the original design and any changes that have been made to a network topology.

*asymmetric switching*    Switches that provide connections between ports of different speeds.

*Asynchronous Transfer Mode (ATM)*    International standard for the cell relay of service types such as voice, video, or data. In ATM, the services are conveyed in fixed-length, 53-byte cells. Fixed-length cells reduce transit delays because cell processing occurs in the hardware. ATM is designed for high-speed transmission media such as T3, E3, and SONET.

*authentication server*    Security server that controls the frequency and timing of challenges to prevent attacks on a network.

*autonomous system*    Collection of networks under a common administration sharing a common routing strategy. Autonomous systems are subdivided by areas. An autonomous system must be assigned a unique 16-bit number by the IANA.

*Autonomous System Boundary Router (ASBR)*    Area border router located between an OSPF autonomous system and a non-OSPF network. An ASBR runs the OSPF routing protocol and another routing protocol, such as RIP. An ASBR must reside in a nonstub OSPF area. An ASBR is also known as Autonomous System Border Router.

*autonomous system number (ASN)*    An autonomous system number is a unique number assigned to an autonomous system for use when routing packets through the Internet.

*auto-negotiation*    A feature of Ethernet switches that allows ports to adjust their speed and duplex settings automatically based on the capabilities of connected devices. Auto-negotiation occurs when a switch port can auto-detect the speed and duplex of the device that is connected to the port.

*availability*    Condition of accessibility.

# B

*backbone cabling*    Physical media that connects wiring closets to each other, wiring closets and the POP, and buildings that are part of the same LAN. Backbone cabling is also known as vertical cabling.

*BackboneFast*    Feature on the switches of a bridge network that provides fast convergence after a spanning-tree topology change. BackboneFast is used at the distribution and core layers to restore backbone connectivity. BackboneFast is Cisco proprietary.

*back-end network*    The connections and network services portion of a WAN that a service provider or ISP is responsible for maintaining between LANs.

*backup designated router (BDR)*    In an OSPF network, the router that is identified to take over if the designated router (DR) fails.

*backward explicit congestion notification (BECN)*    Signal in a frame traveling in the opposite direction of frames that have encountered a congested path in a Frame Relay network. The DTE that receives the frame with the BECN signal can request that higher-level protocols take appropriate flow-control action.

*bandwidth*    1) For digital signals, a measurement of the amount of data that can be transmitted on a given networking medium within a given amount of time. The rated throughput capacity of a given network medium or protocol. 2) Analog bandwidth is the difference between the highest and lowest frequencies available for network signals.

*baseline*    1) A quantitative expression of planned costs, schedules, and technical requirements for a defined project. 2) A baseline is established to describe the "normal" status of network or computer system performance. The status can then be compared to the baseline at any point to measure the variation from the "normal" operation condition.

*bit-oriented*    A protocol that uses bit positions to define characteristics and framing. High-Level Data Link Control (HDLC) is a standard bit-oriented data link layer encapsulation.

*blocked ports*    An STP port designation where the port is set to block traffic to prevent switching loops.

*blocking state*    An STP port state where the port is blocking traffic.

*bounded updates*   Feature associated with routing protocols, such as EIGRP. A bounded update contains specific parameters and is delivered only to routers that require the information.

*bridge ID (BID)*   Identifies a Cisco switch to determine the root bridge, which is the focal point in an STP switched network. The bridge ID consists of a 2-byte priority and the switch 6-byte MAC address.

*bridge protocol data unit (BPDU)*   Spanning Tree Protocol hello packet that is sent out at configurable intervals to exchange information among bridges (switches) in the network.

*broadcast domain*   Set of devices that receive broadcast frames originating from any of the devices within the set. A broadcast domain is typically bounded by routers because routers do not forward broadcast frames unless configured to do so.

*broadcast multiaccess network*   Type of Ethernet link identified by OSPF, which is a standard for a multiaccess network that forwards broadcast traffic.

*broadcast storm*   Undesirable network event in which many broadcasts are sent simultaneously across all network segments. A broadcast storm uses substantial network bandwidth and typically causes network timeouts.

*business continuity plan (BCP)*   Steps to be taken to continue business operations when there is a natural or man-made disaster.

*business enterprise*   Large corporate environment with many users and locations, or with many systems.

*business security plan (BSP)*   Physical, system, and organizational control measures to be taken to protect network and information assets.

# C

*carrier wave*   Signal on which data is modulated and then demodulated in an analog connection.

*cell switching*   Data communication scheme based on fixed-length cell structure. In a cell-switched network, the fixed-length cell achieves a faster speed of transmission than those using variable-length packets. ATM is an example of a cell-switched technology on a network that provides full bandwidth of the link when a station communicates to the switch.

*central office (CO)*   Strategically located facility that accommodates vital devices on a network topology. Typically associated with a telephone company network.

*Challenge Handshake Authentication Protocol (CHAP)*   Security feature supported on lines that use PPP encapsulation to prevent unauthorized access by identifying the remote user. CHAP is a three-way handshake with encryption and enables the router or access server to determine whether a user is allowed access.

*challenge message*   Response sent by a router to establish the identity of the sender.

*channel service unit (CSU)*   Digital interface device that connects end-user equipment to the local digital telephone loop. Often referred to with DSU, as CSU/DSU.

*channel service unit/data service unit (CSU/DSU)*   Network devices that connect an organization to a digital circuit.

*child route*   Subnet route on an EIGRP network.

*circuit switching*   System in which a dedicated physical circuit path exists between sender and receiver for the duration of the connection. Circuit switching is often used in a telephone company network.

*Cisco Discovery Protocol (CDP)*   Protocol on Cisco-manufactured equipment, including routers, access servers, bridges, and switches, that enables a device to discover and communicate with other directly connected devices on the LAN or on the remote side of a WAN. CDP runs on LANs, Frame Relay, and ATM media.

*classful boundary*   Designation of subnets as a single Class A, B, or C network by protocols such as RIP and EIGRP.

*classful routing*   Selecting a path on a network without including subnet mask information. In classful routing, variable-length subnet masks (VLSM) are not supported.

*classless interdomain routing (CIDR)*   Technique based on route aggregation and supported by Border Gateway Protocol Version 4 that allows routers to group routes to reduce the quantity of information carried by core Internet routers. When you are using CIDR, multiple IP networks appear as a single, larger entity to networks outside of the group.

*classless routing*   Feature of a protocol where the subnet mask is sent with all routing update packets. Classless routing protocols include RIPv2, EIGRP, and OSPF.

*classless routing protocol*   A routing protocol that sends a subnet mask with all routing update packets. A classless routing protocol is necessary when the mask cannot be assumed or determined by the value of the first octet. Classless routing protocols include RIPv2, EIGRP, and OSPF.

*clocking signal*   Indicator of the rate at which data moves onto the local loop.

*collision domain*   Network area in Ethernet where frames that have collided are propagated. Repeaters and hubs have collision domains. LAN switches and routers do not.

*committed burst (Bc)*   Maximum amount of data, in bits, that a Frame Relay internetwork is committed to accept and transmit at the CIR. Bc is a negotiated tariff metric.

*committed information rate (CIR)*   Speed, measured in bits per second and averaged over a minimum increment of time, at which a Frame Relay network transfers information. CIR is a negotiated tariff metric.

*committed time (Tc)*   Calculated time interval that data takes to travel a specific distance.

*composite metric*   Method used on an EIGRP network to calculate the best route for loop-free routing and rapid convergence.

*congestion*   Traffic in excess of network capacity.

*content addressable memory (CAM)*   MAC address and port mapping table maintained by a switch. A CAM table is re-created every time a switch is activated.

*contiguous*   Location of a neighboring device. Contiguous means adjacent or next, as with contiguous IP addressing.

*control plane*   Collection of processes that run at the process level on the route processor. Control plane processes collectively provide high-level control for most Cisco IOS functions.

*converged*   Condition in which a group of internetworking devices running a specific routing protocol agree on the topology of the internetwork after a change in the topology.

*coordinated universal time (UTC)*   The international time standard. It is the current term for what was commonly referred to as Greenwich Meridian Time (GMT).

*core layer*   Top layer in a three-layer hierarchical design with the access layer and distribution layer. The core layer is a high-speed backbone layer between geographically dispersed end networks.

*core router*   Router in a packet-switched star topology that is part of the backbone. The core router serves as the single pipe through which all traffic from peripheral networks must pass on the way to other peripheral networks.

*count to infinity*   Situation in which routers continuously increment the hop count to particular networks when routing algorithms are slow to converge. Typically, an arbitrary hop-count limit is imposed to prevent count to infinity.

*customer premises equipment (CPE)*   Terminating equipment, such as terminals, telephones, and modems, supplied by the telephone company, installed at a customer site, and connected to the telephone company network.

**cut-through switching**  Process where data is streamed through a switch so that the leading edge of a frame exits the switch at the output port before the frame finishes entering the input port. Cut-through frame switching enables a device to read, process, and forward frames as soon as the destination address is looked up and the outgoing port determined. Cut-through frame switching is also known as on-the-fly frame switching. Contrast with store-and-forward frame switching.

# D

**data center**  Central management location that monitors all network resources. A data center is also known as a NOC.

**data communications equipment (DCE)**  Physical connection to a communications network in an EIA expansion environment. The DCE forwards traffic and provides a clocking signal used to synchronize data transmission between DCE and DTE devices. Examples of DCE devices include a modem and an interface card. DCE is also known as data circuit-terminating equipment when used in an ITU-T expansion environment.

**data service unit (DSU)**  Digital transmission device that adapts the physical interface on a DTE to a transmission facility such as T1 or E1. The DSU is also responsible for functions such as signal timing. Often referred to with CSU, as CSU/DSU.

**data terminal equipment (DTE)**  Physical connection to the user end in an EIA expansion environment. The DTE serves as a data source, destination, or both. It connects to a data network through a DCE device, such as a modem, and typically uses clocking signals generated by the DCE. Examples of DTE devices include computers, routers, protocol translators, and multiplexers.

**data-link connection identifier (DLCI)**  Layer 2 address that is required for each virtual circuit in an NBMA (for example, Frame Relay) network to reach a destination. The DLCI is stored in the Address field of every frame transmitted. The DLCI usually has only local significance and may be different at each end of a virtual circuit.

**dead interval**  Period of time, in seconds, that a router will wait to hear a hello from a neighbor before declaring the neighbor down.

**default gateway**  Path of a packet on a network used by default, or as the gateway of last resort, when the destination hosts are not listed in the routing table.

**default route**  Path of a packet on a network used by default, or as the gateway of last resort, when the destination hosts are not listed in the routing table.

**delay**  1) Length of time between the initiation of a transaction by a sender and the first response received by the sender. 2) Length of time required to move a packet from source to destination over a given path.

**demarcation point (demarc)**  Indicated point between service provider carrier equipment and CPE.

**denial-of-service (DoS) attack**  Attack by a single system on a network that floods the bandwidth or resources of a targeted system, such as a web server, with the purpose of shutting it down.

**dense wavelength-division multiplexing (DWDM)**  Process that assigns incoming optical signals to specific frequencies or wavelengths of light. DWDM can amplify these wavelengths to boost the signal strength. It can multiplex more than 100 different wavelengths or channels of data onto a single fiber optic link. Each channel is capable of carrying a multiplexed signal at 2.5 Gbps.

**deny**  Rejection of data on a network.

**designated port**  Term used with STP for an interface on a switch that forwards traffic toward the root bridge but does not connect to the least cost path.

*designated router (DR)*   Router designated by the OSPF Hello protocol on a broadcast OSPF network that has at least two attached routers. A designated router generates LSAs. It enables a reduction in the number of adjacencies required, which reduces the amount of routing protocol traffic and the size of the topological database.

*diffusing update algorithm (DUAL)* Mathematical process used in EIGRP that provides loop-free operation at every instant throughout a route computation. DUAL allows routers involved in a topology change to synchronize at the same time, while not involving routers that are unaffected by the change.

*digital signal level 0 (DS0)*   Framing specification when transmitting digital signals over a single channel at 64 kbps on a T1 facility.

*digital signal level 1 (DS1)*   Framing specification when transmitting digital signals at 1.544 Mbps on a T1 facility in the United States, or at 2.048 Mbps on an E1 facility in Europe.

*digital signal level 3 (DS3)*   Framing specification when transmitting digital signals at 44.736 Mbps on a T3 facility.

*Dijkstra's algorithm*   Process used by a link-state SPF protocol to identify all paths to each destination and the total cost of each path.

*disabled*   State of a port when an administrator or switch security has shut it down.

*discard eligible (DE)*   Designation of a packet in Frame Relay networking. A packet with the DE bit set will be dropped first when a router detects network congestion. The DE bit is set on oversubscribed traffic, which is traffic that was received after the CIR was reached.

*discarding state*   State of a port in an RSTP network where the switch does not send a reply. A solid amber LED signifies that discarding is in process.

*discontiguous*   Typically results when subnets from one network are separated by another network.

*distance vector protocol*   Type of routing protocol that uses distance to select the best path. Examples of a distance vector protocol include RIP, IGRP, and EIGRP.

*distribution layer*   Layer in a hierarchical design between the access layer and core layer. The distribution layer interconnects access layer hosts and switches and provides security and traffic management for the core layer.

*divide and conquer*   Troubleshooting technique to resolve a network issue by breaking down the problem into smaller parts that are more manageable by starting in the middle of the OSI model and then working up or down.

*dot1q*   An abbreviation for industry standard IEEE 802.1Q VLAN trunking protocol.

*downtime*   Percentage of time in which a network is unavailable because of administrative shutdown or equipment failure.

*DROther*   Any router on an OSPF network that is not the DR or BDR.

*dynamic NAT*   Network Address Translation process that converts a local IP address to a global IP address by assigning the first available IP address in a pool of public addresses to an inside host. The host uses the assigned global IP address for the length of a session. When the session ends, the global address returns to the pool for use by another host.

*dynamic routing*   Process of finding a path that adjusts automatically to network topology or traffic changes. Dynamic routing is also known as adaptive routing.

# E

*E1*   Wide-area digital transmission scheme used predominantly in Europe that carries data at a rate of 2.048 Mbps. E1 lines can be leased for private use from common carriers.

*E3*   Wide-area digital transmission scheme used predominantly in Europe that carries data at a rate of 34.368 Mbps. E3 lines can be leased for private use from common carriers.

*edge device*   Filter on the perimeter of an enterprise network where incoming packets are passed. Examples of edge devices include a router with a firewall and demilitarized zone (DMZ). Edge devices may be equipped with IDS and IPS to examine and block unwanted traffic.

*electromagnetic interference (EMI)*
Disturbance in an electronic circuit from an external electrical source.

*encapsulation type*    The method of transmission of one network protocol within another. All network transmission protocols use a type of encapsulation. The most common LAN encapsulation is Ethernet (ARPA), and common WAN encapsulations are HDLC, PPP, and Frame Relay. Tunneling uses encapsulation and is the basis of several IP security systems, including IPsec used in VPNs.

*enterprise*    Corporation, business, or other entity that uses computers in a networked environment. The term usually refers to large companies or organizations with complex networks.

*enterprise class*    A class of networking devices with sophisticated features that is designed for high performance and heavy traffic loads typical of an enterprise environment.

*Enterprise Composite Network Model (ECNM)*
Cisco network design that divides the network into functional components while still maintaining the concept of core, distribution, and access layers. The functional components are the enterprise campus, enterprise edge, and service provider edge.

*enterprise network*    Network that integrates all systems within a company or organization. An enterprise network differs from a WAN because it is privately owned and maintained.

*excess burst (Be)*    Number of bits that a Frame Relay internetwork will attempt to transmit after Bc is accommodated. Be data is, in general, delivered with a lower probability than Bc data because Be data can be marked as DE by the network. Be is a negotiated tariff metric.

*excess information rate (EIR)*    Average rate above the CIR that a VC can support when no network congestion exists.

*exit interface*    Location on a router that the data passes through to move closer to the destination.

*extended ACL*    Type of access control list that can filter source IP addresses, destination IP addresses, MAC addresses, protocols, and port numbers. The identification number assigned to an extended ACL can be from 100 to 199 and from 2000 to 2699.

*extended star topology*    Star topology network design that is expanded to include additional networking devices, each of which can have a star pattern.

*exterior gateway protocol (EGP)*    Standard for exchanging routing information between autonomous systems. EGP is an obsolete protocol that was replaced by Border Gateway Protocol.

*external type route (E2)*    Route outside of the OSPF routing domain, redistributed into OSPF.

*extranet*    Network that provides access to information or operations of an organization to suppliers, vendors, partners, customers, or other businesses. Extranet is a private network using Internet protocols and the public telecommunication system to share internal resources. It may be considered an extension of an intranet.

# F

*failover*    Occurrence of a redundant network device performing the load or function of another device automatically if the initial device fails. The failover scheme creates a backup system for mission-critical hardware and software. The objective is to reduce the impact of system failure to a minimum by actively monitoring, identifying, and adjusting to system failure.

*failure domain*    Area of a network that is affected when a networking device malfunctions or fails. A properly designed network minimizes the size of failure domains.

*fast-forward switching*   Cut-through switching method in which the switch forwards the frame before all of the frame is received. Using the fast-forward method, the switch forwards the frame out the destination port immediately when the destination MAC address is read. The switch does not calculate or check the CRC value. The fast-forward method has the lowest latency but may forward collision fragments and damaged frames. This method of switching works best in a stable network with few errors.

*feasible distance (FD)*   Most desirable EIGRP metric along the path to the destination from the router.

*feasible successor*   Backup route identified in a topology table. A feasible successor becomes a successor route if a primary route fails. The feasible successor must have a lower reported distance than the feasible distance of the current successor distance to the destination.

*firewall*   One or more router or access servers designated as a buffer between any connected public networks and a private network. A firewall router uses access lists and other methods to ensure the security of the private network.

*first mile*   Section of physical medium leading from the location of the customer to the central office of a service provider.

*flapping*   1) Problem in routing when an advertised route between two devices alternates between two paths due to intermittent failures on a network. 2) Problem with a WAN interface whereby it is going up and down.

*flat network*   System in which all stations can be reached without having to pass through a device such as a router.

*floating static route*   Path that is manually configured and entered into the routing table that has an administrative distance set greater than the administrative distance of a dynamic route. This route is only used if the existing dynamic route becomes unavailable.

*floods*   Technique used by switches to pass traffic received on an interface to all other interfaces of the device except the interface on which the information was originally received.

*flow control*   Ability to maintain the rate of activity on a network.

*form factor*   Physical size and shape of computer components and network devices. Components that share the same form factor are physically interchangeable.

*forward explicit congestion notification (FECN)*   Signal in a Frame Relay network to inform the DTE that is receiving the frame that congestion was experienced in the path from source to destination. The DTE that receives the FECN signal can request that higher-level protocols take flow-control action as appropriate. As a result of the FECN, the receiving device slows down its requests for data.

*forwarding state*   Process of sending a frame out of a port toward the destination by way of an internetworking device. Examples of devices that forward frames are hosts, repeaters, bridges, and routers.

*fractional E1*   Portion of a high-bandwidth E1 connection offered to a customer by a service provider.

*fractional T1*   Portion of a high-bandwidth T1 connection offered to a customer by a service provider.

*fragment-free switching*   Cut-through switching method where the switch forwards the frame before all of the frame is received but after at least the first 64 bytes is received. The switch does not calculate or check the CRC value. Fragment-free switching is slower than fast-forward but faster than store-and forward.

*Frame Relay*   Industry-standard, switched, WAN standard that operates at the physical layer and data link layer of the OSI reference model. Frame Relay handles multiple virtual circuits using HDLC encapsulation between connected devices. It is more efficient than the X.25 protocol that it replaced.

*frame tagging*   Method used by a Cisco Catalyst switch to identify the VLAN that a frame belongs to. When a frame enters the switch, it is encapsulated with a header that tags it with a VLAN ID.

*full-mesh topology* Network topology in which each device connects to all others using either a physical or virtual circuit. Full mesh provides redundancy in the functionality of the network. It is usually reserved for network backbones because of the high cost of implementation.

# G

*gateway of last resort* Final stop on a route within an enterprise for packets that cannot be matched. This information appears in the routing tables of all routers so that they know where to send packets with an unknown destination.

*Greenwich mean time (GMT)* Time zone located at 0 degrees longitude that sets the standard for all time zones.

# H

*hello interval* Period of time, in seconds, that a router keeps a hello packet from a neighbor.

*hello packet* Packet that is multicast to detect devices on a network and to test the connections. A hello packet is used by a router to determine the best connection available.

*Hello protocol* Standard used by OSPF systems for establishing and maintaining neighbor relationships. The Hello protocol is an interior protocol that uses a routing metric based on the length of time it takes a packet to make the trip between the source and the destination.

*hierarchical design model* Representation of a network featuring an access layer, a distribution layer, and a core layer.

*hierarchical network* Design technique that divides the network into layers to prevent congestion and reduce the size of failure domains. The Cisco hierarchal design model uses core, distribution, and access layers.

*High-Level Data Link Control (HDLC)* Bit-oriented synchronous data link layer protocol developed by ISO. HDLC specifies a data encapsulation method on synchronous serial links using frame characters and checksums.

*hijacking* When a hacker illegally gains access to a system through an authenticated connection.

*hold time* Length of time that a router treats a neighbor as reachable.

*holddown* Placing a router in a state that will neither advertise nor accept routes for a specific length of time, called the holddown period. Holddown is used to remove bad information about a route from all routers in the network. A route is typically placed in holddown when a link in that route fails.

*holddown timer* Timer that determines the holddown period. Holddown is used to remove bad information about a route from all routers in the network. A route is typically placed in holddown when a link in that route fails. With RIP, the default holddown time is 180 seconds, six times the regular update period.

# I

*implicit deny* Last statement of an ACL inserted to block the accidental entry of unwanted traffic. It does not have to be entered when creating the ACL. It is there by default.

*in-band* Management technique for connecting a computer to a network device. In-band management is used to monitor and make configuration changes to a network device over a network connection.

*inside global address* Public-routable IP address of an inside host as it appears to the outside network. Inside global address is an IP address translated by NAT.

*inside local address* Private IP address configured on a host on an inside network. An inside local address must be translated before it can travel outside the local addressing structure to the Internet.

*interior gateway protocol (IGP)* Routing protocol used to exchange routing information within an autonomous system. Examples of IGPs include EIGRP, OSPF, and RIP.

*intermediate distribution facility (IDF)*
Secondary communications room for a building that uses a star networking topology. An IDF has a frame that cross-connects the user cable media to individual user line circuits and may serve as a distribution point for multiple-pair cables from the main distribution frame. The IDF is dependent on the MDF.

*Internet Engineering Task Force (IETF)* Task force consisting of over 80 working groups responsible for developing Internet standards. The IETF is part of the Internet Society, or ISOC, organization.

*Inter-Switch Link (ISL)* Cisco proprietary protocol for tagging VLAN frames on a switched network.

*inter-VLAN routing* Routing between virtual LANs. Specific configuration to switches and routers is necessary.

*intra-area routing* With OSPF networks, the transfer of data within a logical area when the source and destination are in the same area.

*intranet* Networks accessible to internal users of an organization. An intranet is used to share internal information and computing resources.

*intrusion detection system (IDS)* Combination of a sensor, console, and central engine in a single device installed on a network to protect against attacks missed by a conventional firewall. An IDS inspects all inbound and outbound network activity and identifies suspicious patterns that may indicate a network or system attack. It is configured to send an alarm to network administrators when such an attack is encountered.

*intrusion prevention system (IPS)* Active device in the traffic path that monitors network traffic and permits or denies flows and packets into the network. All traffic passes through an IPS for inspection. When the IPS detects malicious traffic, it sends an alert to the management station and blocks the malicious traffic immediately. An IPS proactively prevents attacks by blocking the original and subsequent malicious traffic.

*Inverse Address Resolution Protocol (InARP)* Method of building dynamic routes in a network. Inverse ARP allows an access server to discover the network address of a device associated with a virtual circuit. Inverse ARP is also used in Frame Relay to dynamically map a local DLCI to a destination IP address.

# J

*jabber* 1) Error condition in which a network device continually transmits random and meaningless data onto the network. 2) Data packet that exceeds the length prescribed in the IEEE 802.3 standard.

*jitter* Analog communication line distortion. Jitter can be caused by the variation of a signal from the reference timing positions, network congestion, or route changes. It can cause data loss, particularly at high speeds.

# K

*K value* Numeric value for a composite metric formula in EIGRP to determine the best path to a destination. K1 and K3 are set to 1. K2, K4, and K5 are set to 0. The value of 1 designates that bandwidth and delay have equal weight.

*keepalive* Broadcast sent by one network device to inform another network device that the circuit between the two is still active.

*key* Authentication code that passes between routers in plain text form.

*key exchange* Method for two peers to establish a shared secret key, which only they recognize, while communicating over a channel that is not secure.

*key ID* With OSPF and MD5 authentication, the router uses an algorithm that processes the key, the OSPF packet, and the key ID to generate an encrypted number.

# L

*last mile*   The portion of an ISP or service provider network that connects to the end customer. DSL is frequently referred to as a last-mile technology.

*latency*   1) Delay between the time when a device receives a frame and the time that frame is forwarded out the destination port. 2) Data latency is the time between a query and the results displaying on the screen.

*learning state*   One of four states that a port cycles through when a switch on an STP network powers up. The switch uses information learned to forward frames.

*leased line*   Bandwidth on a communications line reserved by a communications carrier for the private use of a customer. A leased line is a type of dedicated line. An example is a T1 circuit.

*least cost path*   With a link state routing protocol, the path to a destination network that has the highest bandwidth (the lowest sum of link costs).

*legacy*   Older styles of hardware or software that are still being used.

*link*   Network communications channel that includes a circuit or transmission path and all related equipment between a sender and a receiver. A link is also known as a line or a transmission link. With OSPF, a link is synonymous with a router interface.

*Link Control Protocol (LCP)*   Standard that establishes, configures, and tests data-link connections for use by PPP. LCP checks the identity of the linked device, determines the acceptable packet size, searches for errors, and can terminate the link if it exceeds the requirements.

*link-state advertisement (LSA)*   Broadcast packet used by a link-state protocol. An LSA contains information about neighbors and path costs. It is used by the receiving routers to maintain routing tables. An LSA is also known as link-state packet.

*link-state protocol*   Type of interior routing standard, such as OSPF and IS-IS used in a hierarchical network design. Link-state protocols help manage the packet-switching processes in large networks.

*listening state*   One of four states that a port cycles through when a switch on an STP network powers up. The switch listens for BPDUs from neighboring switches.

*load*   Amount of traffic on a network.

*load balancing*   Ability of a router to distribute traffic over multiple network interfaces that are the same distance from the destination address. Load balancing increases the use of network segments, which improves bandwidth. A load-balancing algorithm may use both line speed and reliability information.

*local loop*   Physical line from the premises or demarcation point of a telephone subscriber to the edge of the carrier or telephone company central office. A local loop is also known as a subscriber line and is sometimes referred to as the last mile.

*Local Management Interface (LMI)*   Standard that enhances the basic Frame Relay specification. LMI includes support for a global addressing and support for keepalive, multicast, and status mechanisms.

*logging*   Process of recording and accessing details about packets on a network that have been permitted or denied.

*logical topology*   Map of the flow of data on a network that shows how devices communicate with each other.

*loopback interface*   A simulated interface on a router that can be used for testing purposes.

# M

*main distribution facility (MDF)*   Primary communications room for a building. An MDF is the central point of a star networking topology where patch panels, hubs, switches, and routers are located. It is used to connect public or private lines coming into the building to internal networks.

*Management Information Base (MIB)*
Database of network management information
that is used and maintained by a network management protocol such as SNMP or Common
Management Information Protocol, also known
as CMIP. The value of an MIB object can be
changed or retrieved using SNMP or CMIP commands. MIB objects are organized in a tree
structure that includes public or standard, and
private or proprietary, branches.

*management VLAN*    VLAN1 on a switch. The
IP address of VLAN1 is used to access and configure the switch remotely and to exchange
information with other network devices.

*manual summarization*    Feature on an EIGRP
route where the administrator determines which
subnets on which interfaces are advertised as
summary routes. Manual summarization is done
on a per-interface basis and gives the network
administrator complete control. A manually
summarized route appears in the routing table as
an EIGRP route sourced from a logical interface.

*maximum transmission unit (MTU)*
Maximum packet size, in bytes, that a particular
interface can handle.

*MD5 authentication*    See *Message Digest 5
(MD5).*

*mesh*    Network topology where devices are
organized in a segmented manner with multiple
interconnections strategically placed between
network nodes.

*Message Digest 5 (MD5)*    Method of authentication that requires that each router has a unique
key and key ID. The router uses an algorithm
that processes the key, the OSPF packet, and the
key ID to generate an encrypted number. Each
OSPF packet includes that encrypted number.
The key is never transmitted.

*metric*    Information that a routing algorithm
uses to determine the best route on a network.
Metrics are stored in a routing table. Metrics
include bandwidth, communication cost, delay,
hop count, load, path cost, and reliability.

*microsegmentation*    Division of a network into
smaller segments, usually with the intention of
increasing aggregate bandwidth to network
devices. Switches use microsegmentation to prevent collisions.

*mission critical*    Type of network or computing
process that is vital to an organization. Mission-critical applications that are halted often or for
too long may have negative consequences.

*modulated*    Process in which the characteristics
of an electrical signal are transformed to represent information. Types of modulation include
amplitude modulation, frequency modulation,
and pulse amplitude modulation.

*multicast*    Single packets copied by the network and sent to a specific subset of network
addresses. Multicast addresses are specified in
the destination address field.

*multilayer switching*    Device that filters and
forwards packets based on MAC addresses and
network addresses. A Layer 2/Layer 3 switch is
a multilayer switch.

# N

*named ACL (NACL)*    Standard or extended format ACLs that are referenced by a descriptive
name rather than a number. When you configure
an NACL, the router IOS uses an NACL subcommand mode.

*NAT overload*    Dynamically translates multiple
inside local addresses to a single public address
so that more than one client can access the connection to the Internet.

*native VLAN*    Special VLAN that accommodates untagged traffic. Trunk links carry the
untagged traffic over the native VLAN. On
Cisco Catalyst switches, VLAN1 is the native
VLAN by default.

*neighbor table*    One of three interconnected EIGRP router tables. The neighbor table collects and lists information about directly connected neighbor routers. A sequence number records the number of the last received hello from each neighbor and time stamps the time that the packet arrived. If a hello packet is not received within the hold time, the timer expires and DUAL recalculates the topology. Other router tables include topology and routing tables.

*Network Address Translation (NAT)*    Standard used to reduce the number of public IP addresses necessary for all nodes within the organization to connect to the Internet. NAT allows a large group of private users to access the Internet by converting packet headers for only a small pool of public IP addresses and keeping track of them in a table.

*network attached storage (NAS)*    High-speed, high-capacity data storage that groups large numbers of disk drives that are directly attached to the network and can be used by any server. A NAS device is typically attached to an Ethernet network and is assigned its own IP address.

*network boundary*    Location where route summarization occurs on a boundary router.

*Network Control Protocol (NCP)*    Standard that routes and controls the flow of data between a communications controller, in which it resides, and other network resources.

*network discovery*    Result of dynamic routing protocols enabling a router to share information about reachability and status and to add remote networks to the routing table.

*network maintenance plan (NMP)*    Ensures business continuity by keeping the network running efficiently. Network maintenance must be scheduled during specific periods, usually nights and weekends, to minimize the impact on business operations.

*network management system (NMS)*    System or application that is used to monitor and control managed network devices, such as CiscoWorks.

*network monitoring plan*    Information used by a network administrator to evaluate the condition of a network.

*network operations center (NOC)*    The facility location and personnel in an organization responsible for maintaining a network.

*next hop*    Interface on a connected router that moves the data closer to the final destination.

*nonbroadcast multiaccess (NBMA) network*    Network that does not support broadcasting, such as X.25 and some forms of Frame Relay, or in which broadcasting is not possible, such as an SMDS.

*Null0 interface*    EIGRP installs a Null0 summary route in the routing table for each parent route. The Null0 interface indicates that this is not an actual path, but a summary for advertising purposes.

# O

*Open Shortest Path First (OSPF) Protocol*    Open Shortest Path First routing algorithm for a link-state, hierarchical IGP. OSPF features include least-cost routing, multipath routing, and load balancing.

*open standard*    Protocol or rule available to the public to be applied to a network. An open standard is not proprietary.

*optical carrier (OC)*    Series of physical protocols, such as OC-1, OC-2, and OC-3, defined for synchronous optical network optical signal transmissions. OC signal levels put synchronous transport signal frames onto fiber-optic line at different speeds. The base rate of an OC signal level is 51.84 Mbps for OC-1. Each signal level thereafter operates at a speed multiplied by that number. For example, OC-3 runs at 155.52 Mbps ($51.84 \times 3 = 155.52$).

*out-of-band*    Transmission using frequencies or channels outside the frequencies or channels normally used for information transfer. Out-of-band signaling is often used for error reporting when in-band signaling can be affected by whatever problems the network might be experiencing.

*outside global address*    Public IP address of an external host, as it is referred to on the Internet.

*outside local address* IP address of an outside host as it appears to the inside network.

*overload* Type of network address translation in which a single external public address is used to translate all internal addresses. Also called Port Address Translation, or PAT.

# P

*Packet over SONET/SDH (POS)* Type of networking supported by SONET and SDH that moves large amounts of IP packet data over great distances through fiber-optic cable.

*packet sniffer* Tool that analyzes traffic flows based on the source and destination of the traffic and the type of traffic being sent. Packet sniffer analysis can be used to make decisions on how to manage the traffic more efficiently.

*packet switching* Networking method where nodes share bandwidth by sending packets to each other. Packet switching is a way to direct encoded information in a network from a source to a destination.

*parent route* When default summarization is disabled, updates include subnet information. The routing table installs entries for each of the subnets and an entry for the summary route. A parent route is announced by the summarizing router as long as at least one specific route in its routing table matches the parent route. The parent route is called the summary route, and the child route is called the subnet route.

*partial-mesh topology* Network where devices are organized in a mesh topology with network nodes that may be organized in a full mesh, and network nodes that connected to one or two other nodes in the network. A partial mesh does not provide the level of redundancy of a full-mesh topology and is less expensive to implement. They are generally used in the peripheral networks that connect to a fully meshed backbone.

*Password Authentication Protocol (PAP)* Standard used by PPP peers to authenticate each other on a network. A remote router sends an authentication request when attempting to connect to a local router. PAP passes the password and hostname or username. PAP does not prevent unauthorized access but identifies the remote user. The router or access server then determines whether the user is allowed access.

*permanent virtual circuit (PVC)* Connection that saves bandwidth because the circuit is established ahead of time.

*permit* Allow a process to occur.

*physical addressing* Standardized data link-layer address that is required for every port or device that connects to a LAN. Other devices in the network use these addresses to locate specific ports in the network and to create and update routing tables and data structures. The MAC address is a physical address that is 6 bytes long and is controlled by the IEEE. The MAC address is also known as a hardware address, a MAC layer address, or a physical address.

*physical topology* Layout of devices on a network. The physical topology shows the way that the devices are connected through the cabling and how cables are arranged.

*plain old telephone system (POTS)* The basic analog telephone system that provides land-line service to millions of people worldwide.

*point of presence (POP)* Physical connection between a communication facility, provided by an ISP or local telephone company, and an organization's main distribution facility.

*Point-to-Point Protocol (PPP)* Standard that provides router-to-router and host-to-network connections over synchronous and asynchronous circuits.

*poisoned reverse* Routing update that indicates that a network or subnet is unreachable, instead of just implying that a network is unreachable by not including it in updates. Poison reverse updates are sent to defeat large routing loops. The Cisco IGRP implementation uses poison reverse updates.

*Port Address Translation (PAT)*   Standard used to reduce the number of internal private IP addresses to one external public IP address. PAT enables an organization to conserve addresses in the global address pool by allowing source ports in TCP connections or UDP conversations to be translated. Different local addresses then map to the same global address, with PAT providing the unique information. PAT is a subset of NAT functionality.

*port density*   Number of ports per RU (rack unit) on a switch.

*PortFast*   Enhancement to STP that causes an access port to enter the forwarding state immediately, bypassing the listening and learning states. Using PortFast on access ports that are connected to a single workstation or server allows those devices to connect to the network immediately.

*Power over Ethernet (PoE)*   Powering standard of network devices over Ethernet cable. IEEE 802.3af and Cisco specify two different PoE methods. Cisco power sourcing equipment and powered devices support both PoE methods.

*Predictor*   A compression technique that increases the effective throughput on PPP connections by reducing the amount of data in the frame that travels across the link. The protocol decompresses the frame at its destination. Two compression protocols available in Cisco routers are Stacker and Predictor.

*prefix address*   Pattern that matches the bits of an IP address. For example, 130.120.0.0/16 matches the first 16 bits of the IP network address 130.120.2.23, which are 130.120. In another example, 12.0.0.0/12 matches 12.0.2.3, 12.2.255.240, and 12.15.255.255 but does not match 12.16.0.1.

*prefix length*   Identifies the number of bits used in the network. A prefix length is also known as a network prefix.

*private addresses*   Range of IP address that are reserved for internal use. A private network address is not routed across the public Internet. In IPv4, the ranges of private network addresses are 10.0.0.0 to 10.255.255.255, 172.16.0.0 to 172.31.255.255, and 192.168.0.0 to 192.168.255.255.

*proactive maintenance*   Method for a network administrator to ensure uptime by monitoring network functionality and taking corrective action immediately. Proactive maintenance is performed on a regular basis to detect weaknesses before a critical error that could bring down the network.

*protocol-dependent module (PDM)*   Used by EIGRP to make decisions about specific routing tasks.

*public address*   IP address that is unique and routable across the public Internet.

*public switched telephone network (PSTN)*   General term referring to the variety of telephone networks and services in place worldwide. PSTN is also known as plain old telephone service, or POTS.

*punchdown*   Spring-loaded tool used to cut and connect wires in a jack or on a patch panel.

*punchdown block*   A portion of a patch panel that cross-connects devices, usually for WAN and telephony services.

# Q

*quad-zero route*   Route where the network address and subnet mask are both specified as 0.0.0.0. The command uses either the next-hop address or the exit interface parameters and is commonly used when creating a default route.

*quality of service (QoS)*   Standard for monitoring and maintaining a level of transmission performance and service, such as available data transmission bandwidth and error rate.

*query packet*   Message used to inquire about the value of some variable or set of variables.

# R

*rack unit (RU)*   Standard form factor measurement for the vertical space that computer and networking equipment occupies. A rack unit is equal to the height of 1.75 inches (4.4 cm). A device is measured in RUs. If a device is 1.75 inches tall, it is 1RU. If it is 3.5 inches tall, it is 2RU.

*Rapid Spanning Tree Protocol (RSTP)*
Update to Spanning Tree Protocol standards that reduces the time for connections to be established to switch ports.

*recursive lookup*   Two steps necessary to determine the exit interface for a packet. First, a router matches the destination IP address of a packet to the static route. Then, the router matches the next-hop IP address of the static route to entries in its routing table to determine which interface to use.

*redlines*   Marks on blueprints showing changes in the design.

*redundancy*   Duplication of components on a network, such as devices, services, or connections, for the purpose of maintaining operability if any component fails.

*reference bandwidth*   Parameter related to the OSPF cost metric and used to calculate interface cost. The default bandwidth value calculation of each interface uses the equation 100,000,000 / bandwidth, or $10^8$ / bandwidth.

*reliability*   Ratio of expected-to-received keepalives from a link. If the ratio of keepalives is high, the line is reliable. Reliability is used as a routing metric.

*Reliable Transport Protocol (RTP)*   Cisco proprietary Layer 4 protocol that guarantees delivery and receipt of EIGRP packets for a variety of network layer protocols.

*replay attack*   Malicious process that allows a hacker to gain access to a router using information that is saved and replayed by the hacker as proof of identity.

*reply packet*   Information sent when a query packet is received with EIGRP. A reply packet helps DUAL to locate a successor route to the destination network. Queries can be multicast or unicast. Replies are always unicast.

*reported distance*   Distance to a destination as reported by a neighbor.

*request message*   When a router is started, message sent out by each RIP-configured interface requesting that all RIP neighbors send their routing tables.

*response message*   Reply to a message sent out by each RIP-configured interface requesting that all RIP neighbors send their routing tables.

*RIPng*   Distance vector routing standard with a limit of 15 hops that uses split horizon and poison reverse to prevent routing loops. It is based on IPv4 RIPv2 and is similar to RIPv2, but it uses IPv6 for transport. The multicast group address FF02::9 identifies all RIPng-enabled routers.

*rogue switch*   Unidentified switch on a network.

*root bridge*   Designated packet-forwarding device in a spanning-tree implementation that receives topology information and notifies all other bridges in the network when topology changes are required. A root bridge prevents loops and provides a measure of defense against link failure. A root bridge is also known as root switch.

*root port*   STP designated port that provides the least-cost path back to the root bridge.

*route aggregation*   See *route summarization*.

*route poisoning*   Setting the metric for a route to 16 to stop traffic on the route. RIP sends a triggered update immediately, poisoning the route.

*route summarization*   Consolidation of advertised addresses in a routing table. Route summarization reduces the number of routes in the routing table, the routing update traffic, and overall router overhead. Route summarization is also known as route aggregation.

*router ID*   IP address determined by a value configured with the **router-id** command, a value of the highest configured IP address on a loopback interface, or a value of the highest IP address on any active physical interface.

*router-on-a-stick*   Configuration on the router that determines that if the destination VLAN is on the same switch as the source VLAN, the router forwards the traffic back down to the source switch using the subinterface parameters of the destination VLAN ID.

*Routing Information Protocol next Generation (RIPng)*   See *RIPng*.

*routing loop*   With dynamic routing protocols, when some routers do not have the most current information about the network, routing loops can occur, which is when packets cycle through a series of routers endlessly.

*routing table*   Table stored on a router or other internetworking device that keeps track of routes to network destinations and metrics associated with those routes.

*runt*   Frame that is less than 64 bytes, usually the result of a collision. In fragment-free switching, the switch reads the first 64 bytes of the frame before it begins to forward it out the destination port. Checking the first 64 bytes ensures that the switch does not forward collision fragments.

# S

*segmented data*   Small, uniform parts of data that switch quickly and efficiently between nodes.

*Serial Line Address Resolution Protocol (SLARP)*   Standard that assigns an address to the end point of a serial link if the other end is already configured. SLARP assumes that each serial line is a separate IP subnet and that one end of the line is host number 1 and the other end is host number 2. As long as one end of the serial link is configured, SLARP automatically configures an IP address for the other end.

*serial transmission*   Method of data transmission in which the bits of a data character are transmitted sequentially over a single channel.

*server farm*   Collection of servers located in a central facility and maintained by the central group to provide server needs for organizations. A server farm usually has primary and backup server hardware for load-balancing, redundancy, and fault-tolerance purposes. A server farm architecture provides the operation and maintenance of servers.

*service-level agreement (SLA)*   Binding contract between a network service provider and the end user who requires a certain level of service.

*service provider (SP)*   Organization, such as the local phone or cable company, that provides WAN and Internet services.

*shared secret*   Password known between devices.

*Simple Network Management Protocol (SNMP)*   Standard that allows monitoring of individual devices on the network. SNMP-compliant devices use agents to monitor a number of predefined parameters for specific conditions. These agents collect information and store it in an MIB.

*simple password authentication*   Method that offers basic security to a router using a key to gain access.

*Spanning Tree Protocol (STP)*   Bridge standards that use the spanning-tree algorithm and enable a switch to dynamically work around loops in a network topology by creating a spanning tree. A switch exchanges BPDU messages with other switches to detect loops, and then it removes the loops by shutting down selected switch interfaces.

*shortest path first (SPF) algorithm*   The SPF algorithm is a mathematical process that uses the length of a path to determine a shortest-path spanning tree. An SPF algorithm is used in link-state routing protocols.

*SPF tree*   All paths from a source to each destination and the total cost of each path.

*split horizon*   Routing technique that controls the formation of loops by preventing information from exiting the router interface through the same interface it was received. A split-horizon update is used to prevent routing loops.

*Stacker*   A compression technique that increases the effective throughput on PPP connections by reducing the amount of data in the frame that travels across the link. The protocol decompresses the frame at its destination. Two compression protocols available in Cisco routers are Stacker and Predictor.

*stakeholder*   Person or organization that has an interest in the success of a process.

*standard ACL*   Access control list that accepts or denies packets based on the source IP address. Standard ACLs are identified by the number assigned to them. The numbers range from 1 to 99 and from 1300 to 1999.

*star topology*   Network topology in which devices are connected to a common central switch by point-to-point links. The star topology is the most commonly used physical topology for Ethernet LANs.

*static NAT*   Method in which an internal host with a fixed private IP address is mapped with a fixed public IP address all the time.

*statistical time-division multiplexing (STDM)*   Technique where information from multiple logical channels is transmitted across a single physical channel. STDM dynamically allocates bandwidth only to active input channels, making better use of available bandwidth and allowing many devices to be connected. Statistical time-division multiplexing is also known as statistical multiplexing or stat mux.

*storage-area network (SAN)*   Data communication platform that interconnects servers and storage at gigabit speeds. By combining LAN networking models with server performance and mass storage capacity, a SAN eliminates bandwidth issues and scalability limitations created by previous SCSI bus-based architectures.

*store-and-forward switching*   Technique in which frames are completely processed before being forwarded out of the appropriate port. Store- and-forward packet switching is a process that includes the calculation of the cyclic redundancy check and the verification of the destination address.

*structured cabling*   Using an internationally recognized standard to implement a physical network cabling design.

*stub network*   Network that has only a single connection to a router.

*subinterface*   One of a number of virtual interfaces on a single physical interface.

*subset advertisements*   VTP message that contains new VLAN information based on the summary advertisement.

*sub-subnet*   Further division of a subnetted network address.

*successor route*   Equal-cost, primary loop-free path with the lowest metric to the destination determined by the topology and recorded in the routing table.

*summary advertisement*   Current VTP domain name and configuration revision number issued periodically by a Catalyst switch.

*supernetting*   Process of summarizing contiguous classful addresses given out by the Internet community. An example of supernetting is when a group of Class C addresses 200.100.16.0 through 200.100.31.0 is summarized into the address 200.100.16.0 with a mask of 255.255.240.0. Also known as classless interdomain routing.

*switched virtual circuit (SVC)*   Route that is dynamically established on demand and is removed when transmission is complete. An SVC is used in situations where data transmission is sporadic.

*switching loop*   Causes duplicate frames to be sent throughout a network. A switching loop occurs when there is more than one path between two switches.

*symmetric switching*   Switches that have ports of all the same speeds.

*Synchronous Digital Hierarchy (SDH)*   Fiber-optic carrier standard developed for high-speed digital circuits by the International Telecommunication Union (ITU), documented in standard G.707 and its extension G.708

*Synchronous Optical Network (SONET)*   A high-speed synchronous optical network up to 2.5 Gbps. Specification developed by Bellcore and designed to run on optical fiber. STS-1, which operates at 51.84 Mbps, is the basic building block of SONET. Approved as an international standard in 1988. SONET format has been adopted by common carriers.

*syslog*   Type of message logged and sent to an external server to inform users of various reports in real time.

# T

**T1**    Digital WAN carrier facility that transmits DS-1-formatted data at 1.544 Mbps through the telephone-switching network, with the use of AMI or binary 8-zero substitution coding.

**T3**    Digital WAN carrier facility that transmits DS-3-formatted data at 44.736 Mbps through the telephone switching network.

**telecommunication service provider (TSP)**    Vendor authorized by regulatory agencies to operate a telecommunications system and provide telecommunications service. A telecommunication service provider is also known as a local exchange carrier, telecom carrier, or carrier.

**telecommunications room**    Facility that contains network and telecommunications equipment, vertical and horizontal cable terminations, and cross-connect cables.

**telecommuter**    One who works from a location other than the centralized office.

**telecommuting**    Working from a location other than the centralized office.

**teleconferencing**    Method for a group of people to communicate in real time online.

**teleworker**    Employee who works at a location other than the centralized office.

**teleworking**    Working at a location other than the centralized office location.

**time-division multiplexing (TDM)**    Division of bandwidth to allow multiple logical signals to be transmitted simultaneously across a single physical channel. The signals are then separated at the receiving end.

**time slice**    Period of time during which a conversation has complete use of the physical media. Bandwidth is allocated to each channel or time slot. In standard TDM, if a sender has nothing to say, the time slice goes unused, wasting valuable bandwidth.

**topology database**    Location on a topology that stores SPF tree information. In an OSPF network, each router keeps its own topology database.

**topology table**    One of three tables on an EIGRP router. The topology table lists all routes learned from each EIGRP neighbor. DUAL takes the information from the neighbor and topology tables and calculates the lowest cost routes to each network. The topology table identifies up to four primary loop-free routes for any one destination.

**traffic filtering**    The process of analyzing the contents of a packet to determine whether the packet should be allowed or blocked. Used to control traffic in various segments of the network.

**transceiver**    Device that receives and forwards analog and digital signals.

**triggered update**    Message containing the routing table of a router that is sent to neighboring routers on a network when the router starts up. Triggered updates are also sent due to topology changes or links being dropped.

**trunk port**    Point-to-point link that connects a switch to another switch, a router, or a server. A trunk carries traffic for multiple VLANs over the same link. The VLANs are multiplexed over the link with a trunking protocol.

# U

**unicast**    Message sent to a single network destination.

**update packet**    Message about the network topology sent to a neighbor. The update packet is added to the topology table. Several updates are often required to send all of the topology information to a new neighbor.

**uplink port**    High-speed port that connects to areas that have a higher demand for bandwidth, such as another switch, a server farm, or other networks.

**UplinkFast**    STP enhancement to minimize downtime during recalculation. STP UplinkFast accelerates choosing a new root port when a link or switch fails or when an STP is reconfigured. The transition of the root port to the forwarding state occurs immediately, without going through the normal STP procedures of listening and learning.

# V

*V.35*    ITU-T standard describing a synchronous, physical layer protocol used for communications between a network access device and a packet network. V.35 is most commonly used in the United States and in Europe, and is recommended for speeds up to 2.048 Mbps.

*variable-length subnet mask (VLSM)* Technique used to specify a different subnet mask for the same major network number to identify different subnets. VLSM can help optimize available IP address space.

*vector*    With a distance vector routing protocol, the direction (exit interface) to a remote network.

*virtual circuit (VC)*    Logical relationship created to ensure reliable communication between two network devices. A virtual circuit is defined by a virtual path identifier/virtual channel identifier pair and can be either a permanent virtual circuit or switched virtual circuit. Virtual circuits are used in Frame Relay and X.25. In ATM, a virtual circuit is called a virtual channel.

*virtual local-area network (VLAN)*    Group of devices on a network, typically end-user stations, that communicate as if attached to the same network segment even though they may be on different segments. VLANs are configured on workgroup switches. Switches with VLANs may interconnect using VLAN trunking protocols.

*virtual private network (VPN)*    Network through which data is sent through a public telecommunication infrastructure while maintaining the privacy of the data by creating a tunnel through the public telecommunication infrastructure.

*VLAN ID (VID)*    Identity of the VLAN inserted into an Ethernet frame as it enters a port on a switch.

*VLAN management policy server (VMPS)* Server with a database that maps MAC addresses to VLAN assignments. When a device plugs into a switch port, the VMPS searches the database for a match of the MAC address and temporarily assigns that port to the appropriate VLAN.

*VLAN Trunking Protocol (VTP)*    Cisco proprietary standard that maintains a consistent VLAN configuration across a common administrative domain.

*VTP client*    A VTP mode in which the switch does not create, modify, or delete VLAN information for the VTP domain. It accepts VTP messages from the VTP server and modifies its own database with this information. A VTP client sends VTP messages out all trunk ports.

*VTP server*    A VTP mode in which the administrator can create, modify, and delete VLANs and VLAN configuration parameters for the entire domain. A VTP server saves VLAN configuration information in the switch NVRAM and sends out VTP messages on all trunk ports.

*VTP transparent*    A VTP mode in which the switch ignores information in the VTP messages. It does not modify its database with information received from the VTP server, but it does forward VTP advertisements. A switch in VTP transparent mode will not send out an update that indicates a change in its own VLAN database; therefore, all VLANs created on a switch in this mode remain local to the switch.

# W

*wildcard mask*    32-bit quantity used in conjunction with an IP address to determine which bits in an IP address should be ignored when that address is compared to another IP address. A wildcard mask is specified when access lists are set up. A wildcard mask is used in IPv4.

*wire speed*    Rate that packets are forwarded on a network that is equal to the physical capabilities of the medium.

# Z

*zero CIR*    Excess bandwidth that is discounted when it is available from a Frame Relay service provider. In zero CIR, a user pays a small fee for the capability to transmit data across a PVC at speeds up to that of the access link. If there is congestion, all DE-labeled frames are dropped. There is no guarantee of service with a CIR set to zero.

classful routing protocols, 122
classless routing protocols, 122
pie charts, 127
requirements for, 124-126
sub-subnets, 123
tabular charts, 127

**VMPS (VLAN management policy servers), 87**

**voice traffic, network traffic prioritization, 14**

**VPN (Virtual Private Networks)**
enterprise edge security, 33
IPsec, 17
virtual tunnels, 16

**VTP (VLAN Trunking Protocol), 97**
advertisement requests, 99
client mode, 98
configuring, 99-102
passwords, 344
revision numbers, 98
server mode, 98
subset advertisements, 99
summary advertisements, 99
transport mode, 98
troubleshooting, 343-344

**vtp version command, 344**

# W - X - Y - Z

**WAN (Wide Area Networks), 10, 247**
analog data connections, 251
cell switching, 255
circuit switching, 254
data link layer standards, 251
debugging
*authentication, 373*
*connectivity, 370-372*
demarc, 248
DS0 standard, 249
DS1 standard, 249
DS3 standard, 250
encapsulation
*data link layer, 259*
*Ethernet, 258-259*
*Frame Relay, 271-274*
*HDLC, 260*
*layer 2, 258*
*PPP, 260-263*
first miles, 248
fractional E1 connections, 252
fractional T1 connections, 252
last miles, 248, 257
layer 1 standards, 250

layer 2 standards, 250
leased lines, 254
line characteristics, 250
local loops, 248, 257
long-range communications, 258
packet switching, 255
physical layer protocols, 249
physical link layer standards, 251
troubleshooting
*authentication, 372*
*connectivity, 367-370*

**wildcard masks**
ACL, 291
*filtering specific hosts, 289-290*
*packet-matching, 288*
*statement creation, 288*
*structure of, 287*
converting subnet masks to, 290-291
EIGRP, 190
single-area OSPF configurations, 218-220
viewing, 190

**wire speed, 67**

**wireless traffic, VLAN support for, 102**

**wiring closets.** *See* **telecommunications rooms**